Raleigh and the British Bicycle Industry

Modern Economic and Social History Series

General Editor: Derek H. Aldcroft

Titles in this series include:

Studies in the Interwar European Economy
Derek H. Aldcroft

Whatever Happened to Monetarism?
Economic Policy-Making and Social Learning in the United Kingdom
since 1979
Michael J. Oliver

Disillusionment or New Opportunities?
The Changing Nature of Work in Offices, Glasgow 1880–1914
R. Guerriero Wilson

Raleigh and the British Bicycle Industry:
An Economic and Business History, 1870–1960
Roger Lloyd-Jones and M. J. Lewis

Battles for the Standard:
Bimetallism and the Spread of the Gold Standard, 1870–1914
Edward R. Wilson

The British Footwear Industry
Peter R. Mounfield

Trade Unions and the Economy, 1870–2000
Derek H. Aldcroft and Michael J. Oliver

The British Electronics Industry:
Innovation, Markets and Performance, 1930–97
John F. Wilson

The Seaside, Health and the Environment since 1850
John Hassan

Exchange Rate Regimes and Economic Policy in the Twentieth Century
edited by Ross Catterall and Derek H. Aldcroft

Raleigh and the British Bicycle Industry

An Economic and Business History, 1870–1960

ROGER LLOYD-JONES and M. J. LEWIS,
with the assistance of MARK EASON

Ashgate

Aldershot • Brookfield USA • Singapore • Sydney

Published by
Ashgate Publishing Limited
Gower House
Croft Road
Aldershot
Hants GU11 3HR
England

Ashgate Publishing Company
Old Post Road
Brookfield
Vermont 05036–9704
USA

HD
9993
.B544
R355
2000

Ashgate website: http://www.ashgate.com

British Library Cataloguing in Publication Data

Roger Lloyd-Jones.
    Raleigh and the British Bicycle Industry: An Economic and
Business History, 1870–1960.
    (Modern Economic and Social History)
    1. Raleigh. 2. Bicycle industry—Great Britain—History.
    I. Title. II. Lewis, M. J. (Mervyn J.), 1957– . III. Eason, Mark.
    338.7'6292272'0941

Library of Congress Cataloging-in-Publication Data

Roger Lloyd-Jones, 1944–
    Raleigh and the British bicycle industry: an economic and business
history, 1870–1960/Roger Lloyd-Jones and M. J. Lewis.
      (Modern Economic and Social History)
      Includes bibliographical references and indexes.
      ISBN 1–85928–457–4
      1. Raleigh Cycle Co.—History. 2. Bicycle industry—Great Britain—History.
    I. Lewis, M. J. (Mervyn J.), 1957– . II. Eason, Mark, 1957– . III. Title.
    IV. Series.
    HD9993.B544R355   2000
    338.7'6292272'0941—dc21
                                                                                                99–45176
                                                                                                CIP

ISBN 1 85928 457 4

This book is printed on acid free paper

Typeset in Sabon by Manton Typesetters, Louth, Lincolnshire, UK and printed in Great Britain by MPG Books Limited, Bodmin, Cornwall.

Contents

Modern Economic and Social History Series
General Editor's Preface

Economic and social history has been a flourishing subject of scholarly study during recent decades. Not only has the volume of literature increased enormously but the range of interest in time, space and subject matter has broadened considerably so that today there are many sub-branches of the subject which have developed considerable status in their own right.

One of the aims of this new series is to encourage the publication of scholarly monographs on any aspect of modern economic and social history. The geographical coverage is world-wide and contributions on non-British themes will be especially welcome. While emphasis will be placed on works embodying original research, it is also intended that the series should provide the opportunity to publish studies of a more general and thematic nature which offer a reappraisal or critical analysis of major issues of debate.

Derek H. Aldcroft

Manchester Metropolitan University

List of figures and tables

Figures

Tables

Acknowledgements

There are two outstanding debts which the authors wish to acknowledge. One is to the scholar who should have written this book, A. E. Harrison, whose work on the early bicycle industry is a model of economic and business history at its best. As one of the authors was taught by Tony Harrison at the University of York, there is considerable satisfaction in continuing his work and in drawing attention to his primary research into the bicycle industry. The other debt is to Professor Derek Aldcroft who, after hearing a paper on Raleigh Industries at a Northern Economic History Conference, suggested the idea of writing a business history of the industry, and then helped facilitate a commission with Ashgate Publishing. We would like to record our thanks to Dr Mark Eason who has contributed to the research work, particularly on the BSA records, and produced the original draft of Chapter 4. The various facets of the book have been discussed with a number of colleagues over the past few years; we would particularly like to thank Professor Peter Cain, Professor John Wilson and Dr Andrew Popp who have provided some lively insights into notions such as personal capitalism, industrial districts and business networks. A paper by Professor Cain on the ideas of Ruskin on intrinsic value also provided insights into the notions of quality and craft traditions which permeated the British bicycle industry. We would also like to record the help and assistance of archivists and librarians at Nottingham Record Office, the home of the Raleigh papers, Coventry Record Office and Central Library, and Birmingham Central Library. Our research work was greatly helped by sabbatical terms granted by the Cultural Research Institute at Sheffield Hallam University. Last, and by no means least, our thanks go to Ishbel Lewis, whose proofreading skills and great patience in reading our numerous drafts provided a quality control much in advance of our meagre efforts.

Roger Lloyd-Jones and M. J. Lewis
1999

Introduction: Raleigh and the British bicycle industry

A basic theme of this book, providing the connecting thread through-out, is that of enterprise. For Joseph Schumpeter enterprise was 'essentially about the mechanism of economic change'. Economic and business life is not a passive process, where business firms and other economic agents merely engage in 'smooth and uniquely determined adaptations to changing data'. Rather, the business environment rarely remains stable for any length of time, and if we were to assume that it did we would be distorting the picture of most ordinary business prac-tices. It follows, then, that historical analysis must play a crucial role in understanding the role of enterprise and economic and business change. Entrepreneurs cannot be reduced to the fable of the rational 'economic man', so enshrined by neo-classical economic theory. On the contrary, as Schumpeter reminds us,

> What they [entrepreneurs] really are, how they really work, what it is that conditions their performance and their failure, how they in turn help shape the conditions under which they work, and, above all, whether any significant generalisations may be made about all this, can be gleaned from history alone.[1]

The types of questions that Schumpeter posed, over half a century ago, remain just as relevant today, and they inform our general ap-proach to the study of Raleigh and the British bicycle industry. The role of entrepreneurs in building a new industry, in developing new products and processes, in exploiting new markets and in confronting the chal-lenge of foreign competition, is set within a long-term context. The actual format adopted to explore the development of the British bicycle industry traces the business history of one of its leading firms, Raleigh. The history of this company is then set in the context of more general trends and patterns in the industry's evolution over three chronological periods: 1870 to 1914, 1914 to 1939 and 1939 to 1960. This approach, we believe, allows us to examine Schumpeter's broad questions, and to be consistent with a key objective of the business historian, an objective taken up by John Wilson who argues that we need to 'explain the behaviour of firms over long periods of time, and to place the conclu-sions in a broader framework composed of the markets and institutions in which that behaviour occurs'.[2] Thus, the origins of Raleigh and its rise to become one of Britain's leading bicycle producers in the twentieth century forms the focus of this book. The story is an interesting one, because the company, although it experimented with diversification into other activities such as motor cycle and motor vehicle production, remained committed to a long-term policy of promoting its reputation as a producer of quality bicycles. Raleigh's history is told through a series of case studies which examine its business development, and the entrepreneurial drive of its founders and mentors, Frank Bowden and his son Harold. At the same time, due consideration is given to broader processes of change in the business environment and we focus on market, organisational, cultural and technological developments, as well as examining the consequences of shifting patterns of foreign competition. This is not to suggest that our case study approach offers a solution to D. C. Coleman's 'Catch 22' in which he postulates the dilemma faced by the business historian. The potential richness of a business case study is diluted because of the narrow operational value of the generalisations that can be made, and is limited by the reliance on a detailed, yet necessarily narrow, set of company records.[3] It certainly is the case that this book draws on the extensive Raleigh Archive, which provides a rich source for the empirical detail of this book. Nevertheless, we maintain that the insights gained from a detailed study of Raleigh, juxtaposed with chapters exploring more general developments at the industry level, do help to focus attention on key trends whose impact could be variable across different sectors of the bicycle trade. Thus, we argue in Chapter 2 that an important aspect of the early growth of the cycle industry was the emergence of an 'industrial district' which helped facilitate the process of business networking of bicycle firms in centres such as Birmingham and Coventry. Raleigh, a Nottingham-based firm, was tangential to this development, but this did not seem to have constrained its business performance. At a more general level of analysis we might be tempted to exaggerate the notion of the 'industrial district', while too close a focus on a specific case study might lead to an underplaying of its significance.

There is one important caveat to our methodology. As the bicycle industry developed in the twentieth century, structural change drastically reduced the number of bicycle manufacturers. Consequently, the business relationship between Raleigh and the wider industry becomes increasingly difficult to disentangle. After the end of the Second World War, Raleigh was the one major independent producer left in the industry, and the only other British manufacturers who could effectively challenge its position were the bicycle divisions of two large groups, Tube Investments (TI) and Birmingham Small Arms (BSA). In 1957 Raleigh acquired the bicycle interests of BSA, and in 1960 Raleigh

Industries merged with the British Bicycle Corporation (BCC), the bicycle division of TI. This meant that the British industry was dominated by one producer. In less than half a century an industry which could boast 275 firms in Birmingham, Coventry and Nottingham in 1913, with names as illustrious as Rover, Riley, Morris, Humber, Hillman, Singer, Triumph, Sunbeam etc., was reduced to one manufacturer, albeit one of world prominence.

The above named firms, of course, were synonymous with Britain's early development of motorised transport, and it cannot be too strongly emphasised that a number of cycle firms successfully diversified, and made an important contribution to this new manufacturing sector. For example, Riley, which began its business life as a Coventry ribbon-making firm, successfully evolved from bicycle manufacture to motor cycles to motor vehicle production. In part this diversification, first into motor cycle then motor vehicle production, was a response by the bicycle manufacturers to the challenge presented by cheap mass-produced American machines which flooded the British market at the end of the 1890s, and in the first decade of the new century. This is, however, only part of the story, and it was the profits earned in the cycle business which provided the necessary funds to finance and support the experimental research and development which was necessary to set up initial motor vehicle production (see Chapter 2). This usually meant that it was only those firms with sufficient financial resources, and very patient shareholders, who achieved long-term success, and for the small manufacturer diversification could be a high-risk strategy. But there were always exceptions. William Morris, later Lord Nuffield, who branched out from bicycle manufacture to motorcycles and then to motor vehicles, became one of Britain's most successful businessmen in the first half of the twentieth century. He began his first bicycle workshop in a brick building at the back of his parent's house in Oxford, and used one of the front rooms of the house as a showroom for his bicycles.

William Morris is a reminder, too, of the importance of personal capitalism in British business. It was this form of business organisation which predominated in the early phase of the British bicycle industry, and was characteristic of the organisational culture of Raleigh from its foundation to its loss of independence in 1960. This is a central theme of the chapters which explore Raleigh's business development, and is important for, as Alfred D. Chandler has persuasively argued, the British persistence with personal capitalism damaged Britain's ability to absorb the economic advantages flowing from the innovations of the second industrial revolution, and consequently in the period from the 1880s to 1914 Britain lost out to the USA and Germany in the new sectors of the industrial economy.[4] This hypothesis does not fit the British bicycle industry. As will be shown in Chapter 2, the British industry successfully fought off American competition and the threat of mass-produced standardised bicycles. British manufacturers also competed vigorously with German bicycle-makers in world markets, and by the eve of the Great War had seized back the initiative and were world leaders in the industry.[5] This is not to argue that American management systems were not the most advanced at the beginning of the twentieth century; they clearly were, but it does not necessarily follow that they were ideally suited for the British business environment with its different institutional structures.[6]

For example, even during the difficult business conditions of the inter-war years, as shown in Chapters 4 and 5, entrepreneurs such as Harold Bowden were reluctant to sacrifice their commitment to 'quality products' by going down-market and producing cheap, low-quality bicycles. Indeed, Bowden continued to expound an optimistic philosophy, and as the leading figure in the company he guided Raleigh through a series of ambitious business strategies relating to production development, extensive investment in marketing and a move to diversification into motorised transport, an activity which he decided to abandon in 1934. Bowden typified the personal capitalist, and central to his thinking was the need to develop co-operation with his workforce, and to introduce a labour strategy based on ideas of industrial welfare. Raleigh's experiences in the inter-war years were fraught with difficulties, and there was a variety of managerial twists and turns, but not only did the company survive the competitive test, it also achieved considerable business success which led to its flotation as a public holding company in 1934. The inter-war years did bring considerable structural change in the industry, and the population of firms sharply declined. Large-scale producers came increasingly to predominate, and there was a rise in the importance of trade associations which led to growing business co-operation. This stood in marked contrast to the more cut-throat competition of the pre-1914 period, but as shown in Chapter 5 trade agreements could be undermined by the independent actions of large producers such as Hercules, and Raleigh's attempts to create closer co-operation in the 1930s were constantly undermined. Nevertheless, after 1932 the industry responded positively to the business opportunities opened up by the relatively strong British economic recovery, as firms such as Raleigh, Hercules, and the bicycle divisions of BSA and TI directed their efforts more intensively on the home market. A personal capitalist form of control still persisted, however, in companies such as Raleigh and Hercules, and the style and governance of management was determined by family founders or their heirs. Indeed, even within the larger holding companies of BSA and TI the constituent bicycle firms enjoyed a high degree of autonomy.

While the temporal sequence of this book concentrates on the business activities of bicycle firms during three time periods, we have not overlooked the fact that the bicycle industry made important contributions to the two world wars. For example, during both wars Raleigh produced a range of munitions, including fuses, shell cases, exploder containers and smoke bombs. Indeed, by the end of the First World War Raleigh had become one of the largest manufacturers of munitions in the country. This is not to suggest that Raleigh's contribution to the war effort was simply a patriotic gesture, and George Wilson, for example, who became managing director of the Raleigh Cycle Co. in 1938, kept a strict business relationship with the Ministry of Supply during the Second World War, and he insisted on obtaining 'a firm price for all the articles manufactured by [Raleigh] for the government'. J. A. Phillips Ltd, part of TI's cycle division, produced over 89 million common shells between 1940 and 1945, and converted its plant to produce armour-piercing nose-caps, and a huge volume of components for aircraft. Its pedal and hub assembly shops produced grenades and land mines by the millions, and companies such as Hercules mass-produced components for the aircraft industry, and other branches of the armed services. These examples were typical, as we shall see in Chapters 4 to 7, of many enterprises in the industry who converted their plant to help the British war effort.

At the end of the Second World War the British bicycle industry was dominated by three large firms: Raleigh Industries Ltd, the only remaining independent large cycle maker, and the bicycle divisions of two group organisations, TI and BSA. Apart from the 'big three' the industry was characterised by a large number of small, not to say tiny specialist makers who produced almost exclusively for the sporting and bicycle club market. The industry had become highly concentrated, and it was these three large manufacturers who were to face the main post-war challenge to contribute to Britain's export drive. From the end of hostilities to the mid-1950s the industry was spectacularly successful in meeting its export targets, and this represented a pattern of business performance quite different from the inter-war years. In the 1930s, in particular, bicycle firms had mainly focused their attention on the home market, but by the early 1950s Raleigh, for example, was exporting approximately 70 per cent of its total output. This compared to less than 40 per cent in 1938, and another company, J. A. Phillips, a subsidiary of TI, also expanded its export sales. As shown in Chapter 6, both these companies were active in establishing factories abroad, and exploiting the increased demand in the world for cycles after 1945.

However, during the second half of the 1950s the industry was confronted by increasing international competition, and by 1957 the 'big three' had been reduced to the 'big two' when Raleigh purchased the bicycle interests of BSA. In 1960 the merger between Raleigh and BCC, the cycle division of TI, meant that the industry was now concentrated around one prominent domestic manufacturer. The success of the postwar years, and the failure to meet the aggressive foreign challenge, is examined in Chapters 6 and 7, and we also explore the failed effort to enter the market for mopeds from the mid-1950s. Our historical account effectively ends in 1960, the year when Raleigh and the British bicycle industry became one through Raleigh's merger with BCC, and the story of the post-1960 development requires a separate treatment in its own right.

Notes

1. Quotes from Schumpeter, cited in Swedberg, 1991, pp. 407, 408.
2. Wilson, 1995, p. 1.
3. Coleman, 1987b.
4. Chandler, 1990, p. 237.
5. See Harrison, 1969.
6. See Wilson, 1995, p. 8.

CHAPTER TWO

Boom, bust and progress: the British bicycle industry, 1870–1914

In January 1876 the Coventry Machinist Co. Ltd, one of the very early manufacturers of cycles, advertised their new 'Gentleman's bicycle – the lightest, strongest and quickest machine yet invented'.[1] At this stage, bicycling was almost exclusively a middle- or upper-class activity. For example, the 52 inch 'Challenger' machine, produced by Singer, was being offered second-hand to the public at a price of £14, a sum well beyond the range of the average working-class income.[2] The early bicycle firms had to expand the market and attempts were made to extend sales by offering customers easy terms for repayment. For example, in November 1876 a London dealer, F. Hucklebridge of Chelsea, provided a list of machines ranging from £11 10s. to £12 5s. Customers were informed that these machines could be purchased 'by paying £5 cash, and the remainder in instalments of £2', and a 5s. discount was offered for a cash sale. The promotion of the bicycle was enhanced by the opening of a number of bicycling schools, an important factor given the 'problem of mounting and dismounting', a difficult art especially on the penny-farthing machines. In February 1877 the *Bicycling News* carried an advertisement informing the public of the opening of 'the largest bicycle school in London, 1s. 6d. single lesson, perfect riding guaranteed for 10s., machines for practice 1s. per hour, second hour 6d.'. Further, visitors to Brighton in 1876 were invited by J. G. Harrison, agent for the Coventry Machinist Co., 'to learn to ride a bicycle, in a few hours, at Harrison's bicycle hall'.[3] A 'fad' for bicycles had actually emerged in the late 1860s, based on machines such as the 'boneshaker' and the 'velocipede', which owed their origin to the French designer Pierre Michaux. But the British bicycle industry, in terms of the expansion of new manufacturing firms, did not really undergo major change until the late 1870s and early 1880s.[4]

This delay in the industry's expansion was due to a number of problems which faced entrepreneurs who entered the industry with initial high expectations. The potential for business success was obvious to the early entrepreneurs. Cycling was a novelty and could attract great public interest, as demonstrated by the estimated 16 000 people who turned out to watch the professional mile bicycle championship held at Molyneux, Wolverhampton, on Boxing Day 1876. A year later, the promoters of the new stadium at Bramall Lane, Sheffield, announced that it 'will soon be ready for bicycling'. The original hosts of Bramall Lane were the Sheffield and Hallam Bicycle Club, and only subsequently was football added to the club's title.[5] In response to the growing popularity of cycling as a sport, numerous clubs sprang up in the 1870s. The potential of the cycle to excite the popular imagination in terms of sporting achievement was not lost on the early cycle-makers who focused their sales drive on this area. For example, Thomas Humber's cycling business was aided by his association with F. Cooper of Sheffield. In the 1870s Cooper, 'a keen racing man', had captured a number of prestigious cycle races on Humber machines. In 1877 he joined the firm of Humber, Marriott & Cooper and 'with his splendid reputation as a racing man, opened up a London branch ... thus greatly widening the reputation of the firm which had hitherto been confined to more northerly parts'.[6]

There were clearly forces at work which encouraged the early growth of the cycle industry, but there were also factors which inhibited its more rapid development. Until the introduction of the safety bicycle in 1885, the penny-farthing machines had placed a considerable limitation to the more rapid diffusion of the bicycle. It was prone to numerous breakdowns and accidents for the user were a common occurrence. The cycling press was littered with adverts for second-hand machines due to 'injury' to the original owner, and the art of cycling was not helped either by the state of the roads. The *Bicycling News* warned its readers in January 1876: 'The recent thaw left roads everywhere in a rotten condition. The macadam is in a very slippery state, and the roads surrounding it are so badly ploughed.' The roads around Sheffield, for example, were 'rough and hilly, and somewhat of a cross between Aberdeen granite, coal dust and chalk'. Not surprisingly, makers tended to press upon the public the alleged robustness of their machines. Thus, the New Hollow Spoke Bicycle Co. of Nottingham stated that its machine, 'if judged mechanically', would not substitute 'lightness for strength' and each part was 'designed with a due regard for the strains it will have to bear'. The conditions of the roads forced on makers the need for custom-built machines. Firms advised potential customers that in order to guarantee 'a suitable machine' it was 'advisable to state weight and character of roads where it will be generally used'.[7]

Given these problems, the number of indigenous cycle firms was small in number during the first decade of growth from the late 1860s to the late 1870s.[8] Table A.1 in the Appendix provides a list of most of the early pioneering manufacturing companies. The progress of the industry in its first decade of development was steady rather than dynamic. Nevertheless, progress was being made and, in the summer of

1878, a large meeting held at Coventry brought together bicycle manu-factures, cyclists and town dignitaries, including the mayor and local MP, to promote the development of the industry. The mayor informed the audience that the bicycle trade 'had found employment for many ... of the citizens of Coventry', and he went on to assure the some 300 persons present that the town's bicycle-makers 'meant to adopt every scientific improvement, and to continue to produce the best machines, in which there should be the most endurance, combined with perfection and ease of action'.[9] By the mid-1880s Sir Charles Dilke, a member of the Cabinet and President of the Chelsea Bicycling Club, claimed that the business development of Coventry had been 'greatly revived by cycling'. He estimated that the town 'now had 2,000 of its labour force' located in the industry. Along with the USA, England 'was now at the head of the cycling world'. During the 1880s the numbers employed in the Coventry cycle industry grew rapidly, the estimated number of workers rising from just under 600 in 1881 to 4 059 in 1891.[10] The next section examines the pattern of growth in the industry from its origins to the cycle boom of the mid-1890s.

The pattern of growth, 1870–97

The initial expansion in the late 1860s, which saw the emergence of the first cycle-manufacturing firms, did not, as noted earlier, lead to any spectacular breakthrough of the indigenous industry. Nevertheless, there were spurts of development in the late 1870s, the early 1880s and the late 1880s, before the industry experienced the huge boom of the mid-1890s. The industry was centred in the main manufacturing towns of the Midlands, and Table A.2 in the Appendix shows the growth in the number of firms in the industry from 1870 to 1896. Employment in the industry also expanded. The census of 1881 recorded 1 072 workers in the industry, and by 1891 this had risen to 11 524. Table 2.1 shows the distribution of labour across the main producing areas in 1891, and the concentration on the Midlands is clearly highlighted. By 1895 the la-bour force nearly doubled compared to 1891, and it doubled again between 1895 and 1897.[11]

The boom in the mid-1890s has been largely seen as a consequence of the rise in the popularity of the safety bicycle, especially among women. For example, in 1890 the membership of the British Cycle Touring Club was 60 000, 'of whom over 20,000 were women and women were important members of clubs up and down the country'. This raised cycling to a new fashionable status and expanded the demand for bicycles beyond that of the sporting fraternity. Innovations in the design

Table 2.1   Regional distribution of the labour Force in the UK cycle trade, 1891

Location	Number employed	% of total employment
Coventry	4 059	35.0
Birmingham & Aston Manor	2 575	22.0
London	922	8.0
Wolverhampton	643	5.6
Leicester	215	1.9
Nottingham	204	1.8

Source: Harrison, 1985, p. 43.

of the safety cycle attracted a growing middle-class following as a recreational activity, and 'The new class of cyclists became known as "cads on castors"'.[12] This massive increase in demand led to a proliferation of new firms entering the industry. Rapid growth occurred in an industry with a highly competitive structure, and with little or no barriers to entry. As can be seen in Table 2.2, the number of factories and workshops producing bicycles grew at an enormous rate between 1895 and 1897, the former doubling in numbers over the boom years. The figures for average numbers employed suggests that there were no discernible trends towards large-scale size, and the bulk of the firms in the industry remained very small. Thus, the number of workshop units outstripped the growth of factories over the boom years and workshops employed on average only 5.5 workers in 1897. Factory organisation was also small scale; the average number of factory employers was 26 in 1870 but had only risen to 43 in 1897. Average numbers employed, of course, are only a crude indicator of firm size,

Table 2.2   Growth of the cycle industry in the UK, 1895–97

		Factories			Workshops	
	Number	Total employed	Average employed	Number	Total employed	Average employed
1895	497	20 923	42.1	232	1 318	5.7
1896	721	36 405	50.5	434	2 856	6.6
1897	991	42 775	43.1	746	4 118	5.5

Source: Compiled from Harrison, 1985 p. 45.

and Harrison has pointed out that the expansion of home and foreign demand, associated with the boom of the mid-1890s, had 'helped to produce a number of sizeable enterprises in the cycle industry'. The four largest producers in terms of numbers employed were Humber (1 000), Swift Cycle (1 000), Premier Cycle (1 100), and the largest, Rudge-Whitworth (1 200). At least another eight firms employed between 500 and 1 000 employees, and these included firms such as Singer Cycle, Osmond Cycle and, as we shall see in the next chapter, the Raleigh Cycle Co.[13]

According to Harrison, a number of these larger enterprises were the result of amalgamations, take-overs and mergers. For instance, Humber & Co. Ltd 'was publicly floated in June 1887 to acquire Humber and Co. of Beeston, Nottingham, C. N. Baker's Coventry Cycle Co. and the Express Cycle Co. of Birmingham'. Seven years later, in 1894, five separate Birmingham cycle companies merged to form the Cycle Component Manufacturing Co., and in 1896 the New Rapid Cycle Co. was formed by a merger of Starley Bros with four other companies. One of the most important mergers of the period saw the formation of Rudge-Whitworth in 1894, a merger between the Rudge Cycle Co. of Coventry and the Whitworth Co. of Birmingham. This firm was to become one of the industy's leaders prior to its purchase by the Gramophone Co. of London in 1936, and its subsequent absorption by the Raleigh Holding Co. Ltd in 1943.[14] Its importance during the early years of the cycle industry is worthy of some consideration.

The company's origins can be traced back to developments in the bicycle trade in Coventry and Wolverhampton. The main entrepreneurial figure in its formation was a Coventry solicitor, George Woodcock (b. Coventry 1837, d. 18 May 1891). In 1874 Woodcock had founded the Watch Manufacturing Co. of Coventry, and using his accumulated capital he purchased the cycle factory of Haynes & Jefferies, Spon Street, Coventry, in 1879. He thereby invested in a well-established firm, with a reputation for specialist cycle manufacture. Haynes & Jefferies had not been the first company in Coventry to produce cycles, having been preceded by the Coventry Machinist Co. and Smith & Starley. Nevertheless, the latter two firms had also combined cycle manufacture with the production of sewing-machines, and James Starley, for instance, had also been instrumental in the formation of the Coventry Machinist Manufacturing Co. in 1869, when he had changed the company's name from the Coventry Sewing Machine Co. Thus, Haynes & Jefferies could claim the reputation of being the first firm in Coventry to concentrate production solely on cycles, and when Woodcock purchased the factory in 1879 he formed a new enterprise, the Tangent and Coventry Tricycle Co. In 1880 this firm was amalgamated with

Daniel Rudge, a Wolverhampton cycle manufacturer, and the company's operations were transferred exclusively to Coventry. In 1885, Wood-cock injected fresh capital into the enterprise when he brought in several Birmingham investors and established a limited company, D. Rudge & Co. Ltd. It was this firm which amalgamated with Whitworths in 1894, just prior to the cycling boom. Rudge & Co. was a highly innovative firm, and was, for example, one of the first manufacturers to fit Dunlop pneumatic tyres to its bicycles. It brought to the new merged firm of Rudge-Whitworth a list of patents which included rotary and detachable cranks (1876), Rudge ball bearings (1878), hinged handlebars (1884 and 1885), new rotary brake (1885), Crescent Steering (1886) and Bicycette US (1886). The sale value of the assets of the two companies was estimated at £132 746, and the new company was incorporated with a nominal capital of £200 000, divided into 100 000 ordinary shares of £1 each and 20 000 preference shares of £5 each, the latter entitled to a cumulative dividend of 6 per cent.[15]

This merger proved to be highly successful, and during the first quarter of the twentieth century Rudge-Whitworth was 'the largest cycle and motor cycle manufacturing concern in Coventry'. In 1906, the firm produced 75 000 out of the 310 000 bicycles made in the city during that year, and employed some 2 700 workers. Other large producers in Coventry included the New Premier Cycle Co., with an output of 40 000 machines in 1897, Swift Cycles (formerly the Machinist Co.), producing approximately 35 000 machines in 1896, and Humber, which in 1898 was manufacturing 1 000 cycles per week.[16] Nevertheless, despite the emergence of these industrial leaders, the industry remained highly competitive. Firms required only a relatively small amount 'of capital ... to start in the cycle industry and the ready availability of capital, labour and optimistic entrepreneurs created a situation in which entry was easy, if not always sustained or successful'.[17] Indeed, many firms were to disappear as inevitably the 'boom years gave way to bust', and the industry was faced with considerable problems of adjustment after 1897. But prior to an examination of the post-boom period, the next section will focus on the concept of the industrial district, and explore the development of bicycle manufacture at a local level.

Production and the industrial district

In the early years of the cycle industry in Britain the pattern of development saw the simultaneous development of a whole range of manufacturers producing accessories and fittings for the bicycle, alongside the growth of complete-cycle makers. The development of very large-scale factories, which fabricated the complete cycle, would eventually come to dominate the industry, especially by the inter-war years, but in the early history of the industry, as we have seen, the vast bulk of manufacturers remained small. As Grew has informed us: the small maker relied very largely on 'component makers for his output'.[18] Thus, for example, William Morris, later Lord Nuffield, began a bicycle repair and manufacturing business in Oxford in 1893 with a capital of £4. He would cycle 'as far as Birmingham to get components' and when he acquired them 'he would often work on the job far into the night, sometimes all night'.[19]

The growth of component manufacturers was clearly evident in the main industrial centres of the cycle industry. For example, in 1894 Coventry had, in addition to its 48 cycle manufacturers, 32 component-makers subdivided into 16 different trades, and at the turn of the century Birmingham could boast 189 component-makers alongside its 301 cycle-manufacturing firms. These two centres of the trade did display differences, with Birmingham having a more variegated cycle component sector than that in Coventry. Nevertheless, the latter did become 'well known for the manufacture of frames, bearings, saddles and tyres, as well as other parts used in cycle assembly and this contributed to the industry's overall growth and significance within the city'.[20] Specialist component producers provided an interlocking business environment supplying manufacturers with parts for final assembly. In the actual manufacture of bicycles the maker might purchase a complete frame from one supplier or decide to buy the tubes and lugs and construct the frame himself. Tyres would come from another specialist, as did handlebars, seat accessories, mudguards, gears, chains, etc. The actual work in the factory or workshop consisted 'largely of polishing, enamelling, plating and assembly'. Factories of this type did not 'require a plant of machine tools, a design staff, or much organising ability'.[21] Consequently, firms could be set up with a minimum of capital outlay and, not dissimilar to the early nineteenth-century cotton industry, could rent machinery and premises and rely upon trade credit to tide them over between production and sale.[22] In terms of the design of premises they 'did not have to be particularly specialised' and, for example, 'prior to 1900 some 14 Birmingham cycle and component manufacturers established themselves in premises previously occupied by tailors, drapers and outfitters, and 6 in grocer's shops'. Thus, William Morris's first bicycle workshop 'was a brick building at the back of his father's house in James Street, Cowley St Johns, Oxford. His home became very much a place of business. The front room of the double fronted house became his show room and shop'.[23]

While Morris was to branch out from bicycle manufacturing to motor cycle and motor car production, and become one of Britain's most successful businessmen in the first half of the twentieth century, for the bulk of small firms mere survival was their main ambition. The cycle trade was characterised by a high turnover of firms but, paradoxically, this also eased entry into the industry. As Scranton has pointed out in terms of the Philadelphia textile industry:

> Failed family firms leave behind substantially developed plant and equipment for others to activate; mill space is readily occupied and old machines may be so cheaply bought as to be profitably operable or sufficiently adaptable to be modified for new purposes that eluded their former owners ... collapses may open the way for new starts as much as success offers examples for them to emulate.[24]

Similar to the example of textiles, firms in the bicycle industry had access to second-hand machinery, and this was associated with the high turnover of firms. This may help to explain, at least in part, the spectacular increase in the number of bicycle firms. For instance, Birmingham witnessed a doubling of its cycle-manufacturing units between 1895 and 1898, the numbers increasing from 159 to 309. In addition, the number of fitting and accessory firms rose from 53 to 145 over the same period. The industry displayed a disintegrated system of production, characterised by the continuing existence of small-scale producers in a sector with low barriers to entry. Thus, Harrison's analysis of Coventry and Birmingham trade directories showed that from the 1880s to the turn of the century 1 247 firms entered the cycle, component and accessories industries of the two cities, but 628 failed to stay the course. Further, in Nottingham, in the years between 1886 and 1898, '52 per cent of the new entrants ... endured for no more than four years and only 28 per cent for ten years or more'.[25]

It was sufficient to start business with small and informal sources of initial capital which used local and familial business networks. In Coventry, for example, many cycle firms employed no more than three or four employees, there was little or no use of expensive machinery, no use of depots for distribution, and there was no allowance given for depreciation, repairs or overheads.[26] These small producers, who also characterised the industry in Birmingham, were referred to as 'garretmen', and their continued survival in the cycle trade was in part a result of the support they received from the 'specialist, large scale, cycle component manufactures'. Millward informs us that 'During the course of the boom of 1896–7', small makers with their cheaper products 'were reckoned to have got hold of an abnormally large slice of the cycle trade at a time when many of the largest concerns were tardy in introducing a cheap but reliable machine aimed at a potentially wider cycle public'.[27] This symbiotic relationship is suggestive of the notion of an 'industrial district', and Scranton's concept of 'proximity'. To explore this, we can examine the two key centres of the cycle trade, Birmingham and Coventry.

Scranton has been at the forefront of those scholars who have stressed the importance of focusing 'on the existence of a spectrum of possible approaches to manufacturing ranging from custom and batch work to bulk and mass production'.[28] The development of mass production as a route to modern economic success, particularly from the late nineteenth century, has been articulated in the influential work of Alfred D. Chandler jnr.[29] The route to economic success is associated with the rise of large-scale firms but, as Scranton points out, if we ignore the continued existence of custom and batch production then we are in danger of missing part of the history of industrial capitalism since the latter part of the nineteenth century. It is in this context that the notion of the industrial district acts as a useful methodological device in exploring business change. It raises the important point that there 'may be pathways to industrial capitalism different from but in many ways complementary to the large-scale route identified by ... Chandler'.[30] Studies of industrial districts have shown the importance of clusters of firms at the regional level and the formation of an alternative mode of production to that of large-scale organisation. Scranton, for instance, argues that firms which specialised in batch production methods 'often located in proximity to one another' created inter-firm networks within the industrial district. Such firms can conduct their activities 'most effectively in spaces with densely concentrated specialist firms, each of which may interact with others in fairly complex productive sequences'. These industrial districts emerged in the industrial countries of Western Europe during the early stages of industrial capitalism, and also in the USA.[31]

In the case of the British bicycle industry, there is little difficulty in designating Birmingham as an industrial district, but there are also good grounds for supposing that the rapid development of bicycle production in Coventry during the last three decades of the nineteenth century was facilitated by the advantages accruing from the characteristics of an industrial district. In the latter, the diffusion of good practice and technological innovation in the city's bicycle trade was not simply confined to leading firms such as the Starleys or the Hillmans. Rather, the competitive nature of the industry in Coventry provided a fertile ground for technological change. As Thoms and Donnelly show, in Coventry 'The competitive nature of the cycle trade, stimulated by the practice of introducing revised models for the new season, ensured that changes relating to technical specifications and designs occurred with great frequency'.[32] As Scranton has noted, such competitive factors placed a premium on batch production where firms were required to

meet often specific and 'time-centre needs' based on 'institutional flexibility rather than routinization'.[33] Thus, D. Wright and Sons, bicycle
manufacturers of Coventry, informed potential customers in 1894 that
their 'machines were built to any design', and they could supply 'up to
date cycle fittings ... including the latest Humber-pattern frames made
up for sale with or without wheels'.[34]

In turn, the industrial districts were characterised by the building up
of networks through contractual relations. As Scranton points out,
owners and managers of firms in the industrial district would 'undertake efforts to institutionalise contracts among firms, and between them,
their clients, and workers, so as to create governance mechanisms that
might manage routine relationships or sustain solidarity in times of
challenge or crisis without creating restraining rigidity'.[35] It provided
the opportunity for firms to create networks of trust which could
reduce transaction costs on the market and develop effective flows of
information.[36] Thoms and Donnelly have argued that in Coventry networks between local firms were facilitated through the flow of
information which 'made it possible for many smaller firms', without
the reason to develop their own technical advances, to flourish by
tapping into a pool of 'local intelligence received in a variety of ways'.
In other words, many small firms benefited from the externalities generated at the level of the industrial district, and while a number of firms
used patents to protect their technological information, 'the costs of
registration and defending them in the courts deterred some firms from
making full use of this device'.[37]

In centres of the cycle trade such as Coventry and Birmingham, inter-
firm networks were also facilitated by the diversification of existing
firms into the bicycle trade. The three main sources that provided the
origins of growth for the cycle trade in Coventry were ribbon-weaving,
watchmaking and the manufacture of sewing-machines. For example,
in 1874/75 Coventry had 45 ribbon manufacturers and 150 watch
manufacturers, the latter being subdivided into 11 different
specialisations. These staple trades provided a pool of entrepreneurial
talent, and provided a base of technological knowledge. For example,
as we saw earlier, James Starley, one of the pioneers of the cycle industry, had his business antecedents in the sewing-machine industry, and
was the founder in 1861 of the Coventry Sewing Machine Co. Starley
changed the name of this company to the Coventry Machinist Co. in
1869, and it was this firm which provided the seed-bed for a number of
dynamic entrepreneurs who played key roles in the early development
of the cycle industry. A number of former employees of the company
went on to establish their own cycle firms, and these included George
Singer, William Hillman, and Thomas and John Bayliss. In turn, these

men subsequently 'provided the training which enabled others to branch out as independent bicycle producers'.[38] A network of business experience and learning emerged which was critical to the perpetuation of firms within the early cycle industry.

This pattern of development was further reinforced by the focus of the industry on batch production. The emphasis on batch production and flexible technologies allowed firms to pursue a strategy of business diversification in response to changing market demand. Such flexibility was crucial to the survival of batch producers and, as Scranton points out, for that type of producer 'The selection of plant and equipment becomes less scientific and more a question of judgement ... Selling is no longer a matter of disposing of products already on hand ... It is a question of marketing what the plant can successfully make'.[39] Thus, many cycle firms 'modified their focus of interest according to the structure of demand. These changes not only provided the opportunities for diversification, but frequently made it a condition for survival'. This pattern can be detected in the decision of firms to switch into cycle manufacture in the first instance. The emergence of the Coventry Machinist Co. was associated with the downturn in the sewing-machine industry in the late 1870s, and in 1894 Rotherhams, who were the largest watchmakers in Coventry and the technological leaders, 'turned to the production of cyclometers' owing to the depression in the watch trade. The main firm emerging from ribbon-weaving in Coventry was Riley & Co., but it would appear that watchmaking rather than textiles provided 'a more fertile source of recruitment for the cycle industry'. For instance, the switch to cycle manufacturing by Rotherhams in the 1890s was accompanied by another large watchmaking concern, James Hawley & Sons, who moved into the industry at the same time.[40]

The advent of the safety cycle also provided outlets for component manufacturers to seize the opportunity for diversification and tapping into new markets. A case in point was Joseph Lucas and Son, who were to become major producers of lights for motor vehicles in the twentieth century and could trace the roots of its business success to its early involvement in the cycle industry. Founded in 1875 by Joseph Lucas, a Birmingham metal worker, the company initially produced patented ships' lamps which found a market both at home and in the USA. Nevertheless, the company's early history demonstrates the precarious nature of operating a small business concern during its early years of growth. By the early 1870s the firm was living a precarious existence, starved of both working capital and the resources to expand output, and vulnerable to periodic downturns in demand. The firm survived, however, and the dedication and close attention of its proprietors to the financial needs of the company, together with an understanding of the need to diversify production, ensured not only survival but considerable business success. A close working partnership was formed between Joseph and his son, Harry, the former taking charge of factory operations, while the latter acted as a roving agent, touting for business both at home and abroad. In 1882 Harry was made a formal partner, and under his prompting the firm was quick to seize the opportunity offered for expansion by the innovatory developments in cycle manufacturing in Coventry. Harry wrote to his father that 'We must keep our eyes open for cheap work. It pays best, and I want something for the lads ... We do nothing with the Coventry [bicycle] manufacturers. I'm afraid some of them connect our name with expensive lamps only and don't know or forget we do cheap ones'. Consequently, they produced the '48.5' series model, a lamp which hooked on to the wheel hub of the cycle, and sold at the reasonable cost of 2s. 2d. They also developed a standard series 50 model which sold for 2d. more but came with a brass barrel cycle fitting. In the 1880s the firm gained a reputation for supplying high quality but reasonably priced lamps to Coventry producers, and in 1885 were supplying lamps to Starley and Sutton for their first safety cycle.[41]

The switch from traditional trades to new sectors such as cycles was further facilitated by the structure of Coventry's labour force. The emergence of cycle factories and workshops has been described as offering 'asylums for weavers, watchmakers, and others down on their luck'.[42] The assimilation of these workers into the cycle trades may be accounted for by the type of technology used by early cycle manufacturers. As Harrison has pointed out, the pedal cycle itself was not particularly a 'scientific piece of advanced engineering technology', and certainly its manufacture did not require 'a specific and high grade scientific education and technical training [for] its basic principles to be understood'. In technological terms the manufacture of cycles were 'well within' the reach of the 'artisan and men willing to appreciate its basic mechanised principles by observation and cycle riding experience'. Understood from this perspective 'the cycle industry, as a new industry, was able to take root early and to flourish in ... Britain because its development demanded, technologically, little more than the traditional, empirically-based aptitudes of the British engineering craftsmen, and the ideas of the mechanically-minded man'.[43] Thus, in Coventry, the traditional engineering skills of its labour force gave to cycle firms, in the early stages of their development, a flexibility which could combine the buying in of components with the designing and making of their own tools. For example, George Freeman, born in 1842, 'trained as a loom builder before joining the (Coventry) Machinist Co., where he remained for some years, eventually ending his career as a toolmaker with Rudge-Whitworth'.[44]

The adaptability of the workforce, which this example implies, is consistent with Scranton's view that 'the choice ... between variety and volume had strong technical correlations built into the structure of production'. Scranton holds that 'batch producers relied on general purpose machinery and tools that could be adapted to multiple tasks rather than seeking dedicated mechanisms devoted to accelerating the flow of standard items'.[45] For example, BSA, when it re-entered cycle-component manufacturing in 1893, converted its 'idle shell-making plant', which contained 'row upon row of semi-automatic copying lathes', to the production of cycle hubs. This successful conversion of 60 per cent of the plant for this purpose by the end of December 1893, led the firm to widen the range of manufacture from hubs to 'bottom brackets (complete with axles, chain wheels and cranks), pedals, cycle chains and steel balls'.[46] The diversity of production was also demonstrated by the firm of Humber of Beeston. Formed as the cycling firm of Humber, Marriott & Cooper in 1880, this company, 'Like many engineers of this period ... turned their hands to any product in demand' and, for example, produced lace machines for the well-known firm of Pollard's when the market for lace was buoyant. Specialist machine-makers for the lace trades of Nottingham and district also diversified, often for short periods, into bicycle production. With the lace industry facing periodic recessions in the 1870s and 1880s, specialist firms such as Gambles, bobbin and carriage makers, Jardines, lace-machine makers, and Pycroft, general engineers, turned their attention to the attractions of the cycle market. Cycle construction 'called for mechanical skills similar to those required in the construction of lace and hosiery machinery', and by the third quarter of the nineteenth century Nottingham's reputation as a centre of machine-building excellence was already well established.[47] These firms were pursuing what Scranton has described as a strategy of 'profusion'. That is, they did not focus on the mass volume output of one item but instead produced a 'profusion of goods skilfully made'. Crucial, of course, to the success of such a strategy was the availability of skilled workers 'whose shop floor versatility made productive diversity flexible'.[48] Even in the 1890s, when the impact of the cycle boom strained Coventry's skilled labour resources, the city's 'proximity to the West Midland industrial conurbation was a particular asset' which allowed it to tap into a large pool of skilled labour.[49]

Shortages of skilled labour from the 1890s stimulated local initiatives in technical education in Coventry. As Thoms argues, Coventry, as early as 1914, was recognised as a centre of excellence in the provision of technical engineering in education with the development of technical colleges catering for apprentices and involving close co-operation between employers and the city's educational institutions. A general increase 'of technical education in Coventry coincided with a transformation in the city's industrial base', initially involving the structural transformation from the staple watchmaking and textile trades to cycles, machine tools and motor vehicles. With the decline of the traditional staples from the 1860s the cycle trades provided new opportunities for employment and 'elevated Coventry to one of the most dynamic local economies of the twentieth century'. From the late nineteenth century there was a growing demand for skilled and semi-skilled labour, and from the mid-1890s, as the pool of skill in the staple trades dried up, there were increasing opportunities for local initiatives in technical education and training. At a local level, institutions such as the Coventry and District Engineering Employers' Association and the Coventry Mechanics' Institute became actively engaged from the 1890s in promoting technical education. These initiatives enhanced the general engineering skills of the workforce but, as Thoms points out, in the early years little provision was made for technical education in the industries of cars and cycles, and it was not until 1901, when the Coventry cycle boom was over, that a class at the Coventry Technical Institute in cycle construction was offered. This delay was most probably attributable to Coventry's reliance on importing cycle components from outside the city.[50] As we shall see in the next chapter, the Raleigh Company at Nottingham was equally aware of the importance of component supply and skilled labour within the Midlands industrial district. As its chairman and managing director, Frank Bowden, observed in 1900, the success of the company depended upon its proximity to the component suppliers of the Midlands and upon the personal attention of 'every official in the company – including the Managing Director, Secretary, London Manager, Travellers, Staff ... and Foremen'. In particular, he recognised that their 'mechanics are noted for their skill', and this, combined with personal attention, 'enables us to produce cycles ... that are unequalled in value in proportion to their prices, for correctness of construction, accuracy of detail ... easy running, durability, beauty of finish, and general excellence'.[51]

A final feature of the industrial district worthy of examination is the notion of personal capitalism with its focus on the personal ownership and style of management of a select but clearly defined governance structure. A key structural feature of personal capitalism was the tendency to utilise local and familial sources of capital, and to legalise the firm through the use of partnerships and limited liability, both private and public, which sought to link money with technical expertise.[52] Firms could, and did, metamorphasise their legal form, moving from private to public, and in a number of cases, as we will see in the analysis of Raleigh in the next chapter, from private to public and back again.

Certainly, in the main centres of the trade small firms predominated, and they operated with very limited financial resources. In Coventry, even well-known firms such 'as Rover, Centaur, and Wareman & Hazlewood', had only moderate capital requirements in their early years. For example, these firms cut fixed capital requirements by renting their premises in buildings formerly owned by weavers. This seems also to have been a common feature in Birmingham. A survey of 18 firms listed in the rate books for the Aston district in 1901 showed 11 of them renting premises.[53] Harrison refers to the relatively small-scale nature of 'private incorporations', and one firm in his survey was converted with a nominal capital of just £26. There were of course exceptions to small-scale firms, and the firm of Rudge & Co., for example, raised £68 475 from private sources when it converted to private limited status in 1886. However, Harrison describes this allotment as 'singularly exceptional'.[54] In Birmingham, which overtook Coventry by the mid-1890s as the principle centre of bicycle-making, 'the capital needed for starting up and expanding' a cycle company 'could be found from ploughed back profits and local business contacts'. Indeed, even with the formation of public companies like Raleigh and Rudge-Whitworth in the 1890s, local networks were important for supplying capital for formation and further expansion. Thus, the directors of Rudge-Whitworth pursued an expansionary policy following the cycle boom of the mid-1890s, but informed the shareholders that 'The buildings, plant and machinery have been maintained in a state of high efficiency out of revenue', as well as additions to plant to meet increased capacity requirements. Charles Vernon Pugh, the managing director of Rudge-Whitworth, and the original proprietor of Whitworth's before amalgamation, was a successful Birmingham manufacturer of screws and nuts, and was in an ideal position for tapping into local sources of finance. In 1893 the Whitworth Co. privately issued '£30 000 £1 shares to 58 share holders, 34 of whom resided in Birmingham and were connected with industrial activity and the professions'.[55]

Also important to the early development of firms was the link between financing partners and technical expertise. Thoms and Donnelly provide excellent examples of this link, and show how this business attribute underpinned some of Coventry's most successful cycle enterprises. J. K. Starley, for example, who was attributed with the invention of the safety cycle and who played an instrumental role in the formation of Rover, formed a partnership with W. Sutton in 1873. Their partnership established the Meteor Works which manufactured a highly popular tricycle as well as their famous safety cycle. Most of the capital for this undertaking was supplied by Sutton, who was 'a keen cyclist' and had made his money in Coventry's haberdashery trade.[56] As we shall see in the next chapter, this mix of technical and financial acumen was characteristic of the early development of Raleigh, and further expertise on the sales side of the business was also a common feature of the function of early managers and founders in the industry.

Another case in point was the partnership of William Hillman and William Herbert who united technical expertise with money when they formed the firm of Automachinery Ltd, though this firm may also have relied upon finance capital from outside the city. The attraction of this firm to private investors may well have been related to its technical versatility which meant that it could produce a diverse range of products and reduce the risks involved in capital investment. Thus, the firm pursued the strategy of 'profusion', discussed earlier, manufacturing cycle parts, sewing-machines and roller-skates. During the height of the cycle boom in 1896 the cycle part of the business was hived off to form the New Premier Cycle Co. This company had a labour force of 600 and an annual output of 33 000 cycles, making it one of the largest cycle manufacturers of the time.[57]

These attributes of the early entrepreneurs were reinforced by the familial nature of business enterprise and this was clearly demonstrated in the case of the Herbert Brothers. While William Herbert was actively involved in the Automachinery Co. at Coventry his younger brother, Alfred Herbert, who arrived in the city in 1887, took the post of works manager in the steam-engine building firm of Coles and Matthews. In 1888 Alfred formed a partnership with William Hubbard which took over the business of Coles and Matthews. They now began producing rim-bendings and other components relating to the cycle trade. The partnership was short-lived, but on Hubbard leaving the concern the business was already expanding and successful, not least because Alfred had secured the UK agency for weldless steel tubing from a French patent. This was a product 'much in demand in the late 1880s because of its application to the manufacture of the safety cycle'.[58] The importance of family interconnections to the business success of Alfred Herbert is summed up by Thoms and Donnelly:

> [Alfred] Herbert's family provided valuable assistance in promoting his engineering and business career, particularly his eldest brother William ... William Herbert appears to have been instrumental in securing Alfred's purchase of Cole and Matthews for he arranged for Matthews, who owned the business, to obtain an alternative ... source of income. It was also William Herbert who introduced his brother to the French owners of the lucrative steel tubing patent. William Herbert's cycle interests provided an important source of demand for Alfred's products and when the firm became a limited company in 1894 William appeared as one of the principal shareholders.[59]

The perpetuation of the family role in the cycle industry is also provided by the case of James Starley. Reputed to be the father of the British bicycle industry, he left the Coventry Machinist Co. in 1870 and formed a partnership with another enterprising businessman, William Hillman, to produce both bicycles and sewing machines. Hillman left the firm in 1874 to eventually form a partnership with William Herbert, and founded the Automachinery Co., while Starley established a business relationship with Borthwick Smith to produce sewing-machines, roller-skates and cycles. The firm was incorporated as a joint stock company in 1877, but the business experienced severe difficulties at the end of the 1870s and Starley immediately joined forces with two of his sons, John Marshall and William, to form the specialist cycle firm of Starley Bros. John and William were equipped with the technical knowledge of cycle manufacture and proved valuable assets to the expanding concern.[60]

This family route to business evolution was supplemented in the cycle trade not only by managerial spin-offs, but by what may be termed the cycling club or cycling racing path. Perhaps the most outstanding example of personal capitalism in the cycle trade was that of Harvey du Cros and his seven sons. A Dubliner, of Huguenot descent, he rose from clerk to manager and ultimately to a managing partner in a firm of Scottish paper manufacturers. By the 1870s he was a prosperous businessman and 'a firm advocate of the athletic way of life'. In this, he 'encouraged his sons to be cycle racers and he himself became president of the Irish Cycling Association'. This was the family, of course, which was to be instrumental in the formation of the Dunlop Co. The du Cros connection with J. B. Dunlop, who designed the pneumatic tyre, was triggered by events at Queens College Belfast in September 1889 when, to everyone's surprise, there was a victory in the annual cycle race by a rider on a machine fitted with pneumatic tyres. The tyres were designed by J. B. Dunlop, but were manufactured by the cycle firm of Edlin & Sinclair of Belfast. The success on the racing track attracted keen interest, and Dunlop was persuaded by William Bowden, the proprietor of Bowden & Sweden, cycle agents of Dublin, and J. M. Gillies, the manager of the *Freeman's Journal*, a Dublin newspaper, 'to permit the formation of a separate enterprise to exploit pneumatic tyre production'. In turn, Bowden and Gillies invited Harvey du Cros to join the project, which he eventually acceded to do when he was granted the full control over the new enterprise. The new company was floated in November 1889 with a public subscription of £15 000. Although shares were not fully subscribed for, it allowed the new concern to 'acquire Dunlop's patent of 1888', the cycle-manufacturing business of Edlin & Sinclair, and the Dublin cycle agency of Richard Booth, the latter purchase providing the business premises for the new venture. Trading under the names of the

Pneumatic Tyre Co. and the Booth Cycle Agency Ltd, the initial net profit of these concerns was £2 600 in 1889/90. The potential of the company, and the need for managerial talent, prompted du Cros to pull his seven sons 'out of school or employment and put them into the service of the new company'. The company's potential was not exaggerated, and by 1894/95 net profits had risen to the astronomical figure of £220 000. In 1891, the company had relocated to Coventry, and was refloated as the Dunlop Pneumatic Tyre Co. in May 1896 which 'laid the basis of the du Cros family's entrepreneurial empire'.[61]

By the eve of the great boom of the mid-1890s, the British bicycle industry had taken on a number of distinctive characteristics. A highly competitive industry, with a volatile firm population structure, it had developed business strategies associated with 'profusion', producing a range of different types of products rather than focusing on standardised output. Further, the industry was characterised by proximity with its emergence within distinctive industrial districts which allowed firms the advantages of external economies. Barriers to entry in the cycle industry were practically non-existent; the capital requirements for most firms could be adequately sourced by the local financial network and, while it is true that the industry saw the elevation to business prominence of a number of pioneering industrial leaders controlling large enterprises, the typical firm in the industry was small. Personal capitalism predominated with strong family commitment, or control by a few dominant individuals, and this permeated the governance structure of cycle firms. Nevertheless, the industry was to undergo dynamic change during the boom of the mid-1890s, when the cycle trade experienced an unprecedented demand for its products. The next section examines some of the main features of the boom years.

The bicycle boom, 1895–97

The antecedents of the boom lay in the late 1880s with 'the marriage ... of the diamond framed safety bicycle with Dunlop's pneumatic tyres'. This gave cycling a wider popular appeal and 'precipitated the industry's rapid expansion during the 1890s'.[62] Even before the spectacular bicycle boom of the mid-1890s *The Economist* was referring to the 'Cycle Tyre Craze', and pointing out that some investors had 'proved their gullibility by subscribing to one or other of the highly speculative class of undertakings which have seen the light in the past two or three years'. By the summer of 1893, such was the 'craze' for cycle tyre companies that *The Economist* was concerned by the fact that potential investors had 'been inundated with prospectuses inviting them to provide the capital required for taking-up various patents in cycle tyres'.[63] This first bicycle promotion boom was centred on Dublin, which was not surprising given the success of the du Cros family and their association with the Dunlop pneumatic tyre enterprise, and the fact that 50 cycle manufacturers were located in the city.[64] As *The Economist* noted, share issues quoted on the Dublin Stock Exchange were reaching a 100 to 300 per cent premium, and proving highly rewarding to speculators. However, the journal preached caution, and was concerned that each prospectus issued claimed for its particular tyre a unique set of attributes together with the confident prediction that high profits were a foregone conclusion. In a clear warning to the investing public, *The Economist* claimed that these new companies had nothing tangible to sell, 'except their patents', and it considered that the majority of these possessed 'little value'. *The Economist* listed 13 firms (see Table 2.3) who offered a total capital of £835 000, 'all of which had been formed and most successfully floated'. However, company promoters had got in on the act and intended to take in cash, or shares, £605 000 for patents, the value of which was held to be dubious and, in some cases, litigation was already pending. *The Economist* concluded 'that in all probability the legal profession will be benefited at the expense of the foolish investor'.[65]

This mini-boom demonstrated the speculative nature of investment activity in the cycle trade, but it also proved to be just the precursor for

Table 2.3   Cycle tyre company flotations, January–June 1893

Date of issue	Company	Capital offered (£000)	Purchase price (£000)
18 January	Persil Flexible	170	150
1 April	Seddon's French	50	30
30 May	Sydney Pneumatic	50	40
5 May	Seddon's Continental	35	35
5 May	Puncture Proof	50	20
11 May	Pneumatic Wheel	85	50
18 May	Preston Davies	60	50
27 May	Grappler Pneumatic	75	46
27 May	McDonald's Puncture Proof	35	24
29 May	Surrey Pneumatic	50	35
3 June	Turner Pneumatic	50	30
14 June	Hook Pneumatic	40	30
14 June	Manhole Pneumatic	85	65

Source: *The Economist*, 7 June 1893, p. 728.

an investment mania which was to engulf the cycling trade in the mid-1890s. Rapidly growing domestic demand was accompanied by a rising growth in exports. The value of cycle exports, for example, rose from £1 311 251 to £1 648 861 over the 11-month period ending November 1896, an increase of 25.7 per cent, and export sales for November 1896 totalled £144 120 compared with £80 418 for the previous November. In terms of the total value of British exports, of course, the cycle industry was eclipsed by the traditional staple sectors, and this is shown in Table 2.4. Nevertheless, in 1896 'A substantial increase took place in the value of cycles exported'. This rising export demand was accompanied by an 'enormous' increase in the popularity of cycling which 'caused a constantly increasing demand for machines, with a corresponding increase in the profits of the companies'.[66] As the *Financial Times* reported, in an article on the 'Cycling Boom', in April 1896:

> For some time past the cycling industry has been making enormous strides; the manufacturing companies have been unable to keep pace with the orders, and their shares have been steadily rising in value, in anticipation of the splendid dividends which are in many instances assured. There is at present no indication of any slackening down of popular enthusiasm with regard to cycling.[67]

Rising business confidence triggered a phenomenal increase in the number of cycle manufacturing firms, as well as concerns producing cycle com-

Table 2.4   Rate of change in a range of manufactured exports, for 11 months ending November 1896

Category	Value (£)	% change over December 1895
Cycles	1 648 861[a]	+25.7
Cotton yarn	9 229 958	+7.5
Cotton piece goods	46 940 120	+9.8
Woollen yarns	5 243 136	+6.1
Woollen fabrics	5 831 001	+1.8
Worsted fabrics	7 669 380	−18.3
Total textile	96 646 093	+4.0
Iron and steel	21 853 794	+21.9
Machinery and engineering	15 515 900	+11.7
Coal	14 020 235	−2.0

Note: [a] Disaggregated from carriages.

Source: *The Economist*, 12 December 1896, p. 3.

ponents and accessories. In Birmingham, cycle-manufacturing firms doubled in number between 1895 and 1898, and component and accessory manufacturers almost trebled over the same period. Birmingham itself overtook Coventry as the main cycle-producing centre over the mid-1890s boom years, and this is shown in Table 2.5 which provides data on the distribution of the workforce employed in the cycle trades between 1891 and 1911.[68]

Table 2.5   Percentage of total employed in the cycle trade, England and Wales, 1891–1911

	1891	1901	1911
Birmingham	22.3	23.5	26.5
Coventry	36.1	18.9	16.6
Elsewhere	41.6	57.6	56.9

Source: Millward, 1989, p. 166.

The business optimism amongst established cycle firms can be illustrated by the example of Rudge-Whitworth. Following its formation through amalgamation in 1894 the company made a loss of £27 924 in its first year of operations. In its first annual report of August 1895 this unsatisfactory result was explained by Charles Wallis and Charles Vernon Pugh, the chairman and managing director respectively. They argued that the loss was accounted for by a series of factors caused by the process of amalgamation itself which had caused delays in production and an inability to meet demand during 1895, and a further delay in realising the anticipated economies in production which was the underlying rational of the merger. Nevertheless, business optimism remained high, and as the directors informed the shareholders:

> the demand for ... cycles during the past season has been unprecedented, but owing to the difficulties before alluded to this demand could not be met. The designs and quality have given universal satisfaction. The unusually large orders for contracts already obtained for the 1896 season should secure a largely increased and profitable trade for the ensuing year.[69]

Such optimism was fully justified and buoyant market demand during 1896 created a net profit of £17 767. The company increased output by 45 per cent over the levels of 1895 but orders 'were greatly in excess of even the increased production'. To meet the need for further expansion, the company sold an additional 6 150 £5 ordinary shares to subscribers to meet the needs of investment in additional plant and machinery for the 1897 season. In 1897 the company recorded a net profit of £48 311 and the directors reported that 'The steady progress of the Company has been fully maintained ... the handsome profit shown will be a matter of congratulation for the shareholders, especially having regard to the moderate capitalisation of the Company'.[70]

The example of Rudge-Whitworth illustrates the opportunities presented by the boom in demand, and the high profits that could be reaped by expanding output through increased investment. Nevertheless, the boom was built upon fragile foundations, as the *The Economist* claimed in the summer of 1896. Recognising that cycle companies were busily engaged in production, and that good profits could be made, the journal nevertheless raised concern over the durability of demand for bicycles. Perspective investors were asked to consider the following:

> the great incentive to the demand for this type of locomotion is that it has become a fashionable rage. The vagaries of fashion, however, are as fickle as they are inscrutable ... an industry which is largely dependent upon such an essentially fluctuating condition of things can scarcely be said to afford a fitting medium to investors who are not prepared to run considerable risks for sake of obtaining a large return on their capital.[71]

On the other hand, company promoters had no such qualms concerning the 'vagaries of fashion', and seized on the rising demand for bicycles among the general public. As Harrison points out, company prospectuses attempted to underplay the risks involved in the industry and to persuade potential investors to discount risk by circulating prospectuses 'with the names of aristocrats, willing to serve as company directors'. For example, the Earl of Warwick became chairman of the Singer Cycle Co. in 1896 and the board also included the name of the Earl of Norbury. The former also held a directorship on the board of the British Pattison Hygienic Cycle Saddle Co. Ltd.[72] Indeed, within debates concerning British company law at the time the issue of the prospectus was of deep concern. As one commentator put it in 1900, the character of the prospectus was a 'chief evil' and the preparing of the prospectus was a 'high art' form. This art entailed projecting an inflated image of the company's prospects while, at the same time, 'communicating as little information as possible'.[73] Yet, the prospectus was the main medium of communicating to the investing public, and company promoters focused their attention on bringing cycle firms, particularly in Birmingham, to public issues. In that city alone, during 1896 and the early months of 1897, the conversion of cycle firms was occurring at the rate of about four a week.[74]

The two leading company promoters were E. T. Hooley, a former Nottingham lace manufacturer turned stockbroker, and H. J. Lawson who had arrived in Coventry in the early 1870s and who was involved in a series of company promotions which included most importantly Rudge, Humber, the Great Horse Less Carriage Co. and the New Beeston Cycle and Manufacturing Co.[75] While the value of new share issues in the cycle and related industries 'constituted only a small percentage of the total value of new issues during the peak year of 1896', it did reach 13.4 per cent of the total.[76] In terms of the size of issue, of 193 flotations between 1882 and 1914, 33.6 per cent were for £30 000 or less and 51.8 per cent for £50 000 or less. Harrison claims that a 'striking feature' of the cycle trade was 'the relatively large number of cycle manufacturers entertaining what contemporaries considered to be "small" floatation issues of £30,000 or less'.[77]

The small-scale nature of cycle company flotations came in for severe criticism from *The Economist*, which associated small capital issues with small business organisations. Although agreeing that small private ventures could be 'prosperous', the cycle conversions were condemned as 'quite unsuited for conversion into joint-stock enterprises'.[78] The problem was, according to Harrison, that small conversions, with a capital of £50 000 or less, 'precluded either a stock exchange quotation or a free market in shares'.[79] Such conversion exercises served to featherbed the likes of company promoters such as Hooley and Lawson. According to *The Economist* the cost of incorporation was usually 'out of all proportion to the nominal capitalisation of the company', and in fact such concerns had no need of the influence of the company promoter. Carefully managed and progressive firms, *The Economist* claimed, would have little difficulty in finding the necessary accommodations on reasonable terms 'from their bankers', who were 'only too anxious to lend to customers of good credit and repute'.[80] But it was not only the small fry who were caught in the web spun by company promoters such as Hooley and Lawson. There were larger victims who were all too ready to become entangled, and a classic example is provided by the Humber Co.

In 1892 the founder of this concern, Thomas Humber, retired from the business and Martin D. Rucker became general manager. Rucker was an extrovert, and like many of the early pioneers of the trade he was a keen sportsman. He was described by a contemporary acquaintance 'who knew him well ... as ... recklessly extravagant'. Rucker came under the influence of Hooley and the latter, behind the scenes, began to steer the company in a new direction. Backed by Hooley, the Humber Co. Ltd entered into a series of promotions of subsidiary companies in the USA, Russia, Portugal, Denmark and Sweden, and also established in Paris 'a very sizeable depot of almost factory proportions'. In Britain, the company operated three major producing plants: at Beeston, four miles outside Nottingham, and at Wolverhampton and Coventry, and by the mid-1890s the total output of these factories placed the firm 'among the leaders of the world's cycle makers'. In September 1895 it was proposed that a new company, the Humber Supply Co. Ltd, be formed with a capital of £150 000 consisting of shares of £100 each. The newly constructed company would take over all the trading activities of the Humber Co.'s business, allowing the latter to concentrate on production but also now purchasing from Hooley the business of Marriot and Cooper, Humber's original partners, who still retained the rights to sell the bicycle under the trade mark of the Humber machine.[81]

When Marriot and Cooper had left the original partnership they had established themselves as cycle wholesalers, and as Thomas Humber 'had taken no steps ... to protect his designs, patents or the use of the Humber name on Humber machines', the two partners were entitled to market the Humber cycle on their own under a production licence to Daniel Rudge of Wolverhampton. Thomas Humber attempted to differentiate his machines by calling them 'Genuine Humber' and later the 'Beeston Humber'. In contrast, Marriott & Cooper also promoted the cycle as the 'Genuine Humber' informing customers 'that no make of cycles have attained the popularity ... that Marriott and Cooper's genuine Humbers have in six months'. It was in this complex and somewhat confusing business situation that Hooley proposed to the Humber directors the buy-out of Mariott & Cooper by the new Humber Supply Co. But not all at Humber were in agreement with Hooley, and one director objected to Hooley's plans. His direct line of attack concerned the proposed buy-out of Marriott & Cooper. As he argued, although 'This competition is irritating to us ... they do not do a great deal of business and there is a great doubt as to whether their rights to use the style names is assignable'. The director acknowledged that his 'co-directors do not seem to support my desire that Marriott & Cooper's rights to assign should be thoroughly sifted before he (Hooley) decides on this question of purchasing at the price', and he consequently attacked the proposal on three other fronts. First, he attacked the principle that prices should be fixed between the two companies. In this scheme the existing company would supply machines to the new company at fixed prices, but this opened up questions of equity, with the real possibility that such a price system would ensure that more benefits would flow to one company compared to the other. The consequence of this would be to create 'Conflicting interests ... between shareholders'. Second, the director objected that the creation of a new company 'would materially increase expenses, while the power of administration and control would not be strengthened because the management is limited to the same brain force'. Finally, he pointed out that as Humber shares were, at that time, selling at a 200 per cent premium, it was questionable why they should pay promoters and underwriters their high fees to set up a new company 'instead of adopting the simple process of increasing our capital, if necessary'.[82]

These objections were swept aside, and Hooley himself became involved closely in the formulation of business policy at Humber. Rucker's decision to establish close links with Hooley almost brought Humber down, and was to destroy his career with the company. As the cycle mania 'spent its force', and gave way to business downturn, Hooley's business networks began to unravel, and in 1898 he was declared bankrupt. By 1898 Humber was in serious financial difficulties, but so were speculators such as Hooley and Rucker. Hooley's fall 'cast rumours of corruption on the activities of many prominent men in the cycle trade, Humber men among them, and in particular Hooley's close friend ... Martin Rucker'. The alarm created in the cycle trade led to the fall of Rucker and the entire board of directors at Humber. The new board appointed was confronted with taking drastic action by shutting down all the company's overseas factories, and its plant at Wolverhampton. The flirtation of Humber with speculators such as Hooley brought it close to financial disaster, but the company survived, and went on to adapt, diversify and prosper. But, as the bicycle boom crashed into depression, a good number of the firms launched on the froth of 1895–97 were to sink without trace.[83] This brings us to the crisis in the cycle trade and the years of adjustment after 1897, years too of intense competition, particularly from American cycle-makers who could supply cheap standardised machines at high volume output into the British market.

Crisis and adjustment, 1897–1914

In the summer of 1896 *The Economist* referred to the 'successful flotation of so many cycle companies'. This boom continued in the second half of 1896 and into early 1897 when *The Economist* observed that 'of the making of bicycle companies there is no end, and if recent registrations at Somerset House are to be accepted as the shadow of coming events investors ... are likely to be afforded plenty more opportunities' of placing their capital in cycle companies. Clearly, the boom in cycle company promotions was fuelled by the expectations of high returns, and the 'handsome dividends paid by certain cycle companies' was reflected in the rapid increase in the share price of successful firms. For example, in 1897 Rudge-Whitworth, with unbridled optimism concerning the future, formed a subsidiary foreign trading company, and announced to its shareholders unprecedented dividends for the year ending August 1897 of 6 per cent on preference shares and 10 per cent on ordinary shares.[84]

Nevertheless, *The Economist* had a strong warning for potential investors in cycle companies. Recognising that windfall returns could be made, in certain cases cycle shares being sold at premiums ranging 'from 25 per cent to nearly 400 per cent', there were however considerable risks attached to speculation in newly floated cycle companies. In particular, *The Economist* thought it prudent to inform potential investors that quotations for cycle companies were often 'more nominal than real'. It further maintained that brokers were actually prepared to discourage their clients from purchasing most of the cycle issues 'for the simple reason that the particulars available are generally of a very vague character, and that, even in the cases of well established undertakings, the valuations placed upon the shares freely discount future profits'. Entrepreneurs could, of course, apply for patents to protect potentially valuable inventions, but these were frequently of a temporary nature and were 'being constantly superseded'. Thus, investors could not afford to be sanguine over the outcome of the various cycle promotion schemes, for 'the doctrine of the survival of the fittest' was 'especially applicable to the cycle industry'.[85]

At the height of the cycle craze, supply struggled to meet the buoyant demand, a problem which will be examined further in the case of Raleigh in the next chapter. But the boom also created the means of its own demise, as business optimism in the face of rising demand forced new capacity to come on stream by 1897. New factories were 'started up all over the country', and increased supply was also accentuated by the activities of the 'enormous number of small makers' who now entered the industry, plus the rapid rise of foreign cycle imports. The gulf opening up for the industry was quite clear to *The Economist*: supply would eventually exceed demand, and the ensuing intense competition would force prices to fall sharply. The outcome would be to engender the doctrine of the survival of the fittest, and a good number of the recently floated companies 'will be wiped out of existence'. Added to this problem of potential overcapacity was that of overcapitalisation. Firms which had been floated at the top of the boom based their capitalisation on the high profits earned during the cycle mania. In particular, too many small manufacturers were able to acquire 'ridiculously high terms' for their business, and the new enterprises that emerged from the flotation were, by late 1897, burdened with a capital base which required equally high profits to satisfy the expectations of shareholders in terms of high dividend payments. The profit-earning capability of cycle firms was, of course, conditioned by the continuation of the strong demand which had been at the forefront of the boom but, as trading conditions weakened, the short-term nature of high profits was exposed.[86] Boom now turned to bust, and reflecting on this event in 1922, Sir Harold Bowden, the head of Raleigh, noted that 'In the great company "boom" the Raleigh was swept in with all the others' to the 'ultimate and infinite regret' of the entrepreneurs within the industry.[87]

By the spring of 1897 there were already imminent signs of a downturn in trade. Stocks of cycles were now rising as trading conditions, during what was usually the high season for the cycle trade, were deteriorating. The situation for domestic producers was made all the more serious by the aggressive strategy of American manufacturers who 'flooded the U.K. market' with cheap standardised machines. In particular, the Americans made inroads into the market for women's bicycles which, at the time, was an important market for domestic manufacturers. Although French and German cycle exports rose in the first half of the 1890s, it was competition from the American cycle industry 'which posed the greatest threat to the British industry'. By 1897 there were approximately 700 cycle factories in the USA and the largest maker, the Pope Manufacturing Co., employed in the late 1890s over 5 000 workers, and operated a complex of plants in Hartford, Connecticut, embracing cycle tube, cycle tyre and complete-cycle manufacture. Its estimated output in 1897 was 70 000 machines, and in July of that year it caused a 'commotion' in the trade when it reduced its list prices by 25 per cent. The impact of this decision on British producers was all the more serious because during the height of the mania the 'better class' of maker at home tended to charge 'quite fancy prices'.[88] Such problems were also evident in continental markets. For example, in the French market the head of Raleigh's Paris depot reported in July 1897 that American competition 'was very serious ... and customers would not pay more than Frs 500 at the highest for best grade machines'. He went on to condemn British firms who failed to cut prices and consequently 'lost business'.[89]

The nature of the challenge facing the British industry from the mid-1890s was summed up by *The Economist* in a historical survey of 1925:

> There can be little doubt that British machines were at that time too dear, a very usual retail price being about £15 15s. The Americans applied to the industry the same principles which Mr Henry Ford later adopted in the motor trade. By the production of standardised parts in vast quantities they lowered prices by about 50 per cent.[90]

To meet this challenge British firms would have to respond by 'a general lowering of prices'. The problems facing the industry were, however, compounded by a sharp fall in British cycle exports to the USA. In value terms they stood at over £255 000 in 1892 but had collapsed to only £5 723 by 1898 (Table 2.6). In contrast American cycle exports increased dramatically by 269.1 per cent between the fiscal years 1895/96 and 1896/97, reaching $7 005 323 in the latter year. Britain was by far the largest recipient of American machines, taking 33.9 per cent of the total in 1896/97 compared to 14.6 per cent for Germany and 10.5 per cent for Canada. The Americans successfully exploited weaknesses in the British cycle industry, and domestic manufacturers during the boom were unable to meet customer demand quickly. This, as we shall see, was particularly acute at the Raleigh Co., but it was a general problem which faced the industry, and there were growing complaints of long delays in delivery time, which was not helped by the inadequate provision for stocks during the off-season. Criticism was also levied against the pricing policy of British manufacturers. It was claimed that 'large discounts were given on list prices, irrespective of the amount ordered'. In contrast, American and continental makers adopted a different strategy by using a 'net cash pricing system ... not subject to discount'. In these circumstances contractual trust was diminished, and 'feelings amongst agents and customers, both at home and abroad, began to run high against British manufacturers'.[91]

Table 2.6 Value of exports of cycle and cycle parts from the UK to the USA, 1892–98

	(£)
1892	255 466
1893	200 225
1894	70 744
1895	162 702
1896	187 412
1897	24 308
1898	5 723

Source: Harrison, 1969, p. 291.

The initial response of the British makers to the new competitive challenge of the second half of the 1890s did seem to take on the appearance of complacency. *The Economist*, albeit with the advantage of hindsight, accused the cycle industry of being 'lulled ... into a false sense of security, relying on their perception of their success in the early and mid-1890s'.[92] Among the large manufacturers, with few exceptions, the majority of firms appeared to have believed in the 'indefinite prosperity' of the cycle trade, a fact which was reflected in the inflated capital values of companies floated during 1896 to 1897. In addition to growing competition in the home market, British manufacturers also lost ground abroad, and they were overtaken by the Americans in 1898 and by the Germans in 1900.[93] At first sight, this looks like another example of British entrepreneurial failure during the second industrial revolution of the late nineteenth century. In a new industry, bicycles, British businessmen seemed to fail to respond adequately to the more dynamic enterprise of their American and continental rivals. Such damnation, however, is not as straightforward as it seems, and the British cycle industry fought back vigorously against the competitive challenge from abroad. The American challenge was quickly rebuffed as they were edged out of the domestic market and, particularly after 1906, British makers clawed back the German lead in world cycle markets.[94] The challenge was met by British producers pursuing three basic strategies: a more competitive pricing policy, a shift in the methods of production and diversification into related activities such as motor cycles and motor cars.

The strategy of price cutting was first introduced by Rudge-Whitworth, one of the most successful of the pre-1914 cycle firms. In July 1897 it reduced the price of its special cycle by almost 50 per cent from £30 to £16, and of its standard cycle from £20 to £12. Most other firms, including as we shall see the Raleigh Co., held off reducing their prices until 1898 when the reality of the competitive environment forced on them the inevitable. For example, Raleigh reported in March 1898 that 'Humber's recent drop in price is hurting us to a considerable extent. The American competition is also not yet done with', and this led to an increasing emphasis on producing cheaper models.[95] By the end of 1898 the majority of the leading companies 'were introducing their special cheap machines', and between this date and 1914 the trend of prices in the industry 'was firmly set in decline'.[96] Some firms, such as Singer and the Premier Cycle Co., did attempt to resist this trend, and persisted with a high-price and high-quality strategy. In part, this was related to the high capitalisation of these companies, and their desire to keep up prices was conditioned by the need to generate sufficient earnings to pay shareholder dividends. For example, a review of the business performance of Singer noted the 'apparent impossibility of earning a dividend for their shareholders on the present fabulous capital of £800 000', made up of £400 000 ordinary shares, £200 000 preference shares, and £200 000 capital debentures. Further, *The Economist* calculated that in order to pay its 4.5 per cent debenture holders, and 3 per cent preference share holders, it would have to earn £15 000 before even contemplating dividend payments 'to its long suffering ordinary share-holders'.[97]

As is shown in Table 2.7, Singer's profits deteriorated sharply after 1898, and in 1901 it actually made a loss, as indeed was also the fate of the Premier Cycle Co. which was forced to pay its interest on £100 000 of debenture holdings, and part of the preference dividend, out of the accumulated reserve fund. Singer was also accused by the trade press of depending for too long upon its past reputation of having significantly failed to introduce popular lines and follow the lead of companies such as Humber, Raleigh, Rudge-Whitworth and Enfield. Both Singer and Premier were eventually forced to change their policy radically in 1902, and Singer's managing director, Walter Hewit, announced to the trade that 'a cheaper bicycle was to be produced in the future'.[98] However, for those firms that failed to introduce lower-priced machines bankruptcy and failure were the inevitable outcome. As Table 2.8 shows, there was a significant decline in the number of cycle-makers in the three principal production centres between 1897 and 1913, an unambiguous confirmation of *The Economist's* earlier warning that the doctrine of the 'survival of the fittest' would ultimately prevail. Indeed, in addition to a more aggressive pricing policy, cycle firms needed to

Table 2.7   Profit and loss of the Singer Cycle Co., 1898–1901

	Profit (£)	Loss (£)	Ordinary dividend (%)	Preference dividend (%)	Debenture interest (%)
1897–98	27 053	—	4	5.5	4.5
1898–99	11 798	—	nil	5.5	4.5
1899–1900	12 062	—	nil	5.5	4.5
1900–01	—	1 342	nil	nil	nil

Source: Bicycle News and Motor Review, 1901, 58.

Table 2.8   Number of cycle-makers in Coventry, Birmingham and Nottingham, 1897 and 1913

	1897	1913	% decrease
Coventry	75	49	34.6
Birmingham	309	160	48.2
Nottingham	80	66	17.5

Source: Harrison, 1969, p. 302.

recognise the need for a 'dramatic writing down of capital' and *The Economist* welcomed warmly the capital reconstructions at Humber in 1900 and at Raleigh in 1901 which 'should place the concerns upon a sounder basis'. Further, *The Economist* praised the management at the Premier Cycle Co. in 1903 for its foresight in 'writing down its capital heroically'. This reconstruction meant that the company 'has made quite a promising restart, after getting rid of a composite item of £646,196 of goodwill, works, premises, plant, machinery etc., the separate items of which now stand in the balance sheet for only £59,518'.[99]

While strategies such as price-cutting, cheaper bicycles, and capital reconstruction all helped to restore a degree of confidence in the industry, such entrepreneurial actions were insufficient without quite radical changes in production and product design. For example, a British visitor to the continent in 1895 complained that while European producers tended to keep to 'standard patterns', English makers were too apt to give way 'to the fads and whims of individual customers'. The writer did acknowledge that English cycle manufacturers did not deny that converting to standardised output would bring advantages in the form of the simplification of work at the shop-floor level, and thus lower the costs of production and facilitate an increase in output, but they appeared reluctant to embrace fully such a strategy.[100] Their reluctance, prior to the cycle mania of the mid-1890s, is understandable. As we saw earlier, a commitment to batch production was a perfectly rational one in the context of a market which was relatively limited to 'cycling enthusiasts seeking the latest type of machine and prepared to sell in their old model and buy the latest in the next season's'. It was this type of demand structure which 'encouraged the leading manufacturers to produce high quality machines for high prices, a strategy which militated against mass production'. Pursuing such a strategy allowed firms to extend the market through a policy of product differentiation. Products such as tricycles and quad-cycles were launched and the focus on quality was aided by cycle manufacturers advising customers to avoid low-priced machines. However, the bicycle boom of the mid-1890s 'exposed the limitations' of this strategy.[101] Consumer preferences were changing and the growth of a mass market required a shift in emphasis. The changing nature of the demand function facing firms can be illustrated by consumer preferences in the French market, and this typified changing consumer preferences in many markets including Britain. In 1898 W. D. Bassett, the general manager at Raleigh, and formerly of Humber, visited French manufacturers and dealers. In his report back to the directors he noted 'that the better class of cyclists instead of now buying high grade machines are quite satisfied to accept a cheap mass produced machine, so long as it is a cycle, irrespective of the mark'.[102]

The emergence of a mass market for bicycles meant that firms were now required to produce in quantity, but in the British case without necessarily sacrificing quality.[103]

The British response was to move towards the increased use of machine tools, often adapted from the USA, and to gear production to larger-volume output. For example, the New Hudson Cycle Co. introduced automatic machinery in its plant in 1898 allowing it in December of that year to launch a low priced machine. The profits of the company almost doubled between 1898 and 1899.[104] As Millward has argued, the change in market conditions led firms to recognise that the market required 'low priced machines' and this in turn necessitated a change in attitudes towards methods of production.[105] Of key importance was the relationship between the volume of output and the level of quality. While *The Economist* was quick to condemn the cycle trade for the excesses of the 1890s, it was nevertheless, in December 1900, prepared to give credit where it was due: 'One point stands to the credit of the industry, which is that the quality of the work has been maintained, inspite of unprofitable working, so that the English machine bearing a reputable name is unrivalled for excellence by the products of any other country.'[106] This point is endorsed by Millward who has argued that the post-boom British cycle industry successfully brought in 'a lower priced quality bicycle capable of rebuffing foreign competition on the unprotected home market, and in markets abroad, despite the imposition of foreign import duties'.[107] Certainly exports revived in 1901, and after collapsing from £1 856 000 in 1896 to £531 000 in 1900 they rose sharply by a factor of approximately 3.5 times between 1901 and 1913. Further, retained imports fell sharply from the late 1890s. The share of retained imports as a percentage of exports stood at 30.34 per cent in 1897, but this had fallen to just 8.95 per cent by 1903 (Table A.3 in the Appendix). These improvements in the fortunes of the trade were accompanied by improved selling techniques such as better trade catalogues and easy payment schemes, and by priority being given to the details of production by manufacturers to guarantee 'the general reliability' of British cycle products. Thus Humber, for example, with the appointment of a new managing director, Edward A. Powell, in 1898, immediately rationalised its very wide range of models 'while at the same time the surviving models were brought into line with recent developments in free wheels, better brakes, a variable gear option, and so on'. The company's advertising slogan in 1906 highlights the new emphasis placed on cheaper models and high-quality products: 'To Buy The Best Is True Economy.'[108]

By November 1902, *The Economist*, while warning that 'a good deal remains to be done by many of the cycle companies', nevertheless felt sufficiently relaxed about general conditions in the trade to inform its readers that there was 'a distinct improvement in actual results and in future prospects'. A year later it proclaimed that the cycle trade had 'enjoyed a fairly good season, aided in part, at least, by the additions of motor cycle and automobile production'. It was reported that a 'popular demand is for a motor cycle or car, comfortable to sit in or upon, running silently and reliably, and purchased at a moderate price'.[109] This takes us to the third form of radical adaptation in the industry, the diversification into motor cycle and motor vehicle production. The first attempt to fit an internal combustion engine to a bicycle was apparently attempted by Daimler and Otto in 1886, but the first in public use appeared in Paris in 1895 and was brought to Britain by Humber in the following year. This, however, was too crude a machine for practical development, and the next major event took place in 1897 'when a Paris firm dealing in gramophones introduced the Werner front driven bicycle'. This machine combined ingenuity with an acceptable degree of reliability, and it rapidly 'made a market' for itself. The Werner was initially exploited by the Motor Manufacturing Co. of Coventry, but it also inspired other cycle manufacturers in the city, such as Singer, to go into motor cycle production. Unfortunately, the Singer machine suffered from technical problems, in particular an 'extreme vibration in the engine', and it was not until the Stanley Cycle Show, the main annual exhibition of the cycle industry, of 1899 that the motor cycle was brought to the attention of the public. Firms such as the Ariel Cycle Co. of Birmingham, the Eadie Cycle Co. and Enfield Cycles exhibited motor cycles, motor tricycles and motor quad-cycles at the exhibition. These machines were fitted with French engines made under licence from Dion Bouton patents held in Paris. Another major exhibit at the Stanley Show was a small 'belt driven bicycle called the Minerva' which had been built in Antwerp. The novelty and market potential of the motor cycle led to a number of firms diversifying into its production, and by 1901 'there was hardly a cycle maker who did not list a motor cycle with a Minerva engine' as part of their stock in trade.[110]

The account above of the early development of the motor cycle, by H. Grew, does not, however, allow for the variety of design that appeared at this time. For example, reference has been made to 'the strange recipes for powered machines that emanated from the Humber works ... though no more strange than those of their rivals'. Experimentation was the order of the day, as cycle firms attempted a series of innovations in order to create new markets for their products. Thus, in 1898, Humber's catalogue listed a 'Three Wheel Motor Carriage (for three riders)' but also a 'Ladies' Motor Safety'. The former incorporated a 'two seater fore car with what was basically a pedal cycle frame, handlebars, and saddle tube, topped up by a pillar upon which the rider apparently sat in comfort'. The latter was a somewhat crude model, constructed from a 'ladies' cycle frame', the forepart of which was an ordinary pedal cycle with a motor 'mounted behind the saddle pillar'. These early developments at Humber were curtailed by the débâcle over Hooley's bankruptcy, and the end of Rucker's reign at Humber. The company withdrew from the motor cycle trade, and did not become actively involved in this area again until 1902.[111] The company's re-entry into the trade was successful, and in 1902 they acquired the Royal Warrant for their 'patent motor bicycle', a machine which was well received in the trade press and was described as 'very successful'.[112]

The early part of the twentieth century marked what Demaus and Tarring refer to as the end of 'the early gestation period of motor cycle design'. There was now a more clear understanding of the technical and design potential of the motor cycle which could form a firm foundation for future development.[113] In particular, the early experiments with the motorised tricycle had led to advances in the motor cycle itself, which had made considerable advances. For example, in 1902 the *Bicycling News and Motor Review* claimed that the 'motor tricycle was doomed', its best year was in 1899, when 97 machines were displayed at the National Cycle Exhibition at the Crystal Palace. Three years later, the number of machines exhibited at the National was only nine, and at the Stanley Cycle Show only four were displayed. On the other hand, motor cycles had made 'a considerable advance'. In 1901 there were only ten machines on show at the National, whereas a year later there were 57 machines on display, while at the Stanley Show 110 models were presented to an ever eager public. As the journal argued, 'motor cycles ... are rapidly coming into favour, and now can be supplied at prices which brings them within reach of many riders'.[114]

In addition to motor cycles, some cycle firms also attempted to diversify into the motor vehicle industry. This was particularly the case in Coventry. Firms in the city 'were prepared to react positively to' new demand, and Coventry 'was unique in the number of motor car producers whose origins were located in the cycle industry'. The bicycle firm of Riley & Co., whose business antecedents were originally in the ribbon trades, added to their operations in 1898 the manufacture of motor cycles and cars, and in the same year Humber followed suit. In 1899 these firms were joined by the Allard Cycle Co and the Swift Cycle Co., in 1903 by Lee Francis and in 1904 by Rover. In 1906 Singer began the production of cars, but Triumph did not enter the industry until 1923, and Rudge-Whitworth, one of the giants of the cycle trade, resisted the switch to car manufacture and remained a cycle and motor cycle manufacturer. It would appear that motor cycle production acted as the means of transition from cycles to cars, by acting as a form of technical experimentation. Thus, for example, the manufacture of motor cycles led to experimentations, by firms such as Riley, with motor cycle cars. These could be manufactured using plant originally designed for the production of pedal cycles. The cycle industry, from its origins, had also developed a sophisticated component sector which could be transferred for use in the manufacture of motor cycles and motor cars. The industry made a significant contribution to the development and use of a variety of components, which included 'wheels, ball-bearings, brakes, lighting and chains'. The experimentation and development of cycle gears was of particular importance 'in solving problems concerned with the transmission of power in motor vehicles'. For example, the Quadrant Cycle Co. developed a bicycle gear which was successfully adapted to the motor car, leading to the creation of a subsidiary in 1906 to exploit its market potential.[115]

The development of component production also offered niche markets to small cycle companies, a factor which was important for their long-term survival. For example, the firm of Cluley & Clark of Coventry survived to 1988, and its early involvement in the motor cycle industry provided it with a basis for product diversification. The firm also again demonstrates the versatility of the early bicycle industry. Founded in the early 1890s by a consortium of small Coventry cycle manufacturers, Ernest and Charles Clark, Charles James Cluley, Daniel Blackmore and George Storo Smith, it was not until 1900 that a formal partnership agreement was drawn up. In that year, the company was legally constituted as a partnership with the intention 'to carry on the business of cycle manufacturers, motor car manufacturing engineers, and general machinists'. Shares were divided equally between the partners, with Clark and Cluley being appointed managing directors with responsibility for 'the practical working of the ... business', while Blackmore and Smith acted as sleeping partners, providing advice but not controlling or interfering in the 'partnership business'. Before 1914 the firm concentrated not only on cycle manufacture, but also on supplying components for motors to a number of nascent engineering industries. For example, in 1908 the company was converted into a private limited company to carry on the business of cycle and motor cycle production, repairers of all types of motors, and manufacturers of engines for motor cars and vehicles, aircraft, ships, launches and boats, 'and all implements and components connected with them'. On the eve of the First World War the company was making healthy profits averaging £18 500 between 1913 and 1914. From this diverse beginning the firm continued to pursue a strategy of diversification throughout its history, concentrating on motor manufacturing and components for textile machines in the 1920s, electrical dynamos in the 1930s and, during the Second World War, parts for aero engines.[116]

In part, the diversification into motor car production was a response by the cycle manufacturers to the problems of the immediate post-boom years, not least the challenges presented by cheap mass-produced American machines. At the same time, it was the capital generated by the cycle branch of the business which 'often produced the necessary resources to support research activities and initial production'.[117] This meant that it was only those firms with sufficient financial resources, and 'very patient shareholders', who managed to achieve long-term success. Thus, Enfield's 'were obliged to keep their cycle works as profitable as possible to cover the loss incurred in automobile manufacture'.[118] For the small manufacturer, diversification could be a high-risk strategy; many of these firms 'appear to have faltered in the initial stages of research and development'. Indeed, even long-established cycle companies, such as Cluley & Calcott Bros of Coventry, entered the car market only to find that success was short term. Nevertheless, even the larger firms had to develop the necessary managerial and administrative skills which could provide the business infrastructure to support a move into motor vehicle production. By 1913, firms such as Humber, Swift, Singer and Rover combined relatively high output of both bicycles and motor vehicles, and supported these developments with the use of their purchase and advertising departments to promote sales.[119]

British firms did not, however, in general forego the personal capitalism form of business organisation which, Chandler has argued, inhibited Britain's capacity to exploit fully the innovations of the second industrial revolution.[120] British bicycle producers did not become large multi-divisional corporations, yet they vigorously met the challenge of American competition. This is not to argue that American management techniques were not the most advanced at the beginning of the twentieth century, but rather that they were not necessarily appropriate to the British business environment with its different legal, cultural and economic trends and conditions. As Wilson has reminded us, this perspective is vital to remember when analysing British business history.[121] In less than two decades from the end of the cycle boom, the industry had undergone a radical transformation. On the eve of the First World War Britain possessed a viable bicycle industry which included in its ranks some of the leading cycle companies in the world. The challenge of foreign competition had been successfully confronted, a rapid increase in the volume of output had been achieved without sacrificing quality, and a significant degree of diversification into new sectors, important to the long-term performance of the British economy, had been undertaken. There is little evidence of business conservatism or a gradual adaptation to changed conditions. Indeed, as the next chapter will show, the business activities of Raleigh illustrate the financial and commercial acumen, and the entrepreneurial drive of its founder, Frank Bowden. Under Bowden, Raleigh was to become a world-class bicycle firm.

Notes

1. Coventry Central Library (CRO), Bartlett Collection, *Bicycling News*, 14 January 1876. All references to trade journals in this chapter are to be found at this location.
2. Ibid., 21 January 1876. Prices of second-hand bikes varied from £8 to £14. See ibid., 5 May 1876.
3. Ibid., 1 February 1878, 8 February 1877, 12 May 1876.
4. Harrison, 1985, pp. 42–3. For the development of the Michaux type velocipede by Thomas Humber see Demaus and Tarring, 1989, p. 4.
5. *Bicycling News*, 14 January 1876, 23 February 1877.
6. Demaus and Tarring, 1989, p. 4. As shown in Chapter 3, the sporting aspects of the cycle was also influential in the early development of the Raleigh Cycle Co. under Frank Bowden.
7. *Bicycling News*, 21 January 1876, 27 July 1877, 14 December 1877.
8. See Harrison, 1985, p. 43.
9. *Bicycling News*, 9 August 1878.
10. *Cycling Times*, 20 January 1885; Lancaster, n.d., p. 58.
11. Harrison, 1985, pp. 43, 45.
12. Wigglesworth, 1996, pp. 9, 81. See also Millward, 1989, p. 172.
13. Harrison, 1985, p. 45.
14. Ibid., p. 45; CRO, Rudge-Whitworth Papers, 849, Biography of the Company. The business history of Rudge-Whitworth is also examined in Chapters 4 and 7.
15. Rudge-Whitworth Papers, Biography of the Company, CRO 849/2 Contract for Sale of Rudge & Co. Ltd, August 1887, 849/10, Agreement for Sale and Purchase of Business, 15 October 1894; Nottingham Record Office (NRO), Raleigh Records, DDRN 1/29/1, First Annual Report of the Directors and Statement of Accounts of Rudge-Whitworth Ltd, 31 August 1895; *Coventry Trade and Commercial Directory*, 1874–75, p. 102; Thoms and Donnelly n.d., p. 18.
16. Thoms and Donnelly, n.d., p. 15; Saul, 1968, p. 215.
17. Harrison, 1985, p. 145.
18. Grew, 1921, p. 48.
19. Andrews and Brunner, 1955, pp. 40, 41.
20. *Coventry Complete Directory*, 1894, p. 187; *Birmingham Trade and Commercial Directory* 1901; Thoms and Donnelly, 1985, p. 20.
21. Grew, 1921, p. 48.
22. For examples of renting in the cotton industry see Lloyd-Jones and Le Roux, 1984; Lloyd-Jones and Lewis, 1988, pp. 16, 18, 25.
23. Millward, 1989, p. 167; Harrison, 1985, p. 70; Andrews and Brunner, 1955, p. 40.

24. Scranton, 1989. Again there were close parallels here with the early cotton industry. See Lloyd-Jones and Lewis, 1988, p.198; Farnie, 1979, p. 210.
25. Millward, 1989, pp. 165–6; Harrison, 1985, p. 49.
26. Harrison, 1985, pp. 49–50; Thoms and Donnelly, n.d., p. 15.
27. Millward, 1989, p. 169.
28. Scranton, 1991, p. 28. See also Piore and Sabel, 1984; Sabel and Zeitlin 1985.
29. See Chandler, 1962, 1977, 1990.
30. Lloyd-Jones and Lewis, 1994. See also Piore and Sabel, 1984, pp. 28–9, 104.
31. Scranton, 1991, pp. 35–6. Examples of industrial districts in Europe would be Sheffield, Birmingham, Paris, Lyons, Geneva and Solingen. In the USA, from Worcester to Newark and Philadelphia and West to Cincinnati, Grand Rapids and Milwaukee.
32. Thoms and Donnelly, 1985, p. 20.
33. Scranton, 1991, pp. 29, 36.
34. *Coventry Complete Directory*, 1894, p. 192.
35. Scranton, 1991, pp. 29, 36.
36. See Casson and Rose, 1997, pp. 3–4.
37. Thoms and Donnelly, 1985, p. 20.
38. *Coventry Trade and Commercial Directory*, 1874–75, p. 102; Thoms and Donnelly, n.d., p. 18.
39. Scranton, 1991, pp. 29–30.
40. Thoms and Donnelly, n.d., p. 19; Harrison, 1985, p. 53.
41. Nockolds, 1976, pp. 7, 32, 41–2, 51, 61–2, 72.
42. Thoms and Donnelly, 1985, p. 16.
43. Harrison, 1977, pp. 88, 89.
44. Thoms and Donnelly, 1985, p. 16.
45. Scranton, 1991, p. 38.
46. Harrison, 1985, p. 54.
47. Mason, 1994, pp. 55–6, 260; Church, 1966, p. 243.
48. Scranton, 1991, p. 41.
49. Thoms and Donnelly, 1985, p. 17.
50. Thoms, 1990, pp. 37–40, 51.
51. Raleigh Records, DDRN 4/10/1/6, The book of the Raleigh for the 1900 Season.
52. For an analysis of private limited conversions in the cycle and cycle component industry see Harrison, 1977, pp. 364–6.
53. Thoms and Donnelly, 1985, p. 17; Birmingham Central Library Archives, Birmingham Rate Books, Aston District, 2.
54. Harrison, 1977, p. 365.
55. Ibid., p 366; Millward, 1989, p. 167; DDRN 1/29/3, Third Annual Report of Rudge-Whitworth, 31 August 1897.
56. Thoms and Donnelly, 1985, p. 17.
57. Ibid., pp. 17–18; See also Lane, 1977, p. 66; Harrison, 1985, p. 56.
58. Thoms and Donnelly, 1985, p. 22. See also Floud, 1976, p. 43.
59. Thoms and Donnelly, 1985, p. 22. See also Davies, n.d.
60. Thoms and Donnelly, 1985, pp. 21–2. As we shall see in the next chapter, the perpetuation of the family was clearly important to the early development of Raleigh.

61. Harrison, 1985, pp. 60–62.
62. Thoms and Donnelly, 1985, p. 19.
63. *The Economist*, 7 June 1893, p. 728.
64. Cottrell, 1980, p. 174.
65. *The Economist*, 7 June 1893, p. 728.
66. Ibid., 12 December 1896, pp. 3, 21.
67. Cited in Kynaston, 1996, p. 142.
68. Millward, 1989, pp. 165–6; Allen, 1929, p. 290.
69. First Annual Report of Rudge-Whitworth Ltd, 31 August 1895.
70. DDRN 1/29/2–3, Second and Third Annual Reports of Rudge-Whitworth, August 1896, 31 August 1897.
71. *The Economist*, 16 May 1896, p. 618.
72. Harrison, 1981 p. 175.
73. Rollitt, 1900, p. 13.
74. Cottrell, 1980, p. 174.
75. Thoms and Donnelly, 1985, pp. 36–7. Hooley was a teetotaller who in an earlier life had been a deacon and organist at the Baptist church at Long Eaton, near Nottingham. He was described as 'well dressed and always polite ... too earnestly busy to show any conceit'. He was 'an optimist to the finger tips'. Little is known about Lawson's background. He was, from the late 1870s, a bicycle pioneer, promoting companies whenever and wherever he could. Kynaston, 1996, pp. 143, 145.
76. Harrison, 1977, p. 360. Harrison estimates from *The Economist* and the *Investors-Chronicle* that new issues for bikes and motor bikes in 1896 was £9 267 910, for tyre companies £6 760 000, and tube companies £1 356 000. Ibid., Table 19, p. 354.
77. Ibid., p. 360. Harrison also quotes a contemporary authority, H. Lowenfield, who defined issues of £50 000 to £100 000 'to be small'.
78. *The Economist*, 31 July 1897, p. 1087.
79. Harrison, 1977, p. 362.
80. *The Economist*, 31 July 1897, p. 1087.
81. Demaus and Tarring, 1989, pp. 5–7.
82. Ibid., pp. 5–6; *Bicycling News*, 1885, p. 243; Cottrell, 1980, pp. 174–5.
83. Demaus and Tarring, 1989, p. 7; Kynaston, 1996, p. 143. In 1896 'Several of the jobbers in the Miscellaneous market speedily learnt to specialise in cycle shares and were accorded the nickname of the "windbags".' A series of usually profitable flotations came their way over the ensuing months. Kynaston 1996, p. 143.
84. *The Economist*, 27 January 1896, p. 831, 20 February 1897, p. 274; Third Annual Reports of Rudge-Whitworth, 31 August 1897.
85. *The Economist*, 20 February 1897, p. 274.
86. Ibid., 22 May 1897, p. 742, 21 August 1897, p. 1202.
87. DDRN 7/2/3, Souvenir of the Raleigh Works on the Occasion of the Opening of the New Factory, 5 May 1922.
88. *The Economist*, 21 August 1897, p. 1202; 3 July 1897, pp. 952–3; Harrison, 1969, p. 290.
89. DDRN 1/1/2, Raleigh Cycle Co. Ltd, Directors and General Meetings Minutes, 20 July 1897.
90. *The Economist*, 16 May 1925, p. 956.
91. Ibid., 3 July 1897, pp. 952–3; Harrison, 1969, p. 291.
92. *The Economist*, 16 May 1925, p. 956.

93. Harrison, 1969, pp. 292–3.
94. Ibid., Table 7, p. 293.
95. Raleigh, Directors and General Meetings, 29 March 1898.
96. Harrison, 1969, p. 297.
97. *Bicycling News*, 15 January 1902; *The Economist*, 8 December 1900, p. 1726.
98. *Bicycling News and Motorcycle Review*, 15 January 1902.
99. *The Economist*, 8 December 1900, p. 1726, 16 November 1901, p. 1696, 17 October 1903, p. 1752. For further reconstruction schemes in the industry see H. Miller & Co. (cycle-lamp makers); the Cycle Component Co. and Amalgamated Tyres (formerly the Beeston Tyre Co. of Nottingham), in *Bicycling News and Motorcycle Review*, 15 January 1902, pp. 7, 8–9.
100. Harrison, 1969, p. 289.
101. Millward, 1989, pp. 169–70. For more details concerning product differentiation in British industry see Payne, 1967.
102. DDRN 1/1/3, Raleigh Directors and General Meetings, 18 July 1898.
103. Millward, 1989, p. 170.
104. *Bicycling News*, January 1901.
105. Millward, 1989, pp. 170, 173.
106. *The Economist*, 8 December 1900, p. 1726.
107. Millward, 1989, p. 173.
108. Harrison, 1969, pp. 298–9; Demaus and Tarring, 1989, p. 8; Raleigh Records, DDRN 4/63/1–2, Company Promotion and Design, Advertisement for Humber 1906.
109. *The Economist*, 8 November 1902, p. 1723, 17 October 1903, p. 1753.
110. Grew, 1921, pp. 105–7.
111. Demaus and Tarring, 1989, pp. 11, 12, 14.
112. *The Economist*, 8 November 1902, p. 1722.
113. Demaus and Tarring, 1989, p. 14.
114. *Bicycling News and Motorcycle Review*, 8 January 1902.
115. Thoms and Donnelly, n.d., pp. 19–20; 1985, pp. 24–5.
116. CRO, 1233/107/1 Draft Article of Partnership of Cluley & Clarke, 1900; 1233/105/1 Incorporation of Registration as a Private Ltd Co., 21 December 1908; 1233/87/1, Private Ledger of C. J. Cluley, 1911–34.
117. Thoms and Donnelly, n.d., p. 20.
118. Harrison, 1969, pp. 302–3
119. Thoms and Donnelly, 1985, pp. 14, 26.
120. Chandler, 1990, p. 237.
121. Wilson, 1995, p. 8.

CHAPTER THREE

Frank Bowden and the making of the Raleigh Cycle Co., *c.* 1887–1914

The entrepreneurial spirit behind the foundation of Raleigh was Frank Bowden who was born in Bristol in 1847. His father and grandfather were prominent manufacturers in the city, and Frank was groomed to join the family business. Following the death of his father, however, when Frank was still young, he entered the law profession and was apprenticed to a firm in London. In 1870 an opportunity arose in Hong Kong to advance his career. He applied for a vacancy in the office of the Principal Law Officer of Hong Kong, and was selected out of 500 candidates for the post. Bowden made an immediate impact, gaining a reputation as an astute dealer in stocks and shares and property. By 1872 he was earning a yearly salary of £500 and, backed by his employer, he began to speculate in the Hong Kong property market. 'His clear vision and sound judgement enabled him to conclude deals of a highly profitable nature, aided by the unique opportunities which then existed in the Far East.' In six years he accumulated a substantial fortune but, due to ill health, he left Hong Kong for San Francisco in 1878 where he resumed his legal studies. Bowden was a self-made man, and in 1879 he married Amelia Francis, a wealthy American heiress, and the daughter of Colonel Alexander Houston, one of the original pioneers of the State of California.[1] Thus by the early 1880s Bowden had become a successful venture capitalist, a member of the British *rentier* class which made substantial fortunes in dealing in paper and property.[2] It was this accumulation of funds which was later to provide the financial base for the foundation of Raleigh.

In 1886 Frank Bowden left the USA for France, following a prolonged and serious illness, and was attracted to bicycling for health reasons. As we saw in Chapter 2, a number of the early firms had been established by cycling enthusiasts, and Bowden was no exception. He remained an enthusiastic cyclist throughout his life, and a keen promoter of cycling as a sport, but the business prospects of the cycle did not pass him by. In 1887 he visited the works of Woodhead, Angois & Ellis, a small cycle firm located in Raleigh Street, Nottingham. The firm had first started making cycles in 1886, manufacturing penny farthings, tricycles and the recently introduced safety cycle, and it constituted a classic private partnership. R. M. Woodhead, 'a clever mechanic',

3.1 Portrait of Sir Frank Bowden, *c.* 1918. Photograph from the Raleigh Archive, reproduced courtesy of Nottingham County Archive.

together with Paul Angois, a Frenchman with some engineering and design training, provided the technical expertise, while William Ellis, a small financier, looked after the commercial end of the business.[3]

Two factors attracted Bowden's interest in the business. First, he was aware of the expanding market for the safety cycle, and its future potential. What the company required was a sound campaign of 'advertisement and propaganda' to promote the innovative features of the company's safety cycle. Second, he recognised that Woodhead and Angois possessed the necessary technical expertise to develop the product, and this would allow him to concentrate on the business side of the enterprise. The company was technically innovative, and the machines 'were exceptionally well designed'. Backed by the engineering skills of the proprietors, they had 'improved upon the original design of the safety cycle', introducing the 'standard diamond frame'. The firm was also at the forefront of innovations to increase the speed and reduce the effort in cycling, and had designed the first variant of a gear system, which was later to become a marketing feature of the early Raleigh machines. The individual attention paid to design and construction impressed upon Bowden the possibility of producing quality cycles which could be tailored to the needs of individual riders. Each machine was manufactured to a high standard rather than a low price, and Bowden realised that they could expand sales by developing a reputation for quality and individuality. At the same time, there was a need to reduce prices to competitive levels by increasing output and decreasing the overhead costs of manufacture.[4] Similar to many of the pre-1914 cycle firms, as we saw in Chapter 2, Raleigh was to develop its reputation as a batch producer of high-quality machines.

It was from these small beginnings, claimed Bowden later, that a 'successful company emerged'. In 1887 an agreement was drawn up between Bowden and the proprietors. Bowden consented to supply fresh working capital to expand the business, and it was agreed that he was to have a 'free hand' in the general administration of the concern. A year later, Bowden bought out the one-third stake in the company held by William Ellis, for a sum of £1 000, and also paid £1 000 to the remaining partners to secure an equal partnership. The partnership was placed on a formal footing by the allotment of 10 000 £1 ordinary shares to the partners and directors. Bowden was allocated 5 000 and the remaining 5 000 shares were distributed equally between Woodhead and Angois. The company remained, however, 'a private' partnership, and no shares were allotted to the public. The key managerial figure was Bowden who was 'his own manager, traveller, salesman and accountant'. In particular, Bowden was to provide the capital investment for expansion, although he was also keenly aware of the risks involved. Being a shrewd financier, he premised his investment decisions on the need to ensure business success. To reduce his own personal risk the company was incorporated as a limited company in January 1889 to provide additional working capital. The nominal capital of the company was £20 000, Bowden subscribing £10 000 for £1 ordinary shares, and Woodhead and Angois a further £5 000. In addition, 1 000 £1

founders' shares were allocated, Bowden receiving 642 and the remainder being divided between his co-partners. The remaining 4 000 shares
were advertised in the local press, subscriptions being invited from local
businessmen and small investors. The control of the business was to
remain, however, in the hands of the original proprietors by the legal
rights of their founders' shares. Managerial tasks were also separated,
and strategic management was given to Bowden who was appointed
chairman and managing director, and who took up the majority holding of the newly allotted public subscription. Functional management,
involving the operation of the company, was placed in the hands of
Angois, the director responsible for bicycle design, and Woodhead, the
director in charge of factory management.[5]

Bowden's business strategy was to expand output to meet the increased demand for quality cycles. To achieve this aim the new company
had to expand its factory capacity which was wholly inadequate, both
in scale and design. For example, in 1886 the company produced just
three machines per week, and by 1889 the Raleigh Street factory was a
'greenhouse' and three small workshops. Backed by a small workforce
of 12 men, Woodhead and Angois did most of the work themselves.[6]
Despite the sale of shares to the public in 1889, outside capital for
expansion was minimal, and Bowden's personal commitment to the
programme for expansion, between 1889 and 1891, was crucial. As
Table B.1 in the Appendix shows, the company could not rely on
internally generated funds for finance, as profits, although rising steadily in the first three years of business, remained modest. With limited
resources to plough back into the business, Bowden had to finance the
company entirely, providing both the fixed capital for the expansion of
capacity, and the working capital to sustain trading operations. In 1889
the decision was taken to rent a five-storey factory in Russell Street,
adjacent to the Raleigh Street works, recently vacated by the lacemakers,
Clarke & Co. Initially employing 90 workers, Bowden financed the
installation of new machinery, and by 1891 employment had expanded
to 200, and production was 60 machines per week, making it the
largest bicycle firm in the Nottingham area. Bowden also supplied
injections of working capital, loaning the company £3 000 on a 10 per
cent debenture in 1890. This far-sighted investment strategy was supported by a campaign of 'advertisement and propaganda' to promote
the reputation of their products both at home and abroad. In this
Bowden played an active role, travelling extensively abroad to promote
the company's image. By 1892, Raleigh was employing over 400 workers with an estimated 400 agents all over the world.[7]

Table B.2 in the Appendix shows that the value of Raleigh sales
increased from a mere £7 148 in the first year of business to £17 471 in

1890 and £36 696 by 1891. By the latter date, Bowden realised that any further expansion would require an enlargement of the capital base of the company. Consequently, he decided to place the company in voluntary liquidation and promote a new public company. With the full consent of the shareholders and partners, the 'New Raleigh Cycle Co. Ltd.' was registered in December with a nominal capital of £100 000, divided into 99 000 ordinary shares of £1 each and 1 000 fully paid founders' shares of £1. The purchase price of the business and assets of the old company was £40 012, and the vendors, Bowden and his partners, agreed to sell this to the newly incorporated company. To demonstrate to investors their commitment to the future management of the concern the vendors received shares in the company in consideration of the purchase price, and agreed not to sell these for a minimum period of two years. Thus, 39 012 fully paid up £1 ordinary shares and 1 000 fully paid up founders' shares were allotted to the vendors, the latter not being entitled to any dividend until 10 per cent had been paid on ordinary shares, and provision made to allocate profits to the reserve fund. The flotation of 1891 was designed with the specific purpose of maintaining Bowden as the majority shareholder, and of the 39 000 ordinary shares allotted, Bowden and his wife received 27 000 (see Table 3.1). Following the allocation of 40 012 shares to the vendors, it was proposed to offer 29 988 partly paid ordinary shares for public subscription, the first call for a payment of 2s. 6d. per share scheduled for January 1892. This left 30 000 shares as a reserve of unpaid capital. Of the public subscription of 29 988 partly paid shares, the vendors

Table 3.1 Number of shares allotted on incorporation of Raleigh Cycle Co. Ltd, 1891

£1 founder's shares		£1 ordinary shares	
F. Bowden	692	F. Bowden	19 000
R. M. Woodhead	154	R. M. Woodhead	6 000
P. Angois	154	P. Angois	6 000
		Mrs A. Bowden	8 000
		R. S. Gutteridge	3
		F. Strobridge	3
		M. Bryan	3
		J. Lazonby	3
Total allocated	1 000		39 012

Source: DDRN 10/3/8, Allotment Book, Register of Members and Annual Share Ledger of the Raleigh Cycle Co. Ltd.

applied for 15 300, Bowden subscribing for 10 000, Woodhead and Angois for 1 000 each, and the new directors of the company for 3 300. This left 14 688 shares available for public issue.[8]

Financial restructuring was a key factor underlying the company's business strategy. A priority was 'the power of raising more capital when required for extending what they believe will before long become one of the largest cycle manufacturing businesses in the world'. This was essential to meet an upturn in cycle demand during 1891, and as Bowden pointed out, 'the only problem [was] to turn out machines fast enough'. The public issue of shares would provide 'a broader basis' for the raising of capital, and they appealed particularly to the local public and their own sales agents. There was no attempt to seek a quotation on the stock exchange, but rather the management sought to foster a parochial relationship between the firm and its shareholders. The aim of the limited public issue was to increase 'the number of persons interested' in the business, and to extend within the existing network of influence. For example, by April 1892, when share subscriptions closed, £25 782 had been raised by new share subscriptions, but only £10 082 of the £14 788 public issue shares had been subscribed for. The vast majority of shares continued to be held by those with a direct influence in the firm, and there was only a limited attempt to extend the capital outside the firm. Nevertheless, the public issue attracted 212 subscriptions, mainly for the minimum offer of five shares, and a number of small subscriptions came from agents and customers. The reserve of unpaid share capital, totalling £30 000, however, was seen by the management as a future stock for expansion, which could be called upon when the company required further capital.[9]

A strategy of expansion also required a restructuring of the management of the company. When Bowden had entered the business, the low level of economic activity had allowed him to be actively involved in the sales and operational end of the business. An expanded business now necessitated a 'greater security in management by a larger directorate'. Table B.3 in the Appendix provides a profile of the main directors and managers of the company from 1891. The appointment of Fellows and Lazonby in 1891 would suggest a strategy of recruiting directors with financial connections. Fellows was the manager of Lloyds Bank at Nottingham, and Lazonby was a local banker whom Bowden had first met during his brief appointment in the London law office. The appointment of Sir John Turney, a 'gentleman well known in Nottingham', was clearly dictated by the need to recruit an experienced businessman to help guide executive decision-making. Turney was chairman and managing director of the family firm of Turney Bros, leather dressers of Nottingham, which he had owned and run in partnership with his son and nephew since 1889. Turney's remit was to provide advice on business policy, and one gets a sense that there was an attempt by Bowden to create specialist managerial functions. The leading figure was Bowden, chairman and managing director, and Woodhead and Angois were given responsibility for the operational end of the business, the former being appointed factory manager and the latter works manager with direct responsibility for design. The new management team facilitated the development of the business, and was portrayed to the public as a collection of talented individuals with impeccable business reputations. As the company's French prospectus put it, Raleigh represented 'Une Excellente Speculation'.[10]

Business strategy at Raleigh: building a company name

The company embarked upon a marketing strategy which focused upon expanding sales of quality cycles both at home and abroad. Their marketing programme had three basic, but interrelated aims: first, to position their products on the market by emphasising the quality attributes of the Raleigh machines; second, to penetrate the market by an emphasis on flexible production and a reliance upon constant design innovation; third, to create a network of trust through a policy of meeting customer needs, and developing relations with outside component suppliers. As Kay argues, firms build upon their own perceived capabilities to develop an advantage in the market. For our purposes he identifies three types of capabilities: innovation, which can of course be mimicked by competitors; architecture, the development of relationships with suppliers and customers; and reputation, the selling of 'branded products'. Through enhancing these capabilities the firm attempts to gain competitive advantage.[11] In the case of Raleigh, Bowden began the building of a company tradition which, as we shall see in later chapters, was to permeate the company's history, and guide its strategic direction, well into the twentieth century. The company's promotional drive illustrates the importance attached to quality, and this was matched by a constant attention to design and improvement innovations. A key strength was the talents of Paul Angois, and his designs enabled Raleigh to produce a wide range of differentiated models which were aimed at forging a competitive edge in the market. For example, Raleigh sent 23 models to the Stanley Cycle Show held in London in 1890, and '12 of these machines are from new designs'. Included were an improved version of their tandem safety cycle, weighing 73 lb, and a lighter model weighing 64 lb. Also exhibited was a new 'ladies' safety model and the 'Pathracer, and 15 other patterns of safeties including one with pneumatic tyres'.[12] The 'tailor-made' nature of these products was emphasised by an advertisement for the 'Raleigh No. 1 Rational Light Roadster' for the 1891 season: 'Front wheel made to suit reach of rider, rear wheel in proportion, detachable gears and accessories if requested, at prices from £18 upwards.' The company directed its attention at the top end of the market, and in 1891 the cheapest model offered was priced at 13 guineas, while their 'basic model' sold at £20.[13]

Ingenuity in engineering design, and a close attention to novelty, were key selling points. Raleigh had, from its beginnings, a tradition of producing a quality product, and they are 'always leading with novelties and the latest design'.[14] Although by the time Raleigh was founded, the major engineering developments in bicycle construction had already been undertaken; Raleigh were no mere imitators. Thus, a feature of the early Raleighs was an adjustable back axle and an anti-vibration device on the front. In 1892 the company pioneered the tubular fork crown, which was to become the hallmark of the Raleigh cycle. This consisted of a length of round tube to which the steering post and fork blades were brazed, and it gave to Raleigh machines enhanced steering capability and increased durability. Early Raleigh bicycles and tricycles also used a crude form of gearing system, the 'Raleigh Patented Detachable and Changeable Gear'. This allowed the rider to remove the outside ring of the chain wheel and replace it by either a larger or smaller chain wheel. Though a cumbersome device, compared to the later development at Raleigh of the variable gear system, it nevertheless allowed the cyclist to heighten or lower the gear ratio for different road gradients, and was sold as an attachment for 7s. 6d. each. Raleigh was also one of the first cycle firms to exploit the potential of the pneumatic tyre, patented by John Boyd Dunlop in 1888. Bowden visited Dublin to meet Dunlop in 1891, and despite initial resistance in the cycle trade to the new tyre, he was determined to purchase patent rights, being confident that 'the pneumatic is the tyre of the future, and would soon replace the existing cushion and solid variety of tyres'.[15] Bowden's foresight in anticipating major trends in the industry was a vital asset to the company in its early development.

The reputation of Raleigh was enhanced by the priority given to cycle racing. Bowden entered Raleighs in competitions all over the world, and this was used to promote the company's image. By 1892 Raleigh led the world in the sport with over 2 300 prizes being awarded to riders of Raleigh machines in that year alone. The most spectacular successes went to A. A. Zimmerman, a famous American amateur racer, whom Bowden had persuaded in 1891 to accept the sponsorship of Raleigh. Zimmerman turned professional, and in 1894 won 100 races riding Raleigh machines. The 'prestige this brought to the firm was incalculable'. In 1892 the company opened its marketing campaign by sending to dealers the following message: 'Prizes Open to Raleigh Riders. Whilst declining to employ celebrated path or road racers for the purpose of making records and winning races, we are desirous of encouraging amateurs who buy and ride the "Raleigh" in England or abroad.' Racing offered the opportunity to promote the quality aspects of the Raleigh, and an advertisement of 1891 displayed a fanned hand of playing cards with the names of prize-winning riders, and records broken on Raleigh machines. As the caption noted: 'The Raleigh Winning Hand ... Our Diamonds Are Trumps And Bound To Win'.[16]

During the first half of the 1890s Raleigh built up its marketing organisation. In the domestic market the company established a number of sales depots designed to hold stocks for prospective customers, and in 1892 it franchised agency rights for selling Raleighs on a regional basis. For example, an agreement was signed granting sole agency of Raleigh cycles for Ireland and for Manchester and district to the Dunlop Cycle Co. Ltd, and in 1893 this was extended to include Scotland, Liverpool, Leeds and Bristol. Bowden was also aware of the need to expand their distribution system in export markets, and in the European market Baker and Strasse, a Birmingham import-export firm, was commissioned to organise sales. By the mid-1890s this company was selling Raleighs in Poland, Czechoslovakia, Sweden, Finland, Spain and Portugal. Baker and Strasse acted as intermediaries, rather than selling directly to foreign customers, but they were prominent in establishing a network of distributors in each country, and ensuring a flow of market information to the management at Nottingham. In 1893 Raleigh opened a depot in Paris to facilitate sales in the expanding French market, and links were also forged with London merchants and confirming houses to cover sales in the rest of the world, especially in colonial markets. One of the most successful of these was the confirming house of Levetus & Co., who handled Raleigh's business in the Punjab, Burma, Nepal and their most important overseas market before 1914, India. Their relationship with the London merchants, Agar Cross, also proved fruitful in organising distribution in Argentina and the Far Eastern markets. In Australia, sole agency rights were granted to the Astral Cycle Co. of Melbourne in 1894, and during that year Bowden travelled that country to promote business. The company was prepared to offer flexibility in production, and to tailor products to the individual cultures of different nations.[17]

In the key North American market Raleigh sold through a local agency in Canada, the Braverman Hardware Co. of Hamilton, and in 1891 opened a sales depot in New York run by a manager on a salary of $80 per month, and 5 per cent commission on the entire profits of

the American business. By 1892 the New York depot had been extended into an assembly shop for cycles, parts being procured from the
factory at Nottingham. At the company's Annual General Meeting
(AGM) in September 1892 Bowden forecast that 'New York is now
established and good business ... is now assured'.[18] Bowden's positive
outlook meant that despite high tariffs in the USA it was not deterred
from entering the market early, but the ventures into the US and Canadian markets did not bring the success that Bowden anticipated. Indeed,
as the cycle industry entered the boom of 1895, as we saw in the last
chapter, business confidence was driven up to new heights, but it corre-
sponded at Raleigh with a financial crisis that led to the company's
reconstruction in 1896. Despite Bowden building the firm around its
own strengths and capabilities, Raleigh faced a serious crisis, in which
survival became the main objective. The next section examines this
crisis, and in particular emphasises the problems of the company in
building up sufficient productive capacity, which affected sales in both
domestic and foreign markets.

Missed opportunities and financial distress, 1892–96

As Table B2 in the Appendix shows, Raleigh's sales rose steadily between 1892 and 1894, but stagnated during 1895 when the bicycle
industry in general experienced boom conditions. Indeed, during the
17-month period between September 1894 and January 1896 sales were
only slightly higher than the previous 12-month period, and the management reported that during this time they were instigating a process
of reconstruction which included 'two dead seasons' during the winters
of 1894–95 and 1895–96.[19] Further, profits fell sharply in 1895, and
although they recovered strongly in 1896 the company faced mounting
financial difficulties. Thus, as the cycle boom in Britain escalated, Raleigh
was presented with the task of reconstruction and a shake-up of the
existing managerial structure of the company. What factors led to this
precarious situation?

The necessity for reconstruction demonstrates the instability of the
company's financial position, and in particular the problem of insufficient working capital. The company's production strategy was geared
towards producing sufficient stocks of cycles to meet rising customer
demand, but this entailed the costs of purchasing supplies of components from outside firms, which locked up capital until the sales were
realised. The company thus became dependent upon agents and dealers
to turn over stock rapidly, and provide the necessary revenue to meet
production expenses. Such a strategy brought with it considerable risks.

For example, during 1892 the company increased its stock and work in progress to meet a buoyant demand in the domestic market.[20] The risks of this were evident to Bowden, who complained in September 1892 that dealers were more cautious than manufacturers, and had delayed payments on goods dispatched until they could themselves ensure a sale. This placed the company at the mercy of dealers who could determine the length of payment, and the consequence was that it led to a severe depletion of working capital. These problems were exacerbated by attempts to force cycles on the British and Irish markets by offering credit schemes to customers through the company's recognised dealers and agents. Based upon 12- to 18-month repayment instalments, they were offered as a ploy to sell the company's racing cycles, but the effect of extended credit terms was to delay the receipt of much needed revenue to the company in the short run.[21]

In this situation it was imperative that management provided the necessary working capital to maintain output levels, and ensure that stocks were adequate to meet demand. In September 1892 Bowden called upon the directors and shareholders to meet the future need for working capital by depositing in the name of the company loans for a three-month period at 5 per cent interest. This provided a short-term solution, but by December a further deterioration in revenue forced the management to find longer-term funds,[22] which was achieved in two ways. First, the flotation of the company in 1891 had offered partly paid share capital totalling £29 988, and this was now used to provide additions to working capital. This raised only limited amounts,[23] and the management decided, second, to arrange overdraft facilities with its bankers, Lloyds. Using George Fellows as their contact, he was authorised to open negotiations for an overdraft of £8 000 to meet operating expenses. Lloyds, however, were reluctant to concede to the proposal, and informed Raleigh that the bank required security to sanction overdraft facilities. Bowden's response was to offer security tied to the uncalled share capital reserve of the company, totalling £30 000. Not surprisingly the bank rejected his proposal, arguing that the risk avoidance would be based upon securities which had not yet been redeemed by the company. Further, they pointed out that Raleigh's articles of association did not give the directors the authority to provide security upon the uncalled capital of the concern. The compromise reached in January 1893 was an agreement for the bank to fund the overdraft on the basis of the directors issuing equivalent mortgage debentures on the stock and assets of the company.[24] The financing of working capital thus presented a growing debt problem for the Raleigh management. By 1895 the bank overdraft stood at £15 000, and a second mortgage debenture was issued, making the company directly dependent upon bank financing. But why could not Raleigh increase sales revenue, and thus raise reserves for financing working operations? The answer to this lies partly in the inability of the company to increase output sufficiently to meet rising demand due to capacity constraints, partly to the failure of the business in the North American markets and finally, as we saw in Chapter 2, to the rise of cheaper American competition.

Capacity constraints led to delays in dispatching orders to customers, and resulted in declining confidence on the part of dealers in the ability of Raleigh to deliver promptly. This was caused both by the inadequacies of the existing Nottingham factory to deliver a speedy throughput of output, and by deficiencies in the managerial supervision of operations. The Russell Street factory was not purpose-built for the rapid production of cycles, and its five-storey structure led to problems in the layout of machinery and the general supervision of the work process.[25] Given these spatial limitations, a heavy responsibility for the efficient running of the plant was placed upon Woodhead and Angois. They had to ensure that the factory was organised to produce at optimum levels and to provide regular information to Bowden and the board on operational targets. Indeed, Bowden insisted that the key to business success was a strict supervision of the productive process by his senior managers, but his faith in this system was to be tested to the full. For example, in March 1892 he took his factory managers to task concerning the inefficiency of production. Referring to 'a promise' by Woodhead in September 1891 that a substantial increase in output would be delivered, he complained that 'so far very little actual increase in the number of machines was apparent'. The outcome was a deterioration in the trust of dealers and agents, and 'numerous complaints were being received daily from customers at home and abroad who had been promised better delivery than last year'. In particular, given the company's venture into the US market, the inadequacy of supply led to deficiencies of stock in the New York depot, and customers turned increasingly to domestic suppliers. In July 1893 Bowden reported a net profit of only £3 645 on the year's trading in New York, 'a disappointing result'.[26] The company now experienced the classic problem faced by newly established firms embarking upon a growth strategy, namely a combination of inadequate capital funds and inefficient production facilities. The result frequently is that market opportunities are either not fully exploited or are lost.[27] At Raleigh, these teething problems resulted in tension between Bowden and his operational mangers. In January 1894 Bowden informed the board of the numerous complaints of their main American agent, the John Griffiths Cycle Corporation, concerning delays in delivery. Orders placed by this company in July 1893 were still 'unexecuted', and he directed blame for this delay on the inadequate management of Woodhead. 'Sufficient energy and foresight', he claimed, 'had not been shown in the factory management for the arranging for the output of new season's goods.' Although Bowden knew the limitations of the Raleigh factory, he had clearly targeted his managers to shoulder the blame, and he displayed a side of his character which was contemptuous of individual failure. At the root of this failure was Raleigh's dismal performance in the USA, and its depot and assembly shop in New York was abandoned in August 1893 due to the unprofitable nature of the business.[28]

The failure in the USA was compounded by growing problems in the Canadian market. In August 1894 Woodhead visited the Braverman Hardware Co. in Hamilton, Canada. The intention was to discuss proposals for an extension of the business between the two companies, and on his return he optimistically predicted an expansion of Raleigh sales. There were, however, negative aspects to his visit, and he referred to the numerous complaints received by the Braverman Co. from retailers over the inability to guarantee 'prompt delivery'. Retailers inevitably turned to US suppliers who could 'guarantee' meeting orders on time, and this loss of business was compounded by Raleigh's policy of altering specifications from its trade lists, and the numerous breakdowns, especially in forks and spokes, experienced by customers. As Raleigh faced declining sales in the Canadian market, Bowden again focused the blame on the failure of his managers to ensure prompt delivery. This was clearly an attempt to bring the factory management question to a head, and in a heated board meeting in October 1894 Bowden launched a direct attack, asserting that Woodhead and Angois 'had not shown that degree of initiative, enterprise and enthusiasm which was so essential if progress was to increase'. Both were summarily dismissed from the meeting while the directors discussed their position, and on their return they resigned on the spot.[29]

How far were these managers responsible for the supply problems of the company? The factory, as already noted, was not designed to produce a rapid throughput, and Woodhead, in his defence to the board, also highlighted two additional factors affecting supply. First, he referred to internal constraints relating to the company's strategy of product diversification, the assembling of machines differentiated by design and construction. Bowden, in building up the Raleigh reputation, had placed the emphasis on constant improvement innovations and a constant search for new designs. Given the limitations of plant this strategy was in itself responsible for restricting the supply of output. In January 1894, in response to a stinging attack by Bowden on his competency, Woodhead retorted that the annual changing of models and bicycle specifications required re-tooling of the plant, the

rearrangement of the factory layout, and the changing of the patterns
at the end of each season. In turn this entailed considerable costs in
terms of labour time and disruption to production, especially given
the faults of the factory. The co-ordination of output was also adversely affected by labour disputes during December 1893, which had
disrupted plans for the changing of patterns and resulted in the failure
to meet output targets.[30] Second, Woodhead highlighted external factors outside the direct control of the company. Similar to many of the
pre-1914 British cycle manufacturers Raleigh was not an integrated
production unit, on the model of large-scale producers in the USA.[31]
Raleigh was dependent upon outside contractors for material and
component supplies, and the building up of these relations had been
part of Bowden's strategy of building up the capabilities of the firm. In
March 1892 Woodhead reported the 'difficulty of obtaining supplies
of raw materials and tyres'. For example, orders for 1 000 feet of tube
steel from the Weldless Steel Tube Co., and 500 tyres from Dunlop,
ordered 'some time ago', were still undelivered. The inadequacy of
contractors to supply constrained production, and the company was
also vulnerable to random events which affected their stocks of materials. Thus in January 1894 orders were stacked up because of shortages
of steel tubes caused by a strike in the coal industry. The problems of
supply at Raleigh went deeper than the inadequacies of plant and the
deficiencies of management, and were related to the form of production undertaken by the company. Indeed, for all Bowden's criticism of
his managers he cannot himself be exonerated from some of the responsibility. As we shall see later, these problems continued to affect
the company into the second half of the 1890s.[32]

The damage to Raleigh's reputation in the North American markets,
locations with high potential in the first half of the 1890s, was obviously related to the failure to increase sales and reap high revenue
returns. The problems in America, however, were compounded by growing price competition from larger-scale US producers, and this pattern
was reinforced by the McKinley Tariff of 1890 which raised 'the ad
valorum duty on imported cycles and parts from 35 to 45 per cent'. The
growth of American manufacturers protected by high import duties
meant that Raleigh, along with other British producers, faced serious
difficulties in selling at prices which could compete with the best American machines.[33] The British emphasis on the high-price high-quality
machine, which reflected customer preference in the British domestic
market, rather than the American market, led to a virtual annihilation
of exports across the Atlantic. British exports of finished cycles and
parts to the USA fell to just £70 000 in 1894, and although they revived
in 1895 and 1896 they collapsed again in 1897 (see Table 2.6). Such

was the débâcle of Raleigh's experience across the Atlantic that it retreated from the American market until the early 1930s.[34]

American price competition also affected Raleigh's position in the Canadian market. In his report to the directors in September 1894 Woodhead had argued that the company would be able gain a head start over US producers, and their agents were confident about establishing 'a large trade in Raleighs in British North America, they having been already advertised and pushed'. Further, he argued that the Canadian cycle industry was in its infancy and 'there were only two companies ... who made or partly made cycles'. Raleigh should not, however, be complacent. Woodhead believed that the political climate in Canada was shifting to a more protectionist policy for indigenous industry, and more threatening was the spectre of US competition in the lower-priced end of the market. The fear of prohibitive tariffs was to prove unfounded, as consequently 'tariff arrangements' were deployed in Britain's favour, but between 1895 and 1898 the 'British ... lost the Canadian market almost entirely to the Americans'. By 1894 Raleigh faced deteriorating sales in Canada, shipments falling from £2 723 in 1893 to £2 116, and payments of £1 269 were outstanding on orders taken up. The door was opened to the Americans in the severe trade depression in North America in 1894 which led to a fall in consumer demand. Canadian buyers now turned to the cheaper end of the market to the detriment of the higher-priced Raleighs. As the Braverman Co. argued: 'American made machines ... are inferior and not so popular or well finished as Raleighs, but the price differential was now the key consideration.' Raleigh's policy of creating brand loyalty with its agents through offering differentiated quality machines made little impact on agents who were propelled to concentrate on the most profitable lines. During 1894 Braverman sold 600 US machines, 'second grade eclipses made by a firm at Bevan Falls, close to the Canadian border', and the American advantage was hit home by the provision of liberal credit facilities for buyers. In comparison, Raleigh alienated small retailers 'who are solely aggrieved at our strict terms of credit'. The consequence was, that despite a large investment in advertisement and promotion, Raleigh's ambitions in the Canadian market were frustrated and the agency agreement was eventually ended.[35]

Success for Raleigh was no foregone conclusion, but the setbacks in the North American market need to be juxtaposed with the massive increase in demand for bicycles in the domestic market during 1895. In order to exploit these market opportunities the management embarked upon a policy of reconstruction, the intended outcome of which was to form a new company with an extended nominal capital. As a precursor to the formation of the new company, however, the management had to get its own house in order. This involved three decisions by management concerning long-term strategy. First, on the financial side of the business the company faced the need to overcome its trading debt problems. For example, in February 1895 the company was faced with demands for immediate repayment of £9 000 on bills of exchange due for material supplies. On the revenue side, the Braverman Co. had defaulted on the payment of £11 000 due on cycles received, resulting in an expense of £1 000 to fight a law suit. Temporary relief was provided by a loan of £20 000 based on a second debenture mortgage with Lloyds Bank, a concession which was only given 'after considerable negotiation, and through the mediation of a mutual friend'. The mutual friend in question was E. T. Hooley who, as we saw in Chapter 2, was a prominent promoter of new cycle companies during the boom. Bowden was introduced to Hooley during 1895, and an agreement reached to promote a new Raleigh Company, a scheme which received the approval of the bankers at Lloyds.[36] Second, the prospects of reconstruction offered the possibility of expanding and modernising the existing scale of plant, a decision aimed at confronting the supply constraints of their existing factory. A new purpose-built factory on a 5-acre site at Farraday Road, Lenton, was planned to come into operation during 1896, at a cost of £80 000. The conversion to the new plant disrupted output from late 1894, and production was irregular during the 17 months to January 1896.[37] Raleigh was effectively in limbo during this period as the management made preparations for the new factory, and negotiations proceeded for the reconstruction of the company.

The third decision involved the recruitment of new operational managers to replace Woodhead and Angois. This provided a 'new direction' for the company, and the organisation of production, and in particular the engineering and design side of the business, should be controlled by 'men of vision' who could 'confidently anticipate the trend of design and not merely be content to follow what other manufacturers are doing'.[38] This was a reaffirment of Bowden's belief that the company should commit its future to the quality cycle, and success could be achieved by constant attention to improvement and design. In November 1894 G. P. Mills was enticed by Bowden to join Raleigh from their neighbours, Humber of Beeston, and was appointed as chief draughtsman and later as manager of the new factory. One suspects that Mills did not need much persuasion, Bowden offering him the fantastic salary of £1 000 per annum. Mills was a qualified civil and mechanical engineer, an Associate Member of the Institute of Civil Engineers, and also a successful tandem cyclist, holding the Lands End to John O'Groats record on machines built and designed by himself.[39] Bowden also recruited another 'Humber man', their general manager D. W. Bassett, who was appointed as general manager at Raleigh.[40] These hand-picked men were considered by Bowden as essential to the future of the company, and they were given direct responsibility for the design and layout of the new factory. In 1896 Mills, on a tour of factories in the USA, recruited Edward Glover, an American design consultant who was to be influential in introducing American machine-tool technology in the factory. As Bowden later reflected, the appointment of these men laid the foundation of the company's managerial recruitment policy and defined the personal relationship between strategic management and operational management. It became the practice, he claimed, to bring in people who could be relied upon to answer 'any question of any importance', and we always 'consult our staff of practical young men, who thoroughly understand the business'.[41] These changes at Raleigh preceded the crucial formation of the new company, and its incorporation in February 1896.

A new start: the Raleigh Cycle Company Ltd of 1896

On the 3 February 1896 the Raleigh directors announced to shareholders a proposal for the voluntary winding up of the concern, the appointment of Edward Charles Farrow, the company secretary, as official receiver, and their intention to reconstruct the capital to form a new business concern. Why was this decision taken? The primary objective was to provide additional capital for the construction of a modern factory, 'equipped with all the latest improvements in automatic and other tools, sufficient to double the present output'. Thus reconstruction was aimed at meeting the 'unparalleled increase in the company's business', due to the bicycle boom, and to overcome the inadequacies of the existing factory. Further, the proceeds from the sale of the old company would provide the funds to extinguish the original founders' shares in the company, and by selling shares to the public raise £20 000 to build a reserve of additional working capital.[42]

Raleigh shareholders unanimously agreed to the reconstruction, but this was only achieved after a hard sell by Bowden. Confidence in the management was low, which was hardly surprising given the financial instability of the company during the previous two years. In January 1896 Bowden wrote to shareholders pleading for their support: 'I should like to again see the Directors have the unanimous support of the Shareholders.' As the leading managerial personality, it was left to Bowden to restore confidence, and this was done in two ways. First, he had to demonstrate that shareholders were investing in a viable business concern and that the management had put its own house in order.

Although recognising that the company had encountered serious financial problems during the past year, he projected an image of a management team which had instigated remedial action to tackle the finances of the company. Placing the facts, as he saw them, before shareholders, he claimed that they could now boast a credit balance with the bank of £15 737, trade debts of £9 000 had been paid, the debenture mortgage of £20 000 had been fully repaid, and an £11 000 debt owing to the company had been recovered. As a softener to shareholders, Bowden announced that the £15 737 bank balance would be partly used to pay a final dividend on the old company's ordinary shares of 3s., and despite reconstruction the company declared a profit of £14 536 between September 1894 and January 1896. The company, claimed Bowden, was now ideally placed to meet the rising demand for cycles. The factory presently employed 600 workers, operating on overtime to its fullest capacity, and the general prosperity of trade would ensure the company's stakeholders a profitable return.[43]

Second, Bowden had to satisfy shareholders that the management of the new company would have a full commitment to the running of the concern. In this Bowden's own role was paramount, and he had to allay fears that he was involved in a sell-out. Shareholders had become suspicious that the proposed reconstruction had come on the back of the flotation of the Humber Supply Co., a cycle firm promoted by Hooley and Rucker in September 1895. Rumours spread that Bowden was retiring from active management, and selling out to a management group which would be controlled by a syndicate of large promoters, headed by Hooley and Rucker. The inference was that Raleigh would merge with Humber, and that this would be sanctioned by Bowden who was closely acquainted with the Humber directors. These allegations were fuelled by the earlier association of Raleigh's general and factory managers, Bassett and Mills, with the Humber Co. Bowden vigorously denied these allegations, and in reply to a question from a shareholder he admitted he knew the Humber directors but had never held shares in that company, and neither did Mills and Bassett, who had given Bowden their assurance on this matter. Taking the offensive, he disclaimed the 'erroneous statements' in the press and assured shareholders that the management of the concern was in his own capable hands, being the majority shareholder in the old company. No 'better assurance could be forthcoming of faith in the future ... than the fact that the directors of the company held the majority of the shares', and since joining the concern Bassett and Mills had been large purchasers of shares.[44]

The succession of the existing management team was thus deemed essential to future business success. Bowden would continue to guide the company strategically as managing director and chairman, but would delegate responsibility for the supervision of production and the layout of the new factory to Bassett and Mills. In addition, the board would be strengthened by the appointment of new directors. As Table B.3 in the Appendix shows, only Joseph Lazonby retained his position as a director in the new company, while five new directors were brought in from outside. The background of the new directors clearly indicated the importance of men with a financial and legal background in running the business, and in the appointment of Enfield there was a direct link to Raleigh's bankers, Lloyds. Comprising respectable local men, with financial connections, an aura of respectability was generated to shareholders, and the new directors were to act in an advisory capacity in the running of the concern.[45] Reconstruction itself involved voluntary liquidation and the sale for £180 000 of the concern to a newly incorporated company with a nominal capital at £200 000, divided into 100 000 cumulative 6 per cent preference shares and 100 000 ordinary shares of £1 each. A summary of the reconstruction scheme is given in Table B.4 in the Appendix. Share capital in the old company, totalling £65 800, was converted to share capital in the new company, at an exchange of one of the former for two of the latter. The residue of share capital was then to be allotted to the vendors, principally Bowden, who could dispose of them to the public if desired. The allocation of shares in the new company is shown in Table 3.2, and illustrates the wide dispersion of shares, and the attraction of the company to small investors.[46] Nevertheless, Bowden remained the dominant shareholder, and as can be seen in Table 3.3 the bulk of converted shares were retained by himself and

Table 3.2 Distribution of shareholders of ordinary and preference shares, Raleigh Cycle Co., March 1896

Share category	Number of shareholders	% of total number of shareholders
1–25	135	57.7
25–100	73	31.2
101–500	19	8.1
501–1000	1	0.4
1 000+	6	2.6
Totals	234	100.0

Source: DDRN 10/3/1/3/1 Agreement Between the Old Raleigh Cycle Co., incorporated 1891, and the new Company, incorporated 1896 for the reconstruction of the company, Supplement, 29 April 1896.

Table 3.3 Profile of shareholders holding 100 plus ordinary and preference shares, Raleigh, 1896

Name	Location	Description	Preference	Ordinary
Frank Bowden	Nottingham	Cycle manufacturer	12 801	12 801
Amelia F. Bowden	Nottingham	Married	4 000	4 000
William H. Woodhouse	Nottingham	Coal merchant	1 805	1 805
Joseph F. Youngman	Nottingham	Manager, Nottingham Joint Stock Bank	1 264	1 264
Arthur J. Chamberlain	Nottingham	Solicitor	1 090	1 090
Joseph Lazonby	Nottingham	Solicitor	1 077	1 076

Source: As Table 3.2.

his wife. Indeed, a clear message was given to shareholders that Bowden, as the largest shareholder 'in the old company ... will take shares and not cash in exchange for those they now hold, so far as permitted by the rules of the stock exchange, with which this company must comply in order to obtain an official quotation for the shares'.[47]

The objectives of reconstruction were to expand the capital base of the firm to meet the requirements of an enlarged business, and at the same time ensure a continuity of ownership and control, with Bowden at the head of affairs. With a new board of directors behind him Bowden launched a programme of output expansion to meet the buoyant cycle market of 1896. In February 1896 he outlined the company's strategy to extend the business, increase the output of quality machines to build up stocks, and to introduce new 'up-to-date models', especially the cross-frame cycle designed and patented by Mills. There was a feeling of unbridled optimism, and 'There could be no doubt about success'. Large orders were being received, and the new factory would provide the capacity to supply demand. By April Raleigh was preparing to produce for stock. Large orders for raw materials and components were contracted for, and the factory was operated on overtime.[48] The new factory was central to management's perception of success, and semi-automatic machine tools, of both British and US designs, were introduced to increase efficiency.[49] For example, Edward Glover had designed a process for pressing steel lugs from steel sheets, and using special machinery purchased from the American Ferranti Co. steel lugs, fork crowns and bottom brackets were pressed from a single sheet of steel. This reduced the number of processes in pressing, and also led to the marketing of the Raleigh as the 'all steel bicycle'.[50]

Despite the modernisation of plant, and the pressure of the boom to increase output, the Raleigh management remained committed to quality. Thus, the objective was to raise output without jeopardising the company's reputation as a quality manufacturer at the higher end of the price range. Raleigh was synonymous with 'the finest make of cycles in the world', and this tradition, set by Bowden from his early association with the company, was to continue to dominate management thinking during the cycle boom and its aftermath.[51] Bowden's confidence in Raleigh's production strategy was initially borne out by its business performance during 1896. At the new company's first AGM in October 1896 Bowden announced a net profit of £19 296 (Table B1 in the Appendix), plus £3 349 brought forward from the old company, leaving £22 645 to be distributed as dividends, and to bolster the capital reserve. This satisfactory outcome, claimed Bowden, was the result of the management's commitment to capacity expansion and modernisation, but he also preached financial conservatism to shareholders. If the company was to benefit from the boom they would have to accept lower dividends, and allocate £14 000 of profits to a capital reserve to meet the future demands for working capital in an enlarged business. Bowden warned shareholders that past shortages of working capital needed to be avoided, but he was also keenly aware of the vagaries of the cycle market. Expand, but with caution, was Bowden's philosophy, and he urged shareholders to accept lower dividends in the interests of long-term sustained expansion. Not surprisingly, Bowden's financial strategy, in the context of a boom in bicycle sales, was hardly likely to attract full support from shareholders. For example, in a letter to share-holders in October 1896 he condemned a splinter group of shareholders who, in his view, were working against the long-term interests of the company: 'I feel that the Director's Report to the shareholders is re-ceived with opposite feelings. The firm investment shareholders, and especially the preference holders, heartily approve of the Board's policy in building up a large reserve fund – and the speculators oppose it and desire a large dividend.' The director's report was finally accepted at the October AGM, but a number of shareholders registered their disaproval when Bowden announced his prediction that future dividends on ordi-nary shares would be only 8 per cent.[52] This event hinted at a growing feeling of distrust in Bowden's motives and his business strategy, and as the boom gave way to bust tensions spilt over into the boardroom and jeopardised Bowden's commanding position in the organisation.

Boom, bust and boardroom crisis, 1896–98

In management affairs Bowden demanded strict adherence to the tasks set by him. He expected diligence, both from his operational managers and fellow directors, and the constant supervision of both the produc-tion and financial management of the concern. Bowden provided leadership and direction, and as we have seen earlier was not averse to condemning managerial inadequacies on the spot. Nevertheless, his commanding influence was temporarily broken in late October 1896 when he suffered a serious deterioration in health. Announcing his decision to 'abstain' from the managing directorship, he urged his direc-tors and managers to closely attend to the business, and he proclaimed that the concern had 'proved itself' and the new factory was being 'efficiently' run in the capable hands of Bassett. Retaining the chairman-ship of the company, Bowden travelled to Australia to recuperate, where he continued to work for the company as a travelling salesman. In December Bassett was appointed by the board to replace Bowden as managing director, on the same remuneration, and under his existing contract as general manager with direct responsibility for the supervision of the new factory.[53]

Bowden was later to comment, in 1904, on Bassett's appointment in less than favourable terms. He claimed that it was an attempt to capture the managerial control of the company, and the conspiracy was led by an ex-Raleigh director, Sir John Turney, in collusion with his close friend, E. T. Hooley. Bowden's conspiratorial theory went further, and he condemned certain members of the Raleigh board for using Bassett as the means for acquiring absolute control of 'the company during my long illness'.[54] These claims were made retrospectively and, as we shall see later, at a time when relationships between Bowden and Turney, who was reappointed to the board as chairman in 1899, were at breaking point. Nevertheless, the company records reveal growing turmoil at the boardroom level, which intensified as the company faced mounting financial problems due to the collapse of the bicycle boom. This was to lead to another winding-up in late 1898, and from Bowden's viewpoint was directly related to mismanagement on the part of the board, and in particular Bassett's supervision of the new factory.

In July 1897 Bowden returned from Australia, and was appalled at the state of manufacturing operations, the low level of output of the new factory and the high overhead costs. He was

> much astonished and upset ... that during the past five months the expenses of the company had been exceedingly great, and that there was now an enormously heavy stock of raw materials, cycles and parts, whilst the output in comparison with the large outgoings could only be described as trivial.

These problems were not unknown to the directors, and in March 1897 Arthur Chamberlain had reported on the difficulties in meeting orders, and the 'great discrepancy between the output and the expenses'. He registered his 'great dissatisfaction at the failure of the company to turn out machines more freely', and in combination with his fellow directors, Enfield and Lazonby, roundly condemned Mills and Bassett for the fact that the output of their new factory was no larger than it had been in the old Russell Street works. Increasing overhead charges now became a matter of acute concern. The factory was producing insufficient machines to cover the increased operational expenses, and in April it was estimated that an additional output of 4 000 bicycles per year was needed to cover overhead costs, while the manufacturing reports showed that output was languishing. This was reported to shareholders at the Raleigh AGM in December, where the directors referred to the serious logistical problems of operating the factory during the year. There had been major delays in removing machinery and stock to the new factory, and in installing and arranging new machines. The outcome was 'that output had been comparatively small until May and we could not fulfil half our orders', even though £62 216 had been spent upon the capital account, of which £21 000 was invested in the latest automatic and other labour-saving machinery. From the chair, Bowden apologised on behalf of the board for the fact that net profits were only £19 783, and the appropriation for dividend was no higher than last year, but he had the assurance of his fellow directors that the company was financially sound, and that logistical problems had been rectified.[55] This, however, was a false hope, and the minute books of the board tell a different story.

There were clearly internal organisational problems at Raleigh which were partly responsible for delays in preparing the factory for optimum output. On the defensive, Mills and Bassett explained that the organisation of the factory was not yet complete, and that the layout of machinery was as yet not accomplished. But there were also exogenous factors which were outside the management's control. For example, there were shortages of key labour inputs, and the return of the old problem of insufficient supplies of outside materials. Although by May 1897 the factory was organised for maximum production there were constant delays in the finishing department, and the company had great difficulty in obtaining skilled workers. Craftsmanship and an attention to minute detail were key factors in the finishing stages of production at Raleigh, and thus skilled workers were essential to ensure high-quality output. Shortages of labour inputs were compounded by deficiencies in the supply of nuts and screws which they largely purchased from Shirley, Banks & Co. This company could not supply in sufficient quantities for the enlarged output, and they were supplying only 25 per cent of the company's needs.[56]

This raised a fundamental paradox relating to the randomness of the business environment facing cycle firms. In Bowden's absence the directors had embarked upon a policy of increasing stocks of cycles in expectation of a continued rising demand in the market during 1897. In pursuing this policy they had not counted on the logistical problems of bringing the factory into full operation, and consequently overhead costs had risen rapidly. By the middle of 1897 the management believed that they could rectify this situation by selling accumulated stocks, and by raising the output of the factory which was now ready to produce at full capacity. But as Bassett informed Bowden in July, the factory had come on stream three months too late, and after May 1897 the company was inundated by cancellations from dealers and agents, which represented an 'alarming' state of affairs. The boom had given way to bust, and this changed market configuration 'prevented the output equalling the full capacity of the factory'. Evidence of a downturn in demand had first become apparent in the French market in May when Raleigh's Paris agents, Bruel & Co., reported a collapse in orders for the company's cycles, and noted a rising market for cheaper American and French designs. Raleigh's agents remained optimistic that they could sell 600 Raleighs in the future, but urged that this would necessitate a cut in prices and a vastly increased expenditure on advertisement. Since their failures in the North American arena the French market had been targeted by the company, but the management rejected additional expenditure on marketing, considering this undesirable given the rising expenditure on overheads at the Nottingham factory, and on Bowden's return in July he was faced with the situation that 'Raleigh had lost business because they had not cut down prices to meet ... competition'.[57]

Prospects had also taken a turn for the worse in the Australian market, where Bowden travelled to promote business,[58] and of more concern was the ominous sign of falling demand in the home market, despite efforts to increase sales through an advertisement campaign directed through the trade press and local and national newspapers.[59] An obvious response by management was to produce cheaper lines, and as early as January 1897 Bassett had reported on the 'large demand for machines to be sold at a price lower than our cheapest Raleigh'. Bassett, however, was well aware of the risks of this strategy, and commented on the commitment of their productive resources to stockpiling 'higher grade machines', a policy which would be undermined by placing on the market cheaper cycles, directly competing with their own top-range models, and resulting in falling prices and financial losses on stocks. Downgrading the product clearly contradicted their strategy of quality production, and to reconcile the dilemma Bassett proposed to establish a 'private concern', the Kestrel Cycle Co., to manufacture cheaper models. As he argued: 'It would not do for the Raleigh Company to invoice these machines on their forms – the Kestrel Co. must be a distinctly separate one.'[60]

The estimated cost of producing Kestrels was £7 for machines without brake or mudguards and £7 12s. 6d. with accessories included. The proposed selling price to dealers was £9 10s., less 2.5 per cent discount for cash and, as can be seen in Table B.5 in the Appendix which shows Raleigh prices in 1898, this was a considerable reduction from the company's norm. The Kestrel scheme, however, was scuppered by Bowden, who briefly returned from Australia in January 1897 to attend a special board meeting on the Kestrel proposal. Bowden's objections were not based on a rejection of the need to produce cheaper machines, and he claimed that he had 'always advocated the production of a cheaper bike'. Nevertheless, he considered Bassett's scheme to be somewhat unethical, as 'it was not fair to Raleigh shareholders for a rival concern to be started', and it could not be 'considered as straight dealing'. On his moral high horse, he dismissed the formation of what he considered would become a rival concern and a future competitor. Bowden's intervention demonstrated a strong determination to preserve the Raleigh tradition of the quality cycle, which he saw as the key to business success, but he did propose to the board that they could sell cheaper cycles under the Gazelle trade mark, the patents for which had been purchased by Bowden from the company in 1894. His offer was readily accepted, and the belief was that Gazelle would allow the company a degree of flexibility; the Raleigh factory could concentrate on high-quality machines and Gazelle could be managed by Bowden as a separate concern, producing for the growing trend towards cheaper models, especially in France.[61]

Going down-market was not a guarantee of business success, as seen by Bowden's alarm at the state of the company on his return from Australia in July. The Gazelle business, for example, was viewed by management as of secondary importance to their core business activity of producing quality cycles under the Raleigh name. Produced in the old Russell Street factory, Gazelles were produced using cheap bought-in parts, and there was little commitment to investments in factory modernisation. Gazelle cycles performed poorly in the French market, even though the price differential with its closest local competitor, the Clement Gladiator Co., was minimal, the former selling at 280 fr. compared to the latter at 240 fr. Bruel & Co. constantly complained that Raleigh were not investing sufficiently in promoting the Gazelle, compared to the Raleigh, and noted also the failure to design the machines to meet the requirements of the French customer, who demanded 'horizontal top tubes'. The machines were further condemned for supervision of quality, the 'use of cheap parts' and their unreliability made them a poor market prospect. On their overall business in France, they had by October 500 cycles in stock, sold only 349 during the year, and the Paris depot recorded a loss of £2 900, a fact which Chamberlain regarded as 'extremely disappointing as the shareholders had been told ... that the French business was highly thought of'. Raleigh's technical and labour expertise was geared to producing high-quality cycles, and they did not adapt easily to a commitment to lower standards.[62]

This failure to compete at the bottom end of the market was compounded by the collapse of the demand for higher-grade cycles, which resulted in serious financial problems. It was in this context that Bowden reasserted his influence in the board in July 1897. At the core of Raleigh's problems was now the issue of financial retrenchment. Thus,

Bowden criticised the directors for a free-for-all investment policy in the face of the declining demand in the cycle trade. In Bowden's view market signals were not encouraging but 'despite the company's want of working capital [the directors] were still proposing to extend the factory', construct a new chain-making plant, purchase premises for Gazelle and acquire a business for the production of stampings. These were strategic managerial decisions, but in Bowden's view the wrong ones. The immediate issue, claimed Bowden, was business survival, and he presented to the board a stark choice: should they 'slow down' output or continue to manufacture for stock during the winter months in anticipation of an up-turn in business fortunes in early 1898? In part, the resolution to this question lay outside the confines of the board, for they needed an additional £20 000 to £30 000 to carry on the business during the winter, and 'the most important thing was to satisfy the Bank [Lloyds], to slow down or just go on manufacturing stock'. In September Bowden reported on discussions with Lloyds and the general impression of the bankers was that Raleigh's 'accounts were unsatisfactory'. Thus, 'a great deal of money had been spent – apparently far more than necessary and ... we held a very much heavier stock than we ought'. Reassurances were nevertheless provided by the main office at Birmingham that the bank would not withdraw support, but at the same time they were not prepared to extend loans unless the directors agreed on a strategy for their loss-making factory.[63]

In this situation, it is little wonder that Bowden urged the board in July to adopt a strategy of 'immediate retrenchment', pushing wage costs downwards and rationalising on labour by the introduction of automatic machinery. For example, piece-rate systems were gradually introduced for workers producing component parts for finished cycles, and Bowden urged greater vigilance in the supervision of work to raise productivity and ensure quality. At the insistence of the bank, Bowden brought in an American consultant to inspect the factory. His report highlighted that despite the management's commitment to modernisation the company was not utilising the full potential of the plant. The layout of plant and machinery was condemned as inefficient, in the wheel department there was 'an entire absence of labour saving devices', and the purchase of various outside components was expensive and increased workloads. In frame construction, the failure to use jigs was uneconomical, and the cost of labour in building and fitting the frame at Raleigh averaged 17s., compared to only 5s. 11d. in the USA. Part of the problem at Raleigh was related to the uncoordinated nature of factory operations, which were dictated by the seasonal demand for cycles, and the need to plan production and labour rotas for the coming season. For example, Bassett informed Bowden in July that weekly wages had been reduced from £986 to £777, but 'he thought it inadvisable to make a too sweeping reduction on account of spoiling business for the coming season'.[64] Further, as Millward argues, although a number of Birmingham manufacturers introduced American machine tools in the boom, they were tailor-made to British factory conditions, and thus a great deal of output was lost 'through failing to optimise their use'.[65] These problems were clearly evident at Raleigh, who remained committed to the batch production of non-standardised quality cycles, often using their own technicians to design tools. For example, the company manufactured machines for the Australian market with specially designed handlebars, and reported that until new tools could be procured and modified 'it was necessary to make the handlebars by hand'. The continued reliance on outside component suppliers also created problems, and vertical integration was now restricted by the financial constraints placed on the management. As mentioned earlier, management were planning to extend the plant to produce chains and stampings internally, but Bowden's concerns over the increasing debts of the company put paid to these ambitions. Financial retrenchment involved shelving plans for further modernisation, and a proposed expenditure of £1 000 on additional automatic machinery for the turning department was vetoed by Bowden, as was a projected department for pedal manufacture costing £730.[66]

Constraints on output at Raleigh led to rising overhead costs, and to add to managerial concerns there were escalating labour problems in the factory. For example, in July 1897 Humber had proposed to Raleigh a general lock out of 25 per cent of their men belonging to the Amalgamated Society of Engineers (ASE), a reaction against proposals for a 48-hour week. In response Raleigh joined forces with the Federation of Employers in the lock out, a decision which the management considered would have little affect on their own business, the company only employing 50 ASE members. By September, however, with the bankers knocking on the door, labour unrest was rife. Registering 'losses' in the factory, Bowden condemned the workers who, encouraged by the union, were engaged in making 'the work spin out as much as possible'. Management may well have thought they held the upper hand over labour, but the unions clearly were not to be stampeded. The union coordinated its action, and in August the ASE targeted 120 men working on special machines for the Australian market, and they were 'coerced' to strike by personal acts of violence and demonstrations at the factory gates. The men targeted were finishers, which seriously delayed the production for the Australian orders, and forced management, in turn, to persuade them back by promises of protection and special bonuses. Further, skilled tool-workers were targeted, and although automatic machinery had made it possible to dispose of a great deal of skilled labour in the turning shop, a strike by toolmakers in September severely disrupted output.[67]

Financial crisis became interlocked with a mounting labour crisis, and the latter limited the actions of management to remedy the deficiencies of the factory. Labour unrest brought the decision in September 1897 to close the factory for a six-week period to reduce wage expenses, and to provide an opportunity to sell off unsold stocks of last season's goods. Lurking amongst these problems was the question of bank finance and Bowden's rising irritation with the inadequacies of his own managerial team. For example, commenting on the report by the American consultant on the state of the factory, he claimed 'there had been gross mis-management and inattention to business from the highest to the lowest'. The concerns of the bank could be related to inefficiencies of production leading to a failure to turn out sufficient quantities of cycles. When the 'slump came and orders were cancelled', sales fell sharply 'whilst expenses on the running and capital accounts had been enormous'. Referring to the bank overdraft, he argued that Bassett had informed him that they would not need 'more than £40 000 from the Bank but we had far exceeded that, and were now brought to an absolute standstill unless we should find more money'. In his defence, Bassett, supported by Chamberlain, argued that they could not foresee the slump, and with buoyant trading conditions at the end of 1896 it had been rational to contract out for large supplies of materials, but admitted that with 'the loss of business caused through the delay in getting the factory into order we had over contracted'. In an attempt to placate Bowden, Bassett pointed out that the directors had attended board meetings weekly, and 'had continually before them reports showing the progress of the business'. Why then, retorted Bowden, did the consultant's report show that 'we had too much machinery in some departments – in others we had not enough'?[68]

As tensions in the board rose, the issue of the bank took centre stage. At the board in September, Bowden insisted that the directors must find additional capital to 'carry on the business'; they had a responsibility to shareholders, and they should personally guarantee the money necessary to secure an advance on the bank overdraft, Bowden being 'willing to take on double portion'. At this point, Bowden and Bassett adjourned from the board while 'private' discussions ensued. On Bowden's return he was disappointed to find the directors were not willing to guarantee their own capital in a venture which was in financial difficulties, and in which Bassett's managerial prowess was under question. The decision was therefore taken to negotiate with Lloyds an advance on existing loans based on the security of the Gazelle Bicycle Co. In October this was rejected, and as a drastic measure it was decided to approach the Dunlop Rubber Co. with a request for an advance of £25 000, secured on a second mortgage debenture. It was acknowledged that there would have to be 'a quid pro quo', and the directors sanctioned an agreement to purchase Dunlop tyres. In October Du Cros of Dunlop turned down Raleigh's application on the grounds that they were 'not in a position to lend and thought that the Raleigh Directors and large shareholders should make the necessary financial arrangements'.[69] In November the Raleigh directors were forced to capitulate, and along with Bowden signed an agreement to guarantee personally an advance from Lloyds, by the issue of debenture shares totalling £50 000 which were to be held by the bank.[70]

This provided only a temporary reprieve, for the company continued to face adverse market conditions, and during 1898 the business was affected by cut-throat competition. As we saw in Chapter 2, the British market was flooded by American imports, and in January 1898 Raleigh's order books were one-third down on the corresponding period in 1897. Thus, output was kept small, the company not wishing to expand without more firm orders. With falling orders, the cycle trade entered a period of panic selling, and in March Bassett reported that 'Humber's recent drop in prices is hurting us to a considerable extent. The American competition is also not yet done with'. Companies now dumped unsold stocks on the market at reduced prices, Rudge-Whitworth and Swift cutting in April followed by a further reduction by Humber. In May Humber advertised 3 000 cycles for sale at 'ridiculously low prices', and

> the general trade was being brought to a standstill through the action of the Griffiths Corporation who were offering their stocks of Humbers and Singers and other bicycles for sale by auction all over the country. All this had a very adverse effect on our trade and things were very slack indeed.

The situation was no better in export markets, especially in France, where there was 'the fiercest possible competition', up-to-date machines being sold at £40 per dozen, and cycles with imitation Dunlop tyres at 15s. per pair. Coventry-made Humbers with French Dunlop tyres were selling at £4 each, and the Griffiths Corporation, representing Singer, Swift, Premier, Star and Ariel, were 'offering stock at whatever they can get'.[71] As Bassett claimed:

> I found that the better class of cyclists instead of now buying the high grade machines are quite satisfied to accept a cheap machine ... irrespective of the mark. They also make their machines last two seasons, instead of as hitherto having new machines each year. I was quite surprised to see quite respectable people riding old pattern and practically worn out machines.

He also noted a worrying new trend, with 'hundreds of the swell class of riders' switching their allegiance to motor cycles, and 'it was practically impossible to ... continue in France'.[72] By October the French depot had been sold for £13 500, Bowden remarking that they 'were very well out of France under the circumstances'.[73]

In the hostile market environment of 1898 business survival was paramount, and Raleigh responded by curtailing future capital outlays and restricting the manufacture of 1898 cycle models to 'special orders' only. The factory was now to focus on using up surplus parts from the old models to develop new lines which 'would contain all our improvements'. This decision reflected a belief in a revival in trade during 1899, which Raleigh could exploit by placing on the market new designs, but the short-term crisis of panic selling had also to be tackled. The company was left with large unsold stocks which now had to be disposed of in the short run. This was made difficult in a buyer's market where agents were increasingly determining the trend. For example, Bassett reported that despite lower prices in the domestic market 'agents were determined to clear out their present stock before buying', even though discounts of 10 per cent had been given for guaranteed orders of 12 machines. Agents were 'fighting shy of placing orders for immediate delivery', and further, were increasingly determining the design of models. Thus, in March, although they had 1 500 orders guaranteed, there was an 'unexpected' switch in demand to 'tall frames', a pattern which Raleigh had practically no stock of. This forced the management to sacrifice profit margins by trying to 'coax' agents 'off high frames' through bonuses of 5s. 10d. on every 'standard' Raleigh sold. Market resistance remained high, and as John Handley, the Midlands sales manager, complained, it was 'difficult to introduce new business owing to the high prices of Raleighs, to the fact that they were very poorly advertised, and that no attractive catalogue had been issued'. As Table B.5 in the Appendix shows, Raleigh's sales catalogue for 1898 advertised its lowest priced machine, the 'Radford Make Light Roadster' at £20 but in April this model was being touted to agents at special discounts of £10, and they were prepared to sell 'at any price we can get'. By June 1898 Bassett reported that 'trade all over the country was exceedingly bad, and it was most difficult to make sales'. In desperation, the directors announced a further reduction in prices to the home trade, and informed agents of their intention to introduce a new system of hire purchase.[74]

Some relief was found in export markets, where Raleigh drastically cut prices, for example, producing special export models at £9 16s. and £9 5s., ladies' and gentlemans' respectively. The sales of cycles and sundries abroad amounted to £16 500 for the six months to February 1898, and in April export orders, representing about two-thirds of all orders, were being maintained due to significant reductions in price. Nevertheless, American competition in export markets intensified, and as the management noted, 95 per cent of their foreign business, with the exception of Paris, was conducted on a cash basis, providing the advantage of security, but the 'American houses offer practically unlimited credit'. The company was thus forced to offer more liberal trade credit to foreign agents, a decision which they viewed as entailing considerable risks given the mounting financial debts of the company. Increasing sales, however, were paramount if the company was to survive, for as Bassett put it, 'the more cycles we sell, the lower the expenses will be, thus reducing our gross cost'. Cost reductions were essential given the management's decision to sell cycles at lower prices. Bowden recognised that to compete 'it was absolutely necessary to produce machines to sell at £10 to £14 with which a very large business was now being done throughout the country'. As Table B.5 in the Appendix shows, cycles had been pitched at the upper end of the market, and the company introduced price discrimination, producing 'three grades', varying in price from the 'Nottingham Make', the 'Lenton Make', and the 'Radford Make'. The latter two makes, together with the separate Gazelle machines, were targeted at the lower price range.[75] This would seem to be a positive response to the market conditions prevailing in this period, and the growing demand for cheaper machines, especially from the USA, but management remained reluctant to abandon its commitment to the quality high-grade cycle.

In May 1898 the names Lenton and Radford were abandoned, a decision for which Bowden was 'glad' because it had 'given the impression that these were second and third grade machines, and had been detrimental to the business'.[76] The belief in the quality cycle was deeply embedded in management thinking, and in terms of marketing they continued to promote the ideal that quality represented value for money, regardless of price:

> To-day this famous name is borne by the finest make of cycles in the world ... the popular appreciation of the benefits and pleasures of cycling had reached a point never hitherto approached, the manufacture of Raleighs had been brought to a degree of excellence little short of perfection. The makers of this superb machine are not attracted by the sole desire to build up an enormous business. Their first objective is to produce absolutely the best machine as regards design, workmanship, and material.

This reflected upon the production facilities of the factory and 'expense has been a secondary consideration'. Thus, 'cycles cannot be possibly made to sell at very low prices', despite the 'growing disposition to accept the doctrine that the best is the cheapest'.[77]

The management now faced a fundamental dilemma, in the sense that on the one hand it was imperative that the factory be operated at a level of output which met running expenses, and be instrumental in reducing costs in line with falling prices. On the other hand, entering the cheaper end of the market had to be achieved without damaging the company's reputation for quality. This complex balancing act was frustrated by continued problems on the production side of the business. For example, the company introduced new lathes, drills, presses and jigs, and semi-automatic machinery to reduce skilled labour, with the intention of producing 600 Raleighs and 200 Gazelles per week. By February 1898, however, although Gazelle production was on target, the factory was turning out only 200 Raleigh machines per week. Bowden was less than impressed, and although Mills argued that the introduction of piece rates had reduced costs by 50 per cent compared to day rates, and resulted in increased productivity, he demanded to know why they were producing at levels 400 below the targets set. As Table 3.4 shows, economy in production had been effected, largely with the reduction of skilled labour and wages, but the success of the factory, as Mills argued, 'was now a matter of having the orders in'. However, in May 1898 both Bowden and Chamberlain claimed that even if they could secure orders they 'could not deliver them', and there were still too many non-productive workers, namely foremen and supervisory staff, being employed.[78] According to Bowden, the factory was grossly 'mismanaged', and the company, he believed, was overstaffed with office workers who were 'out of all proportion to the output and that radical reductions ought to be made at once'. Although Bowden had issued a directive to Mills and Bassett to address overstaffing he maintained that they 'should know it was their duty to make every reduction and economy possible ... without any request from himself or any other Director'.[79]

Raleigh was restricted in reducing costs through inefficiencies in the factory, and in addition the commitment to the quality cycle reduced their capability to switch to low-grade cheaper machines. Reputation

Table 3.4 Wages and finished machines at Raleigh, four weeks ending 20 March 1898, compared to similar period in 1897

	Producers' wages (£)	Non-producers' wages (£)	Finished machines
1897	3 963	685	770
1898	2 799	614	1 035

Source: Minutes with Reports, 20 March 1898.

had to be maintained, and Bassett announced that the company was to 'turn out low priced Raleighs' for the 1899 season, under the somewhat dubious title of 'No Name Machines'. These were to be offered to large dealers only to ensure bulk orders, and demonstrates the management's half-way house policy on the question of cheaper machines. 'No Name Machines' were produced from cheaper components brought in from outside, and clearly demonstrated the inefficiencies of the factory to produce sufficient supplies of components. Further, the Gazelle, in which Bowden had invested an additional capital of £9 000, was being made under licence from the Raleigh Co. at 2s. 6d. royalty per machine, but Bowden's ownership of Gazelle clashed with his interests in Raleigh. As Bowden put it:

> how could the Gazelle be carried on without conflicting with the Raleigh Company; if it was desirable for the travellers to be instructed to push Raleighs and to give up Gazelle he had no objection, but wished the Board to do and say only what was best in the Raleigh Company's interests – without regard to the Gazelle.

Consequently, it was decided to supply the cheaper Gazelle with the same components as the 'No Name Machines', and remove the label 'made under licence from the Raleigh Co.'.[80]

The attempt to go down-market could not, however, avoid growing financial problems during 1898. Low sales and defaults by agents on repayments to the company forced the management to pursue 'The utmost economy ... in order to keep the bank balance as low as possible'. By August the overdraft at Lloyds was £58 000, and Bowden informed the board that the bank would not 'sanction the payment of the third mortgage debentures until the remainder of the special loan, now standing at £4 000, which had been secured by the second mortgage debenture, had been paid off'. By October the bank was demanding immediate repayments of £8 000 on the first mortgage debenture of August 1897. Raleigh's solicitor, Jessie Hind, summed up the situation: 'while the step that the Bank had taken might only be a formal one the situation was undoubtedly very serious'. Trading losses for the year were £24 000, 'and the view of the bank was that the Raleigh Company's trade creditors had been paid at the bank's expense'.[81] An ultimatum was presented to Raleigh by Dixon Taylor, the managing director of the Advance Department of Lloyds at Birmingham, to the effect that if the business could not be operated at a profit then it should be voluntarily wound up. The rumour in the trade was that Raleigh 'had the bailiffs in', but the bank felt that it was in the interests of the shareholders to continue the business, albeit after another reconstruction of the company's capital, which was to be sanctioned by the bank. The bank was offering a lifeline to the company, which in the words of Chamberlain would provide 'a new start on much closer lines'. Reconstruction would involve the conversion of shares, the repayment of trade debts, the extension of an overdraft of £30 000 secured by mortgage debentures, and, at the insistence of the bank, the removal of Bassett as managing director, and his replacement by Bowden. Further, the bank insisted that the reconstruction should include a formal amalgamation of the Gazelle business with that of Raleigh.[82]

Bowden was highly supportive of the bank's proposals for reconstruction, but the destiny of the company increasingly revolved around a shareholders' committee chaired by Edward Harlow, a Nottingham stockbroker, and consisting of Sir John Turney, a former Raleigh director, and two local yarn merchants, A. Schmidt and S. Morley.[83] This committee had been formed in January 1898 and was welcomed by Bowden who believed that his company should be scrutinised as they were directly accountable to shareholders. His personal commitment to shareholders displayed the ethical side of his character, and as he claimed, 'everything in connection with the company and its management was being closely watched and criticised and any looseness of management not only caused the business to suffer but had the continuous effect of depressing the shares of the company'.[84] With shareholder confidence in the company waning in October, suspicions aroused by a delay in issuing the annual accounts, the shareholders' committee increasingly took control of the reconstruction of the company, taking on the role of investigating the company's affairs, and formulating the scheme for reconstruction. In November, the committee met with the directors, and Jessie Hind, acting for Bowden who was not present, read prepared statements from him. At issue was Bassett's position as managing director, and Bowden's ownership of Gazelle and its acquisition by Raleigh. The board, with the exception of Bowden's close associate, Lazonby, were reluctant to dismiss Bassett, a decision which Bowden saw as crucial. In a letter read to the board, Bowden argued that Bassett's removal was central to restoring confidence by shareholders in a reconstructed company, but he also referred to the 'general impression ... that for ends of my own (selfish ones of course) I am desirous of supplanting Bassett against the wishes of all Raleigh staff and it is hinted most of the directors'. Having done everything possible 'to work out a scheme for reconstruction for the benefit of all concerned', Bowden now forced the issue by placing the onus for reconstruction directly on his directors: 'I and Gazelle need not figure, or only in a minor part, but they may rely on me seconding their efforts.'[85]

This tactical ploy was designed to appeal to the shareholders' committee, and its chairman, Harlow, had no doubts that Bowden's position in the company was of paramount importance, in particular his personal standing in relation to bank support for the company. Thus,

Bowden was persuaded to approach the bank to 'relax' their terms, and grant a larger overdraft facility of £40 000 for three years, a request which was consented to by Lloyds on the condition that he became managing director. Bassett's days were numbered, and under Harlow's initiative a scheme for reconstruction was finalised which was intended to raise additional working capital, pay off trade creditors and purchase Gazelle from Bowden. Bowden consented to the scheme on the condition that 'arrangements satisfactory to him were made with regard to management'. In December the management issue was confronted, and Bassett, making a final but unsuccessful plea to the shareholders' committee to work under 'new conditions', concluded 'that it was the best thing he could do to resign'. The discussion which followed this announcement illustrates the animosities which had evolved in the board. Interjecting on Bassett's behalf, 'as none of the Directors would speak', Harlow pointed out that it was not a personal matter, but rather 'a pecuniary point of view'. Bassett's resignation would aid the company in obtaining additional capital, and although he had done his best for the shareholders 'certain things had gone on'. In response Chamberlain argued that Bassett should attend the next general meeting to explain the charges which would be brought against him, and that 'the Directors should not be blamed with Bassett'. Agreeing to attend, Bassett then complained that Bowden had not been prepared 'to sit down and discuss matters', to which Bowden replied that 'he could say a great deal but would rather not'! What he did say, however, demonstrated his view that the directors were timid, and he insisted that they should now propose their own motion accepting Bassett's resignation. Reluctantly accepting this, an agreement for reconstruction was signed by the whole of the debenture shareholders in the company, and Bowden was empowered to take charge of the business as managing director from the date of Bassett's resignation.[86]

Bowden's position in the company was now secured, and with Harlow's backing the reconstruction scheme was presented to shareholders. Existing preference shareholders were offered the option of converting their shares into new shares in an incorporated company at 2s. 6d. per share, and paying an additional 2s. 6d. for new shares. As Harlow noted, these shareholders were losing out, as the scheme involved a considerable reduction of capital in the business, and their prior rights to this capital had not been considered. The reduction of capital reflected the depressed conditions of the trade, and the assets of the company had been correspondingly written down from £90 000 to £50 000, and £132 000 standing in the accounts for goodwill and patents had been entirely 'wiped out'. Selling the scheme to shareholders, Harlow guaranteed that a new board of directors would be appointed, and making reference to a past 'want of harmony between the Members of the Board' and a 'weak financial policy', he promised that the new executive would adopt 'a sounder and more economical business policy in the future'.[87] With Bowden firmly in charge, they could be satisfied that the company was a sound investment, and they were acquiring the assets of the old company at knock down values, and the par value of shares in the new company would rise in the future. In the final analysis the shareholders had little option but to accept if they were to safeguard their investments in a company which was in financial jeopardy, and faced the prospects of compulsory liquidation.[88] Raleigh was voluntarily wound up in January 1899, the scheme having been accepted by a majority of shareholders. The new managerial board, headed by Bowden, managing director, and Turney, chairman, also included Harlow as a director.[89] The task facing them was to reforge the company and meet the challenges presented by the collapse of the bicycle boom. In doing this, Bowden was to create the foundations of a family dynasty at Raleigh.

Meeting the challenge: the making of a family business, 1899–1914

By the eve of the First World War Raleigh had become one of the largest and most successful cycle firms in the UK. In this, Bowden's role in directing the company's fortunes was paramount, and represents a classic example of the role of personal leadership in building the reputation of British manufacturing firms. The reconstruction of early 1899 provided the platform for Bowden to launch the company in a new direction. The newly incorporated company had a reduced nominal capital of £120 000, shares distributed pro rata to existing shareholders, and subscriptions of 2s. 6d. per ordinary share raising £25 000, half of which was to be used to pay off the interest of the existing bank debentures, leaving £12 500 for additions to working capital. Financial latitude was provided by the issue of deferred ordinary shares, which allowed the directors flexibility in paying dividends, and provided the means of controlling the appropriation of profits to shareholders. Further, shares totalling £21 000 were left unissued, the directors being empowered to dispose of them, at above par, to raise future additions to capital (see Table B.4 in the Appendix). At the AGM in November Bowden optimistically announced that the company was back on track, and he expected an 'increased demand for Raleigh cycles'.[90]

Bowden's strategy was based on the need to expand output and the reduce the inefficiencies of the factory, which had been central to the company's failings in the past. Expansion was to be financed through retained profits, and the continuation of loan capital from the bank. As Bowden insisted, with intense competition, especially from US manufacturers, output must be raised, costs reduced, and 'Our prices must be lower'.[91] A modernisation programme was launched in late 1899, and aimed at reducing production costs by introducing 'American methods', and reorganising the works on the best American lines as far as practicable.[92] In 1901 the Raleigh factory employed 550 workers in the slack season and 850 in the busy season. The production process began in the drawing office, where the cycles were drawn to scale, 'worked out scientifically', and not 'by rule of thumb, as is still done in many large and most small concerns'. In the turning and press shops, power presses from the USA and toolmaking plant were installed, and converted sheet steel into cranks, brackets, lugs, loops, gear wheels, brake clips and a variety of small parts. Having first tested all material before use, the factory turned out 20 000 machined parts annually, and 'costly machinery' was used for making drills, cutters, reamers and a variety of tools to meet the demands for the implements necessary to produce a range of differentiated cycle models. Apart from the use of American machine tools, the company also bought automatic lathes from Alfred Herberts at Coventry, which largely increased component output and reduced labour costs. Nevertheless, skilled tool-workers were essential to the production process, and these were supervised by a 'master mechanic' who had been trained in the technical schools of Zurich and the workshops of the USA and Germany. The cycle frames themselves were cast from a single sheet of steel, giving their machines the distinction of the 'all steel bicycle', and then put together by the 230 employed in the frame shop who used specially designed jigs to clamp and peg accurately the tubing into place. Frames were then transferred to the brazing and plating department where liquid brazing methods were used to coat the machines. The frames were then returned to the frame shop to be filed and polished, and forks, handlebars and other small parts fitted. Frames and forks were then tested for tracking and accuracy before passing to the plating and enamelling shops. Finally, the assembling and finishing room attached the gear cases, mudguards and pedals, supplied by the gear case shop, and also the wheels and tyres supplied by the wheel shop. Before packaging and distribution, a large staff of employees were responsible for testing the quality and accuracy of machines, an essential process which 'results in perfect interchangeability of parts, and guarantees the true running of our cycle'.[93]

Modernisation at Raleigh clearly did not mean the introduction of the American system of manufacture with its emphasis upon the volume output of standardised components and finished cycles. Rather, the Raleigh system was to integrate machine-tool technology with a continued commitment to skilled labour inputs. Success, claimed Bowden, was to be achieved by a constant attention to detail, and 'We have the finest factory in the world, equipped with the most up-to-date tools and appliances for obtaining accuracy and finish'. The Nottingham mechanic was renowned for his 'skill, and our men have no experience of the jerry built machines that affect other centres of the trade'. Although reducing costs and prices was deemed essential, this was not to be achieved at the expense of reducing quality. Thus, the company continued to differentiate between the Raleigh and the Gazelle brands, the latter targeted at the cheaper end of the market. The Gazelle was clearly distinguished in 'appearance' from the Raleigh and sold at the low price standard of £10 10s., and discounts of 20 per cent were offered to retailers for cash sales. Gazelles offered the possibility of increased turnover which would justify the capital costs of factory modernisation, and the aim was to manufacture cycles of 'exceptionally good value', the machines being constructed using the same bearings and working parts as the Raleigh. By 1901 Bowden could boast that through new techniques in the factory they 'were able to guarantee every cycle to be built dead true and perfectly brazed'. Thus, the cheaper Gazelle could compete favourably with any machine made by rival makers.[94]

As we have seen, quality was an intrinsic company value which was linked to the exchange value of the product through a marketing image which emphasised the best value for money. Cycles were to incorporate the latest designs and gadgetry, symbolised by the introduction of the X-frame cycle, and the development of three-speed gears as attachments. Bowden could also boast that machines would include the Raleigh patented ball-bearing free-wheel gear, a light grade tyre, back-pedalling braking and the new Bowden rim brake, the latter produced by Ernest W. Bowden of London. As agents were informed, these 'novelties and fittings ... will make Raleighs more noticeable than ever', and they could be ensured of a large demand. Raleigh's model range and prices for the 1901 season is shown in Table B.5 in the Appendix. This illustrates the management's commitment to the higher price range, but a comparison of prices with those in 1898 also shows that prices had been substantially lowered and, with discounts to the trade, the net selling price of machines was reduced further. Bowden's recipe for market success was premised upon selling the high-grade image of the company, and this can be seen in his condemnation of small manufacturers who were buying in cheap materials and components from large firms such as BSA, and assembling low-priced machines selling at £6 to £7. The issue here was relative 'safety', and he ridiculed the 'well-to-do people who were satisfied to ride the very cheapest contraptions they can purchase'. The customer, claimed Bowden, was at fault for purchasing down-market, and it was only larger concerns such as Raleigh, using the best material and most modern equipment, who could guarantee machines finished to the highest standard. His scorn, however, was not reserved to the smaller maker, and he quoted an article in the *Bicycling News* of 1901 from a cyclist: 'I have been ridiculed for the tale of the scavenger who saved up for a Beeston Humber, but ... the practice of moneyed men seeking the cheapest brands of low grade cycles seems to me to be as suicidal as it is contemptible.' As Bowden emphasised, to the 'numerous grateful Raleighites', the Raleigh was the 'acme of excellence', and this was reinforced by a 'GUARANTEED FOR EVER' certificate with each cycle purchased.[95] This emphasis on customer satisfaction was reinforced by a greater focus on co-ordinated planning to ensure the company had sufficient components and finished cycle stocks to meet customer needs. Thus, the supervision of the business was tightened, and there was a rigorous scrutiny on a fortnightly basis of production targets which were set in advance.[96]

The attractiveness of the Raleigh was clearly enhanced by the introduction of three-speed gears as attachments to the cycle. The origins of this invention can be traced to Henry Sturmey, a former schoolteacher and editor of the *Cyclist* and the *Autocar*, and William Reilley, a talented engineer. Working separately, they patented their gears and sold them to A. S. Pellant, a London-based cycle and motor dealer, and a renowned trick cyclist. In 1902, Pellant approached Bowden and proposed the formation of a syndicate to purchase the patents and perfect the production of the gears. Fearing that Humber might secure the patents ahead of them, Bowden agreed and experimental work was undertaken by Raleigh to perfect the gear under the direction of James Archer, a foreman engineer. March 1903 saw the formation of the Three-Speed-Gear Syndicate, launched with a capital of £15 000. Bowden acquired the largest share subscription of £2 250, and purchased the patents for a cash payment of £2 000. Bowden became managing director of the Syndicate, and William Reilley was employed to supervise production. The Sturmey-Archer gear allowed the rider to select gears for different gradients, and it was enclosed in a hub shell which made it operational in wet weather conditions. Bowden recognised its potential as a gadget to increase the sales of Raleighs, but it could also bring in new revenue by being sold to other cycle-makers. A special department was created in the factory to produce gears and hubs, £5 312 being spent on plant and machinery by June 1904. The Syndicate was originally operated as a distinct business from Raleigh, the latter manufacturing the gears at a royalty of 2s. 6d. each and taking 25 per cent of output, the remainder being distributed to the trade at a 20 per cent profit upon the cost of production. Raleigh also co-ordinated the marketing end of the business, using its cycle agents to distribute and promote the product, and receiving a 5 per cent commission on sales.[97]

Gears became a profitable part of the Raleigh business, and in May 1905 Bowden sanctioned an additional expenditure of £650 to increase output to 20 000 gears per annum, the existing plant being insufficient to supply the Syndicate to meet the demand in the trade, despite operating on double shifts. With increasing demand Bowden sanctioned an extra £3 000 investment in new plant in August 1905 to produce 30 000 per annum, the whole of which was to be taken up by the Syndicate. Raleigh's share of profits from the Syndicate was also increased from 20 per cent to 40 per cent, reflecting the fact that the Raleigh business was the source of investment capital. Sales of gears rose from 8 200 in 1905 to 19 959 by 1906, Raleigh taking its quota of 25 per cent and the rest being distributed to the trade or held as stock in anticipation of rising demand. In late 1907 the Syndicate called in its unissued share capital of £4 425, and Bowden lent an additional £3 000 at 6 per cent interest to ensure that there was sufficient working capital to continue operations. Sturmey-Archer Gears were now 'world renowned', and an essential attachment to high-grade cycles which allowed the rider to cover 15 to 30 miles per day more than formerly with greater ease. In 1908, the company was re-formed as Sturmey-Archer Gears Ltd, and W. H. Raven who had been appointed as Raleigh's works manager in place of Mills, succeeded Reilley as head of production. The business was finally purchased outright by Bowden in July 1910, and in 1914 sales of cycle gears were valued at £64 291. In 1910 Sturmey-Archer also began to produce hubs for motor cycles, sales of which were valued at £68 442 in 1914 (see Table B.2 in the Appendix).[98]

The production of gear hubs for motor cycles by Sturmey-Archer reflects the growing diversification of British cycle firms into motorised transport following the collapse of the cycle boom, a trend examined in Chapter 2. The opportunities of motorised transport were not lost on Bowden, and as early as 1898 Bassett had urged the directors to act 'quickly' in following the lead of other manufacturers who were taking up the motor cycle business. Experimental work was instigated and the management considered fixing French motors, manufactured by Renaux, Crouau, Dummond, Carno and De Caurville, to their cycles. Raleigh's financial collapse at the end of 1898, and managerial disharmony, delayed any further action, and the matter did not arise again until July 1899 when Bowden proposed that the company should begin experiments with motor cycles and three-wheel cars. This proposal was rejected by Turney and Harlow who felt that before embarking upon a costly strategy of diversification, involving a depletion of working capital, they should first ensure that the factory could turn out cycles in large quantities. Given the earlier problems of the company this caution was sound advice, but there was another element to their objections, and they argued that their priority should be to pay satisfactory dividends to shareholders rather than investing profits in a business which was still in its infancy. Bowden, however, was not to be deterred and although he had no intention to abandon bicycles, his entrepreneurial instincts could not ignore the fact that 'Everyone in the trade ... was taking up the motor industry and it would not do for the Raleigh to fall behind'. He argued that the company should keep up with the general trend towards motorisation and seek new avenues of profit, and if necessary he would finance the venture himself by acquiring personal bank loans. The compromise reached was that Harlow should approach Lloyds with a request for a loan to finance developmental work on motor cycles at Raleigh.[99]

As Thoms and Donnelly argue, 'by the late 1890s the banks were becoming less willing to support cycle firms of almost any description',[100] and Raleigh's overtures to Lloyds met with a negative response. Dixon Taylor informed the board that 'strong application had been made by several cycle firms to the bank to advance money for motor making but the Bank having no faith in the business at present would not make advances'. The continued reliance of Raleigh on the bank overdraft placed Bowden in a non-negotiable position, and the bank rammed home a clear warning: 'In the event of ... Raleigh ... commencing the manufacture of motors [they] would immediately call for the repayment of the first mortgage debenture.' With Raleigh's financial position and expenses being scrutinised by the bank, the management deferred a decision to move into motor car production in 1900, even though they had received a offer from the Caledonian Motor Car Co. Ltd of Aberdeen to produce 100 under licence from them. The bank's caution is understandable given Raleigh's past financial record, and the fact that the cycle trade was slow to recover in the early years of the twentieth century, leaving profit margins low.[101] As Table B.1 in the Appendix shows, net profits were stagnant in 1900, fell in 1901 and, although rising during the next two years, collapsed in 1904. Shareholders clearly lost out, no dividend being paid on ordinary deferred shares, and in 1904 no dividend was paid on ordinary shares.

Summing up the financial position of the company in 1901, Bowden announced that although turnover had increased considerably over 1900, a 'large expenditure' on the factory of £4 226, had been 'charged against profits', and additional share capital had not been issued. He therefore considered it prudent to limit the dividend on ordinary shares to 10 per cent, pay none on deferred shares, and transfer £12 000 of disposable profits to reserve as a sign of the need for additional capital for modernisation and 'bearing in mind the company's indebtedness to the Bankers'. Financial pressures accumulated in 1902 as the company invested £5 000 in the Sturmey-Archer business, and this necessary expenditure, 'To meet the competition', had been provided for out of revenue. Funds at Raleigh were again low, and the competitive environment in the industry, characterised by falling prices, worsened the situation. For example, in December 1901 Bowden noted that Raleigh still had much to do to compete at the cheaper end of the market, the Rover Co. having brought out a machine with rim brakes and free wheel at £10 10s., the Raleigh Co. supplying a 'no name machine at the same price ... to agents, but not fixing a retail price'. Urging the need to reduce prices in 1902 Bowden called for the increased production of cheaper cycles to 5 000 machines for the 1903 season, profits now depending on quantity sales at lower mark-ups. By 1904 price competition had intensified, the management discussing selling cycles at £6 19s. 6d., and Bowden predicting a sharp fall in retail prices for 1905.[102]

With the cycle market continuing to remain flat, Bowden continued to press for diversification into motorised transport. In 1901 experiments were resumed on motor cycles, using motors of the Minerva or Weaver type, and this work continued into 1903, the expenses being paid out of revenue. The company also started producing a small number of 'Raleighettes', three-wheeled motorised cycles. Bowden's persistence in following this route was to attain new sources of profits, but the result was to reduce dividends to shareholders. In 1901 Turney cautioned against unbridled expansion in the face of deteriorating trade conditions, despite Bowden's insistence that they must expand and diversify to survive. A split now opened in the board over the question of using the unissued share capital of the concern to finance expansion, a procedure advocated by Bowden, or the Turney and Harlow alternative which was to continue to rely on bank finance. This rift was temporarily closed by the bank's intervention and a guarantee of the continuation of the overdraft limit of £35 000,[103] but it was the precursor of a much more serious managerial split which occurred in 1903.

At Raleigh's AGM of November 1903 Bowden objected to the re-election of Harlow as a director of the company, and in his place proposed his son, Harold Houston Bowden. Harold left Clare College, Cambridge, in 1899 before graduating, to join Raleigh, and he was apprenticed in the workshops before becoming Raleigh's traveller for Eastern England. Frank's motion to appoint his son was lost, and he later claimed he was 'gagged' at the meeting. Supported by four shareholders Frank now demanded a full poll of all the company's members, the result of which revealed a considerable vote for Harlow. Of the 597 who voted, 185 cast their votes for Harold, and 412 for Harlow.

Frank's one-third share of the voting capital swung the vote, and Harold poled 156 224 votes compared to 125 405 for Harlow. This victory, however, did not ensure an easy transition of boardroom control to Bowden. At a meeting in December, Harold Bowden proposed the appointment of his father as chairman, and the resolution was carried although Turney objected that Harold had not been issued the necessary qualification shares for directorship. Personal antagonisms were rife, and the Bowdens were accused of underhanded behaviour, and Turney concluded with the threat of legal action. Frank's reply was short: 'at your own expense'. A war of words, conducted by circulars to shareholders then ensued. For example, shareholders were informed by Turney that Bowden was using the contest in the board for his own personal ends, and was earning excess rewards through his salary as managing director, and the interest paid by the company on his loans. The conflict rumbled over into February 1904 when, at an Extraordinary General Meeting of the company, Harold was confirmed as a director, following another poll of shareholders, and Frank was officially appointed chairman on the resignation of Turney. The new board consisted of Lazonby, E. C. Farrow, the long-serving company secretary, and Ernest Jardine, a Nottingham machine-maker who was brought in as factory consultant.[104]

Underlying the obvious personal antagonisms in this conflict was the future direction of the company, and Bowden's control over policy-making. The conflicting views of the board were presented to shareholders by Bowden in December 1903:

> In the annual report of 1900 the directors had agreed to raise new capital by issuing the remaining 176 267 ordinary shares of 2s. 6d., for the development of the company's business, however the directors found it possible because of a temporary loan from himself, and in other ways, to finance the company without making the issue. But the continual growth of the business – the purchase during the past year of over £8 000 of new machinery and tools, and the investment of more than £3 000 in retail depots ... have now rendered the provision of more capital necessary especially as the manufacture of gears, motor cycles and Raleighettes has become such an important part of the business, that an outlay of over £10 000 will be required for this new branch alone during the coming season.[105]

Turney and Harlow had certainly not rejected the move to motorised transport, and they had agreed to sanction the purchase of 300 motors to begin production. Nevertheless, they felt that the industry was still 'in its infancy', and that shareholders should not be expected to bear the risk of the venture. From Bowden's viewpoint, however, the alternative to the issue of new share capital was to fall behind their competitors in a new market, and to be increasingly shackled by reliance on bank financing, which was always a precarious policy. For example, John Budd, the manager of Lloyds at Nottingham, had communicated that the bank limit of £35 000 had been exceeded by a small amount during February, March and April, a fact well known to Turney and Harlow through regular reports to the board. According to Bowden this had been misrepresented, and shareholders informed that: 'WE ARE PLEASED TO SAY THAT THE OVERDRAFT HAS NEVER REACHED THE LIMIT.' As Bowden argued, without a personal loan from him of £3 000 the overdraft would have reached £38 905, and Bowden was unwilling to personally guarantee an overdraft of such a magnitude. Indeed, as Farrow pointed out, the bank was insisting that the overdraft should be reduced to £32 500, and with continued expenditure forecast for 1904 they could not rely on the bank.[106]

At stake here were the interests of shareholders on the one hand, supported by Turney and Harlow, and the interests of Bowden's unquestioned financial support of the company. Whatever the merits of the two sides, the managerial conflict certainly presented an unfavourable impression, both to its clientele and to the investing public. For example, Bowden claimed that the company's dismal profit showing was due to the disruption caused by the managerial contest, preventing the managing director and the secretary attending the National Cycle Show, until it was more than half over. Thus, information relating to cuts in prices by competitors had not been picked up, and travellers and agents were consequently confused over Raleigh's future pricing policy. Further, in January 1904 the new directors issued 120 000 ordinary shares to existing holders at 2s. 6d. each, but Turney and Harlow, representing an unelected shareholders' committee, had publicised their intention not to subscribe. This was another example of the policy, claimed Bowden, that 'this Turney-Harlow clique has from first to last pursued to the great injury of the business of the company'. By the end of January only £2 047 of the new shares were subscribed to, 'and of this sum [all] but £274 by Nottingham shareholders'. The 'clique' had clearly been effective in persuading shareholders that Bowden was engaged in pursuing a 'dangerous strategy of expansion' which was not in their best interests. In refuting this allegation Bowden pointed out that they were falsely claiming to be a committee of 'large shareholders' in the business, when in fact the total shareholding of the committee, consisting of 'that notable number 13', was only £1 300, and they had subscribed to the new share issue the measly sum of £8 2s. 6d.[107]

The key to Bowden turning the tide of the contest in his favour was to gain the support of Nottingham-based shareholders. In February 1904 a minority of London shareholders in Raleigh had supported

Turney by signing a requisition, requiring one-tenth of the shareholders in the company, for a second ballot to re-elect Harlow in February 1904. With scant regard for the London interests, Bowden informed shareholders that 'The principal aim of the Turney-Harlow clique of my enemies, who have so little interest in the company, is to make fees for their nominees, and at the same time harass and annoy me'. They were 'useless to this company', and, referring to Harlow, he claimed that he would be better advised to 'utilise his abilities in his special business, that of stockbroker'. Recommending the new management to the shareholders he guaranteed that he, and his 'friends in Nottingham', will provide the additional £15 000 of capital within two weeks. To reinforce this point he launched a bitter counter-attack on Turney's business ethics, and his long-term commitment to Raleigh:

> Turney wants to rule at the expense of the shareholders ... If you want management by Directors, who have as much knowledge of the Cycle Trade as Messrs Turney and Harlow, look at Humber Ltd., where the Directors apparently think a practical Managing Director or General Manager unnecessary, and note the result. That firm has twice our turnover, and yet made only half our profit during 1903. One Humber Director, and I have reason to believe two, are actively engaged supporting Messrs Turney and Harlow.

The choice was thus presented between a Bowden-led strategy of long-term expansion, or to let profits 'slip away' by Turney's 'standstill policy'. As Bowden argued, 'There is no standing still in the cycle trade; we must go forward or go backward, as Sir John Turney is doing with his own company'.[108]

The 'standstill policy' was obviously a reference to the delay in entering the motor market, and by 'veto and delay' Turney and 'his henchman Harlow' were responsible for the low profitability of the company which was exacerbated by entering the motor trade 'two or three years too late'. By the end of 1904, Bowden was firmly in command of the board, and through his own personal investment, and his endeavours to attract subscriptions from his own local contacts, additional shares in Raleigh were eventually fully subscribed to.[109] Yet at the very time that victory was ensured, Bowden turned track, and abandoned the commitment to developing the market for motorised transport, the very issue which had been at the centre of the managerial conflict. At the end of 1904 the company abandoned production of the Raleighette, and ended development work on motor cycles until the First World War.[110] In rejecting diversification, a general trend amongst bicycle firms at this time, Bowden committed the company to the bicycle, and this juggling act is difficult to account for given the complete absence of any discussion in the board minutes. We can suggest, however, that Bowden was becoming increasingly concerned again with the financial security of the concern and his immediate priority became survival in a highly competitive market. The failure of the Raleighette had also demonstrated the risks of entering a new market, a point that Turney and Harlow had cautioned against, and with the bicycle industry in 1904 facing a severe downturn Bowden focused the company's limited financial resources on this side of the business. This can be seen in the drive from 1904 to expand capacity, and to generate a larger share of the market for Raleigh machines.

In April 1904 Bowden reported that the company was directing all its energies to increase sales, focusing particularly on increased expenditure on advertising. This brought immediate rewards in increased sales, but their prospects were threatened by the actions of companies such as Humber and BSA to reduce substantially the prices of cheaper grade machines for 1905. The choice, therefore, was whether Raleigh maintained prices, keeping faith with agents and dealers who held large stocks at existing prices, or followed the lead by competitors and cut prices. Bowden decided to weather the storm, and reasserted his values in maintaining the confidence of dealers. The result, however, was that sales and output fell, and the problems were compounded by a general depression which particularly affected domestic sales for high-grade Raleighs, but was also felt in colonial markets. The resolution to this dilemma rested on the potential of the factory to turn out higher volume, and as Bowden claimed 'The company has never been so well prepared to meet keen competition'. Indeed, by 1905 output had been nearly doubled , and net profits had risen to £6 988 (see Tables B.1 and B.6 in the Appendix). Although profits had nearly doubled over 1904, they remained stubbornly low because the company had finally been forced to reduce prices during 1905 and, despite lower material prices, had failed to reduce costs by corresponding margins. Thus, Bowden decided that to make the business pay in the future the company must aim 'at a much larger output to cover our fixed expenses', provide value for money by constantly increasing quality and introducing improvements, and thus through its reputation gain a greater market share. In this respect Bowden made a firm commitment to the cycle market, and in this decision the full capacity of the factory was directed to this core activity.[111]

Maintaining the full commitment to the quality cycle,[112] output was pushed upwards from 16 555 machines in 1905 to 25 689 in 1906 and, as can be seen in Table 3.5, output had reached 59 219 by 1914. With profits rising significantly in 1906, Bowden celebrated the fact that this had been achieved without any great additional expenditure to plant, tools, power and labour, which diversification into the motor trade

Table 3.5   Output of cycles at Raleigh, 1904–14

Year	Output
1904	9 865
1905	16 555
1906	25 689
1907	28 156
1908	32 577
1909	33 434
1910	38 890
1911	46 075
1912	51 805
1913	57 675
1914	59 219

Source: Book of the Raleigh 1915.

would surely have entailed. With the full capacity geared to cycle output, and the expanding Sturmey-Archer business, Bowden looked optimistically to the future of the company, building up stocks in anticipation of a revival of trading fortunes. Sales were also advanced by the introduction of a gradual payment system, administered via the company's sales depots. Despite the fact that the company was still not paying dividends on deferred shares, and the dividend on ordinary shares had been reduced to 5 per cent, allowing reserves to be increased to £20 000, the increased output still had to be realised through increased sales. At the end of 1906, there was every promise that this could be achieved, cycle sales having shown an increase of 50 per cent between August and December, compared to a similar period in 1905.[113]

Despite a temporary setback to profits in 1907 and 1908, due to severe weather which disrupted sales, profits continued to rise thereafter to 1914 (see Table B.1 in the Appendix). The company's success after 1905 was directly linked to boosting the output of cycles and gears, and at this point Bowden was determined to settle the problems of working capital which had continued to haunt the company since its foundation, and now again threatened his strategy of output expansion. In January 1906 Bowden had proposed that deferred shareholders exchange their shares for ordinary shares, at the rate of one and a half of the latter for one of the former. Shareholders, not surprisingly, were reluctant to comply because share values had risen in just one week from 3s. to 5s. 1d. 'in consequence of speculation in Birmingham'. Bowden, conceding the inevitable, argued that 'it was now useless to approach the Deferred Shareholders on the matter', but reiterated the point that if the company was to expand it was 'absolutely necessary to purchase more machinery, tools and plant for trebling or quadrupling output ... and that for safety more working capital must be provided to avoid dependence on a Bank overdraft, before any dividend could be paid on Deferred Shares'. By November 1907 he was reporting that the company could barely afford a 5 per cent dividend on ordinary shares, and referred to the large sums locked up in the gradual payment system and in stocks of unsold bicycles. Putting it straight to the shareholders, he predicted that without an increase in capital there was little prospect of dividends on deferred shares 'for many years, or until the company could dispose with the heavy bank overdraft which was necessary to carry on the enlarged business'. With falling profits Bowden now realised that he would have to force the issue with the shareholders.[114]

In July 1908 Bowden informed the directors that he had seen the company's bankers on several occasions during the last two years, and they continued to urge a permanent decrease in the company's overdraft. To stave off the bank, Bowden had provided his own personal guarantee for an overdraft of £40 000 in March 1908, but this was to be the limit of his commitment, and 'he should give notice to the bank withdrawing [his guarantee] unless some arrangement was come to whereby he became the purchaser of the company's business, or could be in some other form fully compensated for the risk he was taking'. Laying down his vision of the future, he informed shareholders: 'if the company became a family affair, I could provide a large amount of new capital, and by foregoing dividends for two or three years ... put the business on a sound financial basis'. Using considerable guile he worked his message into a *fait accompli*. All shareholders had received in the past three years was a dividend of 5 per cent, compared to 10 to 20 per cent in other comparable companies, 'principally because we have been working on borrowed capital'. Referring to the precarious environment in which cycle companies operated, he reminded shareholders that many had started with large working capitals in cash, but nearly all had been forced to call up more during the last three years, as prices had fallen sharply. The future of Raleigh was in jeopardy, as expansion had to be maintained, and this could not be achieved by a take-over as locked up capital and heavy debts together with small dividend payments deterred prospective buyers. Bowden offered the way out by proposing a 10 per cent premium on Raleigh ordinary shares, considerably higher than the market price they could realise on the stock exchange, and higher than prices quoted for other cycle companies.[115]

The shareholders were faced with an ultimatum: sell to Bowden at a premium or he would purchase their shares at the existing price. With the almost unanimous agreement of the shareholders in July 1908, the company was wound up voluntarily and sold to Bowden for a sum of £69 733, a 3d. dividend also being paid on ordinary shares. The company was officially placed in Bowden's hands by a deed of transfer in February 1909, and in 1913 a formal partnership agreement was instigated with his son Harold, an event which was to set the agenda for managerial control until the 1930s. Summing up this event, the company's historian, G. H. Bowden, argues that the key motivation was the fact that Bowden was willing to risk more capital in the business, but the shareholders were reluctant, 'and always favoured borrowing it'. As the trade press commented: 'The shareholders have cheerfully allowed him [Bowden] to go on running their property with his own credit and money but now he says, "Hold, Enough!"'[116]

Under Frank Bowden's personal control, with his son in close attendance, Raleigh embarked upon a period of expansion, and with the upturn in trade from 1909 enjoyed considerable business success. Indeed, in that year the company reported that there had been a significant increase in demand for the more expensive cycles, such as the X-Frame Modele Superbe. By 1910 Bowden was celebrating further rises in sales, a fact that he associated with superior quality, and an increased demand for higher priced models. By 1911 he could point to the fact that the company, unlike most large firms in the industry, concentrated solely on cycles, and cyclists could 'rely upon our individual attention to all their needs'. By this date the company was having considerable success with their new all-weather cycles, and had also recaptured the women's market by producing a drop-frame cycle with a light gear case which significantly reduced the weight of the machine, as well as developing special featherweight models for racing. Bowden's commitment to the quality cycle was thus to prove justified, and the company participated fully in the upturn of economic activity in Britain during the late Edwardian period. The company finally utilised its capacity to its full potential and costs fell. By 1908 Raleigh was already selling their cheaper 'standard' model at £8 19s. 6d., and with the upturn in the market thereafter they were fortuitous in being able to maintain prices, and increase sales. As Table B.2 in the Appendix shows, Raleigh cycle sales rose steadily from 1910 to 1913, as did sales of its cheaper Robin Hood cycles, a brand which had replaced Gazelle in 1909. On the eve of Britain's entry to the First World War, Raleigh had become the largest producer of quality cycles in the world, and also a major producer of three-speed gears through its association with Sturmey-Archer.[117] Raleigh, as we shall see in Chapter 5, was to retain and enhance this position during the turbulent decades of the inter-war years.

Notes

1. NRO, Raleigh Records, DDRN 7/2/12, Sir Harold H. Bowden, Manuscript of the History of the Raleigh Company, n.d, Unpublished, pp 1–3; DDRN 7/2/5, Souvenir of The New Raleigh Offices Opened January 1931; Bowden, 1975, p. 13; Harrison, 1984, p. 406.

2. Bowden was to remain an active speculator in foreign securities throughout his life. An examination of his private entries in the Raleigh company ledgers shows that Bowden continued to build upon his substantial investment portfolio, speculating in foreign government bonds, especially in South Asia, and in railway shares. He also invested in British manufacturing companies, for example, purchasing £5 901 of shares in the Dunlop Rubber Co. in 1893 and £7 000 of shares in the saddle company, J. B. Brooks, between 1897 and 1904. DDRN 3/1/1, Ledger of the Raleigh Cycle Co. Ltd.

3. Bowden, 1975, p. 13; Bowden, Manuscript, p. 6; DDRN 10/3/9/3, Prospectus of the Raleigh Cycle Co. Ltd, 1891.

4. Bowden, Manuscript, pp. 6, 10; Harrison, 1969, p. 287; DDRN 4/10/1/1, Advertisement for the Raleigh Safety Cycle produced by Woodhead, Angois & Ellis, 1889.

5. DDRN 2/7/1, Forms of Notices and Cuttings, *Nottingham Daily Express*, 4 February 1896; Bowden, Manuscript, p. 7; DDRN 3/1/1, Company Ledger; DDRN 4/10/1/8, Frank Bowden, in The Book of the Raleigh for the 1904 Season, p. 4; DDRN 7/2/3 Souvenir of the New Raleigh Works, 5 May 1922, p. 3; DDRN 7/2/7, History of the Raleigh Cycle Co. Ltd, n.d; Prospectus of the Raleigh, 1891.

6. Bowden, Manuscript, p. 7; *Nottingham Daily Express*, 4 February 1896. The company's plant was valued at £700, plus £100 for tools, £100 for fixtures and £800 for stock in trade and work in progress. The largest valuation was placed on goodwill, patents and patent rights, totalling £6 217. DDRN 3/1/2, Company Ledger.

7. Frank Bowden in Book of the Raleigh, 1904, p. 4; *Nottingham Daily Express*, 4 February 1896; Bowden, Manuscript, pp. 7–8; Bowden, 1975, pp. 16–17, 25; DDRN 3/1/1, Company Ledger; DDRN 1/1/1–6, Raleigh Cycle Co. Ltd, Directors and General Meetings Minutes 1891–1908, 4 April 1892.

8. Prospectus of the Raleigh, 1891; Directors and General Meetings, 12, 28 December 1891, 4 April 1892; History of the Raleigh Cycle Co. Ltd, n.d.; Bowden, 1975, pp. 16–17, 25. As we saw in Chapter 2, the development of the industry at the regional level was premised upon the retention of personal control.

9. Prospectus of the Raleigh, 1891; Directors and General Meetings, 28 December 1891, 4 April 1892; DDRN 10/3/8 Allotment Book – Register of Members and Annual Share Ledger of the Raleigh Cycle Company Ltd. The use of local business networks for finance was common in the cycle industry, and we would argue was widespread in British business before 1914. See Wilson, 1995, pp. 74–5; Cottrell, 1980, p. 174; Lloyd-Jones and Lewis, 1998b, pp. 56–87.

10. Prospectus of the Raleigh, 1891; DDRN 4/10/1/4/2 The Raleigh Cycle Co. Ltd, Prospectus in French, 1891; Directors and General Meetings, 12, 28 December 1891; DDRN 2/7/1, Forms of Notices and Cuttings, Frank

Bowden, Circular to Shareholders, 27 January 1904; *Nottingham Directory* (1900); Souvenir of the New Raleigh Works, 5 May 1922, p. 3.

11.   The discussion of Kay's ideas is taken from Jeremy, 1998, pp. 166–7. See Kay, 1993, pp. 34–49.

12.   The company also exhibited three different patterns of tricycles, and there was a particular emphasis on the growing market for women's bicycles. Bowden, 1975, p. 16; Bowden, Manuscript, p. 10.

13.   DDRN 4/10/1/2, Advertisement for the Raleigh Rational Light Roadster, 1890; DDRN 7/2/6, Raleigh, Pioneers of Cycle manufacture for 50 Years, Jubilee Souvenir.

14.   DDRN 4/63/1–2, 'What the press say about the Raleigh cycles', *Hull Daily Mail*, June 1907.

15.   Bowden, 1975, pp. 19–20; Bowden, Manuscript, pp. 8–11; DDRN 7/1/23, A Miniature History of the Bicycle.

16.   Bowden, 1975, pp. 18–19; DDRN 4/10/1/3/1, Circular to Dealers, 1892; DDRN 4/10/1/4/3, Advertisement to Dealers 1891.

17.   Directors and General Meetings, 14 November 1892, 2 October 1893, 12 November 1894; Bowden, 1975 pp. 129–30, 133. As Sako, 1992, pp. 40–42 argues, the building up of customer 'trust' may be seen as a 'cultural disposition', and is premised upon 'moralised trading relationships of mutual goodwill'.

18.   Directors and General Meetings, 28 December 1891, 30 September 1892, 26 September 1894.

19.   DDRN 10/3/9/4/1, Prospectus of the Raleigh Cycle Co. Ltd, 1896.

20.   The value of stocks and work in progress in August 1892 was £19 105, compared with £ 8 862 for the corresponding period in 1891. DDRN 3/1/2, Company Ledger.

21.   Directors and General Meetings, 30 September 1892.

22.   Ibid., 30 September, 5 December 1892.

23.   The first call on this capital, a partial payment of 2s. 6d. per share, was called in January 1892, and raised £3 200. This was then followed by a second call to payment in November of that year, and two final payments in both 1893 and 1895. DDRN 3/1/2, Company Ledger.

24.   Directors and General Meetings, 30 September, 5 December 1892, 10 January 1893.

25.   See Bowden, 1975, p. 17.

26.   Directors and General Meetings, 7 March, 20 July 1892.

27.   For a similar example of the problems of new firms in the industry see Harrison, 1982.

28.   Directors and General Meetings, 9 January 1894; Prospectus of the Raleigh, 1896.

29.   Directors and General Meetings, 26 September, 2 October 1894, Bowden, Manuscript, pp. 12–13.

30.   Directors and General Meetings, 9 January 1894.

31.   For example, the largest firm in the USA, the Pope Cycle Co., developed integrated plant for the production of cycle tubes, cycle tyres and the complete manufacture of the cycle. Harrison, 1969, p. 290.

32.   Directors and General Meetings, 7 March 1892, 9 January 1894.

33.   In the American market Raleigh faced similar problems to other British cycle manufacturers. For example, in March 1895 the Griffiths Corporation, which had also purchased the New York selling agency for

Premier, were reporting losses of £53 926 on trading and stock depreciation over the previous 18 months, and their agreement with Raleigh was
brought to an end. The Coventry Machinists Co. also lost £20 000 in
1893/94 and £27 000 in 1894/95, and it created acute financial embarrassment. Harrison, 1969, pp. 290–91, 295–6; Bowden, Manuscript, p. 11.

34. Bowden, 1975, pp. 130–31.
35. Directors and General Meetings, 26 September 1894; Harrison, 1969,
     p. 294. A further advantage of the American producers was their capa-
     bility to supply in volume parts for replacement and repairs.
36. *Nottingham Daily Express*, 4 February 1896; DDRN 2/7/1, Wells and
     Hind (Solicitors), Circular to Shareholders, 30 October 1896.
37. *Nottingham Daily Express*, 4 February 1896; Prospectus of the Raleigh,
     1896.
38. Bowden, Manuscript, pp. 12–13.
39. Mills had originally joined Humber in 1890 as salesman to their London
     depot. His rise in the company was thereafter rapid. In 1891 he was
     promoted to assistant works manager, and in 1892 designed the highly
     successful Beeston-Humber cycle, and was accredited with numerous
     improvements in cycle design. Ibid., pp. 10, 12–13; Bowden, 1975, p. 17;
     Nottingham Daily Express, 4 February 1896; Directors and General
     Meetings, 12 November 1894.
40. Bowden, Manuscript, pp. 12–13. The sales side of the business was also
     revamped by the appointment of Frank Shortland to head the London
     sales depot. Shortland was an experienced sales manager and famous
     cyclist.
41. Ibid., p. 14; Bowden, 1975, pp. 17–18, 19–21; DDRN 2/7/1, Frank
     Bowden, Circular to Shareholders, 27 January 1904.
42. Directors and General Meetings, 3 February 1896; Prospectus of the
     Raleigh, 1896; *Nottingham Daily Express*, 4 February 1896; DDRN
     2/7/1 Frank Bowden, Circular to Shareholders, 4 February 1896.
43. DDRN 2/7/1, Frank Bowden, Circular to Shareholders, 30 January 1896;
     Nottingham Daily Express, 4 February 1896; Prospectus of the Raleigh,
     1896. Bowden confidently announced that shareholders could expect
     dividends in the next year of 6 per cent on preference, and 8 or 10 per
     cent on ordinary shares, after paying a large amount to the reserve fund.
44. *Nottingham Daily Express*, 4 February 1896.
45. Ibid.; Prospectus of the Raleigh, 1896; DDRN 3/1/2/2 Raleigh Cycle
     Co., Agreement for Sale and Purchase of Business Upon Reconstruction,
     4 March 1896.
46. The majority of shareholders came from Nottingham and Birmingham,
     and were drawn from manufacturing, banking and, in the case of inves-
     tors with less than 25 shares, from the professional classes.
47. DDRN 2/7/1, Wells and Hind (Solicitors), Circular to Shareholders,
     30 October 1896; DDRN 10/3/1/3/1 Agreement Between the Old Raleigh
     Cycle Co., Incorporated 1891, and the New Company Incorporated 1896,
     for the Reconstruction of the Company, Supplement, 29 April 1896.
48. Directors and General Meetings, 15, 29 April 1896; Bowden, 1975,
     p. 21. For example, the company placed orders with the Manufacturing
     Tube Co. for 400 000 feet of tube steel for frames, and a further order
     for 300 000 feet with the Weldless Steel Tube Co. A further order for
     500 sets of stampings was also contracted for.

49. Bowden, 1975, p. 21. For an examination of the trend towards intro-
    ducing semi-automatic machine tools in the Birmingham cycle industry
    see Millward, 1989, p. 171.
50. Bowden, 1975, pp. 17–18, 19–21; Bowden, Manuscript, p. 14. This was
    a revolutionary process because other manufacturers used cast lugs which
    produced a less durable product and were prone to frequent break-
    downs.
51. See DDRN 4/10/1/5, The Raleigh Cycle Co., Price List, 1898.
52. DDRN 2/7/1, AGM of the Raleigh Cycle Co., 26 October 1896; DDRN
    2/7/1, Frank Bowden, Circular to Shareholders, 22 October 1896.
53. Directors and General Meetings, 28 October, 22 December 1896; DDRN
    2/7/1 Frank Bowden, Circular to Shareholders, 27 January 1904.
54. Frank Bowden, Circular to Shareholders, 27 January 1904.
55. Directors and General Meetings, 30 March, 13, 27 April, 13 July 1897;
    DDRN 2/7/1, AGM, 30 November 1897.
56. Directors and General Meetings, 30 March, 13, 27 April 1897. As
    Millward, 1989, p. 170, argues, there was evidence of firms such as BSA
    internalising the production of component parts to increase output and
    ensure quality in 1896, but vertical integration in the industry came
    piecemeal.
57. Directors and General Meetings, 25 May, 13, 20 July 1897.
58. The 'cycle craze' also affected Australia, but Bowden reported intense
    competition from US manufacturers, and despite securing an order for
    1 600 cycles he noted that this would have been much larger if not for
    the depression in the Australian market, and the fact that the Griffiths
    Corporation were holding a stock of 700 cycles in their depot 'which
    make the agents hesitant to take up many bicycles for fear of being
    undersold'. Ibid., 13 July 1897.
59. Ibid., 29 June 1897.
60. Ibid., 12 January 1897. The proposed nominal capital of Kestrel was
    £10 000, shares to be subscribed for by Raleigh management and 'staff'.
    It was to be an assembly plant only, selling machines under the Kestrel
    mark, but using components purchased from BSA, and fitting 'second
    grade tyres'. Raleigh would obtain the rights to purchase finished Kes-
    trels at a special 10 per cent discount off 'recognised trade prices', and
    would market the machines for Kestrel on a 5 per cent commission.
61. Ibid., 15 January, 16 February 1897.
62. Ibid., 25 May, 20 July, 12 October 1897.
63. Ibid., 13 July, 14 September 1897. The stance taken by Lloyds was
    hardly surprising, as Raleigh's overdraft in October 1897 was £52 000,
    £12 000 above their agreed limit. An additional overdraft of £3 800 was
    owing by Gazelle, and the company owed creditors £23 000 for materi-
    als and components, making an accumulated debt of £79 000. Ibid.,
    7 October 1897. This state of affairs was conveniently not presented at
    the company's AGM two months later, and it is reasonable to suggest
    that the company's financial affairs were misrepresented.
64. Ibid., 13, 20 July, 28 September 1897.
65. Millward, 1989, p. 171.
66. Directors and General Meetings, 20 July 1897.
67. Ibid., 20, 29 July, 17 August, 14 September 1897. For a discussion of

the labour problems of British industry at this time see Burgess, 1975, p. 58; Garside and Gospel, 1982, p. 104.

68. Directors and General Meetings, 7, 14 September, 7 October 1897.

69. Ibid., 14 September, 7, 15, 26 October 1897. Dunlop's rejection may well have been based on growing conflict between the companies relating to supplies of tyres. For example, Bowden complained of monopoly trading by Dunlop, and under agreements with Raleigh only 3 per cent of cycles were fitted with non-Dunlop tyres. To the annoyance of Du Cros, Bowden and Bassett were influential in persuading the North British Rubber Co. to push their 'Clincher' tyres more strongly to directly compete with Dunlop. Ibid., 8, 14 September 1897.

70. Ibid., 5 November 1897.

71. Ibid., 18 January, 29 March, 26 April, 10, 24 May, 18 July 1898.

72. Ibid., 18 July 1898. French producers were also suffering in their own market, and there were reports of manufacturers dumping cycles into the German market, and Peugeot Freres had 80 per cent of their 1898 production still unsold.

73. Ibid., 25 October 1898.

74. Ibid., 29 March, 26 April, 10, 24 May, 21 June 1898.

75. Ibid., 29 March, 26 April, 10 May, 21 June 1898.

76. Ibid., 10 May 1898.

77. DDRN 4/10/1/5, The Raleigh Cycle Company Ltd (Raleigh, Nottingham, 1898), pp. 7–9.

78. Directors and General Meetings, 5 November 1897, 1 February, 29 March, 10 May 1898. To illustrate his point Bowden, claimed that handlebars were being supplied to Gazelle from Raleigh at 8s. 9d., whereas the former had received a quotation from the Campion Cycle Co. at 4s. 6d. Raleigh handlebars were still being produced by hand 'in our enormous factory while any little firm could produce them ... at half the price they cost us'. Similarly, they were producing pedals at 10s. 6d. per pair, but Humber were paying only 7s. 6d. to purchase them from BSA. Ibid., 10 May 1898.

79. Ibid., 29 May 1898.

80. Ibid., 1 February, 26 April, 5, 26 July 1898.

81. Ibid., 7 June, 19 July, 29 August, 19 October 1898. Trade creditors included a number of outside component firms, £1 600 alone owing to Perry & Co. for pedals. Although Perry were sympathetic to Raleigh's plight they were demanding repayment. Ibid., 25 October 1898.

82. Ibid., 19, 25, 28 October 1898.

83. Ibid., 11 November 1898; DDRN 10/3/4/6/1 Memorandum and Articles of Association of the Raleigh Cycle Co., Incorporated 15 February 1899.

84. Directors and General Meetings, 4 January 1898.

85. Ibid., 15 , 24 November 1898, and letter from Bowden to Wells & Hind, 22 November 1898.

86. Ibid., 29 November, 2 December 1898. See also DDRN 2/7/1, Bowden, Circular to Shareholders, 23 November 1903.

87. DDRN 2/7/1, Harlow, Circular to Shareholders, 17 December 1898. Financial mismanagement at Raleigh was also the conclusion of *The Economist*, 10 December 1898, pp. 1760–62, who referred to the company having a carry over of £2 200, and a reserve fund of £20 000 at the

beginning of 1898, 'the whole of which has disappeared'. The financial management 'was inherently wrong', and although the company 'succeeded in bolstering it up for a while ... the truth was bound to come out sooner or later, and a bad season brought matters to a climax'.

88.   As Edward Farrow, Raleigh's secretary, put it: 'unless these proposals can be carried into effect, there does not appear any alternative but the compulsory liquidation of the company, in which case we fear that the creditors and shareholders would get nothing'. DDRN 2/7/1, Farrow, Circular to Shareholders, 15 December 1898.

89.   DDRN 2/7/1, Farrow, Circular to Shareholders, 19 January 1899.

90.   Directors and General Meetings, 18 February 1899; Memorandum and Articles of Association of the Raleigh Cycle Co. Ltd, Incorporated 15 February 1899; DDRN 1/39/1–2, Raleigh AGM, 3 January 1899; 14 November 1899; DDRN 10/3/13/1–58, Certificates for Issue of Third Mortgage Debenture; DDRN 10/3/1/4, Memorandum of Agreement Between Raleigh and the Lloyds Bank for Issue of third mortgage, 1899. The company's debts were paid off by existing debenture holders in the old company exchanging them for like debentures in the new company, and a new debenture, with the power to raise £40 000, was issued as security for the extension of the bank overdraft, to pay 5 per cent interest per annum, and held by the trustees of the bank.

91.   Directors and General Meetings, 27 April 1899.

92.   Ibid., 21 December 1899. Prior to this, Mills had visited the USA to examine various automatic toolmaking factories.

93.   Bowden, 1975, p. 26; Bowden, Manuscript, p. 15; Book of the Raleigh 1900, p. 5, 1901, pp. 5, 37, 1904, pp. 4–22, 1906, p. 3.

94.   Book of the Raleigh 1900, p. 5, 1901, pp. 5, 37. In 1899 five Gazelle models were produced, ranging in price from £10 6s. 3d. to the cheapest model at £7 10s., the latter fitted with lower grade Warwick tyres, rather than Dunlop. DDRN 2/7/1 The Gazelle Cycle Co. per Frank Bowden, 23 January 1899; Newhall & Mason, Manufacturing Chemists, Promotion to Retailers, 1899; DDRN 2/7/1, Report of Directors, 1st AGM 14 November 1899.

95.   DDRN 2/7/1, Raleigh Cycle Co. to Agents, July 1899, p. 15; Book of the Raleigh, 1900, pp. 11, 13, 1901, pp. 17, 37; DDRN 4/63/1–2, Cycling, 27 November. 1913.

96.   In particular Mills was expected to set output targets and material costs well in advance, which were then sanctioned by the directors. For example, to meet a target of 12 000 machines in 1900, the company purchased materials well in advance and Mills was instructed not to allow weekly output to fall below 400 machines. For 1901 10 000 sets of parts were sanctioned to meet an expected output of 16 000 cycles. See Directors and General Meetings, 14 December 1899, 8 March, 21 June 1900.

97.   Ibid., 27 March, 28 April, 1 May, 30 October 1902, 28 June 1904; DDRN 1/23/1, Sturmey-Archer Gears, Minutes, 27 February, 10 March 1903; Bowden, 1975, pp. 23–4; Bowden, Manuscript, pp. 17–20; DDRN 7/1/19/1–3, The Raleigh Concise History of the Bicycle, p. 3.

98.   Directors and General, 9 May 1905, 17 August 1905; Sturmey-Archer Gears, Minutes, 17 August 1906, 19 November, 17 December 1907, 21 October, 11 December 1908, 20 July 1910, 8 March, 5 November 1912.; DDRN 4/63/1–2, East Anglia Daily Times, 1907.

99. Directors and General, 21 June, 19 July 1898, 7 July 1899.

100. Thoms and Donnelly, 1985, p. 28.

101. Directors and General Meetings, 20 July 1899, 13 July, 17 August 1900.

102. Ibid., 5 December 1901, 10 April 1902, 16, 28 August 1904; Raleigh AGMs, 14 November 1901, 11 November 1902.

103. Directors and General Meetings, 28 February, 7 March, 22 August, 14, 30 October 1901; Raleigh AGM, 7 November 1903.

104. Directors and General Meetings, 17 November 1903 and Result of Poll Notified to Shareholders, 24 November 1903, 3 December 1903, 5 February, 8 February 1904; DDRN 2/7/1, Frank Bowden, Circular to Shareholders, 23 November 1903.

105. DDRN 2/7/1, Frank Bowden, Circular to Shareholders, December 1903.

106. DDRN 2/7/1, Frank Bowden, Circular to Shareholders, 23 November 1903; Directors and General Meetings, 3 December 1903.

107. Directors and General Meetings, 3 December 1903; DDRN 2/7/1, E. C. Farrow, Circular to Shareholders, 7 January 1904; DDRN 2/7/1, Frank Bowden, Circular to Shareholders, 27 January 1904.

108. DDRN 2/7/1, Frank Bowden, Circular to Shareholders, 27 January 1904. Bowden also condemned the profit record of Turney Bros which, 'Although a public company ... no reports or accounts of meetings ... are ... allowed to be published'.

109. DDRN 1/39/6, Report of Directors, 1904.

110. Bowden, 1975, p. 28.

111. DDRN 2/7/1, Raleigh AGM, 5 December 1904, 4 December 1905.

112. For example, referring to the fact that some firms had stopped producing cycles at prices above £16, he claimed this 'was not the high water mark'. The company continued to produce its modele superbes at £25, with accessories included in the price, and special lamp, bell, gold or silver plated name and address plaque. Book of the Raleigh for 1905, p. 3.

113. DDRN 2/7/1, Raleigh AGM, 5 December 1906.

114. Directors and General Meetings, 25 January 1906; DDRN 2/7/1, AGM, 20 November 1907.

115. Directors and General Meetings, 18 July 1908; DDRN 2/7/1, Frank Bowden, Circular to Shareholders, 4 June 1908.

116. DDRN 2/7/1, Frank Bowden, Circular to Shareholders, 4 June 1908; DDRN 10/3/4/13–15, Agreements between Frank Bowden and the Raleigh Cycle Co., 18 July, 17 August 1908, Directors and General Meetings, 30 July 1908; Bowden, 1975, citing Cycle and Motor Trades Review, pp. 28–9; DDRN 7/2/7, History of the Raleigh Cycle Co. Ltd.

117. Book of the Raleigh, 1908, 1909, 1910, 1911, 1912; Bowden, 1975, p. 33.

CHAPTER FOUR

The 'golden age' of cycling: depression and recovery in the inter-war years

This chapter surveys the key developments in the British bicycle industry between 1918 and 1939, and begins by exploring the problems encountered by firms during the inflationary boom between 1918 and 1920. The boom was followed by a severe depression from the middle of 1920, and the industry had to meet the challenges of the depressed economic climate of the 1920s. The market for cycles picked up from the mid-1920s, only for business confidence and profits to again take a severe jolt in the world economic depression of 1929–32. However, the industry fought back and recovered rapidly after 1932 as sales rose in both domestic and foreign markets. The years leading up to the Second World War may be described as a 'golden age' for cycling, and by 1936 it was estimated that there were 10 million cycles in use in the UK, and there was a rising demand overseas, especially in colonial markets.[1] Not all trends were positive in the 1930s, and in particular the emergence of Japan as a serious competitor placed pressure on British cycle firms to adapt and exploit the available market opportunities. Thus, firms modernised plant to reduce costs and prices, and innovated in marketing to increase sales. By the end of the 1930s the industry was on a sound footing, but had also undergone a series of significant changes.

The inter-war years saw a trend in the cycle industry towards increased business concentration, a pattern which mirrored that of British business in general.[2] By the end of the period the industry was dominated by a few large firms, notably Hercules, the largest British producer, J. A. Phillips, an operating company of Tube Investments (TI) acquired in 1919, BSA Cycles, and Raleigh Holdings Co. This trend of structural change will be examined, and it will be argued that merger activity to achieve greater vertical integration in the industry was limited. In family firms, such as Hercules, individual interests militated against merger, but we will also argue that vertical integration was slow because of the persistence in the industry of dependence on outside component suppliers, and the effects of trade agreements, a response to intense price competition, as a means of alleviating the problems of cut-throat competition.[3] Structural change did not mean a departure from traditional forms of business organisation, and personal capitalism, with its links to family, remained well entrenched throughout the period. Nevertheless, the industry responded and adapted to the economic environment, and in two key strategic areas, technological development and marketing, showed a highly positive attitude. In particular Hercules and Phillips 'were to become giants in the industry, marketing cheap mass-produced bicycles'.[4] The former developed mass-production systems, and through lowering the price of its machines it rapidly became a formidable competitor in the 1930s. This company represented the cheaper end of the cycle market in Britain, whilst other firms such as Humber, BSA and Raleigh enhanced their competitive capabilities by expanding output without reducing the quality and status of their cycles. As we will show in the case of BSA Cycles, an operating company within a larger group organisation, going down-market could create tensions between the parent and the subsidiary business. Certainly, not all firms survived the competitive test, and in particular we will examine the demise of Rudge-Whitworth, one of the early pioneers of the British cycle industry. This company provides an example of missed opportunities during the interwar years, which negated its ability to exploit the market opportunities of the 1930s. We begin our investigation by examining the impact of the First World War on the industry, the problems of readjustment and the onset of the depression.

War, readjustment and depression, 1914–20

At the outbreak of the First World War the British bicycle industry had found itself in a strong competitive position, and firms within the industry made a rapid response to harnessing their productive resources to the war effort.[5] Their contribution took two basic forms: first, they supplied bicycles, and in diversified firms motor cycles, which were specially designed for military purposes; second, plant was converted for the production of munitions. To meet these demands the industry responded by recruiting more unskilled labour, a process known as dilution, and by investing in enlarging plant and in increasing automation.[6] By 1916, as the war intensified, the industry faced mounting pressures to increase military output, and often cycle production had to be cut back. For example, Charles Vernon Pugh, the chairman and managing director of Rudge-Whitworth, informed his shareholders in 1916 that they had received a large volume of 'important munitions contracts', and this had raised output to record levels. However, he noted with some dismay that 'the output of the company's staple products has been and remains practically suspended'. This continued at Rudge-Whitworth for the remainder of the war, and in 1918 the value of cycle sales was just £7 841 (see Table C.4 in the Appendix). Similarly Gerald Oscar Herbert, the joint managing director of the Coventry Premier Cycle Co., announced in 1917 that the company's net profits, of only £2 786, were restricted by government controls 'which have prevented the company from obtaining further supplies of materials for maintaining the manufacture of cycles'.[7] Nevertheless as Millward argues, the war 'accelerated the growth of many of the leading bicycle companies', and employment at BSA, for example, rose from 3 500 to 13 000, and the technology and skills employed in bicycle production were easily convertible to 'munitions and aeroplanes'.[8] By 1917, however, the strain of war was beginning to tell on a number of cycle firms, and in particular munitions work was leading to rising overhead costs and falling profits. This was the case at Raleigh, as we shall see in the next chapter, and the problems were outlined by Cecil Twist, the other managing director of Coventry Premier, who claimed that:

> By reason of the small proportion of machinery to the total plant of a factory equipped for the manufacture of cycles, it is impossible to occupy fully such a factory on the production of munitions, the output of which is entirely dependent upon the machine shop. We undertook the maximum amount of munitions work last year with the result that the factory equipment and space which could not be employed on this class of work has not yielded the same return as if utilised in the manufacture of the company's usual products [cycles].[9]

By the end of 1917 cycle firms were under increasing pressure to return to their traditional product lines, as the price of munitions contracts fell, and the continuation of government restrictions on supplies affected their ability to utilise fully capacity on both munitions and cycles, a situation which worsened as munitions contracts fell in 1918. The problems of the industry were intensified by the loss of export markets during the First World War and, as Table C.1 in the Appendix shows, the volume of British cycle exports fell from 147 633 machines in 1913 to 58 878 in 1916, and by 1918 to just 28 000. This 80 per cent fall by 1918 was also accompanied by declining exports of cycle parts, and the overall export demand position facing the industry was not a favourable one. In this situation there was a varied response by businessmen in the industry to the return to peacetime conditions. Some, like Sir Hallewell Rogers, chairman of BSA, took a positive view of the post-war future of the industry. Acknowledging that the transition from war to peace would not be easy, he nevertheless believed that the war had created a pent up demand for British cycles, and export markets would be quickly restored as major manufacturing nations, such as Germany would be effectively knocked out of the market. Such was his confidence in the future of the industry that he committed BSA to an expansionary programme to meet the post-war domestic and overseas demand, and by 1919 BSA had constructed new factories at Small Heath, Birmingham for a larger volume output of both cycles and motor cycles.[10] The company was quite likely drawn into this strategy by the fact that profits rose considerably during the war (Table C.3 in the Appendix) and they were able to plough back profits in the expansion of plant.

As will be seen in the next chapter, Harold Bowden at Raleigh also committed his company to expansion at the end of the war, but the market environment facing firms was uncertain and often confusing. Thus other manufacturers viewed the post-war situation less favourably, and John J. B. Arter, the chairman of the Jane Cycle Co. of Birmingham, warned shareholders in August 1918 of the 'uncertainty of the future', and the 'goodwill of the company has been materially injured by setting aside their own trade, and it will be expensive to recover'. In particular, he pointed to the disruption of world trade, which would take time 'to recover to anything approaching normal conditions', and he claimed that the war had materially damaged those cycle companies that were successfully developing before 1914, and those that were formed during the war. Arter, realising the highly competitive nature of the cycle industry, went on to predict that older established firms would 'face a great deal of financial strain', while newly formed businesses during the war would 'go under'. Of particular concern to Arter was the economic efficiency of the industry, and the impact of external factors such as taxation and the price of fuel and transport. As he claimed, 'The factors which are most uncertain are the prices of materials, the rate of wages in relation to output, and the extent of Imperial and local taxation, apart from the cost of monopolies such as gas, electricity and transport'.[11] Anticipating inflationary pressures in the economy, he warned that 'No selling price can be safely fixed, as forward contracts for materials and supplies have practically been unobtainable'. What concerned him most was the productivity of labour in relation to wage rates, and he argued that 'The rate of wages is certainly advancing, particularly for unskilled and semi-skilled work, the working hours are shorter and the output is falling, so that work done in the same time is substantially less than in pre-war days, which is the most vital and difficult feature of the situation'. Central to this message was the view that to meet foreign competition effectively would require co-operation between capital and labour, and a 'full days work for a fair and full days pay'.[12]

The warnings of businessmen such as Arter had considerable predictive power for they focused on the problems which were to confront the industry in the immediate post-war era. Britain and the world economy was to experience a brief inflationary boom and then slide into a sharp depression. Initially cycle exports recovered rapidly after 1918. By 1920 cycle exports were 12 000 machines higher than the pre-war peak in 1913, and between 1918 and 1920 the trend in the value of exports was highly impressive, registering an eightfold increase (Table C.1 in the Appendix). Nevertheless, cycle production remained constrained by shortages of vital raw materials, power supplies and labour. The effects of this were twofold: first, it prevented manufacturers from taking full advantage of the potential demand for their products, creating a window of opportunity for foreign manufacturers to exploit as their plant came back on stream; second, it pushed the price of raw materials and labour inexorably upwards. In turn, rising costs were passed on to consumers through higher prices, and this accounts for the large increase in the value of cycle exports immediately after the war. The consequences of post-war shortages and inflation were reported by Rudge-Whitworth in 1919. Charles Vernon Pugh informed shareholders that the company was unable to present its accounts because of unsettled payments for munitions contracts and, although the company had resumed cycle production, shortages of supplies of materials and labour had resulted in output progressing 'much more slowly than is desirable'.[13] The directors of BSA Cycles also complained that despite substantial investment in extending plant they were unable to meet the demand for their bicycles because of shortages of raw materials and rising power costs, notably electricity and gas, the prices of which were pushed up by the local supplier, Redditch District Council.[14] BSA's investment strategy was frustrated by supply constraints and rising costs, and their whole programme was threatened in 1920 when cycle assemblers at their Redditch factory struck for higher piece rates in January. A matter of three months earlier Rogers had welcomed what he saw as 'the hearty co-operation of labour', but this now proved to be illusionary. The management held out for a month, but shortages of labour forced them to capitulate in February 1920, and concede to the demands of the AEU for higher rates. The outcome of these rising costs was that BSA bicycles were selling at prices which were 100 per cent above pre-war levels, and not surprisingly Rogers felt let down by the 'continued failure of the two human elements in industry to find some means of adjudicating between them when their material interests conflict'.[15] In April 1921 cycle and motor cycle workers struck in Coventry for over one month, causing widespread disruption to output, and the coal strike of the same year forced a number of firms to cease production temporarily.[16]

During the inflationary boom wages within the cycle industry increased dramatically, and cycle firms were forced to steadily increase the price of their products. For example, in 1918 the average price of a British bicycle in export markets was £7.25, but by 1921 it had risen by 34.5 per cent to £9.75 (Table C.1 in the Appendix) As Rogers at BSA was well aware, price inflation after the war had led to a deterioration in real earnings compared to pre-war, and he 'did not grudge the increase in wages'. Nevertheless, he urged employees to co-operate fully with management and improve productivity. By 1920, as the management of the Royal Enfield Company were well aware, the 'cycling boom' had created a large demand for cycles but they now had 'to meet a great deal of foreign competition'. The inflationary boom damaged the competitive position of the industry, and when the depression hit from the middle of 1920 manufacturers faced acute problems. By the late spring of 1920 the management of BSA Cycles were concerned that 'in certain markets orders for pedal cycles are being cancelled on account of the high prices of our machines'. This typified the dilemma of the industry, for with rising production costs the management were forced to announce that the price of their three-speed gear hubs were to increase from 28 to 33 shillings, and this was to be followed by a general rise in the prices of cycles. The outcome of this was that by the summer of 1920 there was a collapse of orders in the domestic market, and also from importers in Japan, Scandinavia, France and Italy. BSA held off reducing prices, and in these circumstances orders continued to fall throughout the autumn and factory overheads began to rise as capacity was under-utilised. Rogers reported in November that foreign competition had quickly re-established itself, the industry was slipping into the grips of an acute depression, and there was a 'dramatic contrast between conditions today and those prevailing a year ago'.[17] The next section examines the performance of the industry in the 1920s and 1930s, and demonstrates that the industry, despite two severe shocks, in the early 1920s and again in 1929–32, performed adequately in this period.

The performance of the cycle industry, 1920–39

As boom gave way to depression in 1920 the industry was faced with three problems. First, domestic sales declined, and the industry was faced with competition in the home market from cheaper foreign makers. As the *Motor Cycle and Cycle Trader* noted in April 1922:

> It has been a bit of a job getting the market back to English bicycles, as there was a long period during the war when we had to buy from the United States the public have kind of got the idea that there are no other bicycles on this market than this class of stuff.

The impact of cheaper competition in the home market was intensified by the actions of domestic manufacturers who responded to falling demand by slashing prices. For example, Rudge-Whitworth cut its cycle prices from £15 15s. to £12 in March 1921, and although companies such as BSA, Enfield, Humber and Raleigh colluded to maintain a 'no reduction' policy in April, price-cutting continued to intensify. The actions of domestic producers in cutting prices was compounded by increased foreign competition in the home market: 'The demand for lower prices has caused a large number of alleged cheap bicycles – some of them of foreign origin and thrown together in the most slip-shod style – to be put upon the market.'[18] Second, British exports collapsed from 159 698 machines in 1920 to 39 117 in 1921, and as prices were cut the drop in value was even more dramatic (Table C.1 in the Appendix). Although the volume of cycle exports had almost recovered its lost ground by 1923, the value of sales remained well below the figures prevailing in 1920, as increased sales were gained only by reducing prices. Exports were a vital component of demand for the industry, and although the domestic market was still the main target of producers, and as Major J. D. Barnsdale, a director at Raleigh, claimed in January 1922:

> the business, in a normal year, comes along at a time of the year when the home trade is at its lowest ebb. The truth of this was never so much realised as when the foreign trade was cut off with such appalling suddenness last year. Since then manufacturers have tried all sorts of ways to regain the business, but by reason of the extraordinary state of conditions in certain countries, the business was not really there to be had, and the question of price and quality scarcely entered the matter.

Competitive pressures were particularly acute in colonial markets, and they were literally flooded with cheap foreign machines. In Britain's most important foreign market before the war, India, there was a growing incursion from cheaper Japanese manufacturers.[19] As we saw in an earlier chapter, a number of cycle manufacturers had moved into motor cycle production before the war, but this business did not provide a business opportunity which could counteract the downturn in the cycle market. As can be seen in Table C.1 in the Appendix the value and volume of British motor cycle exports fell sharply in 1921, and remained depressed throughout the 1920s.

Third, the onslaught of depression was not helped by government policies in the 1920s which further constrained the ability of manufacturers to export and left the door open to foreign imports. Thus, British producers had to contend with stiff tariff barriers abroad, and unlike the motor car industry, which was protected by a 33.3 per cent import tariff under the McKenna Duties of 1915, which were further extended under the Safeguarding of Industry Act of 1921, the cycle industry had no such protection.[20] Further, demand in colonial markets was constrained by the 'prevailing financial stringency', and depreciated currencies on the Continent made British exports there less competitive.[21] The industry's export position, and that of other staple export sectors in the 1920s was, if anything, worsened by the decision to return to the Gold Standard at the pre-war parity in 1925. This may well have overvalued sterling against the dollar by approximately 10 per cent, and against a basket of European currencies by 20 to 25 per cent. This placed exports at a cost disadvantage, and by the same token it made cycle imports into the UK market cheaper.[22] In turn, the cycle industry had to compete in an unprotected market. It could be argued that free trade benefited cycle manufacturers by allowing in imports of cheap foreign steel, but in reality the industry was largely dependent upon domestic supplies which they considered to be of a superior quality, and in which cycle firms had developed networks through local steel suppliers, built upon mutual trust.[23]

Given these constraints, it is quite remarkable that Britain's cycle manufacturers performed so well during the 1920s. The worst period was unquestionably between 1921 to 1924, and as can be seen in Table C.3 in the Appendix profits were restricted, and in some years firms recorded significant losses. Cycle imports also rose, and domestic and foreign demand remained constrained.[24] Nevertheless, by May 1925 *The Economist* was reporting a 'Record Year' for the cycle industry, and rejoiced in the fact that cycle sales in both imperial and foreign markets were rising. The cycle firms of Coventry and Birmingham were operating at 'full pitch' and *The Economist* praised the industry for meeting the challenge of low-priced competition through a 'policy of producing a sound, standard machine at a price low enough to be well within the reach of the vast majority of potential customers in this and other countries'.[25] As can be seen in Table C.1 in the Appendix, the average price of an exported machine fell from £9.75 in 1921 to £4.70 in 1925, and by 1929 to just £3.78, overall a fall of 61 per cent. We will examine the reasons behind these price falls later, but certainly a contributory factor was the weakening strength of the engineering unions, and their inability to push costs upwards. For example, in Coventry the AEU was soundly beaten in the lock-out in the engineering industry in 1922, and with rising unemployment the bargaining position of labour deteriorated.[26] By the end of 1923 the free trade *Economist* was already presenting the motor cycle and cycle industry as a paragon of British excellence. Condemning motor car manufacturers for hiding behind the shelter of protection, its 'beloved quack medicine', *The Economist* argued that the motor cycle and cycle industry 'laughs at foreign competition either in the home of foreign markets', and their reputation for quality machines, together with increased efficiency in production, had resulted in a resurgence of the industry's business performance. Referring to the pedal cycle industry, *The Economist* concluded that 'Here ... is the best evidence of what even those melancholy Midlanders can do when they are left unspoilt by the debilitation of tariffs, and bend their minds and bodies to the task of establishing and maintaining a world trade'.[27]

By the beginning of 1924 cycle producers had broken out of the depression, and despite the contraction in exports in 1926, which coincided with the general strike and the impact of rising raw material and power costs, the trend in both the volume and value of exports was upwards to 1929. Certainly in export markets the industry displayed considerable robustness, and this stands in marked contrast to the general performance of British exports in this period. As Broadberry argues, 'the most disturbing feature of Britain's industrial position between the wars was the stagnation of exports'; British exports did not regain their pre-war levels throughout the period, and in 1929 they 'were only 81.3% of their 1913 value'.[28] The British bicycle industry is a clear exception to this general trend, but nevertheless the profitability of the industry, especially in the 1920s, was far from satisfactory. Profits for companies such as Rudge-Whitworth, Hercules and Phillips remained low in the 1920s, as sales were increased at the expense of reductions in prices, and as will be discussed in the next chapter, a similar pattern was experienced by Raleigh.

The progression of the industry in the 1920s was brought to an abrupt halt by the great depression of 1929 to 1932, and British cycle exports fell by 65 per cent in volume and by 73 per cent in value (Table C.1 in the Appendix). The industry was faced with acute problems, and both foreign and domestic demand fell. To combat this firms pushed prices down further, with the consequence that profits were substantially reduced, and in some cases simply collapsed. Companies such as Rudge-Whitworth, Hercules and New Hudson all experienced net losses as demand continued to be depressed. The depression experienced by the industry was intense, but fortunately relatively short-lived. In early 1932 the trade press were already talking about a 'bicycle boom', and the possibilities for the rapid recovery of the industry.[29] Indeed, by March 1934 *Bicycling News* claimed that 'It is probable that no section of British trade has shown greater progress during the past year as the bicycle industry'.[30] The recovery proceeded on two fronts, the foreign and domestic. In foreign markets the volume of exports rose from the low ebb of 1932 in each consecutive year up to 1936, by which date it had passed 500 000 machines and had recovered to the figures for 1929. (Table C.1 in the Appendix). Export data is unavailable for the post 1936 period, but figures for the sales of Raleigh and Humber cycles in foreign markets (Table D.7 in the Appendix) show a continuation of the upward trend to 1939, with the exception of 1938 which saw a short, but sharp economic recession. As *The Economist* pointed out in 1935, the industry had responded to the depression by increasing efficiency and output, reducing costs and prices, and counteracting foreign competition. Thus, competitors on the Continent were unable to compete with British price competition, British manufacturers exporting machines priced on average at £3 each, and French and German exports dwindled to a mere 10 000 each. An important characteristic of the industry's export performance in the 1930s is shown in Table 4.1. In 1930 82.5 per cent of British cycle exports were being shipped to the Empire, and by 1936 this stood at almost 85 per cent. This represented the breakdown of international trade into various regional blocks, and in some cases the complete withdrawal of certain countries, such as Germany, from the world market. The importance of the Empire as a British regional trade block can be contrasted with the artificial restrictions placed on the 'natural expansion' of world exports in the form 'of high tariffs, quotas [and] import licence systems'. Thus, although consumers on the Continent 'were anxious to purchase British bicycles ... they were prevented from doing so by the totally inadequate quotas permitted to importers'.[31]

Second, there was a marked revival in home demand after 1932, which provided the main platform for recovery. In 1935 it was reported that since 1929 the number of pedal cycles in Britain has increased from 6 million to 10 million, and in 1937 *Bicycling News* claimed that 'there are nearly 100 per cent more cycles on the road today than in 1929.

Table 4.1   Volume and value of UK cycles exported to Empire and non-Empire markets, 1930–36

	No. to Empire	Value to Empire (£)	No. to non-Empire	Value to non-Empire (£)
1930	203 867	772 963	43 280	172 438
1931	146 331	512 039	26 619	95 552
1932	133 010	413 129	31 064	106 438
1933	168 408	455 350	36 217	124 249
1934	231 798	613 846	50 358	166 719
1935	309 231	829 442	68 070	223 222
1936	439 170	1 141 925	80 003	251 734

Source: Bicycling News, 1 July 1937.

Motor cars have not increased to anything like that percentage in the same period. It is true to say, therefore, that this is a cycling era'. *The Economist* was equally positive in late 1934, and it argued that as bicycle imports into the UK usually formed 'a negligible feature of Board of Trade returns', then British manufacturers were benefiting from a growing demand for their products, and it was a 'golden age of cycling' which found 'gratifying expression' in the profits of Britain's cycle companies.[32] This optimism was certainly reflected in the profits of companies such as Phillips and Hercules, both of which rose substantially between 1932 and 1934. However, in the case of the latter company, which had become Britain's largest producer of standardised models by the 1930s, the profit performance up to the Second World War was somewhat disappointing. We shall return to examine this issue later, but it is important to note at this stage that competitive success, particularly in the domestic market was not simply conditioned by price, but rather by the ability to continue to sell highly differentiated quality products, and quality producers such as Raleigh, who epitomised the higher end of the market, displayed higher profitability in the 1930s than mass producers of cheap machines such as Hercules.

This may well tell us something important about the characteristics of the domestic cycle market in the 1930s. Two underlying forces were operating to promote the increased demand: first, the continuing need for bicycles as a functional mode of transport; second, the growing popularity of cycling as a leisure and sporting pastime. Paradoxically, bicycle manufacturers benefited from the depression, which had severely undermined business and consumer confidence, and in particular had increased fears of job insecurity and the possibility of lower future earning capacity. In such an environment the majority of people were reluctant to purchase higher-value commodities such as cars and motor cycles, which were still the preserve of the middle-class in society. In consequence, cycles made significant gains at the expense of more expensive modes of transport, and in particular made inroads into the utility market for motor cycles. As *The Economist* claimed, the bicycle was important in the growth of suburban areas in Britain, and they attributed the increased sales of cycles to the 're-housing of many people on estates outside urban boundaries at some distance from work'. Improvements in road conditions, and a fall in cycle prices made the cycle even more attractive, and 'encouraged the working and lower middle classes to journey to and from work by cycle'. The *Motor Cycle and Cycle Export Trader* also commented on the changing habits of the population, and what looked like a 'waning industry' a few years earlier, as cycles faced competition from buses and motor coaches, 'is now healthy again'.[33]

In contrast to pedal cycles there was a contraction in the market for motor cycles, a business which a number of cycle manufacturers were also engaged in. BSA, for example, complained that the demand for motor cycles in the 1930s was only a fraction of what it used to be, and it was pointed out that in the 1920s their output was the equivalent of the total sales of all motor cycles in the UK for 1934.[34] As can be seen in Table C.3 in the Appendix, BSA profits fell in both 1934 and 1935, and the company's motor cycle business was constrained by a falling demand from the better off in society, who were increasingly attracted by products such as the 'baby car' which squeezed the demand for top-quality motor cycles. Raleigh too abandoned its motor cycle business in 1934, to concentrate their activities upon the rapidly growing cycle market, and we will explore that decision in the next chapter.

As *The Economist* noted in 1935, the pedal cycle 'had a certain virtue as a means of exercise which the motor cycle lacked'. This takes us to the growing trend during the inter-war years towards the bicycle as a commodity which incorporated the 'possibility for pleasure rather than for pure utility'. Indeed, the inter-war years were the 'golden age' for bicycle touring, and the 1930s saw the renaissance of cycling as a sport. Cycling clubs were established throughout the country, and as the directors of BSA cycles acknowledged, they had an appeal to a wide age group, from 12 to 60 years of age, and enabled 'all classes of people to enjoy the pleasure and health attained by cycling through Britain's beautiful countryside'.[35] Millward has argued that during the inter-war years 'cycling became an affordable pastime for the majority of the population'. Cycling and cycle clubs found a particular appeal among women, and manufacturers, such as Hercules, were quick to take note that of 'the huge increase of cyclists' a 'large proportion ... are women'. Cycling, in many respects witnessed a revival and became a fashion and leisure pursuit, a factor which, as we saw in Chapter 2, had been important for the early development of the industry. Products dictated by the whims of fashion, of course, are prone to sharp changes in fortunes, a fact noted by *The Economist* in 1934. Thus, although the revival of the industry in the 1930s was due to exogenous factors relating to the changing market environment, the industry could not sit back and be complacent, particularly as Japanese makers were competing rigorously in terms of price.[36] Cycle manufacturers had to exploit the market opportunities, and this was achieved by increased efficiency which enabled them to reduce prices, maintain the quality standard of the product and pursue innovative marketing techniques. Before we examine these factors, there is a need to explore the changes in the structure and organisation of the industry, and the slow development in the industry of vertical integration.

Structure, organisation and vertical integration in the inter-war bicycle industry

The general structural trends in the cycle industry are shown in Tables 4.2 and 4.3, which examine the population of firms in the two main centres of the trade, Birmingham and Coventry. The number of firms in the industry fell, and this was part of a trend which saw the industry by the 1930s become increasingly concentrated in the hands of a few large firms, prominent amongst them being the Hercules Cycle and Motor Co., a mass producer of standardised cheaper models, J. A. Phillips & Co., a large producer of components and cycles and a subsidiary of TI, Raleigh Holdings Co. Ltd, and the bicycle division of BSA. Sir Harold Bowden, the leading personality at Raleigh, noted in 1934 that the industry had increased substantially in scale since the war, a trend he expected to continue for the next 50 years.[37] Bowden's prediction was, in fact, already a reality by the 1930s, and by 1935 70 per cent of all employees in the British bicycle industry were employed by the three firms of Hercules, Raleigh and BSA. Larger firms now predominated, and 57.7 per cent of workers were concentrated in firms which employed over 1 000.[38] By 1935 large producers such as Hercules and Raleigh accounted for approximately half of the total sales of British bicycles, and other firms such as BSA, Enfield and New Hudson accounted for a further third.[39] To a large extent increasing concentration was accounted for by market factors associated with the depression, and many smaller and medium-sized producers failed the competitive

Table 4.2 Number of cycle manufacturers in Coventry, 1920–39

1920–21	1923–24	1929–30	1935–36	1939–40
49	37	32	24	24

Source: Compiled from *Coventry Trade Directories* for 1920s and 1930s, various dates.

Table 4.3 Number of cycle manufacturers in Birmingham, 1920–39

1920	1925	1931	1937	1939
132	122	67	44	44

Source: Compiled from *Birmingham Trade Directories* for 1920s and 1930s, various dates.

test, whilst other firms such as Singer, Riley, Swift, Rover and Triumph exited the industry and concentrated on motor cycles and motor vehicles. Nevertheless, increased concentration was identified with two important characteristics of the industry during this period. First, firms grew predominately through internal expansion, rather than by merger. With the notable exceptions of the acquisition of Phillips by TI in 1919, the Raleigh take over of Humber Cycles in 1932 and the acquisition of John Marsh & Co., the manufacturers of the renowned Sunbeam Cycles, by the Matchless Motorcycle Co. in the late 1930s, mergers in the industry were a rare occurrence. As a consequence the managerial organisation of firms remained much the same, and personal capitalism, with its association with family founders and heirs continued to predominate.[40] Why was this the case?

Millward has claimed that 'widespread individualism mitigated against a general merger movement' in the cycle industry.[41] Despite a growing trend towards merger in British business during the 1920s,[42] the cycle industry was not characterised by intensified merger activity, and this may well be the result of the retention of family control in the organisation which inhibited formal merger. The importance of family managers in the continued direction of larger cycle companies is demonstrated in the case of Hercules which became Britain's largest producer of cycles by the 1930s. The company's origins were in Birmingham, and the firm was founded in September 1910 by Edmund and Harry Crane with a capital of just £124. During its first year of business Hercules produced 1 000 cycles from two rented rooms, assembling the frames in the street. From these small beginnings it rapidly expanded, and in 1923, with a revival in the cycle trade, the company expanded into a new factory in Rocky Lane, recently vacated by Dunlop. By 1929 the company had opened a new factory at Manor Hill, and was providing employment for over 10 000 workers. Under the direction of its family founders Hercules rose to become the largest cycle firm in the world by the early 1930s, and its development was financed through the ploughing back of retained profits.[43]

The management of Hercules remained committed to retaining their independence, and in 1937 a proposed merger with the Raleigh Holding Co. was abandoned at the last moment, Edmund Crane fearing that his control of the company would be weakened in a larger organisational group. Thus The Economist argued that a promising merger opportunity, which offered the prospects of integrating the activities of two of the largest producers, Raleigh concentrating on high-grade cycles and Hercules on the lower end of the market, was lost. It concluded that 'merger negotiations of this kind invariably partake of the nature of secret diplomacy [and] the reasons for abandonment are presumably substantial'. A close personal identification with the independence of their firm was clearly evident at Hercules, and the individualistic characteristics of family managers were an element in the limited merger activity in the cycle industry. In 1928, with rumours circulating in the press that Raleigh was to be acquired by an American consortium, Harold Bowden, in a firm rebuttal, commented that it will 'remain a family concern'.[44] The bicycle industry seems to have been influenced by a business culture that placed a heavy emphasis on family control, and this may well have acted as a constraint on the initiation and diffusion of organisational innovation.[45] The individualism of the industry also frustrated attempts by holding companies such as BSA to acquire a number of smaller companies. In 1937 BSA was proposing to purchase a cycle manufacturer who could produce a cheap cycle for export markets in India and South Africa. Its operating company, BSA Cycles, instigated negotiations with a number of firms, including New Hudson, but none of them could be persuaded to relinquish their independence prior to the Second World War.[46]

It would appear that the individual aspirations of personal business leaders, with a strong cultural attachment to their family firms, may well account for the low levels of merger activity in the industry. The effect of this was that vertical integration, and the internalisation of all production processes in a single business unit, remained low. Consequently, even large firms such as Hercules and Raleigh continued to rely on outside component suppliers and forewent opportunities to reduce transaction costs on the market. Indeed, attempts at Raleigh to internalise operations led to problems of co-ordination, as we shall see in the next chapter. The continued dependence on outside suppliers, however, was a rational response to the institutional environment in which cycle firms operated, and this was characterised by the continued existence of long-established producers of components and accessories in the trade. As Asa Briggs has argued, during the inter-war years in Birmingham there were linkages between 'related groups of industries' and, rather than firms internalising all operations in a single factory, there was a continued reliance on independent auxiliary firms. This, of course, was a 'legacy of the past', but it could bring advantages by replicating 'without conscious effort the main advantages of a large single plant, the physical juxtaposition of consecutive services and auxiliary services which reduced costs of transport and frequency of contracts'.[47] Table 4.4 shows that although the number of accessory and component suppliers in Birmingham contracted during the inter-war years, they still remained an important sector of the trade even in 1939.

An insight into the activities of such firms may be provided by the example of Accles and Pollock of Oldbury, Birmingham. This firm

Table 4.4   Cycle accessory and component manufacturers in
Birmingham, 1920–39

	1920	*1931*	*1939*
Cycle accessory manufacturers	80	74	65
Cycle component manufacturers	148	126	90

Source: Compiled from *Birmingham Trade Directories* for 1920s and 1930s,
various dates.

developed as 'makers and manipulators of weldless steel tubing', and
their strategy typified that of many component suppliers who aimed 'to
be as useful as possible to the cycle and allied trade without encroach-
ing on their legitimate domain'. As the company emphasised: 'We do
not build cycle frames or cycles, and we have never done so, nor are we
connected with any cycle manufacturing concern.' Nevertheless, they
informed the cycle trade that they could supply them with 'everything
for frame construction and also other items which make up the complete bicycle', and these included 'polished and plated handlebars, seat
pillars, trapped chains and seat stays'. The company offered a 'large
and varied assortment of designs for selection' and their handlebars
could be supplied in 'both the reversible and adjustable types, and ...
with a bend of any shape'. Recognising that some companies preferred
to make their own handlebars, they nevertheless publicised the fact that
they could provide services through their 'unrivalled facilities for ma-
nipulating tubing'.[48]

Firms such as Accles and Pollock demonstrate the continued importance of component supply firms to the industry, and they developed
through building up mutual interdependence with manufacturing firms,
a factor as we saw in Chapter 2 which was a key attribute of industrial
districts. As Lazerson has argued, firms in cities such as Birmingham
appear to have benefited from 'economic relations based on co-operation
and trust'.[49] The industry also witnessed the growth of large component
suppliers, such as J. A. Phillips, a operating company of TI. This firm
did move into cycle production in the late 1930s, but for most of the
inter-war years its main business was as a supplier of a variety of
components to the trade. In 1922 the management had committed the
firm to a long-term strategy to develop its business of supplying 'general
accessories to the factors of the motor and cycle trades', and in particular handlebars and pedals.[50] Unfortunately, there are no records available
to examine the relationship of Phillips to the larger TI group in this
period, but we can surmise from other sources that Phillips remained,

more or less, an autonomous business firm within the group. TI was formed through a consolidated merger of five firms in 1919, including Phillips, and its objective was to rationalise the precision tool trades. In 1930 the parent holding company controlled the activities of numerous manufacturers in the Midlands, including Babcox and Wilcox, and in that year it acquired the Talbot Stead Tube Co. and Stewarts and Lloyd, the latter being an old-established firm which produced bulk steel for tubing. Hannah has pointed out that TI was 'little more than loose confederations of subsidiaries, and it may be reasonably doubted whether such a structure can have achieved many of the potential economies of large scale'.[51] Phillips supplied a range of components to the cycle trade, and at the height of the depression in 1931 its chairman, J. H. Aston, rejected a move by his fellow directors to integrate forward into the production of complete cycles for the export trade. He argued that they were maintaining sales at present by supplying cheaper components to British producers and colonial makers, and in the latter the company was developing a profitable business in providing 'export parcels' for assembly, which included frame tubes, produced by TI, wheels, tyres, saddles, chains, handlebars and brakes. By 1935 the company was profitably selling complete sets of parts, and had forged a profitable market with merchants in the Irish Republic.[52]

In this context, the advantages to be gained from vertical integration were not immediately obvious from a business point of view, and in the cycle trade this was demonstrated by the business strategies of Hercules and BSA. The former company was, despite having in its title the name of the Hercules Cycle and Motor Company, predominately a bicycle producer. The strategy adopted by the company was to sell at the cheap end of the market a more standardised cycle, especially in the 1930s when as we have seen there was a growing universal demand for cycles. In the 1920s Hercules introduced mass production techniques, and in 1929 was turning out more bicycles than any other producer in the industry, manufacturing in that year 300 000 bicycles. By 1933 the company sold nearly 500 000 bicycles, and this was 'the greatest years output of any one cycle manufacturer in the history of the world'. Two years later Hercules could boast an annual output of 600 000 bicycles, twice as many as its nearest rival Raleigh. Edmund Crane, the leading entrepreneurial figure at Hercules, was acutely aware of the economies of scale that a large output could provide, and he informed agents that 'It costs far less per cycle to manufacture and distribute half a million cycle than it does 10 000'. By producing large-volume output Hercules was able to reduce significantly unit costs, and to sell cheaper cycles, but the company continued to rely on outside component suppliers such as Accles and Pollock and Phillips, and for the supply of gears, as we shall see in the next chapter, on Sturmey-Archer. As Crane claimed, the manufacture of large quantities of cycles required high-volume supplies of materials and components, and economies could be gained through bulk purchasing from established suppliers who could also guarantee 'the highest quality' at the 'lowest possible price'. The existence of an established network of suppliers effectively discouraged management from internalising operations through vertical integration, and Hercules bought in its steel tubing from Phillips, its tyres from Dunlop and its chains from the 'worlds largest chain combine'. Such economies in supply and manufacture enabled Hercules to sell its cheapest models at prices below £3, and to become a formidable competitor in the cycle market of the 1930s.[53]

BSA provides a somewhat different slant on the issue of the advantages of increasing vertical integration in the industry. BSA Cycles, unlike Hercules, was an operating company controlled by the parent holding company which had interests outside the bicycle industry. This company attempted a strategy of vertical integration, but as we shall see this was not necessarily the route to business success. In 1917 BSA comprised four main departments: armaments, cycles, motor cycles and machine tools. In that year the management decided to pursue a strategy to expand the various branches of the business through investment in new plant and equipment, and through the acquisition of companies engaged in kindred or complementary trades. This plan was implemented in the early 1920s and brought forth a need to reorganise fundamentally the structure of the company. In October 1920 BSA was formed into a holding company to co-ordinate more effectively the activities of its various enlarged divisions, and separate subsidiaries were formed: BSA Cycles to produce cycles and motor cycles, and BSA Armaments and BSA Tools. These operating companies were directly controlled by the parent company, under the direction of Sir Hallewell Rogers and Sir Albert Eadie.[54]

Rogers and Eadie had been at the helm of the company since 1907, and it was their aim to direct the strategy and centralise control over their group of companies. In effect, the aim was to limit the autonomy of its subsidiaries, including BSA Cycles. Although the reorganisation involved the formation of three separate companies, 'the control of these companies will remain as heretofore in the hands of the main board'.[55] The operating companies were allowed their own management boards, but the subsidiaries were subordinated to the wider interests of the parent company, and there is little evidence of the delegation of strategic decision making to divisional managers. Eadie and Rogers continued to maintain their own personal control of executive decision-making. It was these two managers who shaped the strategy of BSA

Cycles during the inter-war years, and the overall impression is that their influence on the subsidiary was less than positive. We shall examine the tensions between the senior management and its subsidiaries in the next section, but the key issue at this stage was the decision by Rogers and Eadie, in 1919, to acquire two Sheffield steel firms, William Jessops & Sons and J. J. Saville's, and to integrate backwards into steel production for a variety of products. Integration backwards would have the advantage of providing BSA Cycles with a regular supply of good-quality steel, and reduce dependency on market transactions through outside suppliers. Thus, the management could boast that steel for BSA Cycles 'comes from their own works, and their foundry make their own forgings', and in promotional terms this was used to sell the quality attributes of their cycles.[56] The efficiency gains of this policy, however, and the assumed advantages of quality control, are difficult to detect. Although there is no direct evidence on transaction cost economies for BSA, the qualitative evidence would suggest that the acquisition of its own steel supplies did not create substantial economies. For example, both Jessops and Saville's were well renowned producers of high-quality crucible steels, and both were early pioneers in specialist steel manufacture. However, as Tweedale argues, they failed after the war to invest sufficiently in electric arc technology, and thus produced at much higher costs than other producers in either Sheffield or Birmingham.[57] Thus, internal purchasing from acquired companies would seem unlikely to have resulted in substantial transaction economies, and it is reasonable to assume that the management would have been better off to have followed the strategy of companies such as Hercules, and transact on the market. Further, BSA Cycles found it difficult to procure the quantity of castings that it required, and the cost of its raw materials was rising rather than falling. As BSA attempted to meet the challenge of low priced competition from volume producers like Hercules in the 1930s, it faced increasing problems in reducing costs to competitive levels. Finally, it is highly debatable whether BSA had the organisational capabilities and understanding to develop effectively a strategy of vertical integration, and as late as 1938 the management reported that the company needed to reorganise its information flows between its various divisions, and to introduce 'better accounting and costing systems'.[58]

The BSA example suggests the limited advantages of internalising operations in the cycle industry, and the advantages of contracting out for component supplies was reinforced by trade agreements between specialist component suppliers and between established cycle manufacturers. As we shall see in the next chapter, attempts to develop formal agreements for fixing prices of finished cycles in the depression of the early 1920s, and again in the 1930s, were prone to failure, although companies such as BSA and Raleigh did conclude personal agreements for maintaining price stability. Thus, the trade press in June 1932 displayed a photo of Harold Bowden on the yacht of Commander Herbert of the BSA Company, and noted that they represent companies who 'work on parallel lines – both ranges are similar – and when the lowest price of one range was reduced last October the other followed suit'. Price agreements between large cycle manufacturers could be highly personal, and often of short duration. Nevertheless, component and accessory manufacturers did participate in collusive agreements 'with the object of preventing undue price-cutting' through the establishment of minimum selling prices in the domestic market. A number of associations, of varying degrees of longevity, were established during the 1920s to maintain the selling prices of free wheels, gears and coaster hubs. Collusion did not only come in the shape of trade associations based upon minimum selling prices, and in 1923 Raleigh's associate company, Sturmey-Archer, informed the directors of BSA that, if they were to stop producing three-speed gear hubs, a Sturmey-Archer speciality, Sturmey-Archer would in turn discontinue the making of coaster hubs, a speciality of BSA. In addition, Sturmey-Archer promised to supply BSA with three-speed hubs at a specially negotiated price. The response of BSA was not initially positive, but in 1927 they finally entered into an agreement to discontinue the sale of three-speed hubs for a period of 15 years, in exchange for an annual payment of 5 per cent on the extra sales that Sturmey-Archer would make. At the same time, BSA also thrashed out a deal with the Villiers Engineering Company and the Coventry Chain Company, under which it agreed to discontinue the sale of free wheels so long as these companies paid it ½d. to 1½d. per wheel for each wheel sold over a specified minimum. Such deals reduced competition in the cycle component and accessories market and enabled suppliers such as the Coventry Chain Company to survive a difficult period.[59]

The growth of trade associations was a general trend in British industry during the inter-war years, and as Kirby has observed, the inter-war years were 'marked by the spread of collusion and cartel formation'.[60] Much of the literature on trade associations has been negative, and economic historians have suggested that such associations 'underwrote inefficiency by preventing the exit of high cost producers'.[61] Nevertheless, the impact of trade associations in the supply of components to the British cycle industry may have had positive effects. In an industry where even large firms such as Hercules purchased components from a number of local firms, the use of trade agreements to fix prices created stability in the market, and the fact that cycle producers were able to reduce the price of finished cycles from the early 1920s suggests that there was no adverse effects to the industry through monopoly control over key supplies. Most trade associations did break down, as one or other of the members sold at a price beneath the specified minimum. Nevertheless, individual firms could use their membership of an association in a positive manner. BSA, for example, retained membership of the various free-wheel, coaster-hub and motor cycle associations until 1927, at which point it decided to break free. This decision was informed by the closure of BSA's Redditch works and the concentration of cycle and motor cycle production at its Small Heath plant. This rationalisation of capacity saved the company at least £40 000 per annum at Redditch alone, and allowed for a reduction in overhead costs at Small Heath.[62] BSA used its membership of the trade association as a protective shield, behind which it could begin to rationalise production, reduce costs and improve productivity.

The low level of mergers and vertical integration in the industry, we would argue, was due to a number of factors, the most important of which were the persistence of personal control in organisations, and the high level of interdependence with component suppliers reinforced by collaborative trade agreements. Nevertheless, the industry not only survived but prospered in the post-1932 period, and in meeting the challenge of the depression, and the need to reduce costs and selling prices, it responded positively. This, however, raised issues concerning the traditional emphasis of the industry on high-quality cycles, and it is to this issue that we now turn.

Quality versus quantity in the British cycle industry

The rise of large firms in the cycle industry should not disguise the continued survival of a thick undergrowth of smaller specialist firms which concentrated on developing niche markets. There were still in existence at least a thousand smaller firms involved in the manufacture of specialist cycles, cycle accessories and cycle components.[63] The very fact that volume producers such as Hercules developed standardised models created opportunities for small makers to satisfy the demand for more specialist cycles. As Soltow has argued, small firms can acquire 'a strong position by adapting to a niche in the market'.[64] For example, the market for racing cycles remained highly specialist, and could offer substantial rewards to small producers. Thus, the Saxon Cycle Engineering Company of London manufactured racing cycles which were 'better, faster and lighter' than those produced by larger producers.[65] There was also a specialist market for carrier cycles for the retail trade, and this offered a market for 'specifically designed' cycles for 'carrying goods'. During the inter-war years the James Cycle Company supplied thousands of shops and chain stores with these cycles, and they were manufactured from first class materials, and tailored to meet the variety of patterns and minor modifications that were required by customers. Craft built, utilising the company's '50 years experience', these cycles competed favourably with larger producers.[66]

The focus of specialist producers was upon quality and product diversity, rather than quantity and standardisation, a strategy summed up by the manufacturing slogan of the James Cycle Co.: 'Not how cheap but how good.' For much of the inter-war period James Cycles experienced little competition in the carrier market, and in 1937 *Bicycling News* claimed that there was a growing demand for these cycles and larger producers were no longer interested in competing at this end of the market. Although the trend in the industry was towards increasing scale, small firms continued to survive and prosper. Indeed, the emphasis on quality was not abandoned by some larger producers, and this impacted upon the strategies of production and marketing in large firms. Companies such as Raleigh, Humber and BSA continued to produce high-quality cycles, despite reductions in prices. As *Cycling* reported in 1932, referring to the policy of Hercules to increasingly concentrate on standardised lines, 'the keener type of rider searching for something daintier has gone to the small assembler rather than the mass producer', and they noted that the new range of models by BSA, Humber and Raleigh are counteracting the trend.[67]

The decision to maintain output at the quality end of the market could, of course, be fraught with difficulties. A clear case in point is the tensions which emerged in BSA from the 1920s, and the following section will concentrate on the experience of this company. The objectives set for BSA Cycles by the senior executives, Rogers and Eadie, in the 1920s were to focus on two product lines, bicycles and motor cycles, and to develop sales to large customers, notably government departments both in the UK and abroad. As Morley has argued, 'BSA's real successes during the 1920s and early 1930s came from supplying large numbers of machines to organisations that ordered in relatively high volumes'. In 1919 the Post Office provided BSA with a contract for 1 500 bicycles, and throughout the inter-war years it continued to be an important customer. In addition BSA cycles and motor cycles were also used in public services throughout the world. The Soviet Union, for example, became a major client, and in May 1924 the government placed an order for 1 000 cycles, followed in June by another order for 2 300. In 1925 the company received an order from the Soviet Union for 4 000 bicycles valued at £32 000.[68]

The second plank of the BSA strategy was to focus attention upon increasing motor cycle output. In 1919 the directors of the parent company were confident that the future lay with the motor cycle rather than the humble pedal cycle, and therefore the management of BSA Cycles were urged to allocate a large proportion of its research budget and manufacturing resources to the production of motor cycles. The result was that by 1924 the company was recognised as the leader in the motor cycle industry, manufacturing and selling a variety of models wider in range and much greater in number than any of its competitors. However, the company remained a very large producer of bicycles, and between 1920 and 1935 it approximately doubled its weekly output from 2 000 to 4 000 machines. Such quantities meant that BSA remained a major player in the bicycle market. This was just as well for, although the demand for motor cycles grew during the mid to late 1920s, in the great depression of 1930–32 the market for motor cycles, as we saw earlier, collapsed, and in an environment of financial stringency the public turned to the bicycle. BSA's success in establishing itself as the nation's leading motor cycle manufacturer did not bring the rewards it anticipated. Up until 1935 the market for motor cycles continued to contract and what BSA got for its dedicated investment in motor cycle research and production was an increasing share of a declining market.[69] The directors had underestimated the competition that would emerge from automobiles during the inter-war years and, just as importantly, the growth in the demand for pedal cycles. Fortunately BSA's twin-track strategy meant that its bicycle division was in a position to exploit the market opportunity offered by cycles, especially in terms of reducing prices in line with demand. Exploiting the market, however, was no easy task, and the company was now obstructed by its past association with producing cycles at the top end of the market. Consequently, BSA Cycles were faced with major problems in adapting its cycle range to a business environment whose distinguishing characteristic was limited purchasing power.

At the Olympia Exhibition in 1920 Rogers declared that the strategy of BSA Cycles would be based upon the production of bicycles that would strictly maintain the usual BSA guarantee of quality. He claimed that they wanted to offer the public a bicycle that was 'superior to any other bicycle on the market'. As the boom collapsed, and foreign competition drove prices downwards, the management of BSA Cycles began to question the wisdom of this strategy. The works manager, Bailey, informed Eadie and Rogers that BSA's high prices, *vis-à-vis* its competitors, were resulting in the cancellation of orders. He therefore requested that the company be allowed to put a cheaper lower-quality bicycle on the market. Rogers and Eadie were reluctant to accept this request, but eventually sanctioned Bailey to design a model that 'could be produced at substantially lower cost than the present models'. However, they were wary of chasing prices downwards, and they warned him that 'the BSA standard of workmanship must be maintained'. This severely constrained the extent to which Bailey could go down-market, but he did design a new 'gun finish bicycle', and he claimed that existing plant and equipment could be used to produce approximately 2 000 of these machines each week. Rogers, and particularly Eadie, were not at all comfortable with the launch of this new cycle, which they feared would damage the good name of the company. Indeed, once it had been designed Eadie expressed the opinion that the future of BSA Cycles lay in the opposite direction, and the company should focus upon the development of deluxe models. These would be supplied with three-speed gears and additional accessories which were previously sold as extras on standard machines.[70]

There was clearly a tension between the parent company and the management of the subsidiary as to the future direction of BSA Cycles. Bailey found that BSA Cycles could not manufacture the new gun finish model as cheaply as he had anticipated, and it finally retailed at £14 14s., a price that made the bicycle uncompetitive with those provided by other manufacturers, both domestic and foreign. From its inception BSA had focused upon the manufacture of high-quality products, and under the control of Rogers and Eadie the firm's excellent apprenticeship programme had built up a stock of well-trained skilled workers who were committed to the high quality of the company's products. In addition, it had developed stringent quality control tests which had made the progress of work through its factories slow. Writing in 1920 Bailey acknowledged that the technology, labour inputs and the organisation of work at BSA meant that the company found it difficult to compete with manufacturers at the cheaper end of the cycle market. BSA's pre-war profitability had been built upon product quality, and the directors were not convinced that changes in the business environment warranted a shift in their strategy, or indeed that they would be capable of change. In order to explore whether such change was feasible, and or desirable, they agreed to allow BSA Cycles to enter into an arrangement with the Hercules Cycle Co., under which Hercules manufactured a machine built to BSA specifications bearing the BSA trade mark, but with a distinguishing blue band. This arrangement appealed to the parent board, because it enabled BSA Cycles to distance itself from this cheaper article but test the argument that changes in the business environment required a move down-market.[71]

The Hercules-produced BSA cycle was known as the 'empire' model. As its name suggests, it was deliberately targeted at colonial markets where purchasing power was severely constrained. Hercules was able to produce this cycle at £7, a price considerably beneath anything that

BSA had achieved at that point, and it met with considerable success. It was this success that informed Eadie and Rogers decision to break finally with the past and allow BSA Cycles to begin manufacturing their own 'empire' models in 1925. Unfortunately, BSA was never able to meet the price level attained by Hercules, and Bailey left the company frustrated over the policy of senior executives in the organisation. In particular, he was adamant that the company had pursued the wrong policy, and by focusing on quality had neglected the market trend towards lower prices. As late as 1937 the board of the parent company was still debating the question, but they felt justified, through the company's long association with the quality bicycle, in reiterating the message that BSA 'could not build a cheap cycle in the same works together with the better article'. The compromise outcome was a decision to acquire a cycle firm that could be employed to produce cheaper machines, and during the Second World War BSA acquired an interest in Eadie, Ariel and New Hudson.[72]

The commitment of firms such as BSA to the traditional attributes of the cycle does not, however, indicate a failure on the part of British cycle firms, for as we shall see in the next chapter, Raleigh, who reduced prices and maintained quality, did successfully compete with mass producers such as Hercules. An examination of the profit record of the two companies in the 1930s (Tables C.2 in the Appendix and 5.5) shows that Raleigh outdistanced Hercules by a considerable margin in this period. Although Hercules adopted mass production technology and concentrated increasingly on standardised output, to meet the demand for lower priced cycles, it was still forced to acknowledge that quality was still central to success, and its standard models were 'subject to stringent metallurgical tests [which ensured] a degree of rigidity and strength that [enabled] the company to give 50 years guarantee with every cycle'. This allowed the company to push home its major selling point: 'It is an old notion that for an article to be the best, it must be the most expensive. Twenty-five years ago this may have been true, but today it is absolutely indefensible.'[73]

British cycle firms maintained their traditions for quality, and attempted to achieve and maintain price competitiveness by modernising plant and machinery. The use of automatic and semi-automatic machinery in the bicycle industry was stimulated by the demands of the First World War, and BSA Cycles, for example, made the 'fullest use of the skills which had been learned in the efficient mass-production of precision weapons'. BSA believed that cycle manufacturers should 'avail themselves to the full of what modern science could give in the way of mechanical solutions to engineering problems', and similar to other producers it invested heavily in automatic machinery. The increased use of automatic machinery was accompanied by an increased focus upon flow production technology, and manufacturers such as Raleigh and Hercules had installed conveyor belt systems by the late 1920s. Other cycle manufacturers employed industrial consultants to identify means of speeding up production. Lucas, for example, the cycle and motor cycle accessories manufacturer, employed consultants from the French Beddaux Company to implement a system of work organisation which was extensively adopted by the Birmingham engineering trades, and focused attention upon the elimination of unnecessary movements and operations. Of crucial importance to the development of mass production techniques, and the faster flow of throughputs was an increased focus upon standardisation. BSA cycles for example was able to provide cycle spares which fit 'precisely where it [was] intended without modification or lapping in'. Prior to the First World War, such interchangeability had been far less common.[74]

There were, however, limits to the adoption of mass-production techniques and standardisation. The cycle industry, like most other British industries, had traditionally been geared towards meeting the needs of 'highly differentiated regional markets both at home and abroad'.[75] Cycle firms manufactured a very wide range of models which would cater for all different classes of rider.[76] The need to produce a wide range of cycles mirrored the need to produce a wide range of cars in the British motor industry, a factor considered by Tolliday and Zeitlin. This resulted in British cycle and car firms adopting a similar compromise between batch and mass production. It was flexibility that mattered, and 'Production methods ... remained less rigid and capital intensive with more adaptable equipment ... and greater use of hand labour in assembly'.[77] The customers of the British cycle industry, at both home and abroad, demanded different models. The Australian cycle market, for example, demanded models with reversible handlebars. The mass production of a very narrow range of models was therefore inappropriate, competition continued to be by model and the finer details of design not simply by price. This is not to imply that price competition was not a major consideration, and leading firms were encouraged to focus their production methods on more basic models. Still, the need to maintain a wide range of patterns meant that mass production in British cycle firms was given a distinctly British flavour. Moreover, British firms were keen to ensure that all their bicycles received a sound rust-proof finish and they were prepared to slow production down to ensure this. They did, however, increasingly look to develop new processes that would improve the quality of the finish whilst at the same time speeding up this vital stage of production. Hercules, for example, pioneered the latest liquid presses and adopted the Coslet process in order to deliver a silver-polished rust-proofed finish on their bicycles. This process gave the best finish to cycles up until 1937, when Raleigh developed the Spa Bonderising technique, 'the most important advance since the introduction of the free wheel'.[78]

Innovation in processes and works organisation was mirrored by innovation in product design and finish. Fundamental product innovation was noticeable by its absence because, as the journal *Bicycling News* pointed out in 1937, the trade had reached a stage where 'design cannot be greatly changed except in detail and finish'.[79] Within these parameters, however, British firms were extremely innovative. This is perhaps not surprising, given that, according to Rosenberg, what British industry excelled at was 'sub- or improvement-innovations', that is, slight modifications to existing products and processes that would enable them to meet new customer needs.[80] The editorial for the 1924 Olympia Show, for example, commented upon the general increase in attention being given by cycle manufacturers to lightweight bicycles. These cycles incorporated a shorter wheel base and a more upright steering head, with 26-inch diameter wheels and tyres. Many firms also looked to improve their gears and lighting systems, and in 1937 Raleigh, whose policy was to be 'in the forefront of cycle manufacturing progress', developed the dyno hub. This gave, for the first time, a permanent lighting system which was costless to operate, had no moving parts and created no friction.[81]

The emphasis on novelty in design innovation was a strategy, which as we shall see, was highly successful at Raleigh. Further, the quality and design parameters of the British cycle had to be effectively communicated to the public. During the great bicycle boom of the 1890s marketing had placed an heavy emphasis on women cyclists. In the 1930s this still continued to be the case, and in 1934 Hercules claimed that the huge number of female cyclists was the outcome of their desire for 'freedom, action and adventure'. It added that 'they want to be out doors escaping from the monotony of pent up places and ordered routine. The bicycle is almost ideally the instrument of the modern girl [it] enables [her] to follow entirely her own ideas'. Indeed, it concluded that it was the cycle that had so 'emancipated women'. The bicycle was marketed as a fashionable product for women, and movie stars were increasingly used in bicycle advertisements. On the surface the message propagated by these advertisements was that cycling was a healthy and enjoyable pastime, but the sub-text suggested the product was a fashion item. This sub-text was reinforced by the growing popularity of fashion clothing that was specifically designed for the cyclist who 'wants to be noticed'. The Hercules promotion campaign, for example, emphasised that women's cycling shorts had diffused into other sports, such as tennis, and freed women from more traditional and cumbersome clothing.[82]

Not all were convinced by the notion of the bicycle as a fashion item, and *The Economist* was concerned that fashions have the habit of both coming and going, and argued that the burgeoning demand for cycles 'must inevitably suggest the risk of a "craze" which will pass'. It dwelled on questions such as how long 'expansion' demand could be expected to continue, and how far it would ultimately be maintained by replacement demand. These were questions which it found exceedingly difficult to answer. Nevertheless, it concluded in the mid-1930s that the leading bicycle manufacturers appeared to offer a sound investment opening. Two major factors informed this conclusion. First, the recognition that cycling would always provide an effective means of exercise and recreation, and therefore this facet of demand was of a 'permanent rather than a ephemeral character'. Second, the growing export of British cycles which we have already discussed. But there were lurking dangers on the horizon, and by the mid-1930s there was a 'growing trade menace' in the shape of Japan, which became a major player in the manufacture of bicycles. From 1929 to 1934, Japanese bicycle exports, which retailed at one-seventh of the price of Coventry cycles, increased in value from £56 000 per annum to £353 000 per annum. Such an increase did not go unnoticed, indeed it caused some disquiet amongst the business élites in the Midlands. However, the response of manufacturers to this threat varied. A very few manufacturers sought to compete with this new threat by reducing product quality and in 1937 *Bicycling News* could argue that 'in recent years the finish of some British cycles' has 'left much to be desired'. Instead of applying a copper-nickel, copper-chrome finish, it argued some manufacturers had deposited chromium on the raw material with the inevitable result that it soon rusted. Moreover, it alleged that in certain instances instead of several coats of enamel being applied to bicycles 'no more than two were given in order to cut costs and fight off Japanese competition'. Nevertheless, most manufacturers, though disturbed by the emergence of Japanese competition, were confident that since 'Japanese exports were competitive with British products in price rather than quality ... no lasting danger existed from this source'.[83]

Cycle firms had to be alive to the challenges of the inter-war years, and a failure to exploit new technology, maintain quality and innovate in marketing could inevitably lead to failure. A classic case in point was the long-established firm of Rudge-Whitworth, one of the pioneers of the British cycle industry, and we will conclude this chapter by a brief examination of its demise. The decline of this well-respected firm in the depression of 1929–32 sent shock waves throughout the industry. According to Reynolds, the story of this firm's decline was 'one of missed opportunities and no small amount of bad luck',[84] but we will argue that it could have been avoided had the company pursued a business strategy that was more appropriate to the scale of its operations, and the shifts in the business environment. During the inter-war years, as Table C.3 in the Appendix shows, Rudge-Whitworth sold far more bicycles than motor cycles. However, under the direction of its managing director, John Vernon Pugh, who had succeeded his father in 1921, the directors of the company spent considerable sums of money on the research and development of motor cycles with a very limited market. In what can only be described as a bizarre decision, the management spent much time and effort in developing motor cycle sidecars which were 'water-worthy canoes'. The directors argued that these sidecars gave 'the river man a new mobility', in that he could travel by motor cycle and then traverse water with his adaptable sidecar.[85] Not surprisingly the demand for such products was not great, and research and development on such niche products was a misallocation of scarce resources for a company of Rudge-Whitworth's size and low profits (see Table C.2 in the Appendix). Also mistaken was the commitment of the company towards cycles such as the Aero Special, which were designed for racing rather than utility or recreation. The Rudge-Whitworth organisation may have enjoyed an enviable reputation for its successes in cycle and motor cycle races throughout the world, but its failure to cater for more standard models by the early 1930s put the company under increasing pressure.[86]

As early as 1924 the managing director had recognised that they were not selling enough cycles and motor cycles to carry the heavy overheads associated with research and development but there was no fundamental shift in strategy until it was too late, and as the market for motor cycles crashed in 1930 so to did the company's profits. In 1932 John Vernon Pugh was forced to put the company into voluntary liquidation, and an advisory committee, consisting of the company's bankers, accountants and suppliers, was put in place to devise a rescue package.[87] This committee reported a damning indictment of past managerial failure in 1933:

> The records and financial history of the Company show that it possesses a large volume of business, and that its name and repute are valuable assets. It suffers from lack of up-to-date methods, noticeably an adequate costing system; its Coventry factories are old-fashioned: at least one of its … main lines of manufacture [motor cycles] should have been abandoned several years ago: and the administration and commercial management of the concern requires strengthening.[88]

The advisory committee also noted that there had been a substantial underinvestment in advertising cycles, while resources had been directed to promoting motor cycle sales which had not even covered the costs of advertising (see Table C.3 in the Appendix). The company was reorganised under a new managerial team, streamlining of production introduced, and £6 000 spent on bringing plant up to date. This was an inconsequential sum, and from 1932 to 1935 the company continued to operate at a loss. In 1936 Rudge-Whitworth was acquired by the Gramophone Company, a somewhat strange purchase which was explained as an attempt to acquire the 'summer trade' of a cycle company to counter the seasonal fall in trade in electrical products such as gramophones. This take-over meant new management were installed, the plant in Coventry was dismantled and removed to Hayes in Middlesex, and finally the company ceased to produce specialist motor cycles.[89] Rudge-Whitworth was eventually acquired by the Raleigh Cycle Co. in 1943 and, as we shall see in the next chapter, the failure of Rudge-Whitworth to meet the challenges of the inter-war years stands in marked contrast to the initiatives of the Raleigh management during this period.

In summary, the bicycle industry overall emerges from the inter-war years with some merit. Product and process innovations were accompanied by aggressive marketing in both domestic and colonial markets, and the industry clearly beat off continental challengers. The spectre of Japanese competition did emerge during the 1930s, but with most of the leading producers remaining wedded to a quality product the industry played its part in what was a relatively robust British economic recovery. In addition, despite the considerable structural change which the inter-war depression inevitably brought, the personal capitalism form of organisation persisted, and continued to allow the leading firms to exploit the 'golden age' of cycling. No more so was this the case than at Raleigh, to which we now turn our attentions.

Notes

1. Bowden, Manuscript, p. 35.
2. For a discussion of these general trends towards larger scale in British business see Hannah, 1976, pp. 179–84; Wilson, 1995, ch. 5.
3. As Jeremy, 1998, p. 209 argues, in the 1930s 'business opinion shifted ... away from ideas of rationalisation and merger towards collective agreements and cartels as the best way of restricting competition and holding up prices and profits'.
4. Millward, 1989, p. 175.
5. For a general account of the impact of the war on the British economy see Millward, 1972.
6. BSA Bicycles Trade Catalogue, 1919, p. 2.; BSA Group News, no. 17, June 1961, p. 12; Ryerson, 1980, pp. 42, 68.; Bowden, 1975, pp. 39–42; Millward, 1989, p. 175.

7. DDRN 1/29/22, Annual Reports and Balance Sheets of Rudge-Whitworth, 31 July 1916, 29 October 1917, 18 November 1918; DDRN 1/35, Coventry Premier Ltd, Directors' Report and Balance Sheet, 31 July 1917.
8. Millward, 1989, p. 175.
9. Coventry Premier, Directors' Report, 31 July 1917.
10. *The Economist*, 11 October 1919, p. 587.
11. DDRN 1/36, Jane Cycle Co. Ltd, Directors' Report and Balance Sheet, 31 July 1918. The reference to 'Imperial' taxation is an interesting one, and clearly refers to the expectations of cycle manufacturers in restoring key markets abroad in the Empire.
12. Ibid.
13. Bowden, 1975, p. 42; Rudge-Whitworth Annual Reports, 20 November 1919.
14. Solihull Record Office, BSA collection, BSA 20, p. 16. For example Redditch Council increased electricity prices to BSA by 15 per cent in 1920.
15. Ibid., pp. 20, 26, 37–44; *The Economist*, 11 October 1919, 7 February 1920. As we shall see in the next chapter, at Raleigh the labour strategy of the company was premised upon a managerial philosophy of co-operation which, as the depression of 1920–21 took hold, worked well.
16. *Labour Gazette*, April 1921, p. 202; BSA 21, p. 85.
17. *The Economist*, 11 October 1919, p. 586, 6 November 1920, p. 839; *Bicycling News and Motor Cycle Review*, 14 April 1920; BSA 20, pp. 31, 40, 51.
18. *Motor Cycle and Cycle Trader*, 14 April 1922; DDRN 1/2/1–6, Raleigh Cycle Co. Ltd, Board and General Meetings Minutes with Fortnightly Reports, 23 March, 16 April 1921; *Aberdeen Evening Express*, 30 October 1921.
19. Barnsdale 1922; *Motor Cycle and Cycle Trader*, 14 April 1922; *Bicycling News and Motor Cycle Review*, 25 February 1920.
20. For an examination of the tariff debate in the British motor car industry see Church, 1995, pp. 13–16. For a general discussion of the tariff question in the inter-war years see Marrison, 1996; Capie, 1983.
21. *The Economist*, 7 February 1920.
22. See Peden, 1988, p. 8. There is some debate on the 10 per cent overvaluation figure; see Aldcroft, 1986, pp. 32–3.
23. Watling, 1937.
24. For example, imports of cycles increased from £217 000 in 1909–13 to £293 000 in 1919–23, and in the single year of 1924 to £343 000. *The Economist*, 16 May 1925, p. 956.
25. Ibid.
26. See Donnelly, Batchelor and Morris, 1995.
27. *The Economist*, 1 December 1923, pp. 955–6. See also *The Economist*, 10 May 1924, p. 945.
28. Broadberry, 1986, p. 67.
29. See *Irish Times*, 15 February 1932.
30. *Bicycling News*, 18 March 1934.
31. *The Economist*, 30 November 1935, p. 1060; *Bicycling News*, 1 July 1937.
32. *The Economist*, 30 November 1935, p. 1059, 8 December 1934, p. 701; *Bicycling News*, 8 July 1937.

33. *The Economist*, 30 November 1935, p. 1060, 12 January 1935, p. 121; *Motor Cycle and Cycle Export Trader*, 16 February 1934. For a discussion of the development of consumerism in the inter-war years see Bowden, 1994.
34. *The Times*, 11 October 1934.
35. *The Economist*, 12 January 1935, p. 121, 3 November 1934, p. 837; Beeley, 1992, p. 99; *Motor Cycle and Cycle Trader*, 10 January 1936.
36. Millward, 1989, p. 171; *Hercules Cycle Magazine*, 1934, p. 28; *The Economist*, 3 November 1934, p. 387; *Bicycling News*, 1 July 1937.
37. Bowden, 1934.
38. Florence Sargent, 1933, pp. 24, 87–9, 116.
39. *The Economist*, 30 November 1935, p. 1060.
40. *Bicycling News*, 9 September 1937; Millward, 1989, p. 175; Beeley, 1992, p. 99.
41. Millward, 1989, p. 175.
42. Hannah, 1976, pp. 92–100; Wilson, 1995, p. 133; Jeremy, 1998, pp. 206–9.
43. DDRN 7/3/3, September Story: A History of Hercules.
44. *The Economist*, 2 February 1937, p. 379, 11 February 1937, p. 259; Bowden, 1975 p. 50.
45. See Wilson, 1995, p. 116.
46. BSA 619, Notes of Parent Board Meeting of BSA, 12 January 1937.
47. Briggs, 1952, pp. 296–8.
48. BSA 1244, Tubing and Tubular Parts for Cycles 1920, as Produced by Accles and Pollock Ltd, pp. 1–2, 24.
49. Lazerson, 1988.
50. DDRN 1/18/1, Director's Minute Book of J. A. Phillips & Co., 14 February, 17 March 1922.
51. *The Economist*, 18 October 1930, p. 723, 29 November 1930, p. 1020, 5 December 1936, p. 490; Hannah, 1976, p. 199; Jeremy, 1998, p. 203. On acquiring Stewarts and Lloyds the 'modus operandi' was a 'fusion of interest', TI concentrating on the finishing end of the business by the production of 'precision or highly manipulated tubes' supplied by the newly acquired company. The two companies, however, retained their 'separate identity', the deal allowing for 'permanent liaison'. *The Economist*, 18 October 1930, p. 723.
52. Philips's Minute Book, 3 March 1931, 25 November 1935.
53. *Bicycling News*, 30 January 1929; *Hercules Cycle Magazine*, 1934, p. 4.; *The Economist*, 2 February 1935, p. 259.
54. *The Economist*, 11 October 1919, p. 586.
55. Ibid.
56. *Motor Cycle and Cycle Trader*, 14 September 1934.
57. See Tweedale, 1995.
58. *The Times*, 2 November 1938; *The Economist*, 11 May 1929, p. 1079.
59. *Motor Cycle and Cycle Trader*, 17 June 1932; BSA 22, Minute Book, 24 July 1925, 20 April 1923, 22 September 1927.
60. Kirby, 1992, pp. 644–5. It is estimated that by 1943, 60 per cent of Britain's manufacturing output may have been 'subject to restrictive agreements'.
61. Broadberry and Crafts, 1990, have argued that family firms often sheltered 'from hostile take over' through membership of trade associations.

62. BSA 22, 25 November 1927.
63. *The Economist*, 30 November 1935, p. 1060.
64. Soltow, 1980, p. 195.
65. *Cyclist*, 3 November 1925.
66. DDRN/25, 1930 Advert for James Carrier Bicycles and Tricycles.
67. Ibid.; *Bicycling News*, 29 July 1937; *Cycling*, 28 August 1932.
68. Morley, 1991, p. 16; BSA 22.
69. Ryerson, 1980, p. 46; BSA 20, pp. 52, 53, 55; BSA 619, Management Minutes, 13 November 1935.
70. *The Economist*, 6 November 1920, p. 840; BSA 21, 30 July, 21, 15 October 1920, 21 March 1921.
71. BSA 21, November 1920; BSA 22, 26 September 1924; BSA 20, p. 52; BSA 1242, How BSA Bicycles Are Made, 1920.
72. BSA 22, 24 July 1925; BSA 619, Notes of a Board Meeting, 29 November 1938; Morley, 1991, p. 17.
73. *Hercules News*, 1934, p. 4.
74. Millward, 1989, pp. 173–5; Ryerson, 1980, pp. 26, 41; *The Economist*, 3 May 1924, p. 930; Briggs, 1952, p. 282; BSA 1989, The People's Century: Birmingham 1889–1989, p. 25.
75. See Piore and Sabel, 1984, p. 29.
76. *Cyclist*, 8 March 1939.
77. Tolliday and Zeitlin, 1986, p. 3.
78. *Cyclist*, 8 March 1939; *Bicycling News*, 2, 9 September 1937; Tolliday, 1986, pp. 37–40; *Hercules Cycle Magazine*, 1934, p. 4.
79. *Bicycling News*, 16 September 1937.
80. Rosenberg, 1994, pp. 14–15.
81. Beeley, 1992, pp. 99–100; *Bicycling News*, 22 September 1937.
82. *Hercules Cycle Magazine*, 1934, p. 28.
83. *The Economist*, 3 November 1934, p. 837, 12 January 1935, p. 121, 30 November 1935, p. 1060; *Bicycling News*, 1 July, 16 September 1937.
84. Reynolds, 1977, preface.
85. *The Economist*, 3 January 1925, p. 29.
86. DDRN 1/44, Report and Recommendations of the Investigating Committee of Rudge-Whitworth, 6 February 1933.
87. *The Economist*, 3 January 1925, p. 29; DDRN 1/44, Circular from Investigators' Committee of Rudge-Whitworth, 20 March 1933.
88. Report and Recommendations of Investigating Committee.
89. DDRN 7/3/8, Special Binder – Rudge-Whitworth Ltd and its Acquisition by the Raleigh Cycle Co. Ltd.

CHAPTER FIVE

From father to son: Harold Bowden and entrepreneurial 'optimisim' at Raleigh, 1914–39

'Any industry was the creation of a mind. Some men remained employees all their lives; others like Lord Nuffield, the late Lord Leverhulme, or Sir Herbert Austin, created work for thousands.' This endorsement of the virtues of individual leadership in industry was made by Sir Harold Bowden in 1934. Bowden claimed that there were four key factors accounting for business success: 'The Four Ms of industry – men, management, machinery and money.' The key factor for Bowden was the individual talents of leading figures in the company who created the 'organisation' and directed strategic decision-making.[1] Harold had been the leading figure at Raleigh since 1916 when he was appointed, with his father, joint managing director. With the death of Frank Bowden in 1921 he was to assume direct personal control, and to lead Raleigh through the difficult times of the inter-war depression. Raleigh not only survived, but achieved considerable business success. Such was the resurgence of profits after 1932 that the company was incorporated as a public holding company, the Raleigh Cycle Holding Co. Ltd in 1934, with Harold Bowden as chairman and managing director. Harold retired as managing director in 1938 (but remained as chairman) to be replaced by George Wilson, a long-serving company man who had been groomed for the job. In 1937 Raleigh celebrated its jubilee, and the management could look back with satisfaction on the company's progress during the previous two decades, and its rise to become one of the leading cycle manufacturers in the world.

As Roy Church claims, a 'family controlled enterprise ... refers to a firm in which the founders and their heirs recruited salaried managers but continued to be influential shareholders, held executive managerial positions, and exercised decisive influence on company policy'. Founding entrepreneurs, and their successors, can shape 'not only the structure of the organisation but the character of relations among those employed, and explicitly or implicitly establish the images, symbols, and ritual associated with the firm's activities'.[2] This chapter will examine Bowden's managerial philosophy as the company struggled to respond to the depressed economic climate after 1920, and will demonstrate

5.1   Photograph of Sir Harold Bowden, *c.* 1931. Photograph from the Raleigh
Archive, reproduced courtesy of Nottingham County Archive.

how his personal leadership was central to business survival and success. Bowden's management philosophy was influenced by the values
passed down from his father, in particular the premise that business
success was based on the retention of the company's core value of
quality output. Bowden's continued optimism in the cycle market was a

key factor in Raleigh's survival and prosperity, but he also launched the company on a strategy of diversification into motorised transport after the war, a policy which was deemed essential given the problems in the bicycle market in the early 1920s. Product diversification, however, was abandoned in the mid-1930s as Bowden redirected the company back to its core product, the bicycle, a decision which was to have long-term implications for Raleigh in the 1950s and 1960s. To begin our analysis of Raleigh's business strategy in the inter-war years the next section examines the impact of the First World War on the company, and the problems of readjustment in the post-war inflationary boom to 1920.

War and readjustment, 1914–1920

The immediate effect of the war was to give a significant boost to Raleigh sales. In September 1914 the government contracted for several thousand cycles, and due to shortages of petrol a large number of motorists returned to bicycles for economy. Responding to demand, Raleigh introduced a number of new models, including a special model for the police force, priced at £7 10s. and the 'Scout' and 'Military' models priced at £8 10s. and £6 10s. respectively. Raleigh continued to produce large numbers of cycles until the end of 1915, selling 40 803 quality cycles during that year alone despite 75 per cent of the factory and its workforce being concentrated on munitions production. As the management commented, 'It is a remarkable fact that while several firms manufacturing lower priced bicycles ... during the last two or three years found themselves in difficulties owing to the falling off in ... demand ... the Raleigh Company has, notwithstanding the price of its cheapest machines, shown a rapidly increasing demand for them'. At the end of 1915 Raleigh's model range was streamlined, the company concentrating on the most popular lines, and women were increasingly employed due to shortages of male workers. By this time the pressures of war demands were impacting upon their cycle business, and they were forced to abandon the production of Sturmey-Archer gears because the plant and machinery were exclusively engaged in war work.[3]

Raleigh contributed to the war by supplying shell fuses and cases and magazine pans for the Lewis machine gun. At the end of 1914 Frank Bowden made the patriotic gesture of volunteering the company for war work, as he firmly believed that the war would be one of attrition. In 1915 he was made a baronet for his services to the nation. To increase munitions output the management made large investments in extending plant and machinery, especially after 1916 when war demands intensified. Through introducing automatic machines the production of fuses was substantially increased, and the management found that their existing machinery for bicycle component manufacture was ideally adaptable to the manufacture of munitions. Automatic machinery in the Sturmey-Archer department was converted for the mass production of fuses, and giant presses for stamping parts from sheet steel were converted for the manufacture of magazine pans for machine guns. Technology at Raleigh was flexible, and the management believed that investments in munitions work could provide a stock of equipment which could be quickly reconverted to cycle-making after the war. In 1915 Raleigh had employed 2 000 workers, but by the close of hostilities the workforce had increased to 5 000, making it one of the largest munitions manufacturers in the country, and potentially one of the largest cycle producers in the world. Its potential cycle output in 1918 was 50 per cent greater than in 1914.[4]

As Table 5.1 shows net profits fell slightly in 1915, accounting for only 9.14 per cent of total sales, and this was due to the transition of the company's plant to full war production. During that year munitions production was constrained as the factory was converted, and in 1916 the management invested an additional £13 245 in new plant together with £5 554 in purchasing land for expansion. The company continued to sell cycles after 1915, and they also produced motor hubs for the trade, but it was munitions which accounted for the bulk of sales, and the company received generous government contracts. At the peak of munitions sales in 1917, Raleigh sold a total of £829 098 (Table 5.2), and profits had also risen to £251 362, or 21.27 per cent of total sales. Profits for the Bowdens escalated during the war, and dividends rose from 20 per cent in 1916 to 35.7 per cent in 1917 and 33.3 per cent in 1918. The owners received a total of £212 095 in dividend payments between 1916 and 1918, and the financial outlook for the company

Table 5.1   Net profits and as percentage on sales, Raleigh, 1914–1918

	£	% of sales
1914	49 512	14.32
1915	40 127	9.14
1916	191 075[a]	19.67
1917	251 362	21.27
1918	151 740	13.77

Notes: [a] Profits after 1916 subject to reductions for munitions levy and excess profits tax.

Source: DDRN 1/40/5–8, Auditors Reports and Balance Sheets, 1914–18.

Table 5.2   Sales on Raleigh trading account, 1915–18 (£)

	1915	1916	1917	1918
Raleigh Cycle Co.	78 223	108 855	71 780	78 227
Robin Hood cycles	33 935	26 175		
Easy payment	5 833	3 530	3 385	149
Motor hubs	53 064	57 030	83 244[a]	73 662
Sturmey-Archer gears	25 262	986	498	155
Munitions	75 830	632 761	829 098	748 114
Consignments	392 403	93 511	98 311	125 353

Notes: [a] Also now including the sale of countershaft gears.

Source: DDRN 3/1/3, Accounts Journal.

looked increasingly promising as large sums were also accumulated in capital reserves.[5]

During the war strategic management at Raleigh rested in the hands of a small group of directors, headed by the Bowdens. In 1915 Frank secured the family succession by registering Raleigh as a private limited company, and the newly incorporated business started with a capital of 240 000 £1 shares divided equally between father and son. Succession was secured by agreements giving Harold the right on the death of his father to purchase his shares for a nominal payment of £50 000.[6] In early 1916 he became joint managing director, and in 1918, with failing health, Frank retired from this position, though remained chairman until his death in 1921. The family directors were supported on the board by two co-directors, the long-serving Joseph Lazonby, and a Nottingham solicitor, Douglas McCraith. Operational management was devolved to Harry H. Monks, general manager, and W. H. Raven, works manager[7] (for a profile of key management figures at Raleigh, 1914–39, see Table D.1 in the Appendix). By October 1917 the directors were already considering plans for post-war reconstruction, and despite rising profits there was considerable concern over the future prospects of the company. In particular Harold felt that government policy was sending the wrong messages to business, and he condemned their action in allowing a continuous rise of wages while at the same time reducing the prices on the renewal of munitions contracts.[8] With the spectre of wage-cost inflation facing them, and with rising overheads as munitions orders fell, Harold pessimistically concluded that

It is ... obvious that we shall have the greatest difficulty in even making pre-war standard profits. Our financial position c.c. the Bank Balance today is the same as it was on July 25th, three

months ago, so that apparently no available profits have been
realised for this considerable period – a great contrast to a year or
two years ago.

Central to Harold's thinking was the need to return Raleigh rapidly to
its core activity of cycles, 'the most remunerative Department at present
time', and to discontinue munitions production as soon as possible.[9]

Harold's forecast was correct, and profits fell sharply in 1918 (Table
5.1). In 1917 there had been rumours in the trade that Raleigh would
be forced to abandon the manufacture of bicycles, an allegation vigorously denied by Frank. He informed the trade that 'cycles are our
standard ... and that in the main our agent's living depends on it'.
Acting quickly, Frank approached the Ministry of Supply in early 1918
for permission to import key materials from the USA to ensure a quick
return to cycle production, and to avoid laying off workers. This was a
sign of forward thinking, and the management also planned to diversify
into motor cycles, which they saw as a profitable new market after the
war. Experiments with motor cycles began in 1916, and they also
designed a prototype Sturmey-Archer two-speed countershaft gearbox
for light motor cycles, complete with a kick-start mechanism and anti-
backfiring device. In May 1918 Raleigh announced its intention to
manufacture a 5 hp machine with twin cylinders and a Sturmey-Archer
three-speed gearbox. The increase in the output potential of the concern, and the introduction of sophisticated machinery, persuaded the
Bowdens that there was a need to utilise the plant fully to produce a
variety of products, as well as to expand the production of bicycles.[10]
Management's outlook was again optimistic, but reconstruction in the
climate of the post-war boom proved more difficult than expected.
Their ambitions were frustrated by two main factors, one relating to
labour relations, and the other to the problems of contracting out for
material and component supplies.

The demands of the war for full-time operations entailed heavy depreciation of machinery, and re-equipping the factory was an immediate
priority. Labour issues immediately arose as delays in re-equipping
occurred because of the slow pace of work. Attempts to introduce more
rigid supervision culminated in a strike by moulders in September 1919.
This event was an example of deep-rooted labour problems, and there
were particular difficulties in implementing systems of piece rates which
Frank Bowden saw as essential to increase work effort. In July 1919 the
decision was taken to accelerate the move back to piece rates, and this
was accepted by the shop stewards' committee who commented that
they should return to the pre-war situation where only 25 per cent of
workers were on day rates. They further agreed to meet the management 'half way' and 'to consider any case in which they thought piece

rates were extortionate'. This seemed to signal a co-operative attitude, but the AEU, despite Raleigh granting an advance in rates by 20 per cent for frame-makers, buffers and glaziers, continued to hold out, and the full return to the piece system was still in abeyance in November. Limited progress was also due to the practice of personal negotiation with various segments of the workforce, and thus the management's policy was implemented piecemeal. For example, charge hands applied for a minimum wage in September, and were persuaded to accept piece rates on the basis that they would be set at a 'suitable minimum'.[11] Labour held the upper hand at Raleigh, and this reflected the general increase in union power during the war, especially in the engineering industries.[12] The outcome of this was an 'alarming' increase in wages from 1918 to 1920.[13]

There was no attempt at Raleigh to introduce Fordist labour principals involving a high degree of supervisory control over the workforce.[14] Piece rates were merely assumed by management to be the best method of obtaining increased effort, and this was central to their ambitions to expand output. Indeed, labour disputes constrained their strategy of output expansion, and there were serious stoppages at the factory. Sturmey-Archer gear production was curtailed in March 1919 at a time when an order was secured from Triumph for 4 200 gear cases. This stoppage resulted from a demand by turners to maintain day rates, and to receive higher wages, and although the stoppage was brief this action 'meant that output targets for gears and cycles had not been met' by April. According to Frank and Harold, on their regular factory inspections, work effort and morale were low, and this was related to inadequate supervision by foremen. Restrictive practices also frustrated the management. Thus, Harold enquired why machine operators in the turning shops 'were idle for long periods, and why one man could not work 2 machines'? Raven replied that the 'Trade Unions strongly opposed the idea'. Key groups of workers in the factory also had the ability to determine conditions. For example, by August 1919 the management were desperately attempting to start producing motor cycles, and new piece rates were applied to all departments with the exception of motor cycles who would be paid on day work, and supervised by foremen and not charge-hands.[15] The labour issue in the factory led to both rising costs and restricted output, and the problem of raising output levels was compounded by external supply problems.

Throughout 1919 there were shortages of supplies of sheet steel, pedals, hubs, disks for countershaft gears, and mudguards. This was partly due to internal limitations, the factory lacking the capability to manufacture materials and components on a large enough scale, forcing Raleigh to rely on numerous outside suppliers. For instance, the company had no plant installed for producing pedals and mudguards, and delays in procuring supplies outside held back the production of cycles. The damage of this to Raleigh's sales position was demonstrated by the decision of the management to turn down a lucrative order to supply 4 000 cycles to the Post Office in June 1919.[16] Further, in the production of countershaft gears the demand was greater than the supply due to continuous delays in component supplies.[17] With domestic shortages, Raleigh turned to importing supplies of gear hubs, ball bearings and spokes from the USA, but on testing these were found to be of unsatisfactory quality. There were also serious problems in acquiring nuts and screws, specially cut to gauge for Raleigh's requirements, and supplies received from Whitworth's of Birmingham were unsuitable, and also had escalated in price since 1914.[18] Raleigh was clearly caught in a situation of escalating transaction costs as its plant was not fully integrated to produce sufficient supplies of components internally, and given the general shortages affecting British industry after the war, and rising costs, their transaction cost problems were intensified. Indeed, the continuation of the company's commitment to top-range cycles worsened the transaction cost problems. For example, by May 1919 Raleigh was producing 900 cycles per week and had 13 000 current orders on the books, 20 per cent of which were for high-grade models. Consequently it was decided to concentrate the limited output on quality machines, but as Raven pointed out these machines demanded high-quality components which were in short supply, and thus 'the finishing of these machines hindered output generally'. Raleigh was, however, reacting to positive market signals, and there was a rising demand for higher-grade machines which could command high prices, and thus by December there was a further priority given to these machines.[19]

Responding positively to these constraints, the management commissioned a new machine shop for manufacturing gear hubs, and a plant for producing specialist screws and nuts and bolts. They also installed plant to produce mudguards, sanctioned an investment of £5 000 for a modernised department for manufacturing wheels and three-speed gears, and purchased additional machinery for raising the processing of steel tubing by 50 per cent, the latter being imported from Germany together with increasing imports of steel. Perhaps most importantly, the management were determined to diversify into motor cycle production, which had been delayed due to the capacity constraints of the factory. As Raven argued, agents 'were very anxious to have particulars of our programme and ... promised substantial support'. Consequently, in November 1919 the management decided to build a large factory extension to house a specialist department for the production of motor cycles and countershaft gears.[20] This was an ambitious long-term strategy for expansion, but in the short run the company still faced difficulties in acquiring plant for its policy of internalising component production. For example, in April 1919 the management sanctioned an expenditure of £13 776 on new machinery for motor cycle production, but by June this had still not been ordered because they assumed that prices for US machine tools would fall, and they were subsequently awaiting the outcome.[21] However, as government planning controls were abandoned after the war the policy of 'business as usual' created a chaotic situation,[22] and thus paradoxically the end of government planning made business planning more difficult. Thus, Raleigh's attempts to internalise production by importing machinery from the USA was curtailed because of unfavourable exchange rates, and they were forced to resort to buying second-hand machinery disposed of by the Ministry of Munitions. In December Raleigh imported new Cincinnati Milling machines, despite the unfavourable rate of exchange, noting that this was a one-off purchase given the high cost of importation.[23]

The scheme for reconstruction, involving the build-up of capacity and diversification, was clearly constrained, and given the difficulties of the business environment in the immediate post-war era it is difficult not to conclude that the management's strategy was somewhat overambitious. A target of 1 000 cycles per week had been set for March 1919 but this was only barely achieved by July, and its ambitions to enter the motor cycle market were delayed until September, when three machines were prepared for the National Motor Show, and 1 000 sets of parts were ordered allowing a limited output of 20 per week. Nevertheless, the management entered 1920 in a mood of optimism which reflected a general belief in rising demand for their products, the company predicting that sales would top 100 000 cycles during the year, despite the fact that rising costs had pushed prices up to record levels, machines selling at over £20. 'There is going to be a boom ... a big boom in cycling', echoed the trade press, both in domestic and foreign markets. Responding to this general impression Raleigh extended and modernised, and in early 1920 large orders for cycles and gears flooded in. New milling and drilling machines, costing £8 743, were installed and by mid-1920 a steady output of 2 000 machines per week had been achieved, although this was still insufficient to meet demand. In April the company began to turn out larger numbers of motor cycles, and appointed H. R. Holland from BSA as departmental manager.[24] However, as Raleigh prepared to expand its capacity further, the short boom gave way to a severe economic downturn and the management was faced with a severe crisis. By July 1920 there was a 'general slackness in the cycle trade', and by September the company was 'carrying an enormous stock of rough partly finished and finished goods, which coupled with a marked fall in the number of orders lately received, threatened a considerable strain on the Company's finances'. This outcome was the consequence of accumulating stocks of materials in early 1920 in anticipation of shortages and rising prices, and finished cycle stocks had also been accumulated to meet expected rising demand during the 1921 season.[25]

Falling demand brought the inevitable reaction. Output was cut as a consequence of high wage costs, rising material prices, and the escalating running costs of the factory as turnover fell. Cycle production fell from 2 000 to 1 000 per week in July with an adverse effect on overhead costs. With a continued fall in the market 400 workers were temporarily laid off in September, and Frank vetoed an earlier decision to invest £20 000 in a new stamping plant for countershaft gears. Retrenchment was the order of the day, and Raleigh's plight was worsened by intensified price competition as demand fell. For example, Major J. D. Barnsdale, appointed as a director in 1919, noted that low prices were being offered by BSA for their gears, and urged that Raleigh would have to follow if they wished to 'take a percentage of their business.' In October 1920 the management was forced to reduce cycle prices by 10 per cent, which brought forth an increasing urgency to introduce economies in production.[26] The need for economy is indicated in Table D.4 in the Appendix. Prime costs as a proportion of sales rose between 1914 and 1915, as the factory was converted to munitions production, but fell in the next two years as output and sales expanded rapidly. However, in 1918 prime costs rose as labour and material costs increased, and by 1920 had reached 61.53 per cent of total sales and consignments. In particular, productive wages increased, rising from 24.52 per cent in 1918 to 28.20 per cent by 1920, and factory running charges rose from 20.42 per cent to 21.60 per cent during the same period. Although 1918 sales levels were maintained in 1920 the gross profits on the factory were clearly lower.

With turnover dropping to uneconomic levels, the issue of payments to labour became a priority. As Frank pointed out in October 1920, Raleigh's overheads were out of all proportion to the productive wages being paid, and non-productive wages, which included payments to foremen, charge-hands and office workers, had risen rapidly.[27] As we have seen, Raleigh was in a weak position in labour bargaining after the war, but there was also a managerial philosophy operating which determined that labour matters could be solved by co-operation.[28] Thus Frank argued that the company could weather the depression through co-operation with labour, and he would personally talk to the men and instil in them the need to reduce costs and increase production.[29] Initially this proved a forlorn hope, as labour resisted a 15 per cent reduction of piece rates in countershaft gears in December, and only accepted following the threat of a shutdown.[30] As the crisis hit Harold Bowden was to take direct control over Raleigh's fortunes, and to set an ambitious strategy for meeting the challenge of the depression. Before exploring Raleigh's strategy in detail we need to set the context by examining Harold's business philosophy, and its implications for Raleigh.

A philosophy of optimism: Harold Bowden leads the way

In April 1921 Frank Bowden died aged 74. The reins of control passed to the now Sir Harold Bowden who received half the shares in the company, the remainder being divided between Frank's sister and his grandson. Raleigh, in the words of F. C. Bush the general manager, was a lasting 'monument to his [Frank's] memory', and under Harold's guidance he hoped 'the company would continue to hold and enhance its proud position'. Harold had no doubts about the seriousness of the task that faced him:

> He was called upon to take control of the company's affairs at a most difficult time [but] aided by the willing and unselfish services of all members of the staff he would be able to steer the company safely through the storm of depression which is now passing over the country.

Earlier in January Harold had informed the board that there was an urgent need to reorganise the factories, and warned that they were facing serious financial difficulties following heavy payments for labour and materials. Harold's immediate priority was survival, and he urged rigid economy in every direction, especially targeting wages, which 'should be reduced to the lowest minimum'.[31] This seemed to be a continuation of the policy of retrenchment, but Harold determined that Raleigh should take the lead, and he prepared Raleigh for a long-term strategy of expansion and modernisation based on his philosophy that the depression could only be overcome by a positive attitude by business.

In early 1922 Harold outlined his philosophy, based on Raleigh's own ambitious strategy of expansion and modernisation. His thinking clearly delivered a message to the cycle industry, and British business in general, on how the malaise of depression should be met. In 1921 he had been elected President of the British Cycle and Motor Cycle Manufacturers' and Traders' Union (BCMMTU), and became a mouthpiece for the industry.[32] The solution to existing business problems, he believed, lay with businessmen themselves, who had become paralysed by the severity of the depression. Calling for a 'revitalised Spirit of Optimism' he referred to the fact that 'I am an optimist – my father ... was an optimist – and that accounts for no small measure of our success'. British businessmen were 'mesmerised ... to their own undoing, and to the detriment of commerce generally', by the 'idea ... that the world is suffering from general and individual pauperism, and that the people cannot buy'. Condemning this attitude he stated that 'I will not allow myself to be misled. Money has not gone into thin air. It is still on the earth, although in many countries it has depreciated in value'. They had to combat the 'chief disease' of lower-priced foreign competition which was aggravated by a higher cost of production and adverse foreign rates of exchange. Business obviously had no control over exchange rates, but pursuing his optimistic tone he argued that industry itself could do much to overcome the depression.[33]

Based on his own strategic decisions at Raleigh he outlined a number of policies to overcome the depression. In the first place there should be a commitment to invest in modernisation. This was 'fundamentally right', and Raleigh itself was prepared to launch a 'tremendous output'. Admitting that this involved a calculated risk, Raleigh having consider-able excess capacity because of falling demand, he argued that this was a positive rather than negative factor. Viewing the depression as cycli-cal, he claimed that over-capacity acted as a 'stimulus' to entrepreneurial endeavour to increase sales. This in turn required a focus on raising quality which should be supported by investment in marketing and promotion.[34] Bowden was no naïve optimist, and in July 1922 he addressed the BCMMTU on the question of cheap American cycle and motor cycle imports. A powerful message was delivered:

> In the great cities of the Midlands and the North of England there are manufacturing houses where the business has been handed down from father to son, where there is a family pride in the family products, where the reputation of the house stands before profits or anything else. It is by these firms that the reputation of British industry has been, and will be maintained, and as long as this spirit exists in Britain we need fear no challenge to our commercial pre-eminence.

This statement, celebrating the British attachment to personal capitalism, typified Raleigh's own historical commitment to the values of quality. For Bowden it was the combination of product quality with the craftsman-ship of the British worker that was the key to meeting the American challenge.[35] This message was taken up by his fellow director, Barnsdale, who argued that in foreign markets 'British quality is appreciated to-day ... as much as ever, and in this respect it is only fair to the British workman to say that at last we are getting back to pre-war efficiency and quality'. If companies such as Raleigh could guarantee quality then the only obstacle that remained was to cut costs and prices.[36]

Cutting costs to allow competitive pricing, especially with the USA, related to a second concept in Bowden's philosophy, the need for co-operation with labour. Both Bowden and Barnsdale emphasised a progressive policy towards labour, a philosophy of co-operation not confrontation. These values, he claimed, had been built up over time at Raleigh, and had become deeply embedded in the thinking of management. 'The founder of the business always desired to foster that personal contact and sympathy between those who stood in authority, and those who bore the heat and burden of the day, and this was instilled in his son at an early stage.'[37] This represented the evolution of company culture at Raleigh which placed a heavy emphasis upon a reciprocal loyalty between workers and management.[38] These values were to guide company policy in relation to labour, and Bowden believed that co-operation could be enhanced by communicating basic business relations to the workforce:

> much of what passes as unreasonableness amongst workers is really lack of knowledge. Facts and figures that are trite and common to directors and managers are, in the main, unknown to workers. And the heads of business cannot imagine such common place factors, which they are handling every day, should be obscure to others under the same roof.[39]

Under the slogan of 'A fair day's pay and a fair day's work', he urged businessmen and workers to 'Get rid of all the fantastic schemes for bringing utopia in five minutes'. The only route to recovery was 'hard, honest work, self denial and mutual effort. So shall we win through to the prosperous times that loom ahead of us'. These values of co-operation were to become deeply embedded in the company's culture over time, and became for Bowden a vision of the future of industrial relations in Britain. For example, in 1934 he informed the Birmingham Rotary Club that he hoped that 'employers and employed in all industries would realise that their interests were not opposed but identical'.[40]

Bowden's business philosophy set the context for strategic action at Raleigh from the early 1920s to 1934 when the company was converted to a public limited holding company. Alfred D. Chandler has identified two types of managers, the entrepreneurial manager and the operational manager. The latter applies to those managers who are responsible for the 'day-to-day activities and tactical decisions of the enterprise', while the former 'decide the long-term goals of the enterprise'.[41] Bowden set the strategic direction of the firm and constituted a classic example of a business leader who shaped the framework of development to such an extent that Raleigh became synonymous with Bowden. It was Bowden, influenced by his philosophy of optimism, who was to set the long-term goals of the company. The overall strategic objective at Raleigh was to expand output and increase market share by reducing the price of high-quality cycles, and its associate products, gears and motor cycles. To meet this objective Raleigh pursued four interrelated strategies: a progressive labour policy, a production policy involving modernisation of plant and vertical integration, a focus on creating a market image to increase sales of quality cycles, and diversification into motorised transport and components. The latter strategy, as we shall see, created problems of production planning at Raleigh, and this was one of the factors which led to the abandonment of motorised production in 1934. Each of these strategic objectives will now be examined in turn.

Raleigh's labour strategy, 1920–34

The immediate priority at Raleigh was to reduce wages to meet price competition. In March 1921 Raven informed the board that 'The stress of price competition is compelling certain cycle manufacturers to reduce their prices', and unless wages were brought down Raleigh's competitive position would be undermined. Referring to the 'sensational' reduction in cycle prices by Rudge-Whitworth from £15 15s. to £12, Bowden argued that production costs were now of 'paramount consideration', and should be reduced by 20 per cent for materials and 15 per cent for labour. By May this had become more urgent as Raleigh was forced to cut export prices and 'consequently it is imperative that costs of production are placed on a lower basis as soon as possible'. Labour and material costs, he claimed, had risen by approximately 161 per cent between 1914 and 1921, while prices had risen by only 81 per cent.[42] To survive the competitive test Raleigh would have to persuade workers that it was in their mutual interest to accept reductions, and Bowden set forth to implement his ideas of co-operation in the company. Given the labour problems at Raleigh since the war the management played their hand cautiously. For example, in January 1921 Bowden and Raven obtained an agreement with the foremen and other 'leading hands' to take greater responsibility in the supervision of work. This involved discharging a number of charge-hands and store assistants who worked under foremen, the latter being made directly responsible for supervision. The management objective was to increase work effort through more direct supervision, and foremen were guaranteed that their wages would not be cut. Further, the workforce were given guarantees of employment and, despite the serious difficulties of the company in January, the factory was kept open, the decision being taken to reduce temporarily the production of cycle components which were in large stock. Thus workers were put on a four-day week, and toolworkers were to be offered a 'premium' bonus on production to replace the present fixed bonus of 50 per cent. Management were clearly using the threat of redundancies to enhance their bargaining position, and also giving sweeteners to selected groups of workers. The threat of redundancies, however, was a powerful bargaining tool, and in April day wage rates were reduced from 42s. to 36s., the AEU consenting in exchange for a managerial promise to avoid laying off workers.[43]

The threat of unemployment clearly placed management in a stronger bargaining position, but Raleigh continued to pursue, when possible, a conciliatory attitude to the workforce. For example, in June 1921 the management reported that they had decided not to join a proposed employer's lock-out in the engineering industry after personal negotiations with the shop stewards. The culmination of this dispute occurred in 1922, and led to a general lock-out by the Engineering Employers' Federation of AEU members, which Holland saw as a 'desire on the part of the Union to interfere with the managerial functions of the works at which their members were employed'. Raleigh again sat on the fence and, whilst giving tacit support to the Federation, refused to become directly involved. The overwhelming victory by the employers, however, led to a weakening of the unions and, in June, Holland was able to report that the weak position of labour had allowed him to negotiate revisions in rates in a number of departments.[44] But Bowden's persistence in personal negotiation had paid dividends during 1921, and he continually forced home the message that workers must accept the economic realities of the time.[45] This was demonstrated in July when, with the depression intensifying, the management introduced short-time working in a number of departments, a policy which remained in force until October when the company planned to build up stocks and launch a new reduced price programme for 1922. Implementing the programme required labour co-operation, and Bowden offered the unions a quid-pro-quo. Raleigh would cut by 50 per cent the percentage of profit normally added to the cost of manufacture and guarantee full work, in return for a 20 per cent reduction in piece rates. Bowden's personal intervention in labour negotiations culminated in a speech to the full workforce in October. Putting forward the company's offer he paraded in front of the assembled workers an equivalent German cycle retailing at £6 10s. compared to Raleigh's cheapest model at £14. The choice was a straight one: accept wage reductions or the works would have to close. The workers voted for acceptance, and the AEU, clearly in a no-win situation, duly ratified the agreement. This was an important turning point in industrial relations at Raleigh, and reinforced management's belief in their personal style of management. The company immediately launched its new programme, offering a low priced model at £10 10s. 'to meet the want of those who cannot afford the £14 14s. to 20 guineas of the Standard Raleighs'. In announcing the return to full time work the *Nottingham Guardian* condoned Raleigh's 'public-spirited view' and the fact that they had taken the bold step of locking up capital in building up stocks now rather 'than to follow the usual practice of waiting till the Spring when the demand for the company's products is always at the highest'.[46]

'Public spirited' this may have been, but it was also crucial for business survival during another critical period of the company's history. On his fortnightly inspection of the factories in early 1922 Bowden noted that 'The old tone of indifference was less apparent and everybody seemed to be taking a keener interest in their work'. In May 1922 the company opened a major factory extension and Bowden celebrated the revived fortunes of the company during the first part of the year. Recognising the risks they had taken in building stocks and spending a 'large financial outlay' on expansion, he emphasised that the new 'team spirit' in the company was a key factor which had allowed them to reduce cycle prices by 25 per cent, and thus expand sales in 1922. By early 1923 Bowden was confidently predicting that 'The tide is rising rapidly over the sands of British trade; the demand for British goods is increasing from every part of the world'. Forecasting a 'cycle boom' during 1923 he emphasised that success could be achieved through a combination of modern production methods with the efforts of skilled workers to increase productivity. 'Nothing is so good that it cannot be bettered', he claimed, and the 2 000 employed were producing 70 000 cycles per annum compared to the same number producing 40 000 two years ago. As he concluded: 'Get the highest possible quality, lower the prices to the smallest point consistent with a commercial profit, look into every item of management ... pull together and we shall see such prosperity in the near future as this country has never yet known.' Raleigh now continued to employ its workforce full time to lay in stocks of cheaper cycles for the 1923 season.[47]

Raleigh's labour policy can thus be seen in a positive light in the sense that it was crucial to competitive success in the hostile trade environment of the early 1920s. The policy also had longer term implications, and set the tone of industrial relations by reinforcing the managerial values of co-operation and personal bargaining through consultation with shop-floor committees. Employment relations were determined by Bowden's commitment to policies of industrial welfare, and in the 1920s he gained a national reputation as a promoter of this ideology towards labour.[48] In 1922 Raleigh established a welfare department, which included a hospital and rest room. The aim was 'to care for the physical, mental and moral welfare of the employees'. The company motto was that 'no worker is a mere number, but a living, pulsing human co-worker in the effort to provide the great public ... with the best article that can be produced at the lowest possible price'. By 1924 the management had introduced a workers' benevolent fund, the company subscribing ½d. for every 1d. donated, and in 1926 they devised a scheme for workmen's compensation insurance and profit-sharing. The latter scheme was an attempt to use bonuses across the workforce to increase work effort, and to instil a sense of mutual interest between management and labour. The bonus was to be paid pro rata to employees with 12 months' service, and the fund for distribution was linked to profit performance based on the starting year of 1925–26. Profit sharing was applied to all workers who were not paid by bonus or commission payments, and allowed management to dispense with complex negotiations amongst various groups of workers for bonus payments, although they were maintained for foremen and supervisors, as the management had earlier decided, in 1922, that increased labour efficiency could be improved by a 'healthy rivalry between the foremen of the various departments', who were given direct responsibility for rate-fixing.[49]

Welfarism was clearly an attempt to produce increased efficiency and to create harmony in employment relations. On the latter front, the strategy had some success, and, combined with the weakened state of the unions in the engineering industry, allowed management to force through its policies. Raleigh experienced a relatively peaceful period of industrial relations throughout the inter-war years. During the General Strike of 1926, for example, direct participation by workers was minimal, and the main costs of the national industrial action were secondary.[50] Nevertheless, despite relatively harmonious industrial relations, the workforce continued to command a direct say in the implementation of new work practices and negotiations over rates. In particular, there was resistance from skilled workers which typified the problems associated with the personal style of labour relations adopted. For example, in January 1924 Holland received a deputation from skilled day workers requesting increases in pay, which he rejected on the grounds that they were already receiving 8s. per week more than the district rate, and 7s. more than paid in Coventry and Birmingham. However, he offered the compromise of moving to piece rates, on which, he claimed, they 'would be able to considerably increase their wages'. Negotiations broke down as workers continued to resist the management's insistence on reducing day workers to the ultimate minimum. Again, in October 1925, the company announced that it was following the procedures adopted at Triumph, and placing toolmakers on piece rates and introducing schedules of repetitive work. The shop stewards' committee refused, and a compromise was only reached after Bowden's personal intervention, toolmakers remaining on bonuses, while tool-setters moved to the new system. With the recovery of the cycle industry from the mid-1920s, the issue of rates and work systems became a major concern to management at Raleigh. The central issue was productivity. Raleigh was paying higher piece work rates than companies such as Enfield and Rudge-Whitworth, and 'Comparison has proved that our present piecework prices are more than double those in existence before the war, whilst our operatives' wages are also more than double pre-war, and this in spite of the fact that the cost of living is now recorded as being 76 per cent above pre-war'. During 1926 a number of long-drawn out negotiations took place for productivity deals in return for a commitment not to reduce piece rates for 12 months.[51]

In November 1926 Bush and Holland visited the works of Citroën and Peugeot in France and Holland and commented that they had a number of natural advantages over their British counterparts, most notably cheaper labour and power. They also noted that in terms of labour effort there was 'a total absence of that ca canny spirit which is so evident in this country'. Nevertheless, they found that the general organisation of plant was not as good, but they did use conveying systems, although some were 'of a very primitive character', and they used a larger proportion of female workers than British firms. These visits were a learning curve for Raleigh, and they increasingly introduced unskilled female workers into the assembly shops, on the same principle as Peugeot's plant at Velintiginey. Annual bargaining rounds were instigated in 1928, piece rates being fixed for 12 months, with the management gaining the right to review these in the light of introducing new machinery. In the same year Raleigh appointed a consultant from Industrial Psychology, a consultancy organisation, Bowden remarking that 'his work would bring good results'. This reflected the management's attachment to a welfarist policy, the consultant being instructed to investigate the factory's internal transport system, 'mess room habits', the condition of workers in the tool room, and systems of lighting, ventilation and sanitation in the factory.[52] By the early 1930s Raleigh had also established a wide range of sporting and recreational clubs in the company to develop a 'healthy team spirit', and could boast that 'from the management to the newly-joined errand boy all are alive to the fact that welfare is synonymous with progress'.[53]

The management may well have celebrated the virtues of industrial welfarism, but this is to ignore continuing difficulties in maintaining the commitment of workers. For example, by the late 1920s the issue of work practices was of major concern, as Raleigh planned to introduce overhead conveyor systems into the finishing and annealing shops, which were eventually completed by December 1928. This involved an increased flow of production and impacted upon Raleigh's systems of quality control. For example, in May 1927 the management approached Viles and Ridgeway, factory consultants, who referred to the fact that Raleigh's recent reductions in piece rates, and decreases in the hours worked in the tool room, had reduced worker motivation and led to a lower standard of work. The management recognised that this might be a factor, but felt that the key problem 'was not due so much to a cheese-pairing policy as to slackness on the part of certain sections of the works'. As a result of the conference, Holland made a personal plea to all foremen, and impressed upon them the need to maintain 'the Raleigh standard, which can only be done by increased accuracy in production and greater diligence in the viewing controls'. As Holland argued in January 1928, supervision of labour remained a continual problem and 'he was seriously watching the question of quality and had taken all possible steps to maintain the Raleigh reputation and to eliminate all causes of complaint'.[54]

The assessment of the success of work relations at Raleigh needs to be tempered with a certain degree of caution, but what was not in doubt were the capabilities of management in instilling in workers the need to face economic reality in the face of periodic business crises. Thus, in February and March 1931, with the depression severely affecting sales, the company announced the introduction of short-term working, and the cutting of salaries of all works staff and management by 10 per cent. Management at Raleigh led the way and the company, similar to the early 1920s, negotiated reductions in rates to force down labour costs and substantially reduce prices. The company announced in October 1931 its new cheaper 'Popular' cycle, selling at £4 19s. 6d., and this had been made possible 'by a sacrifice on the part of the personnel of the company from the directors downwards, of a portion of their remuneration'. In fact, piece rates had been reduced by 12.5 per cent in August, and this, coupled with the introduction of new machinery, meant that Raleigh was able to reduce prices substantially, and by early 1932 the management could confidently predict that 'the demand for Raleigh cycles will exceed the supply'.[55] Raleigh's labour strategy was closely linked to a policy of factory modernisation and the instalment of new machinery. In his speech of 1934 on the 'Four Ms of Industry' Bowden referred to press comments by the radical politician, Sir Stafford Cripps, that the capital value of industries had been created by workers. In reply he argued that 'This is pure doctrinaire nonsense. To say that all wealth is produced by labour is as true as to say that all motor cars are run by petrol'. Business success, for Bowden, required a combination of modern machinery with a co-operative labour force, backed up by the organisational skills of managers, and the entrepreneurial skills of business leaders to finance new developments.[56] This takes us to Raleigh's second strategic objective, its policies for production.

Production policy, 1920–34

'Labour rather than being the sole producer of wealth is only one of several factors and the part they play is diminishing more and more.' So argued Bowden in 1934, referring to the importance of machinery, the third 'M' of industry, in creating the conditions for the competitive success of British industry. He argued that increased mechanisation was inevitable, and in Raleigh's experience the 'money' for investment had been provided from the success of the company in expanding sales, and ploughing it back into expansion and modernisation.[57] From the early 1920s Raleigh developed an ambitious and expansive programme of modernisation which had three interrelated aims: first, to invest in process technology to increase productivity and reduce overhead costs, and to allow increasing vertical integration, this being supported by an emphasis on developing systems for planning and co-ordinating output; second, an expansion of Sturmey-Archer gear production to meet the demands both of Raleigh itself and the trade in general; third, a continued commitment to product development and an attempt to lead the market in the fashion for quality cycles. As we shall see, the emphasis on quality determined the pattern and pace of plant modernisation at Raleigh, and was to be a central theme of its marketing strategy.

During 1921 Bowden and his works managers had visited the Ford plant in Detroit to examine production methods. Clearly impressed by what they saw, Bowden considered the introduction of assembly-line systems at Raleigh but dismissed its full application. In the first place it was not appropriate to Raleigh's commitment to non-standardised production, and second, he considered that the cost of installation was prohibitive given the financial difficulties of the company in 1921. Nevertheless, the management were clearly attracted by the vast use of automatic machine tools at Ford and, despite finances being constrained, Bowden decided that the company would work on smaller profit margins to ensure the 'necessary capital outlay' for modernisation. This decision brought forth a major 'reorganisation' of cycle production, aimed at facilitating the flow of production, reducing the processing of materials, and developing 'manufacture in a steady forward line'. Raleigh also introduced new automatic machine tools, of both British and American design, to facilitate the assembly of the numerous components which went into the final cycle, a process which required a large workforce of skilled machine operators. The continued use of skilled labour was determined by the quality attributes of the product, and the large number of components which were used to fabricate the cycle. For example, a liberal estimate of parts in the production of the average cycle was 500, but Raleigh machines consisted of 1 411 parts, and if fitted with a Sturmey-Archer gear, 1 515 parts. As Bowden was at pains to point out, the modernisation programme 'was no blind mass production stunt, where a piece of iron went in one end and came out the other'. Rather, they integrated modern methods with the 'old system of employing a craftsman's skill to fashion an individually perfect machine, but kinks in internal transport, loss of time, etc., were reduced to the absolute minimum'.[58]

Modernised plant was also installed in a new extension to the Sturmey-Archer department, opened in February 1921. This allowed the company by May to announce that the extra charge for a three-speed gear attachment to its bicycles would be 36s., a drop of 28 per cent on its 1920 prices. Raleigh was selling the attachment at 'practically cost price, the company hoping to recoup itself by the greatly increased demand'.[59] This was still high, compared to the pre-war price of 21s., but 'The great reduction in prices ... should have the effect of making it practically universal; at any rate with everyone who wants his or her cycling made easy'. Under the headline of 'No Depression', *Cycling* argued that the new Sturmey-Archer department was necessary to keep pace with orders, 'and is the best possible reply to those pessimists who argue that the cycle industry is played out'. With a capacity to produce 250 000 gears per annum, and covering 32 000 sq. ft, the Sturmey-Archer department was equipped with the latest automatic machinery to produce cycle gears, tricoasters, a three-speed hub with a coaster brake, and two- and three-speed countershaft gears for motor cycles. Increasing automation enabled greater standardisation of parts, and in the machine shops a network of conveyors supplied parts to the factory. Not all processes, however, were simultaneous and although the production of hubs was standardised the finishing of the gears was still left to skilled assemblers who fitted the parts, and required 'dexterity and accuracy'.[60] With the revival of trade in 1923 and 1924 Raleigh was selling large numbers of three-speed cycle gears and tricoaster hubs to Rudge-Whitworth, Enfield, Challenger and Humber.[61]

In May 1922 Raleigh opened its new factory extension, built at a cost of £250 000. The overall capacity potential of the Raleigh factory at Nottingham was now 100 000 cycles per annum, 15 000 motor cycles, 250 000 three-speed gears for cycles, 50 000 countershaft gears for motor cycles and 100 000 gear cases. This was a demonstration of management's commitment to a programme of expansion to cut costs, reduce prices and increase sales to overcome depression. It was also a commitment to diversification, a strategy which we will return to later. By separating the motor cycle from the pedal cycle division, the management aimed at increasing the efficiency of both operations. The extended plant, with its 'immense number of automatic machines', allowed Raleigh to develop 'the quantity production of parts for cycles, motorcycles, and gears'. Increased factory space also enabled vertical integration, and drawing machines were installed which enabled the factory to process steel tubing from sheet steel.[62] The objective of management was to enhance their competitive position and 'to bring down the factory running charges' by forcing economies in all departments. The expansion and modernisation drive, as we have seen, was coupled with reduced rates of pay, and by 1923 this had paid dividends. In that year labour output per worker increased by approximately 50 per cent, and rising productivity and falling costs were transmitted into price reductions across the range of Raleigh cycles. For example, Raleigh's cheapest cycle, its 'Popular Gents', was reduced by 20 per cent, from £10 10s. to £8 10s. in 1923, and by 1924 was selling at £8.[63] By 1927 this was selling at £7 17s. 6d., and as Table D.2 in the Appendix shows, there was a wholesale reduction in prices on all Raleigh machines. At the top end of the market, the 'Modele Superbe' had been reduced in price, and was now fitted with additional features such as the Terry's spring saddle, and greater attention was given to the 'finishing stages'. Bowden confidently predicted that 'The factory only needed to expand its labour force to meet almost any demand'.[64]

With the revival of the cycle market after 1923 Bowden's optimism proved justified, and in 1924 the factory produced 90 000 cycles, and the management sanctioned £55 000 to build another extension to raise output to 120 000 and to increase the output of gears. Raleigh also invested in developing new models and new construction designs. For example, they introduced chrome plated bicycles, lighter construction, attractive colours, rustless rims and spokes, and better quality tyres and saddles. These 'all helped to create a natural demand for the company's products from every class of rider'.[65] Raleigh was at 'the forefront' of developments in lightweights, and these were supplied with a new Sturmey-Archer three-speed gear hub, 'greatly improved in detail and one and one half pounds lighter'. The lightweight models were particularly adaptable to racing machines, a range which Raleigh had dropped during the war but now re-entered, producing an advanced design at a modest price of £11 5s. With a light and lugless, but rigid frame, it was acetylene welded and required expert workmanship in construction. At the 1924 Cycle Show, Raleigh were praised for 'constantly seeking to improve their all-steel range of bicycles in detail', and at the 1926 show 'a new kind of quick releasing fork-end was a novel feature of the North Road Racer'.[66]

Despite considerable investment in expansion, modernisation and product innovation, the performance of Raleigh's cycle business was somewhat disappointing. The fragmented information on profits and sales is shown in Tables D.3 and D5 in the Appendix. Cycle sales increased from £199 116 in 1923 to £280 617 in 1925, and then showed a remarkable acceleration to £743 302 in 1926. At this date cycle sales accounted for 46.85 per cent of total factory sales, but this represented the peak and sales fell sharply in 1927 although they remained over £500 000 until 1930. Sturmey-Archer cycle gears also proved popular, and sales rose from £61 209 to £112 008 between 1923 and 1926. Sales fell slightly in 1927 but were boosted thereafter by the completion of a trade agreement between Raleigh and BSA. The latter withdrew from the market, and gave to Raleigh the exclusive rights to supply them with gear hubs, Raleigh paying a 5 per cent commission on additional turnover through the arrangement.[67] By 1927 Sturmey-Archer was producing 3 000 cycle gears per week, and they obtained large orders from Peugeot in Paris, and from other cycle companies in Britain.[68] By 1928, cycle gears represented nearly 30 per cent of the net factory profits on sales. In contrast, however, profits on the cycle business were disappointing between 1927 and 1929, and fell from 15.27 per cent of sales in 1926 to 8.45 per cent in 1929, and then crashed in the depressed environment of 1930 to just 0.91 per cent. The low profitability of the cycle business was related to falling revenue as prices were cut, but also to the problem of the rising factory operating costs, or what the management referred to as running charges. For example, as Table D.6 in the Appendix shows, running charges rose dramatically in 1927 to 93 per cent of productive wages, and again in the depressed year of 1930 they reached 84.18 per cent. These increases in operating expenses caused serious concern, and at the board's fortnightly meetings were the first item on the agenda. In particular management became obsessed with overheads, which they defined as the ratio between total productive and non-productive wages at a given period. Overheads were the main component in the cost of production, as illustrated in Table 5.3, and in December 1926 Bowden warned that they must eliminate 'all unnecessary overhead charges'. This was clearly not achieved, and in May 1929 Holland reported that overhead charges had increased from a yearly average of 26 per cent in 1924 and 1925 to 31 per cent, 33.57 per cent, and 34 per cent respectively in the three years to 1928. The problem, claimed Holland, was the failure to co-ordinate a regular flow of production in the factory, and work was

Table 5.3 Distribution of costs on various Raleigh products, 1924 (%)

Product	Material Cost	Labour Cost	Tyres	Overheads
Popular Gents cycle	28.6	17.8	12.6	41.0
OHV Model motor cycle	40.2	15.7	6.0	38.1
7 hp motor cycle	41.4	14.2	6.3	38.1
Sturmey-Archer Featherweight gear	27.5	23.1		49.4
Sturmey-Archer LS gear	34.5	20.2		45.3
Sturmey-Archer BS gear	33.8	20.6		45.6

Source: Calculated from Minutes with Reports, 28 July 1924.

regularly disrupted because of changing machinery and layout to meet the demands of producing a differentiated range of cycle models. Co-ordination of production planning was clearly a problem at Raleigh, and, as we shall see later, this was exacerbated by an over-commitment of the factory to motor cycles and countershaft gears which held up component supply.[69]

As the depression took hold in 1930 the question of overhead costs became a prime concern, and, in conjunction with reductions in rates to labour, the management embarked on a further programme of plant modernisation intended to increase the flow of production, reduce running charges and force increased sales by reducing bicycle prices. Bowden had earlier been cautious about the introduction of conveyor belt systems in the factory, due to the high costs of funding the investment from internally generated profits. By 1928, however, the management had recognised their potential for increasing the flow of production, and conveyor systems were partly introduced, being installed in the finishing and annealing shops. The severity of the depression, and the need for price reductions, brought this earlier decision to its logical conclusion. With 'cost-saving ... of such paramount importance by the end of 1931' Bowden decided to extend the network of conveyors. By March 1932 the first mile of an overhead factory conveyor system, running through all departments, was in full operation, and new plant and machinery were reducing costs, 'not by cheapening the product but by utilising the most scientific methods of production'.[70] In October 1931 *Bicycling News* reported a 'substantial reduction' in Raleigh prices, their 'Popular Model' being retailed at £4 19s. 6d., a price still ruling in 1934. Price reductions, Bowden argued, had been enabled by investment in 'modern machinery' and this was accompanied by design innovations.[71]

In 1934 a cheaper Raleigh was still retailing at £1 above the standard for the trade, which stood at £3 19s. 6d., but design improvements allowed the company to compete favourably with lower-priced mass producers such as Hercules, and also smaller specialist makers. For example, in 1931 they launched the 'Record Raleigh', and it was noted that 'There has for many years been a tendency for big makers to confine themselves to the more standardised machines, and the keener type of rider searching for something daintier has gone ... to the small assembler, rather than to the mass producer ... The new Raleigh machine changes all this'.[72] Product differentiation became an even more valuable asset to their competitive success. As the *News Chronicle* reported in November 1931: 'Britain still leads', and the Cycle and Motor Cycle Exhibition would display 'striking advances in the design and manufacture of bicycles', including the use of special molybdenum steel to produce greater lightness and strength which met the requirements of 'the general boom in open air life and of cycle touring in particular'. To succeed, cycle firms had to be ahead of the game in producing new designs, and Triumph was introducing a new light standardised model with bright colour schemes, and the Hercules Co., 'whose output is the highest in the world', were exhibiting models of all types costing £5 or less.[73] Raleigh's management were clearly aware of these trends, and expanded output was accompanied by increased quality control in the factory. In 1932 it was reported that the company 'have brought the manufacture of their machines up to such a standard of perfection, that there are many features of the Raleigh which distinguish it from ordinary bicycles, and have made Ride a Raleigh quite distinct from Ride a Bicycle'. The emphasis on producing the quality bicycle was also crucial in facing up to cheaper foreign competition, especially from Japan. In January 1934 Bowden referred to claims that cheap, low-quality, Japanese cycles were 'flooding ... overseas markets'. Taking the example of Ceylon to counter these claims, he argued that British imports during 1933 totalled 26 259 rupees, compared to just 3 585 for Japanese machines, and Raleigh exported over 50 per cent of the total to this market. Bowden argued that he had attempted to secure a Japanese cycle in Britain, but could not do so, and was not to be 'intimidated'.[74]

Raleigh's commitment to capturing the quality cycle market was demonstrated by its acquisition of the trade marks of Humber's cycle subsidiary in February 1932. Humber production was transferred to Nottingham, and in Bowden's opinion was an 'important addition to Raleigh, Gazelle and Robin Hood Cycles and provided the firm with a programme which could deal with competition at various prices in all markets'. The Humber deal was clearly a process of rationalisation, the Humber Co. closing what it saw as a loss-making factory in Coventry and transferring to the modernised Raleigh plant. Humber was a quality producer, and Raleigh had made links with the firm in the 1920s through agreements to supply it with Sturmey-Archer gears. Humber machines possessed unique features which added to Raleigh's quality cycle range, and followed from the management's belief that although the products of cycle-makers were becoming more standardised and similar in appearance, differing only in detail, the Humber was not in this category. In particular, it offered Raleigh the opportunity to exploit Humber's duplex fork construction for the frame, a feature which had been introduced in 1933, and aimed at the 'privileged few', but could now be standardised on all machines given the increased production facilities that Raleigh offered. Humber sales showed rapid progress. Domestic sales rose by 53.9 per cent in 1933, and in the following year by 49 per cent. Export sales also increased, rising by 73 per cent in 1934.[75]

The Humber acquisition represented a clear commitment by management to increase the diversification of its cycle range further. Raleigh remained committed to a strategy of non-standardisation, and this brought costs as well as benefits. For example, the *Motor Cycle and Cycle Trader* claimed in 1934 that Raleigh 'may be impugned for listing a tremendous number of models', as 'anything off standard' negated efforts to implement co-ordinated planning based on standardised production. In 1934 Raleigh offered for the following season 50 different models, and Humber's range extended to 56. Raleigh were not standardised mass producers, but this could bring advantages, and as the *Motor Cycle and Cycle Trader* noted, Raleigh was building its reputation amongst agents and dealers and meeting customer demand for a variegated product:

> From the agents' standpoint it is easier to sell a completely specified and illustrated model as an entity than it is to ask the customer to conjure up what the 'so and so' would look like if it had fitting A in place of fitting B ... and so forth. From the factory end, it is far simpler and more expeditious to deal with an order for a definite model than it is to search through a complicated sheet, possibly with omissions or errors, to arrive at the complete specification that may be desired by the customer ... the number of machines may appear tremendous, such drawbacks as there may be from the stocking angle are largely offset by other considerations, particularly the easing of sales resistance.

The *Motor Cycle and Cycle Trader* concluded that 'the 1935 Raleigh programme, in common with its forerunners, is planned to avoid the off-standard bogey as far as is humanly possible'.[76] Raleigh's production policy, although not without its drawbacks, demonstrates a highly progressive management who were prepared to invest in modernising the factory within the limits of the company's commitment to product differentiation and the quality cycle. The success of this strategy depended upon a complementary policy of marketing the company image and capturing an increasing share of the market for high-quality machines.

Marketing a tradition: Raleigh's sales policy, 1920–34

Raleigh's marketing and sales policy was based on its historical reputation as a quality producer of cycles. In 1922 Bowden outlined Raleigh's future marketing strategy. Advertisements were to be used as a means to 'educate' the public in recognising the value of quality in relation to cheaper foreign models, and 'Advertising and selling are now our concentration points'. Bowden had been influenced by American sales methods, and in 1923 he visited the USA with a delegation of British businessmen to study 'sales propaganda' there. Influenced by American ideas Bowden hyped up Raleigh's promotional image. For example, the company informed agents of the importance of 'Making Your Own Advertisements Attractive', and they provided a series of standardised publicity blocks which celebrated the quality and durability of the Raleigh, and presented images appealing to boys and girls, outdoor pursuits, family values, and the spirit of adventure. A range of gadgets was also being offered to agents at under cost price for exhibition. The Raleigh paraphernalia included Christmas cards, playing cards, calendars, headed letter paper, match booklets etc. In 1921 the company launched its 'Big Window Dressing Week' for all Raleigh agents throughout the country, an event which was to occur annually. There were also collaborative events with popular magazines, and *Tit-Bits* sponsored an annual competition with prizes for the first person to stop a guest Raleigh rider. The company also advertised extensively through national newspapers and hoardings, and erected neon signs in Piccadilly Circus. The Raleigh sales catalogue was the centre-piece of Raleigh's promotional campaign, and they employed top illustrators to design elaborate front covers, often depicting women in their captions. The 1922 edition was applauded in the trade press, and 'The Raleigh Company know how to produce an attractive catalogue, as well as make excellent cycles'.[77]

Raleigh's sales policy entailed more than just a glossy image, and required a heavy financial commitment in an attempt to create brand loyalty with agents and dealers. During 1921 and 1922 Raleigh spent an estimated £100 000 on advertisement both at home and abroad, and the promotion drive was supported by collective action in the industry. The BCMMTU provided funds to promote the cycle as the cheapest and most convenient form of transport, and also for recreational and health reasons.[78] As Table D.5 in the Appendix shows cycle sales rose steadily from 1923 to their peak in 1927. The fall off in sales after this date prompted another promotional drive, and as can be seen in Table 5.4 advertisement expenditure rose to just under £90 000 in the depressed climate of 1930. There was a conscious effort to create networks of loyalty and trust with agents, especially in the face of adverse market conditions. This objective was set as early as 1921 when intense price competition threatened to undermine the goodwill of agents. Raleigh consequently delayed cutting prices until the following year on the grounds that it would reinforce the cyclical downturn of prices which the industry was facing, and would lead to agents incurring losses on stock bought at higher prices set in October 1920. This was an attempt to create reciprocal loyalty with those who had a stake in the fortunes of the company, and Bowden boldly announced that 'Neither could we, nor should we, follow the example of Rudge-Whitworth' and cut prices. Agents and depot managers were brought into decision-making through Raleigh's annual sales conference, which discussed pricing and product ranges for the forthcoming season, and with the support of BSA, Enfield and Humber, Bowden was able to announce a 'No Reduction programme'. In 1923 Bowden promised agents 'forceful advertisement and ... efficient sales methods', and reminded them to 'PUSH RALEIGHS – REMEMBER YOUR INTERESTS ARE OUR INTERESTS AND OUR INTERESTS ARE YOUR INTERESTS'. In announcing price reductions for that year the trade was informed that 'The company is pursuing its consistent policy of giving its patrons the full benefit of all reductions in cost of production'. In an attempt to foster increasing brand loyalty new agency agreements were contracted, whereby a minimum quantity of cycles were to be purchased, Raleigh paying a commission on machines sold, and allowing main agents to supply sub-agents at a small commission.[79]

The key selling point of the Raleigh was its reputation for quality, and as we have already seen Bowden had no intention of steering the

Table 5.4   Raleigh factory selling expenses on advertisement, 1925–30 (for year ending August)

	1925	1926	1927	1928	1929	1930
Total (£)	61 786	69 962	79 541	78 153	76 472	89 738
% of productive wages	22.15	23.3	34.29	26.68	29.96	38.8

Source: DDRN 3/11/1, Auditors Reports and Accounts 1926–30.

company down-market. Price reductions would have to be introduced through economies in production and Raleigh would 'not contemplate ... the sacrifice of quality'. To reinforce this they had reintroduced in 1921 a limited quantity of their high-quality cross-frame cycle, retailing at £25, to meet the demand of the more discerning cyclist. This was described as 'the connoisseur's bicycle', expensive to produce, and not made by Raleigh at a profit, but simply in response to a small demand for a novel cycle.[80] Despite reducing the price of cycles the Raleigh standard was all important, and this was reinforced by the production policy of constantly updating designs, and offering the latest gadgetry. In the depression of 1929–32 Raleigh's marketing strategy was clearly directed to differentiating its products. As the company reduced prices to meet competition the management embarked upon another extensive sales drive. Offering no deposit payments under their gradual payment business, which had 60 000 accounts by 1933, they hammered home that the Raleigh represented 'the finest value for money'. For example their increasingly popular sports range was intended to 'reduce prices to enable the purchase of the finest class of machine to be within the capabilities of all keen cyclists'. A company poster displayed four hammers with the captions 'RIGID', 'RAPID', 'RELIABLE', 'Raleigh'. 'Keep hammering it in ... RALEIGH FOR QUALITY.' In 1932 Raleigh could boast that cycle sales had 'overshadowed' those of 1931 by 82.6 per cent, and a key factor of this success was the maintenance of goodwill with dealers. As the management claimed: 'Raleigh's sales effort for next season is going to make things hum' and with the 'whole-hearted co-operation' of agents and dealers 'together we'll beat any slump and put any sales record in the shade'. With Raleighs selling at lower prices, they intensified their sales drive by an extensive advertisement campaign which emphasised the quality aspects of the product, and differentiated the product in the market. The success of the campaign was demonstrated by the fact that they sold 50 000 machines more in 1934 than in any previous year, and the export trade had increased by 32 per cent.[81]

The emphasis of the company's sales drive in the period up to 1934 was largely directed at the domestic market, but the management did not ignore foreign countries. For example, in 1922 special representatives were sent to a variety of foreign markets to provide information on market potential. Where exchange rates allowed, and 'where currency was not hopelessly depreciated', the company launched an aggressive marketing programme, supplying catalogues in Spanish, French and Dutch, 'a procedure that might well be copied by other British makers'. The company also saw the need to move into colonial markets, with particular attention being paid to African and Far

Eastern markets in 1922, designing machines tailor-made for these locations and placing the emphasis on a cheap but strongly built cycle. By 1928 the company had achieved a large increase in exports to British East Africa, 'where it was the ambition of every native to own a Raleigh which ... had become known as a symbol of quality'. In 1926 the decision was also taken to produce cheap cycles for West African markets. African markets, however, provided some problems for the company's commitment to the high-quality cycle, consumers demanding cheaper-priced machines. Thus, in the West African market, where Raleigh faced intense competition from low-priced competitors such as Hercules, the decision was taken to produce the forks and frames only, and purchase other finished parts from outside. This suggests that Raleigh's component production capabilities were inadequate to produce finished cycles down-market, and wheels and cranks were supplied by the Chain Wheels Co., mudguards from the Cromford manufacturing Co., seat pits from Heaton Ward, handlebars and brakes from the Bowden Brake Co., pumps from W. Lowe & Co., saddles and tool bars from Leatheries Ltd, and rubber pedals from J. A. Phillips. By the late 1920s the company had also targeted the Argentinian market, opening a branch office in Buenos Aires in 1928 with a capital of £35 000.[82]

In 1933 Raleigh also re-entered the American market, which it had abandoned during the cycle boom of the 1890s. In 1932 Raleigh had conducted a survey of the American market which had concluded that due to the severity of the depression, and the trend towards motorised transport, their prospects in the market were limited. They were then contacted by an American bicycle enthusiast, Hamilton Osgood, who had come to appreciate the commercial potential of the Raleigh during his undergraduate days at Oxford. Although management were sceptical of Osgood's intentions to sell Raleighs in the USA, he was granted permission to establish offices in Boston as sole distributor of the company's cycles. Sales were limited, but there was an appreciation of the lightweight character of the Raleigh machines, in comparison to the heavy models produced by American manufacturers. Raleigh established a niche market for quality cycles, and Osgood developed important retail connections with Abercrombie & Fitch, a New York chain store.[83] As we shall see in Chapter 7, the American market was to become Raleigh's main target in its post-war export drive.

Raleigh's marketing policy was central to its survival and success in the inter-war years, and it was partly based on following its past tradition for quality and excellence. The *Motor Cycle and Cycle Trader* had no doubt about the progressive nature of this policy. In 1932, referring to the fact that the company had spent £1 million on its 'educative policy' of promoting the higher-grade cycle, they argued that to the three R's which symbolised Raleigh publicity, 'Rigid, Rapid, Reliable', should be added a fourth, 'Romance ... a glamour that colours the Raleigh history of the past and the enterprise of the future'.[84] The marketing of the Raleigh cycle was clearly a success in the long run, but the company's ambitions to diversify into motorised transport raised problems relating to the co-ordination of production at Raleigh, and having pursued this policy Bowden abandoned it in 1934.

Raleigh and motorised transport, 1920–34

The opening of Raleigh's major factory extension in May 1922 signalled a commitment to a diversification policy which entailed an emphasis on producing motor cycles and countershaft gears, the latter via its Sturmey-Archer trade marks. The expansion was purpose built to accommodate this new business, and was given a high priority by management. Why did Bowden and his management advisors take this decision? First, they clearly believed that diversification was a means of alleviating the depressed market for their 'staple product', the cycle. The flexibility of technology, it was argued, would allow diversification, and this would enable the factory to utilise its full productive capacity in the production of a range of products. The new enlarged factory was prepared to produce an annual output of 15 000 motor cycles, 250 000 three-speed gears for cycles, 50 000 countershaft gears for motor cycles and 100 000 gear cases, as well as 100 000 cycles. Management thus hoped to gain internal economies of scale through the full utilisation of plant, and to create flexibility in production by co-ordinating output by switching into what they perceived to be the fastest growing areas of trade. Second, the management saw the potential of opening a niche market for itself in producing a range of lightweight quality motor cycles. There was a belief that they could create a market on the back of the company's reputation as a quality-cycle maker. As can be seen in Table D.2 in the Appendix, Raleigh produced a range of motor cycles for the 1923 season, but its main ambition was to break into the market for lightweight machines, which were highly popular in the early 1920s. Raleigh's 2.75 hp lightweight was targeted at solo riders, the larger machines being heavier and more suitable for sidecar attachments, and between 1922 and 1925 Raleigh sold some 15 000 machines between 2.5 and 7 hp. Third, the management saw the opportunity of increasing the Sturmey-Archer business by exploiting the large demand, both at home and on the Continent, for countershaft gears by the motor cycle trade. For example, the company received large orders for this speciality from British firms such as Triumph, Norton, Ariel and Sarolea, and there was also a considerable demand by manufacturers in Belgium, Scandinavia and, particularly, Germany. Such was the demand in 1923 that the factory could not keep pace with the rush of orders. Finally, the management saw the potential for utilising its already extensive marketing network for developing sales of motor cycles and gears. Thus, the agency system could be effectively employed to push a range of products from cycles, motor cycles and gears. The aim was an integrated marketing policy, and to enhance their reputation Raleigh entered numerous motor cycle races and trials, and two famous riders, Hugh Gibson and Amy Cottrell, were engaged to ride for the Raleigh team, and to head the Raleigh Competition Department.[85] How successful was the company in pursuing its policy of diversification?

The expansion of motor cycle output in 1922 immediately brought economies which enabled Raleigh to reduce the price of their 2.75 hp motor cycle from £68 to £55, and their new 'all chain' version was sold at only £60. As can be seen in Table D.5 in the Appendix, motor cycle sales in 1923 were £115 237, and contributed 21 per cent of the total sales of all products in that year. This justified Raleigh's commitment to diversification, and revenue was boosted from sales of motor cycles, and particularly from countershaft gears which contributed 30 per cent of total sales in 1923, compared to the contribution of cycle sales at 37 per cent. Thus, although the cycle trade was rising by 1923, the management had created a potentially profitable business in ancillary products. Diversification also allowed flexibility in the planning of output, which, given the cyclical nature of markets, was conducted on a short-term basis. Product flexibility enabled them to switch factory output into areas which the management viewed as the most profitable, and this was sanctioned at the company's regular fortnightly meetings. This demonstrates a strict monitoring procedure of both market conditions and operational policy, and the objective was to co-ordinate production with orders and existing stocks, figures which were regularly made available to the board. By way of illustration, the following examples will suffice. In August 1923 cycle stocks were low and with orders rising rapidly it was decided to sanction the machining of an additional 2 000 sets of cycle parts, and raise the assembly of finished machines from 1 000 to 1 500 per week. In contrast, stocks of countershaft gears were high, and it was decided to cut down production to the actual number of orders received. These adjustment decisions occurred on a fortnightly basis, and taking another example, Holland informed the directors in July 1927 that 'In view of the shortage of orders for cycles and motorcycles it was decided to cut down the former to 1 500 per week whilst motorcycles were to be assembled in accordance with orders actually received'. However, 'The prospects of

Sturmey-Archer are brighter and it was decided to continue working full time on 3-speed hubs and endeavour to increase our stock of that component to 50 000 pieces'.[86]

In the depressed climate of the 1920s flexibility was a strategy which enabled management to regulate, at short notice, the output of the factory across varied product lines. The success of the strategy, however, was problematic, as it also brought additional costs in terms of internal problems relating to the co-ordination and planning of component supplies. For example, countershaft gear sales rose from £162 800 in 1923 to £246 399 in 1925, when it represented 33 per cent of total factory sales. Thereafter sales remained at this level until rising spectacularly to £316 499 in 1928, but then fell back again to a low of £189 143 in 1930, representing 16.86 per cent of total factory sales. Nevertheless, this product made a significant contribution to net profits, and even in 1930 this stood at 19.29 per cent compared to just 0.91 per cent for cycles and a loss of 7.23 per cent for motor cycles. The latter's contribution to net profits remained modest throughout, despite sales accounting for 30.7 per cent of total factory sales at the peak of 1928 (see Tables D.3 and D.5 in the Appendix).

Raleigh's entry into motor cycles occurred in a period of stagnant demand for the industry, and when price competition, on both the domestic and foreign fronts, was intense. New entrants, such as Raleigh, faced the problems of overcoming the competition posed by long-established firms in the industry, and William Joynson Hicks, then Parliamentary Secretary to the Department of Overseas Trade, informed the BCMMTU in 1922 that 400 British firms were engaged in the manufacture of motor cycles and component parts, and he regretted the decline in export markets. 'Trade is no longer national, it is international' he claimed, and he estimated a 20 per cent decline in prices during 1922. Addressing the same audience, Bowden admitted that Raleigh faced formidable problems, and the depression had left little surplus income to purchase motor cycles, and thus the appeal of the cycle to classes hardest hit by high unemployment. Indeed, in 1923 the company had difficulty in disposing of its 5/6 hp machines, and eventually were forced to sell its stock to wholesalers at a 33.3 per cent discount. Sales resistance to Raleigh machines remained high, and in 1925 Holland reported that motor cycle 'orders were not coming in according to expectations', and they were temporarily discontinuing the assembly of 2.75 and 3 hp machines which were over-stocked. The management had become locked into a product in which it had invested considerable resources in developing, and which it now became reluctant to withdraw from. For example, in 1925 they introduced a newly designed 2.25 hp model.[87] Orders did pick up and as Table D.5 in the Appendix shows sales rose in 1926.

Nevertheless, Raleigh's attempts to compete on the basis of batch producing specially designed motor cycles could only achieve limited success. Profits were affected by intense price competition from established manufacturers. For example, attempts at price fixing by the BCMMTU in 1923 proved futile, and Bowden reported that an existing agreement had been broken by Triumph. Following their lead, all signatories of the price maintenance agreement had given notice of withdrawal pending further negotiations, and Raleigh was going it alone. In May 1923 the management noted that 'Several competitive firms had reduced the price of their lightweight motorcycles', but the management believed that even at their present prices they 'were still giving better value for money than any of our competitors'. By late 1923 BSA, Raleigh's main competitor in the lightweight 2.25 hp category, announced drastic cuts in prices, and forced Raleigh to consider offering additional rebates to agents. This was considered inappropriate, and Raleigh decided to increase expenditure on advertising, targeting large towns through extensive bill-posting. Price competition remained intense during 1924 and 1925, and Bowden was continually frustrated in his attempts to negotiate price agreements. However, with a severe decline in sales in 1925 an agreement was reached with Triumph, BSA and the Douglas Motorcycle Co. for the fixing of prices for the 1926 season. The agreement aimed to ensure the 'stable conduct of manufacture' and to prevent 'the financial loss that would flow from undirected competition and price cutting among themselves'. The trade was well aware that price-cutting was 'suicidal', and price schedules were to be maintained, uniform cash discounts and rebates co-ordinated, and they were to 'act in co-operation'. This agreement was extended in 1927 but by this stage Raleigh's capacity to produce motor cycles was already under severe pressure. In 1927 Bush noted that the disappointing profit figures were due to restricted output because of the scarcity of parts which were being channelled into other product lines, the need for excessive replacement parts and a huge investment in advertisement to push the machines. In 1928 the step was taken to limit the range of machines to three standard models, a 2.48 hp machine, a 4.98 hp single valve (SV) with larger tyres and a 4.98 hp overhead valve (OHV), all fitted with a new mechanical lubricator and stronger stand. The latter two, however, were to be produced to order only.[88]

Pursuing a strategy of production flexibility was one thing, but it presented a need to co-ordinate the component supply of the factory. We have seen earlier that by the late 1920s the management were keenly aware of the rising overhead costs of the factory, and this was exacerbated by their commitment to motor cycles and countershaft gears. Of particular concern was the co-ordination of numerous stocks of components for different products and models, and the transport of these components to the various departments. In 1928 Bowden recognised these obstacles and appointed a 'first class' production manager, J. M. Lees, to revamp their systems of production planning. His first recommendation was to establish a planning department to co-ordinate the supply, and costing of components in the factory which were wholly inadequate. The movement of stocks, work in progress and finished parts were scrupulously recorded, but the auditors' report of 1929 was less than complimentary, and the system was described as unsatisfactory. The records of the planning department did not tally with the records of storekeepers, 'and even records in the planning department did not coincide'. Although the auditors agreed that the intention of the planning department was 'excellent', there was a 'large margin of error'. Attempts to plan production were clearly frustrated by the inability of the factory to co-ordinate adequately component supplies internally across a range of products, and there was a recognition that they had over-extended the factory's capacity. For example, in August 1928 Lees was instructed to plan for a production of 135 000 cycles for the 1928–29 season, but commented that 'It is expected that there will be difficulty in stocking our full requirements of complete bicycles'. Factory storage space was at full stretch and stockbuilding cycles was frustrated by the need to accommodate motor cycles and parts. Further, in October 1928 Bowden referred to the difficulty in supplying ample supplies of tools from the toolmakers, and argued that if work could not be speeded up they would be forced to acquire supplies from outside. In reply, Holland argued that tool workers 'were considerably handicapped by the large variety of gear box work for motorcycles passing through the shops at the present time'. Delays in the factory impacted upon their core business of cycles, and in 1928 and 1929 the output of Raleigh's new 'club model' bicycle was restricted due to shortages in the supply of sundry components caused by delays in the factory.[89]

The onslaught of the depression of 1929 severely restricted motor cycle sales, and profits tumbled. Yet the management did not fully abandon this business, although output was severely cut and the range of models rationalised.[90] For management the motor cycle business offered prestige, and further the company still had ambitions to extend its trade in countershaft gears. Sales of these gears fell in 1929 and 1930 as the motor cycle industry felt the full brunt of the depression, but by this stage Raleigh had aspirations to develop the Sturmey-Archer side of the business in Germany. In 1927 the management had committed Raleigh to extend sales in this market, and supplied not only countershaft gears but also motor cycle engines and gearboxes. In August of that year Bush and Holland visited the cycle and motor cycle works of Elite, Wanderer,

Victoriawerke and Triumphwerke at Nuremberg to study production methods. They reported that 'Generally speaking ... the German firms are no more and in most cases less up to date than we are in England'. This prompted Raleigh to open negotiations with Victoriawerke for the licensing of their patents for liquid brazing, and the management confidently predicted that 'the present motor cycle boom in Germany will last four or five years'. In November 1927 Raleigh produced 1 000 specially designed engines for the Victoriawerke, and in December they sent an engineer to Nuremberg to supervise the assembly of countershaft gears. This led to the opening of a factory in Nuremberg in October 1929, a joint venture by Raleigh and Victoriawerke, directed at avoiding rising tariffs in Germany. The factory was run under the name of Sturmey-Archer Gears Ltd for the purpose of assembling engines and gears in Germany from parts supplied by Raleigh at Nottingham, and also using gearboxes and other parts supplied by two German firms, Nordesta and Montan. German workers were trained by Raleigh engineers in production methods and quality control, and it was estimated in 1930 that 50 per cent of all motor cycles in Germany were fitted with Sturmey-Archer gears and engines.[91]

By 1930 the Nuremberg factory was producing 12 000 engines for Germany, and the Nottingham factory was also providing 6 000 for Raleigh machines and a further 1 500 for the Coventry Eagle Co. By 1931, however, the German operation was showing a considerable loss and was abandoned in early 1932. The depression in Germany was obviously central to this decision, but Raleigh also saw a substantial decline in the demand for countershaft gears and engines in Britain, and in July 1931 both were curtailed as unprofitable.[92] The company continued to produce a limited number of speciality motor cycles until the decision was made to abandon this finally at the end of 1934. The management showed a reluctance to abandon the business, not surprising given the heavy commitment of resources to its development, but Raleigh's venture into motorised transport was given a final twist in 1931 by the decision to manufacture a delivery van, the 'Raleigh Karryall'. This was targeted at small traders, and was promoted as an economical means of transport. Economy in transport was used as a slogan by Bowden to promote sales of the company's cycles, and the decision to produce vans was based on a similar notion that they represented an alternative to more expensive conveyances. For example the 'Karryall' was promoted as the ultimate in economy, capable of 50 miles to the gallon, and subject to a motor tax of only £4 per annum. Retailing at 75 guineas, Raleigh boldly informed dealers that they were 'Supreme in the world of light transport', and would cut delivery costs by half. A similar belief was prevalent in the decision to produce the 'safety seven', a light 3–wheeled car selling at 90 guineas in 1933. This promised 'Motoring for all … with safety and economy', and was later in 1935 sold for a brief period as a saloon model.[93]

Niche markets of this type could be exploited in the short run, but motorised vehicles were not the mainstay of the company. The Raleigh factory in 1934 was actually described as 'a car factory within a factory', practically every part of the car being built in-house, but sales were 'disappointing', and 'a modern motor works of this size cannot be conjured out of air in five months'.[94] At the same time, the cycle market recovered rapidly after 1932, and so did the demand for Sturmey-Archer cycle products. In early 1934 the *Motor Cycle and Cycle Trader* reported on Raleigh's decision to 'completely' abandon motor cycles 'as unprofitable', and noted that this decision was taken in the light of the fact that 'what looked like a waning industry a few years ago [cycles] now looks healthy again'.[95] The management continued to persevere in popularising its light three-wheeled vehicles until late 1934, when the decision was finally taken to concentrate solely on the cycle business. Bowden was now fully convinced that Raleigh's future lay with exploiting the expanding market for cycles, and if this was to be achieved they would have to focus resources on their traditional product. Sustaining diversity, Bowden recognised, would require a complete organisational restructuring, which he was not willing to contemplate. The past experience had convinced him that they could not compete with larger producers, and as he argued, 'several of these products demanded entirely separate staffs and departments for manufacturing, selling and distribution', but 'it was felt that better financial results might be obtained by concentrating the entire resources and energy of the works to one product only – the bicycle and its accessories'. This was also a clear recognition of the planning problems which the company had encountered, but abandoning motorised transport also brought considerable risks. It was a 'bold step', and it was estimated that it would reduce turnover by £1 million and had to be 'compensated for by increased cycle sales'.[96] As the *Financial News* commented in May 1934 Raleigh's production of 200 cars per week was putting enormous pressure on the cycle department, and they cited Bowden's vision that the increased demand for cycles was 'no passing phase' as there was 'a general desire for healthy exercise at an economical price'.[97]

By 1935 Raleigh had become again a specialist producer of bicycles and cycle gears. The rapid recovery from the depression had justified Bowden's commitment to the cycle market, and reductions in selling prices had increased turnover substantially. During 1933 and early 1934 'an ever increasing stream of orders' had demonstrated the need to produce cycles on a more intensive basis all year round, and Bowden recognised that plant would have to be fully utilised to this end. Bowden was responding to changing customs in the domestic market, where sales had previously been concentrated into a three-month period around Easter. However, the changing attitudes of cyclists was making demand 'an all-the-year round business', and better road conditions and the rust protection of cycles had reduced the seasonal peak demand. To ensure sufficient capacity, and take advantage of future opportunities, Raleigh invested £80 000 in new plant during 1933, and this 'forward policy' was adopted to meet the 'Boom in Bicycles'.[98] At the same time, the management launched Raleigh as a public holding company, and the final section examines this decision, and analyses the performance of the concern down to 1939.

Going public, 1934, and business performance to 1939

In February 1934 a major event occurred in Raleigh's history: it was converted into a public holding company. This decision was premised upon the record sales and output which Raleigh had achieved during 1933, and there were high expectations that the profit outlook was buoyant. At Raleigh's AGM of December 1933 Bowden proudly announced record profits and an annual dividend of 20 per cent. He intimated that the time was right to consider a public flotation and, on the 13 February 1934, £2.25 million shares were offered to the public in the Raleigh Cycle Holdings Co. Ltd, which included Sturmey-Archer, Humber and the trade marks of Gazelle and Robin Hood Cycles. The flotation was warmly received by *The Economist* which claimed that the export trade in cycles was steadily improving, 'economies in production and organisation' introduced in 1933 were bringing reduced costs, and profits had correspondingly risen during the year, as shown in Table 5.5. *The Economist* noted, however, that the chief assets of the company were the Raleigh Cycle Co., and its tangential business Sturmey-Archer, and 'The existence of two separate companies – an operating and a holding concern – would appear to serve, at the moment, no concrete purpose', except in allowing the publication of a consolidated balance sheet to shareholders, and thus providing them with a more accurate picture 'of real earnings power etc.'. Whatever *The Economist* may have thought, just four days after subscription lists were opened the offer was closed because the issue was oversubscribed. Investors clearly viewed the company as a progressive concern in which future profits were guaranteed. The formation of a public holding company did not lessen the family commitment to the firm, and at the first meeting of its board on the 13 February Bowden was duly appointed

Table 5.5   Profits of operating companies, 1931–33, and consolidated
net profits of Raleigh Cycle Holdings Co. Ltd, 1934–44

	Net profit	% distributed as dividend
1931	23 555	
1932	73 576	
1933	201 542	
1934	333 986	11.0
1935	370 785	15.0
1936	473 481	22.5
1937	451 087	25.0
1938	376 515	20.0
1939	430 163	20.0
1940	471 035	20.0
1941	458 746	20.0
1942	480 829	20.0
1943	530 253	20.0
1944	500 968	20.0

Source: Figures for 1931–33, *The Economist*, 17 February 1934; for 1934–
44, Bowden. Manuscript, p. 33.

chairman and managing director. The holding company board also
consisted of George Wilson, a former manager at Sturmey-Archer who
had been made a director of the Raleigh Cycle Co. in 1931, and the
long-serving Frederick Bush. Sir Connop Guthrie, a representative of
Suffolk Trust Ltd, the company which had promoted the Raleigh flotation, was also appointed in an 'executive capacity'.[99]

Bowden continued to play an active role in the strategic management
of both the holding company and the operating company, the Raleigh
Cycle Co. Nevertheless, the minute books of the latter clearly reveal
that strategic decision-making was devolved down to Wilson who took
over as general manager with executive authority in 1936, on the
retirement of Bush. Wilson was a salaried manager but was described
by Bowden as 'a Raleigh man', and he was clearly being groomed by
him for succession. In 1938 Bowden retired as managing director of
Raleigh Cycles Ltd, aged 58, and Wilson was appointed in his place.
Nevertheless, Bowden retained the managing directorship of the holding company, and also the chairmanship of Raleigh Cycles. Indeed, he
was unwilling to relinquish 'his final say in the running of the company'.[100] By the mid-1930s Bowden had realised that he needed to
devolve responsibility more, and apart from his increasing reliance on

Wilson, he brought in new personnel such as R. L. Jones, works manager, and A. E. Simpson, sales manager, as well as maintaining his confidence in W. H. Raven, the head of the cycle department, and a 'working director'.[101]

The performance of the company after 1934 displays a high degree of success. Table D.7 in the Appendix shows sales and production figures between 1935 and 1939. Sales of both Raleighs and Humbers rose substantially between 1935 and 1937, before being halted by the short domestic and international recession of 1938. Further, as export markets recovered, foreign sales increased after 1936 and represented 29 per cent of total sales by 1937. Sturmey-Archer sales also accelerated, rising from 536 316 gears in 1935 to 600 884 by 1937. As sales rose so did production, and total output rose from 332 376 machines in 1935 to a peak of 473 864 in 1937, a 42 per cent increase. Profits also remained buoyant and rose to a peak of £473 481 in 1936, and despite the fall in the recession of 1938 recovered again in 1939 and 1940. The profit record was certainly a justification of investors' confidence in the company on the subscription of shares in 1934, and Raleigh enjoyed a highly prosperous period in its history. Profits recovered after the crash, aided by a revival on both the domestic and international fronts, and provided an endorsement of the management's decision to commit the company to the cycle industry. At Raleigh's annual conference of dealers in October 1934 Bowden informed the 800 delegates that the output of Raleigh machines was now 300 000 per annum, selling at an average price of £6 17s. 6d., and they were fully committed to gaining an increasing share of the market. Disclaiming reports in the press that the industry was a spent force, he announced a £100 000 investment in new plant, and claimed that there were approximately 10 million cyclists on the roads of Britain, one in five of the population, and 'millions of men and women rely on their bicycles as a means of transport or healthy recreation'.[102]

Raleigh's decision to concentrate on bicycle production allowed it to focus 'the energies of the staff and the capacity of the works entirely on cycles, supported by a wide and intensive advertising campaign'. Increasing sales of both cycles and gears 'more than counter-balanced the loss in other directions', and with rising profits the management was able to reinvest these resources in further plant modernisation and product development. Specialisation in cycle manufacture allowed the company to continue its policy of vertical integration, and with an enlarged output, as Bowden argued, 'a period has been reached in the company's history whereby it would pay to manufacture practically everything that went into the making of a bicycle except such specialities as tyres and saddles'. In 1936 Raleigh constructed a special tubing department which used automatic machines to weld and polish some three and a quarter miles of tubing a day for cycle frames. Conveyor systems were also extended in the factory, and the latest automatic machinery for plating and dustproof enamelling installed, as well as an investment of £40 000 in a new plant for producing freewheels. In 1936 Raleigh extended its cycle product range, producing 50 models in that year, 'and others were manufactured to meet the demand for special types of machines in vogue in foreign countries'. For example they introduced a new 'juvenile model' and broke strongly into the specialist market for sports models, attaching specially designed gear hubs at 'competitive prices' to 'popularise them'. This typified the management's continued commitment to meeting the demands of the cycling public, and 'the company was able to cater for every class of cyclist, with prices that ranged from £4 19s. 6d. to £8 8s. 0d.'. Developments were also made in electric dynamos for cycle lighting, and Raleigh patented its dyno hub in 1936, in collaboration with H. Miller & Co. Ltd of Birmingham and G. W. Rawlings of Kenilworth in Warwickshire. By 1938 Raleigh was producing 300 per week from a purpose-built factory, costing £13 000, and although at this stage the dyno hub was fitted to Raleighs and Humbers only, they were increasing output with the objective of establishing a position in export markets, and as a supplier to the domestic trade.[103]

By the late 1930s Raleigh represented the state of the art in high-quality cycles and accessories. Consistent with the traditions of the company, the Raleigh was 'individually produced in the world's largest and best equipped cycle factory. It is quality-built in every detail by expert craftsmen using only the finest tools and materials'. This endorsement of its 1937 models was a testimony to management's emphasis upon design innovation, its cheapest model retailing at £4 19s. 6d., with added features at no extra cost. These included stronger forks, rubber handle grips, 'special aero saddles', all chromium plated parts, and 'exclusive frame design for easy running'. In promotional terms the company was selling a quality product based on an 'exclusive design', developed through 'years of experience in producing quality machines'. Thus, as a company advertisement proclaimed: 'Models built from standard parts can never be designed on individual lines to give you perfect performance such as you get on a Raleigh.' Raleigh maintained its craft traditions and, despite facing competition from mass producers at home and abroad, they survived and prospered. This, however, did not come without the costs of reducing potential operational efficiency. We have commented earlier on the problems of co-ordinating production in the factory, and these difficulties remained deeply entrenched. For example, W. H. Raven reported in 1937 that:

> In order that the works shall be in a position to concentrate to a
> greater degree on one particular line of work at a time it was
> decided that the Depots should be fully stocked immediately, thereby
> giving the works a larger assortment and a larger number of orders
> to work on.

The problem, however, was the continued production of numerous
non-standard products, and this was recognised by A. E. Simpson,
Raleigh's sales manager. Commenting on the increasing use of flow
production techniques, he 'hoped the day was not too far distant when
we could supply to the depots whatever stocks suited the factory to
produce, and the depots would be automatically stocked by the factory
working to a programme that suited its requirements'. As he noted,
however, the benefits of mass production systems were negated because
they produced numerous different lines, and 'At the present time it is
scarcely possible to see two consecutive machines of the same type
passing along the conveyors'.[104]

But the exclusivity of design was the key selling point of the Raleigh,
and this was the relationship which had been built up with dealers.
Indeed, the recovery of the bicycle market was characterised by the
substitution of a buyer's market with a seller's market, and Raleigh
regained the upper hand. For example, in 1938 Raleigh announced the
launch of its 'Dealers' Aids Service', and a 'Dealers' Local Co-operative
Advertising' scheme. Advertisement costs, amounting to 50 per cent of
expenditure, were guaranteed to be paid by Raleigh, based on dealers
advertising '100 per cent Raleigh'. This was clearly aimed at securing
brand loyalty, but created tensions with dealers who argued that they
were being imposed upon. Raleigh ignored these claims, recognising
that their cycles were in high demand. This was most aptly demonstrated by Raleigh's decision in 1936 to break its traditional code of
marketing exclusively through appointed agents and dealers, and to
forge agreements with large retailers, such as Halfords and Currys, for
guaranteed bulk orders. Ignoring the pleas of a number of agents that
this would damage their business, Wilson argued 'that the large number
of cycles which we could sell to Currys would more than counteract
any loss which might be sustained through malcontents'. This clearly
represented a switch in policy away from the traditional notion of
building up relations with numerous agents, and as Wilson argued,
their position was 'strengthened by the fact that we are producing a
bicycle which is generally in demand'. The majority of agents were
consequently persuaded to accept the new arrangements.[105]

In this Raleigh was responding to the increasing concentration of the
industry on a few large, but powerful competitors by the 1930s, most
notably BSA, Phillips and Hercules. Raleigh was now included amongst

the most prominent of these large producers, but despite growing co-operation in the industry Raleigh still faced intense competition from cheaper mass producers such as Hercules. A solution, of course, was to merge interests, and in 1935 Bowden, Wilson and Guthrie opened negotiations with Edmund Crane, the proprietor of Hercules, to buy out the business. Negotiations broke down at the last moment, but the offer represented Raleigh's perception of the perceived competitive threat Hercules represented. In particular, Hercules was proposing to develop a rival three-speed hub to Sturmey-Archer and threatening to substitute this for supplies obtained through Raleigh. This represented a consider-able loss of business, and as Guthrie argued it was now imperative that they should increase sales further, by 50 000 cycles per annum, to compensate for the loss of the Hercules business, 'and all legitimate steps should be taken to do so'. After the failure of the negotiations with Hercules Wilson eventually finalised a trade agreement which guaranteed that Hercules would take a minimum of 25 000 hubs from Raleigh, but relationships between the companies were strained to break-ing point.[106]

The competitive threat from companies such as Hercules was central to Raleigh's decision in 1936 to invest directly in an assembly plant in the Republic of Ireland. In collaboration with the Dublin merchant house of W. H. Cooper & Co., who marketed Phillips and Hopper cycles there, they formed Raleigh Industries Ireland Ltd with authorised capital of £15 000. Exploiting generous grants by the Irish government to employ local labour, the Irish company began operations in early 1937 and assembled 1 000 machines per week, from parts supplied by Nottingham, down to the eve of the Second World War. As Wilson argued, this was an important step and should secure Raleigh's position in the Republic against competition from Hercules, Phillips and Hop-per. But competitive pressures were building up elsewhere, and during the sharp recession of 1938 tensions between Raleigh and Hercules hit boiling point. At the end of 1937 Raven reported that the home market was slowing down, and this represented an opportunity to move more into export markets. By February 1938, however, Wilson was con-cerned that export orders were falling, and this was particularly the case in the important Indian market where Hercules, followed by Phillips, had cut prices and created 'a state of uncertainty, resulting in merchants holding up instructions for delivery'.[107] The threat of price-cutting was also prevalent in the domestic market, and the usual dilemma now faced management: cut prices and thus quality, or maintain them and face a declining share of the market. The dilemma was compounded by rising material and labour costs in 1938 as the re-armament drive intensified. One solution was found in the reintroduction of the Gazelle cycle range, which was used to sell lower-quality machines at equivalent prices to those of Hercules, Enfield and Hopper. By May however sales had worsened, and Wilson argued that Raleigh was 'suffering this year from the over-buying of last year' and the company was forced to introduce alternate weekly work patterns.[108]

In the depressed market of 1938 attempts at price collusion were frustrated by the actions of Hercules. Thus, in May 1938 Bowden met with BSA to discuss prices for 1939, but noted that Watling and Brotherton of Hercules had 'definitely refused to come into any price agreement for next season, and they have threatened to put on the market a machine at £2 19s. 6d.'. As he argued, it was 'useless' to determine prices without knowing the position of Hercules. With disappointing sales, especially from their arrangement with Currys, 'the opinion was hardening' nevertheless, 'that we should under no circumstances drop below the figure of £5 5s. 0d. and we should maintain the price and quality of our product irrespective of what the Hercules Company proposed to us'. In June Raleigh was forced to lay off 1 000 workers because of the fall of orders, and in September 1938 the BCMMTU decided to commit the trade to maintaining prices for the 1939 season, regardless of the acceptance of Hercules. The outcome of this competitive game, however, is not fully known because economic conditions recovered sharply in 1939 as the economy moved closer to war. By September 1938 Wilson could announce the resumption of full-time working, tenders for cycles for the armed forces were flooding in, and by November Raleigh was receiving orders for munitions work, of which it had been providing limited amounts since 1937.[109] The competitive forces operating in the industry, and the position of the large producers, were finally to resume in the post-war era, and Raleigh's part in this story is examined in the final chapters of the book.

Notes

1. Bowden, 1934.
2. Church, 1993, p. 18; Church, 1996, p. 565. The importance of the role of family founders in shaping the history of British business enterprise is well documented in the literature. For example, see Coleman, 1987a; Payne, 1984; Jones and Rose, 1993.
3. Bowden, 1975, pp. 39–40, 43; DDRN 4/10/1/39, Abridged List of Raleigh Prices for 1916, published in 1915.
4. DDRN 7/2/3, Souvenir of the Opening of the New Raleigh Works, 5 May 1922, p. 3; Bowden, Manuscript, pp. 24–5; Bowden, 1975, pp. 40, 44.
5. DDRN 1/40/6, Auditors Report with Balance Sheet, 1916; DDRN 1/2/1–6, Raleigh Cycle Co. Ltd, Board and General Meetings Minutes

with Fortnightly Reports, 12 December 1916, 20 September 1917, 16 December 1918.

6. Minutes with Reports, 29 January, 4 February 1915. To secure family progression Harold had no authority to transfer shares without the prior consent of his father during his life.

7. Ibid., 9 February 1916; DDRN 10/3/4/18/1, Memorandum of Agreement Between Frank Bowden and Harold Bowden for Purchase of Shares in the Raleigh Cycle Co. Ltd, 5 February 1915; DDRN 7/2/7, History of the Raleigh Cycle Co. Ltd, n.d.; Bowden, Manuscript, pp. 23–4.

8. Minutes with Reports, 29 October 1917. For example, in October 1917 the weekly wage bill was £2 500 higher than the corresponding month in 1916, and in July 1917 the Ministry of Munitions had contracted for fuses at 6s. each, compared to 7s. 9d. ten months earlier.

9. Ibid.

10. Bowden, 1975, pp. 40, 43–4.

11. Minutes with Reports, 19 July, 13, 28 August, 16 September, 21 November 1919.

12. See Donnelly, Batchelor and Morris, 1995.

13. Minutes with Reports, 22 January 1920.

14. See Church, 1995, pp. 23–4 for an examination of the debate on the introduction of Fordism in the British motor car industry. The general impression is that Fordism, with its implications for a tight supervision of the work process had a limited application in British industry before 1940. See also Gospel, 1992; Wrigley, 1993; Lewchuck, 1987.

15. Minutes with Reports, 13, 20 March, 16, 28 April, 28 August 1919. Attempts to recruit lower-paid women workers on night shifts also contravened the regulations of the engineering trade. See Minutes with Reports, 18, 30 July 1919.

16. Ibid., 13, 27 February, 17 May, 25 June, 28 August, 16 September 1919.

17. Ibid., 18 July, 28 August, 6 October 1919. For example, Raleigh was unable to meet targets for an order of 5 000 countershaft gears from Triumph because of a five-month delay in delivering disks by the Ferodo Co.

18. Ibid., 30 July, 16 September, 22 October, 6, 21 November 1919, 14 May 1920.

19. Ibid., 27 May, 13 June, 19 July, 13, 28 August, 18 December 1919.

20. Ibid., 3, 4 July, 22 October, 6, 21 November, 18 December 1919.

21. Ibid., 28 April, 25 June 1919.

22. For an examination of the role of government after the war see Pollard, 1983; Glyn and Booth, 1996; Middlemass, 1979.

23. Minutes with Reports, 18, 31 December 1919.

24. Ibid., 13, 27 February, 19 July, 25 September 1919, 22 January, 6 February, 4 March, 16 April 1920; Bowden, 1975, pp. 44–5.

25. Minutes with Reports, 20 June, 1 July, 30 September 1920.

26. Ibid., 16 July, 30 September, 14 October 1920; DDRN 5/1/3, Raleigh Newspaper Cuttings, *Motor Cycle and Cycle Trader*, 20 May 1921.

27. Minutes with Reports, 14 October 1920.

28. For example Raleigh had resisted collusion with the Engineering Employers Federation in setting piece rates in June 1919 on the grounds that it would reduce the personal co-operation between Raleigh management and its employees. Ibid., 13 June 1919.

29. He was dissuaded from doing this by Harold who argued that this was 'a contentious matter and would ... be prejudicial to Sir Frank in his present state of health'. Ibid., 29 October 1920.

30. Ibid., 10, 31 December 1920.

31. Ibid., 13 January, 5 May 1921; Bowden, 1975, pp. 45–6; *Irish Cyclist and Motor Cyclist*, 4 May 1921.

32. Harrison, 1984, p. 408.

33. Bowden, 1922. On exchange rates Bowden called on government to abolish all war debts and 'to take such action as is possible and advisable'.

34. Ibid.; *Motor Export Trader*, 24 February 1922.

35. *Motor Export Trader*, July 1922.

36. Barnsdale, 1922. For example, due to unfavourably exchange rates and rampant inflation in Germany the price of a Raleigh machine was a staggering £120, nevertheless the 'Germans are glad to pay it to get the famous all steel bicycle'. *Nottingham Evening Post*, 22 June 1921.

37. Bowden, Manuscript, p. 16.

38. See Lloyd-Jones, Lewis and Eason, 1999.

39. Bowden, 1922.

40. *Lincoln, Rutland and Stamford Mercury*, 24 February 1922; Bowden, 1934. For an excellent examination of the evolution of managerial labour strategies in British business see Gospel, 1992. Similar views to Bowdens were advanced by industrialists such as Dudley Docker. See Davenport-Hines, 1984, pp. 73–7.

41. See Jeremy, 1998, p. 382.

42. Minutes with Reports, 9 March 1921; Bowden, 1975, pp. 46–7; *Motor Cycle and Cycle Trader*, 20 May 1921. Bowden also condemned the efficiency of workers: 'the present efficiency of our workmen as compared with pre-war stood at approximately 75 per cent; whilst on the other hand the present cost of production, both in bicycles and gears, was two and a half times the amount paid in 1913'. Minutes with Reports, 9 November 1921.

43. Minutes with Reports, 13 January, 9, 23 March, 6 April, 5 May 1921; *Police Chronicle*, 22 April 1921; *Motor Cycle and Cycle Trader*, 20 May 1921. A reduction of 12s. 6d. per week for toolmakers was also negotiated, backed up by a guarantee of full-time work. Minutes with Reports, 9 March 1921.

44. Minutes with Reports, 16 June 1921, 10 May, 21 June 1922.

45. For example, in February and March he personally appealed to the Sturmey-Archer department that they must 'meet the challenge'. Countershaft gears were selling at £8 5s. compared to other makers at £6, and cycle gears would have to be reduced to 25s., 'the maximum figure at which it is found possible to do business'. Ibid., 21 February, 15, 29 March 1921.

46. Ibid., 13, 27 July, 24 August 1921; *Nottingham Guardian*, 8 October 1921; *Motor Cycle and Cycle Trader*, 28 October 1921; *Aberdeen Evening Express*, 30 October 1921; Barnsdale, 1922; Bowden, 1922; Bowden, 1975, p. 47.

47. Minutes with Reports, 16 February 1922; *Nottingham Journal*, 5 May 1922; Bowden, Manuscript, p. 27; *Evening Standard*, 24 January 1923; *People*, 31 December 1922.

48. Harrison, 1984, p. 408. During the inter-war years a number of British companies introduced 'welfarist strategies' as part of industrial relations policy as merger activity increased the scale of organisation. For an examination of the creed of industrial welfare in British business see Wilson, 1995, pp. 159–60; Jones, 1983; Morris and Smyth, 1994; Fitzgerald, 1988.
49. *Accelerator*, August 1922; Minutes with Reports, 7 September 1922, 23 September 1924, 24 February, 24 April, 7 December 1926.
50. For example, the company had to reschedule work hours because of the disruption of transport. On one day only was Raleigh directly affected, when 37 per cent of employees struck on union instructions. Operations were, however, indirectly affected, through the continuation of the coal strike which affected supplies to the work and adversely affected rail transport and the dispatch of goods. Minutes with Reports, 6, 26 May, 7 June 1926.
51. Ibid., 31 January 1924, 30 September, 20 October, 20 November 1925, 26 May 1926.
52. Ibid., 29 November 1926, 21 February, 1, 16 May, 13 June; 13 July 1928.
53. *Indian Cycle and Motor Journal*, May 1931.
54. Minutes with Reports, 25 May 1927, 18 January 1928, 5 December 1928.
55. Ibid., 4 February, 3, 18 March, 4 September 1931, 21 January 1932; *Motor Cycle and Cycle Export Trader*, 22 August 1931; *Bicycling News*, 14 October 1932.
56. Bowden, 1934.
57. Ibid.
58. Bowden, Manuscript, p. 26; Bowden, 1922; Bowden, 1975, p. 63; *Leeds Mercury*, 25 May 1921; *Motor Cycle and Cycle Trader*, 19 August 1921; *Constabulary Gazette*, 19 November 1921.
59. *Leeds Mercury*, 25 May 1921.
60. *Cycling*, 24 February 1921. The Sturmey-Archer factory was described as 'Magic in the Making', having 'Machines with Everything but Minds'. Steel plates and bars were converted into gears 'with a minimum of human guidance and a maximum of mechanical work by tools that show all the precision of the perfect machine, coupled with something uncannily like the trained intelligence of the skilled engineer'. Hubs were pressed from steel blanks, having first been tempered, and at each stage of the process the pieces were annealed in large ovens, by experienced workers using rule of thumb, so that its temper would be suited for the next stage of the process. See *Cycling*, 19 May 1921; *Irish Cyclist and Motor Cyclist*, 25 February 1921.
61. Minutes with Reports, 4 January, 17 May 1923, 26 March, 16 April 1924.
62. Bowden, Manuscript, p. 27; *Nottingham Journal*, 5 April 1922; *Garage and Motor Agent*, 13 May 1922; *Motor Cycle and Cycle Trader*, 12 May 1922.
63. Minutes with Reports, 7 September 1922; Bowden, 1975, pp. 48–9; *Indian Cycle and Motor Journal*, February 1923.
64. Minutes with Reports, 26 July 1923.
65. Ibid., 26 March, 16 April 1924; Bowden, Manuscript, pp. 26–7. Raleigh

developed the 'rustless cycle' in 1921, the frame and parts being boiled in a chemical solution to charge the surface of the steel with a phosphate that would not oxidise, and covered with an elastic enamel which was rubber based, and finally covered with two coats of superfine finishing enamel. See *Cycling*, 13 January 1921.

66. Bowden, Manuscript, p. 52; Bowden, 1975, pp. 49, 53; CTC *Gazette*, February 1921.
67. Minutes with Reports, 25 May 1927. The agreement also involved collusion on the technological side, BSA providing Raleigh with 'all facilities for inspecting their manufacturing methods and costings and we are also to provide them with similar facilities'. Negotiations with BSA had first began in 1923 but no agreement had been reached. Ibid., 3 May 1923.
68. Ibid., 15 June 1927.
69. Ibid., 22 December 1926, 29 May 1929.
70. Ibid., 23 August 1928; Bowden, 1975, p. 63; *Motor Cycle and Cycle Trader*, 4 March 1932.
71. *Bicycling News*, 14 October 1931; Bowden, Manuscript, p. 33
72. *Motor Cycle and Cycle Trader*, 12 January 1934; *Cycling*, 28 August 1931.
73. *News Chronicle*, 5 November 1931.
74. *Donegal Democrat*, 6 February 1932; *Motor Cycle and Cycle Trader*, 12 January 1934; *Financial News*, 14 May 1934.
75. Bowden, Manuscript, p. 31; Bowden, 1975, p. 64; Minutes with Reports, 12 February 1932; *Motor Cycle and Cycle Trader*, 1 December 1933, 24 August 1934.
76. *Motor Cycle and Cycle Trader*, 7 September 1934.
77. Bowden, 1922; Minutes with Reports, 12 January 1922, 14 February 1923; DDRN 4/64/1/2–4, Promotional Material for 1926–28; *Swindon Evening Advertiser*, 1921; *Motor Cycle and Cycle Trader*, 6, 20 May 1921; *Clarion*, 10 March 1922. The 1922 catalogue depicted 'a beautiful girl riding out of the picture ... on a perfectly drawn bicycle, with an old world village as a background'. The use of women in promotional campaigns was common, and 'Rosie Raleigh', was used as the image 'of their famous girl cyclist'. See *Indian Cycle and Motor Journal*, February 1923; *Birmingham News*, 23 February 1922.
78. Bowden, Manuscript, p. 26.
79. Minutes with Reports, 6 April 1921; DDRN 4/64/1/1 Promotional Material, 1923; *Indian Cycle and Motor Journal*, February 1923; *Motor Cycle and Cycle Trader*, 6 October 1922.
80. *Police Chronicle*, 22 April 1921; *Motor Cycle and Cycle Trader*, 20 May 1921; *Constabulary Gazette*, 22 January 1921.
81. *Nottingham Evening News*, 1 November 1933; *Nottingham Evening Post*, 3 October 1934; DDRN 1/11/2, 1/14, 1/15, Circulars to Dealers, 1932–33; *Bicycling News*, 16 December 1931; Bowden, Manuscript, p. 33.
82. Bowden, 1922; Bowden, Manuscript, p. 28; *Lloyds Sunday News*, 20 November 1921; Minutes with Reports, 21 June 1922, 3, 29 November, 22 December 1926, 17 February 1927, 2 March 1928.
83. Bowden, 1975, p. 135.
84. *Motor Cycle and Cycle Trader*, 6 May 1932.
85. Bowden, 1975, pp. 48–9, 136; Bowden, Manuscript, p. 27; *Indian Cycle*

and Motor Journal, February 1923; *Irish Cyclist and Motor Cycle,* 3 August 1921; *Motor Cycling,* 30 March 1922; *Motor Cycle and Cycle Trader,* 29 June 1921; Minutes with Reports, 20 December 1922, 4 January, 17 May 1923.

86. Bowden, 1975, pp. 48–9; Minutes with Reports, 16 August 1923, 13 July 1927.

87. *Motor Cycle and Cycle Trader,* 30 November 1922; Minutes with Reports, 26 July 1923, 18, 25 February 1925.

88. Minutes with Reports, 9 November 1922, 3 May, 25 October, 14 November 1923, 12 August, 15 September 1925, 15 June, 16 November 1927, 1 May, 13 July 1928; DDRN 10/1/1/20 Agreement between BSA and Others, 24 September 1925.

89. Minutes with Reports, 2 February, 14 March, 17 April, 13 June, 28 August, 10 October 1928, 12 February 1929, DDRN 3/11/1, Auditors Report and Accounts, 1929.

90. Minutes with Reports, 29 December 1929.

91. Ibid., 17 August, 4 September, 16 November, 14 December 1927, 30 October 1929; Auditors Report with Accounts, 1930; Bowden, 1975, p. 136; Bowden, Manuscript, p. 30.

92. Minutes with Reports, 29 July 1931, 21 January 1932.

93. Bowden, Manuscript, pp. 31–2; Bowden, 1975, pp. 61, 64; DDRN 1/13 Promotional Material Sent to LDV agents, October 1932. The 'Safety Seven' was a 742 cc twin-cylinder convertible four seater, with a three-speed gearbox, and a top speed of 55 mph. Fuel consumption was 50–60 miles to the gallon, and it was advertised as 'The cheapest car in the world to run', and retailed at 100 guineas with a £4 road tax. DDRN 1/19 Promotional Material Sent to Agents 1935.

94. *Motor Cycle and Cycle Trader,* 18 May 1934.

95. Ibid., 16 February 1934.

96. Bowden, Manuscript, p. 35; Bowden, 1975, pp. 65–6. The equipment and stock of the car department was purchased by T. L. Williams, the Raleigh manager, who removed them to a factory at Tamworth and eventually produced under the name of Reliant.

97. *Financial News,* 14 May 1934.

98. *Motor Cycle and Cycle Trader,* 16 February 1934.

99. Bowden, 1975, p. 65; Minutes with Reports, 20 December 1933; 13 February 1934; DDRN 1/3/1 Minute Book of the Raleigh Cycle Holding Co. Ltd, 13 February 1934; *Star,* 13 February 1934; *The Economist,* 17 February 1934, p. 1104, 24 February 1934, p. 422.

100. Bowden, Manuscript, p. 38; Bowden, 1975, p. 68. Bowden, as we shall see, in Chapter 7, remained an important figure in the company until he retired as chairman in 1955, and even then he was made honorary president until his death in 1960.

101. Minutes with Reports, 31 May, 29 June 1938; Bowden, 1975, p. 66.

102. *Daily Herald,* 4 October 1934; *Nottingham Journal,* 3 October 1934. Bowden estimated that with a large number of cyclists on the road, and an average life expectancy of a cycle of five years, if the present high demand continued there would 'be a need to provide 2 million machines per annum', apart from the export trade 'which was steadily improving'. He also called for government to promote cycle paths or roads as on the Continent.

103. Bowden, Manuscript, pp. 35–7; Minutes with Reports, 12 February, 9, 19 March, 17 April, 7, 19 May 1936.
104. *Daily Mail*, 22 April 1937; DDRN 1/27, 'An Explanation of Why the Raleigh Runs so Easily', 1930s; Minutes with Reports, 21 January 1937.
105. DDRN 1/22, Raleigh Dealers Sales Promotion 1938, DDRN 1/24, Dealers Local Co-operative Advertising Scheme, October 1939 to September 1940; Minutes with Reports, 7, 16, 30 January 1936.
106. Bowden, 1975, p. 65; Minutes with Reports, 20 February, 24 April 1935.
107. Bowden, 1975, pp. 136–7; Minutes with Reports, 21 July, 27 November 1936, 1 December 1937, 3 February 1938. In the Indian market Raleigh cycles were selling at 15s. and 18s. above those of Hercules and Phillips respectively. Minutes with Reports, 7 September 1938.
108. Minutes with Reports, 26 April, 11 May 1938.
109. Ibid., 26 May, 29, 7, 24 September, 3 November 1938. Bowden, Manuscript, pp. 38–9.

CHAPTER SIX

Progress and challenge: the British bicycle industry in the post-war years, 1945–60

In April 1944 a social survey in Britain interviewed a sample of 2 862 adults across a spectrum defined by gender, socio-economic grouping, and geographical location. The survey provides a useful insight into the cycling habits of the British populace, and tells us something about the pervasiveness of the bicycle in British life on the eve of the post-war era. Of those interviewed, 26 per cent possessed a bicycle, and 3 per cent used cycles belonging to others. Thus we can reasonably assume that during the early 1940s one in four British people owned a bicycle. The survey also showed that cycling was not evenly distributed across the population, and that there were quite marked differences in bicycle use by different groups. The pattern is illustrated in Table 6.1. Bicycles clearly had an instrumental use, 27 per cent of workers regularly cycling to work, and for those in agriculture, the munitions industries, building and transport, and clerical occupations the percentage was higher. Other distinct patterns which emerged were that a higher proportion 'used bicycles in the middle than in the highest and lowest economic groups', men were significantly more likely to use bicycles than women, and British cycling had a distinct regional pattern to it. Bicycle use was more

Table 6.1 Bicycle use in Britain, 1944

	% Using or possessing a bicycle	Number on which survey was based
Men	42	1 197
Women	19	1 065
Workers	38	1 886
Non-workers	10	976
Urban areas	27	2 290
Rural areas	35	572

Source: 'Social Survey of Bicycles in War Time Transport', *Board of Trade Journal*, 12 January 1946, p. 24.

popular in East Anglia (agricultural and flat), the south-central region (flat), and in the heart of the bicycle industry in the Midlands (also flat), than in Scotland, Wales and the North East of England.[1]

This survey was also of considerable marketing interest to the bicycle industry, but the authors of the report added the caveat that 'cycling habits vary seasonally and also the changing composition of the population as demobilisation proceeds is likely to alter the proportion using bicycles'.[2] The industry could not sit back and contemplate the return to peace without considering the changed domestic environment. In addition, the report was a domestic survey, and said nothing about foreign trends in bicycle usage. In the post-war world, the rallying cry to British industry was to increase exports in a drive for economic growth. Business activity, compared to the inter-war years, switched away from domestic to foreign markets, and while it did not neglect the home front, the bicycle industry was to play its full part in the post-war export drive. It is to this development that we now turn.

The bicycle industry and the post-war export drive

At the end of the Second World War the bicycle industry in Britain was dominated by three large producers. These were the holding company of Raleigh Industries, an exclusive manufacturer of cycles,[3] and two other 'group' organisations who ran large bicycle divisions, Birmingham Small Arms (BSA), and Tube Investments (TI). The latter consolidated its position as Britain's largest cycle producer in 1946 with the acquisition of the Hercules Cycle Co. Ltd for £3.25 million. TI was a engineering concern concentrated in the Midlands, and in 1952 had 36 operating companies and employed a total of 32 000 employees. The chairman of the concern was Sir Ivan Stedeford, 'a trained engineer and the son of a Methodist minister', and in 1946 he informed the public that TI was acquiring in Hercules 'probably the largest producer of bicycles' in the country. At the same time, he reassured the bicycle trade that TI would remain committed to the interests of the bicycle industry, and the cycle division would guarantee the continuation of these supplies.[4] Apart from the big three, the industry also had a large number of specialist producers supplying bicycles for sport and, in addition, toy companies such as Tri-ang produced tricycles for the children's market. Nevertheless, the structure of the industry was highly concentrated in the hands of three large firms, and it was these which were to meet the challenges of the post-war export drive.

The need to expand exports from British industry was a consequence of the enormous costs that the Second World War had imposed upon

British finances. As part of its wartime funding Britain had sold assets held abroad to the value of £1.118 billion, and the effect of this was to cut by half the net income received from abroad compared with the level of 1938. Further, the rise in the price of essential imports had reduced the net spending power of this income, and the external problem facing the country was further compounded by the rise in sterling balances held in London by mainly Commonwealth countries. Over the period of the war, Britain's indebtedness to these countries rose from £476 million to £3.55 billion. The loss of foreign income from abroad, and the huge increase in indebtedness which faced the new Labour government, forced politicians to secure a huge short-term loan from the USA. But in the longer term, salvation could only be ensured by a significant increase in British exports.[5] The target adopted was a 75 per cent increase in exports over the levels prevailing in 1938, and this increase was essential if the country was to import its food and raw material requirements without enduring a massive balance of payments crisis. As the Board of Trade proclaimed in 1946: 'Industry must fit itself for this national task by the best research, industrial design and salesmanship that was possible.' At the same time, there was a warning that there was a need to maintain 'our reputation for quality and value', and businessmen were advised that it would be inadvisable to take advantage of a 'seller's market to palm off inferior goods on our overseas customers', a tactic which would do 'a great disservice to the nation'.[6] Translating this message to the bicycle industry, this meant that increased volume output must not be at the expense of quality and, while the industry should not neglect the home market, a higher proportion of output was required for exportation.

During the war itself, the bicycle industry had made an important contribution to the nation's munitions requirements. For example, J. A. Phillips, the Birmingham bicycle and component maker, who had been taken over by the TI group in 1919, had produced over the war years some 89 million common shells. By the conversion of its 'No. 1' machine shop the firm also produced armour-piercing nose caps and 'literally millions of aircraft parts', and its pedal and hub assembly shops had produced grenades and land-mines 'by the millions'. Similarly, Hercules had produced millions of components for the aircraft industry, and for inclusion in a variety of munitions.[7] These enterprises were typical of many firms in the industry who converted plant to meet the demands of war, and as plant and labour were diverted from cycle production it is not surprising that cycle exports fell back during the first half of the 1940s. Table 6.2 shows the decline in British bicycle exports, and makes a comparison with three other consumer goods industries between 1938 and 1945.

Table 6.2   Exports of selected consumer goods, 1938–45 (£000)

	Foreign countries		British countries		Total	
	1938	1945	1938	1945	1938	1945
Bicycles	486	265	1 189	1 031	1 675	1 297
Cutlery	3 451	3 293	5 576	6 713	9 028	10 006
Electrical goods	4 150	3 745	9 280	9 886	13 430	13 632
Pottery	3 264	5 406	6 346	7 604	9 610	13 010

Source: The Economist, 20 April 1946, p. 643.

While bicycle exports had fallen by 22.5 per cent, those of pottery had risen by 42 per cent, and although electrical goods had remained almost static, the exports of cutlery had risen by 10.8 percent. Despite this trend, *The Economist* was somewhat bullish about the prospects of export growth for the post-war bicycle industry. In a statement, very much the product of its own time, it proclaimed that 'The logical development after a recovery in every country is a refrigerator in every home or a bicycle in every native hut'. *The Economist* predicted that comparative advantage would flow to those industries which were engaged in light, repetitive, assembly work for the manufacture of durable goods such as cycles, cutlery, wireless (radio) apparatus, pottery etc. These industries could expect a brighter future in world export markets than Britain's older heavy industries.[8] To reap the rewards from this window of opportunity, the bicycle industry needed to switch rapidly back to the production of cycles for peacetime requirements by converting existing plant and/or investing in new facilities. It needed to adapt quickly to recapture the lost foreign markets of the war years, and also to consolidate its stronger position in Commonwealth/Empire markets. Sir Ivan Stedeford, the chairman of TI who had consolidated a number of cycle manufacturers into its group of companies, was confident that his company would be at the forefront of the post-war production and export drive. He informed the trade in January 1945 that 'The factories in our cycle division will be able rapidly to effect a change-over to their full peace-time production – immediately they are permitted to do so'. He was adamant that his company would play its full part in rebuilding British trade, and he held out good prospects for business with Russia where missions had already been sent out 'to examine market conditions on the spot', and they also intended visits to South America, Canada, India, South Africa, the Near East and Europe.[9]

The focus on expanding export markets by TI was complemented by technological developments in its bicycle divisions. For example, the subsidiary J. A. Phillips, described by *Cycling* as 'renowned the world over' for its bicycle components, was one of the first concerns in the industry to introduce post-war designs, placing on the market their new alloy pedal, the 'Philite', when the war was still on. Phillips also brought out in 1945 a new brake, and was developing a new centre-pull calliper which was claimed to be of 'a unique design'. They had also in preparation a new ultra-lightweight hub which they were planning to market. By the autumn of 1946 the reconstruction programme at Phillips appeared to have made considerable advances. R. H. Thomas, in a survey of the company's factories at Smethwick (Bridge Street), and Handsworth (Downing Street), commented on the introduction of new machine tools in the automatic shop which had totally replaced pre-war machines. In addition there was re-tooling throughout the No. 1 machine shop, five lines of new semi-automatic machinery were about to be installed in the plating shop, and the No. 2 machine shop was fully 'engaged in general work, having completely changed over from the making of rocket projectiles'. Thomas concluded his survey on an optimistic note, claiming that the conversion from war to peace was 'complete', production had reached satisfactory levels, and he anticipated that when the reorganisation programme was fully installed production would 'soar to even greater heights'.[10] While Thomas's account of the rapid process of conversion at Phillips demonstrated the flexibility of British producers, it nevertheless tended to omit serious problems faced by the company. A much needed dose of realism was provided by James (Jim) Boulstridge who had become chairman of Phillips Cycles during the war.

Boulstridge was one of the leading personalities of the post-war cycle industry, being one of the 'younger executives', and a figure who had 'risen to be one of the most influential'. The son of a Warwickshire mining engineer, he started his career in that industry, then moved into the shipping trade before joining J. A. Phillips, a highly autonomous company within the TI group, in 1924. In 1932 he was appointed the company secretary, and subsequently became a director and managing director. Boulstridge was also linked to other companies within the TI group, including the Hercules Cycle Co., Phillips Cycle Co. of South Africa Ltd, and was a director of the main board of the TI holding company. His role on these other boards was a co-ordinating one, and he exercised no direct managerial role until the cycle division of TI was restructured in the mid-1950s. Nevertheless, in the early years after the war he was recognised as a manager who knew 'his factory inside out'.[11] Compared to the earlier account by Thomas, Boulstridge took a more realistic view of the issues surrounding reconstruction, and his position was also less optimistic than that taken by his immediate superior, Ivan Stedeford, the chairman of TI. In the latter part of 1946 Boulstridge claimed that there was a need to place a high priority on a programme of expansion aimed at 'speeding up output', but admitted that there had been an 'apparent slowness in meeting current demands for cycle components'. This was a consequence of 'unexpected difficulties arising in the change over from war to peace production, and delays in the delivery of new plant and machinery'. Further, the reorganisation and re-equipment of the factories, to which an expenditure of £500 000 had been committed, had been held back by bureaucratic red tape. Commenting on government controls over building construction, he informed the bicycle trade that 'Phillips have been trying, unsuccessfully, for two years to secure a licence for buildings which are essential to the [reconstruction] plans'.[12]

Adjustment problems were not confined to TI's bicycle divisions, and in March 1946 Sir Bernard Docker, chairman of BSA, announced that his company's bicycle plants 'were now starting on peace production', and were producing 'better bicycles ... on a larger scale' than ever before, but by January of the following year the plants were running into the problem of inadequate supplies of fuel in the form of coal, gas and electricity. This was in part a consequence of the terrible winter of early 1947, but Docker was clearly frustrated by the fact that his cycle divisions 'had more orders for home and exports than they could meet quickly owing to restricted output'. These problems were compounded by a lack of adequate supplies of steel, and at TI, for example, Stedeford complained of supply problems in the latter months of 1946, and noted in October that 'steel supplies had for some time been insufficient to keep the group's manufacturing capacity fully occupied'.[13] As we shall see, the issue of steel supplies proved to be a protracted problem for the bicycle industry in the post-war years.

There were clearly problems of adjustment, related to supply-side constraints, following the end of the war. Although these held back the reconstruction programme in the short run, the longer-term prospects for the bicycle industry were bright. Market conditions appeared to favour the industry, and Stedeford proclaimed that the 'outlook for bicycle production is set fair on the demand side'.[14] Further, firms such as BSA and TI had done well out of the war, and possessed the necessary funds to finance reconstruction. For example, TI's profits had increased threefold between 1939 and 1946, rising from £867 794 to £2 567 602. In December 1946 Stedeford announced a £6 million group modernisation and development plan, £500 000 of which was to be allocated to J. A. Phillips. He prided himself that: 'Thanks to the conservative financial policy over the years, and its unwavering adherence to the principle that profits should be ploughed back into the business and strong reserves accumulated, TI was in a favourable position of being able to finance their very considerable programme out of existing funds.'[15]

Stedeford was quick to point out that the acquisition of the Hercules Co., in September 1946, out of liquid resources, was an important part of the programme devised for the bicycle divisions. Hercules was a large producer of bicycles, and had made a rapid reconversion to peacetime conditions under the capable leadership of Sir Edmund Crane, who had originally founded the business with his brother, Harry, in 1910. The take-over by TI effectively ended family control, and the business was placed 'under the able directorship of Arthur Chamberlain', the great-nephew of Joseph Chamberlain. Acquisition created new opportunities, not least 'bringing within reach on a unique scale all the economies inherent in the co-ordination of mass cycle component manufacture with that of the complete bicycle'.[16] Thus, the cost of producing cycle components was predicted to fall as their supply was increased, both to the group's own cycle division as well as to the bicycle industry more generally. The group would benefit from internal economies of scale, and in addition external economies would be generated for the industry as a whole.

By the last quarter of 1947 the TI bicycle division was exporting approximately 75 per cent of its output, and it had become a widely held opinion within the industry that the Ministry of Supply would have to increase the allocation of steel to bicycle manufacturers, even if this was to be at the expense of other industries who did not have a large export business. In December 1947 Stedeford welcomed a government decision to give the cycle industry priority for the supply of raw materials because of its export potential. He was magnanimous in his announcement that TI was the 'world's largest cycle and cycle component producing unit, with the biggest and most valuable export business', and 'the British cycle industry as a whole had firmly established its roots in most of the international markets'.[17] Within two years of the end of the war, the export capacity of the industry had far surpassed its pre-war levels, as shown in Table 6.3.

By the end of 1947 cycle exports had reached their target of 60 per cent of the total output of just under 3 million units,[18] and exports of completed cycles were valued at £11.8 million in the first nine months of 1948, in addition to components valued at £3.6 million. By the late 1940s the industry's largest markets were in the less industrialised nations, such as India, Pakistan, Malaya and the African colonies. This market penetration was, in part, helped by the absence of Japanese competition which 'before the war made so great an appeal to the

Table 6.3 Pedal cycle production and market distribution, 1938–47
(average production, thousands per month)

	1938	1941	1947	% change 1938–47
For export	31.0	92.8	123.2	+297.4
For home market	134.0	83.1	84.3	–37.1
Total	165.0	175.9	207.5	+25.75

Source: Record and Statistical Supplement to *The Economist*, 1948, p. 524.

uninstructed native cyclist'.[19] The switch to export markets, although successfully meeting government targets, did leave the industry vulnerable to external factors. Boulstridge, in the Phillips company magazine, *Newsreel*, informed the workforce in April 1948 that he was approaching the year with 'a feeling of trepidation', and this was shared with other directors and managers. The problem, as Boulstridge saw it, was that overseas markets were steadily closing against the company, effectively shifting the focus to a buyer's market. At the same time, raw materials were becoming more difficult to obtain, and this market was increasingly moving towards a seller's market.[20]

Boulstridge's fears were partly related to his concerns over the trend of growing nationalism in some of their best markets, as foreign governments attempted to encourage local assembly. Such fears were not allayed when in 1949 the Indian government raised tariffs on British goods from 24 to 60 per cent, but the three largest producers, TI, BSA and Raleigh Industries, responded by setting up their own plants in India for the assembly of finished cycles from components supplied from Britain.[21] Indeed, Boulstridge's anxieties concerning 1948 proved to be somewhat premature, and in October he was boasting to the *Birmingham Mail* that Phillips had secured export orders worth £500 000 for 79 000 bicycles placed during the week ending 21 October. The orders had 'come from firms all over the world', and it was the 'greatest amount of work for a single week they had ever handled'. Provided sufficient steel could be procured, he felt confident 'that we shall go a long way to securing this valuable exchange for the country'.[22] By the end of the year the firm was exporting between 9 000 and 10 000 bicycles per week, and Hercules and BSA were 'also making large and increasing exports of cycles'.[23] As we shall see in the next chapter, Raleigh also placed a high priority on exports.

How do we account for the British success in the export of cycles in the immediate post-war years? A simple demand-supply approach goes some way in providing an answer to this question. On the demand side, an estimate by the Board of Trade, based on the normal consumption per head of the world's population at the end of 1946, concluded that due to the shortages of the war years the shortfall of bicycles in the world was in the order of 50 million. This opened a window of opportunity to British producers to satisfy this demand, especially as the capacity of the Germans and Japanese to supply bicycles was severely curtailed. Before the war these two countries were the world's leading exporters. In 1938, for example, they had exported between them in the region of 4 million cycles per annum. Post-war Western Germany had begun bicycle production in 1946 as part of its economic reconstruction programme, but the Board of Trade felt confident that its industry would not be in a position 'to compete in the open market for a considerable time', and at that time the Japanese had not even approached the levels of recovery apparent in Germany. The opportunity was there for the British cycle industry to penetrate new markets, and to regain lost ground in established ones. For example, in 1938 the Japanese had accounted for 13.3 per cent of total cycle imports into British East Africa, and were second only behind the British.[24] British manufacturers now had a major opportunity to increase their market share, and as the Board of Trade pointed out, British East Africa had a population structure of 30 000 to 40 000 Europeans, 250 000 to 300 000 Asians, and 13 million Africans, the latter representing a sizeable body of new consumers. During the war, income levels in Africa had risen, partly due to the rapid increase in expenditure by the military services. Real incomes were also protected by price controls over basic commodities. Thus, there was a rising demand for cheap to medium-priced consumer goods such as bicycles, and the African consumer also had a clear preference for a quality item, a characteristic of the British cycle industry since before the First World War. As Board of Trade officials were quick to point out: 'the African was a keen judge of quality, viewed particularly from the point of view of reliability, and it must be emphasised that poor quality goods are not required'.[25]

After the Second World War the British bicycle industry concentrated on two key markets: the hard currency markets, especially the dollar markets of North America, and the Commonwealth/Empire markets. The need for hard currency, especially dollars, was not of course unique to Britain in the immediate post-war years, but the fiasco of British dollar convertibility in the summer of 1947, when a good deal of the loan negotiated by John Maynard Keynes in the previous year had been wasted trying to defend the indefensible, brought home the need to maximise our exports into the North American markets to earn dollars. By the early 1950s the USA had become the largest single market for British bicycle exports, taking approximately 10 per cent of the total sales of £24 million, and in terms of volume exports to the USA increased from approximately 15 000 in 1948 to 500 000 in 1955.[26] Table 6.4 shows the top three foreign markets in 1952. In that year, 276 000 British bicycles were sold in the USA, and the expectation was that sales would rise to 350 000 during 1953. This was 'A remarkable achievement', claimed *The Economist*, 'in a country where so many working men have their own cars'.[27] In fact, the buoyancy of the American market became particularly important in 1953 for the rise in sales to the USA was in stark contrast to overall bicycle exports which fell to approximately 2 million units compared to 2.8 million in the previous year. In consequence, a number of cycle companies introduced short-time work and there were fears of redundancies in the first half of 1953. For example, the Hercules Cycle Co. introduced a four-day week in January for 1 500 workers; the Unique and Unity Cycle Co. of Birmingham introduced a four-day week for its 190 workforce and made 35 workers redundant; Phillips dismissed nearly 200 workers from its factories in Newtown, Montgomery, and Smethwick near Birmingham in mid-January. An official of the Unique and Unity placed the blame for the company's difficulties on the problems of export markets which were 'Bad', and in his opinion the position the trade faced 'could not be worse'. He held out little prospect of improvement in 'the near future', and this pessimism was reiterated by a spokesperson from Hercules who claimed that since the introduction of a four-day week 'the industry's general position had remained static'.[28]

Table 6.4   Main British markets for bicycle exports in 1952

	% of total exports by volume	% of total exports by value
USA	9.85	10.4
British West Africa	6.32	—
Malaya	3.60	—

Source: *The Economist*, 21 November 1953, p. 609.

A main cause of the problem was the imposition of import restrictions by many countries as a consequence of rising financial difficulties following the end of the Korean War boom. Responding to the redundancies at Phillips, Boulstridge informed the *Evening Dispatch* that 'The simultaneous slowing down of many of the world's principal cycle buying markets makes it inevitable to declare a number of workers redundant. It is very deeply regretted and the decision, unavoidable as it was, has been taken with great reluctance'.[29] Boulstridge held out the hope that the situation would only be of a 'temporary nature', but he noted that several large markets, including India, Pakistan and Indonesia, had closed. In addition, embargoes were placed on imports into Argentina, the Brazilian market was constrained because of currency difficulties and the rise of indigenous cycle production, and New Zealand and Australia had suspended licences to import. It was now acknowledged amongst the industry's business leaders that 'the restrictions could be removed only by negotiations on a government level'. As the trading situation deteriorated, 2 500 workers at both Phillips and Hercules factories signed a petition calling for government action to alleviate the industry's problems.[30]

But the difficulties facing the industry were compounded by two other factors. First, there were clear signs that Japanese and continental competition was presenting a growing threat, one estimate suggesting that Japanese bicycle components, particularly chain wheels and cranks, were some 50 per cent lower in price than those produced by British suppliers. Second, the option of British manufacturers switching to the domestic market was inhibited by high levels of domestic purchase tax.[31] For example, Boulstridge complained that purchase tax 'had played its full part in placing bicycles beyond the reach of so many who needed them and had also interfered with the normal rhythm of retail and wholesale buying'. Relief for the industry did come in April when the budget reduced purchase tax from 33.5 to 25 per cent, a decision which prompted Boulstridge to announce that the Phillips factory in Newtown was to return to full work, and led him to predict that 'The public, trade and manufacturers all will appreciate the concessions made by the Chancellor'. Indeed, the company's plant at Smethwick had been in the process of returning to full-time work since February, and a spokesperson informed the press that 'different departments will return to normal working in stages'. Boulstridge viewed the problems of early 1953 as a short-run cyclical downturn, a consequence of the pattern of demand facing the industry, which had built up to extraordinary levels since 1945 and had been accompanied by speculative stockbuilding.[32] By the early 1950s this pattern had run its course, and there was a return to a more normal seasonal trend, where demand peaked in the second half of the year, but this longer-run change ran in conjuncture with the temporary financial difficulties faced by a number of importing countries. This had created severe short-term trading problems for industries with a high propensity to export, such as bicycles. The problems of 1953 were in reality a precursor of things to come, as the industry faced severe problems from the mid-1950s, and a challenge to its world leadership.

The challenge to the British bicycle industry in the 1950s

By the second half of 1953 the industry did indeed experience a distinct upturn in trade, and firms such as Phillips were boasting about their order books being full.[33] In the two years after 1953 the industry experienced an upsurge in output, the total production of UK cycles rising from 3 million units to 3.56 million in 1955. In 1953 the British bicycle industry was the largest producer and exporter in the world. Output increased from 2 996 000 machines in 1953 to 3 156 000 in 1954, a rise of 5.3 per cent, and exports of British bicycles and parts represented approximately 70 per cent of the world's exports of these goods.[34] Commenting on the performance of Phillips, one of Britain's leading export firms, in 1953, the *Motor Cycle and Cycle Export Trader* stated that the company was 'continuing their successful efforts to raise still higher the standard of British bicycles beyond the reach of foreign competition'.[35] However, British dominance in the export trade was to be short-lived, and from the mid-1950s the situation turned sour for British producers and output fell back to 2.5 million units by 1957. The industry was reduced to two main producers, the bicycle division of TI, which was named the British Cycle Corporation (BCC) in 1956, and Raleigh Industries which had also acquired a number of producers. For example, in 1957 Raleigh purchased the bicycle division of BSA, which also included Sunbeam Cycles Ltd and New Hudson Cycles Ltd, the latter representing subsidiaries of BSA since their acquisition in 1943. In 1953 the main operating company of BSA had segregated the bicycle side of its organisation, which was subsequently operated as a separate entity.[36]

The turnaround in the fortunes of the industry was a result of a combination of external and internal forces over which firms such as BCC and Raleigh had only varying degrees of control. In terms of external factors, exports came under increasing pressure following the prosperity of 1953–55, and fell by one-seventh between 1956 and 1957. In 1957 Sir David Eccles, the President of the Board of Trade, acknowledged in Parliament that the 'export of bicycles had dropped', and this had also been evident between 1955 and 1956 when the total number of machines exported fell from 2 351 000 to 2 006 000. In 1956, the *Manchester Guardian*, under the headline of 'Now Cycle Firms Are Worried', warned that 'The chill wind of foreign competition is now blowing more keenly about export markets'.[37] The broad pattern of exports was affected by three main factors: problems in the important American market; growing foreign competition, especially the re-emergence of Germany and Japan as major competitors; and the rise of import substitution in markets outside Europe and the USA.

In the American market it appeared that the British bicycle industry became a victim of its own success. In 1955, one-quarter of the industry's direct exports were going to the USA, and they had risen by over 400 per cent since the end of the war.[38] This level of market penetration alarmed US bicycle producers, who embarked upon an aggressive lobbying of Congress and the Eisenhower administration to remedy the situation. For example, H. M. Palin, the director of the British Cycle and Motor Cycle Manufacturers' Union, informed journalists on the eve of the International Cycle Show of 1954 that 'American manufacturers had been conducting a campaign against British machines and had applied to the US Tariff Commission for protection'. He went on to observe that it was 'very disheartening for the British bicycle industry to be faced with this attempt to exclude it from a market which it has been at great pains to cultivate, not only in the national interest but in accordance with US Government policy to encourage trade between our two countries'.[39] Palin's remonstrations proved to be of no avail, and the outcome was a rise of one-third in the custom tariff on imported cycles into the USA. *The Economist* acknowledged that British producers had tried to avoid becoming too dependant on one or two large overseas markets, but in the early 1950s, 'when the South-East Asian, East African, and South American markets started to slacken, the bright prospect of the large North American market became too attractive to ignore'. Following the rise in the US tariff, British bicycle exports were halved, but the imposition of import controls does not tell the whole story, for German and Dutch bicycle exports replaced the British as the largest suppliers of complete machines and components and accessories. The British industry's share of the US bicycle market fell from 85 per cent in 1951 to just 26 per cent by 1957.[40] Therefore, the second problem faced by British manufacturers was their failure to compete effectively against the resurgence of other nations in the field of cycle production.

By the mid-1950s this situation had become acute and, in particular, the emergence of German and Japanese competitors pressed heavily on British producers. British bicycle manufacturers were caught in a double-bind. On the one hand German producers were hurting the British in the USA, while on the other hand the Japanese had reappeared as powerful competitors supplying both components and finished machines to countries in South-East Asia and East Africa.[41] The window of opportunity which had opened up for the British industry in the years immediately following the war had been firmly closed by the mid-1950s. This problem was compounded by a number of less developed countries, which had previously provided important markets for British cycles, embarking in the 1950s upon programmes of import substitution, which was made possible because of the relatively simple technology involved in bicycle production. The industry produced 'a remarkably efficient and inexpensive piece of machinery', but allowed for little room for improvement. Cycle design tended to focus on pseudo-innovations which attempted to improve appearance, comfort, and the number of accessories, but it was not technically demanding to reproduce robust, reliable and, above all, cheap machines. Further, the manufacture of bicycles does not require a complicated or heavily capital-intensive industry, and consequently 'it is one of those things to which a country reaching out for quantity production in industry casts its hands'.[42] A simple product life cycle model will show that industries will tend to migrate to lower wage economies where local and small-scale assembly can develop using imported parts and components.[43] The Japanese, of course, were quick to seize the opportunity to supply bicycle components and, in addition, they also benefited from lower wage costs than British component producers.

This is not to suggest that the British were complacent, or gave up mounting a counter-challenge. Both TI and Raleigh Industries were not slow in establishing overseas production capabilities following the end of the war. For example, TI set up production facilities in India, where the company's subsidiaries were already producing cycle saddles, chains and lamps. In the late 1950s its bicycle division, BCC, took a half share in the Ceylon Cycle Co. of Colombo 'which was laying itself out to supply the island's requirements of bicycles'. Similarly, Raleigh followed a strategy of acquiring overseas production capacity, and like TI opened factories in India and South Africa, countries where Phillips and the Hercules Cycle companies also had plants. Raleigh also had foreign trading subsidiaries in Europe and North America, and had built up an extensive network of foreign dealers, numbering some 10 000 by 1953.[44] Despite these initiatives, however, problems still remained. As Stedeford, TI's chairman, admitted in 1958, despite only a moderate trade recession in South Africa there had nevertheless been a serious fall in the demand for cycles. Consequently, their two subsidiaries, Phillips (South Africa) and Hercules, 'had another difficult year'. Although the recession in the South African market had been moderate, what concerned Stedeford was that it had aggravated a deeper underlying problem facing the industry. The regrettable position of the South African cycle industry, he claimed, was that it had 'a productive capacity in excess of, perhaps almost double, the market's foreseeable requirements'.[45] As the world manufacturing capacity for bicycles increased in the 1950s, British producers found themselves confronted by long-term structural problems. In effect they were caught in a vice-like grip, squeezed on the one hand by powerful German and Japanese competitors, and on the other hand constricted by the emergence of new low-wage competitors in both Eastern Europe and Asia.

Given these problems in export markets, was salvation to be found by an increased focus on the domestic market? In 1953 Boulstridge, the managing director at Phillips, highlighted the importance of the domestic British market for the future of the industry. Warning against discounting the domestic market in favour of export-led growth, he informed manufacturers that 'Without a healthy home trade a healthy export business cannot progress'.[46] Yet the performance of his own company in the home market was less than satisfactory. For example, Davis, a director of Phillips, criticised the performance of the company in 1955 in exploiting the home market. In particular, he noted a 'deterioration in our services to the home market since August this year compared with 1954'. The information available to the management showed that the delivery of cycles was 38 per cent down on the corresponding period in 1954, and what caused concern was the assertion that 'the company had lost business ... due to delays in deliveries'. As Davis concluded, their inability to deliver on time affected 'Company goodwill and the prospects of future business'. A prime cause of slow delivery was the company's over-commitment to the export sector. As Boulstridge claimed, the inability to supply the home market satisfactorily was conditioned by 'the very necessary emphasis which had been placed on executions of contracts for the export dollar markets, coupled with delays which had been experienced in delivery of supplies from the component factories'. But the company's problems in supplying the domestic market went deeper than this, and reflected the discrepancy in the company's production methods and its output planning. For example, Boulstridge admitted that there were imbalances between the capabilities of the new 'complex plant' introduced on the shop-floor, and the efficient operation of the tool room at their factories. The latter was 'not keeping pace with the overall development of the business', and Boulstridge acknowledged that this important department was 'under-staffed'. Somewhat contradictorily, he claimed that restrictions 'of tool-room employees is a sound policy', and reluctantly he accepted that 'modern development may merit a possible revision of the policy', and he sanctioned the engagement of 'additional and high class craftsmen'.[47] On the one hand, the company was introducing modern production methods but, on the other hand, given the range and quality of products it was producing, there was still a requirement for the production of its own specialist tools. The initial strategy was to reduce this dependence by cutting the number of tool-workers, a consequence of their higher wage costs and the power of labour in bargaining, but effectively the company was responsible for its own shortcomings by creating production imbalances. Clearly, there were supply-side constraints operating at Phillips, and we shall return to this issue later when we consider the company's production and organisational strategy in the 1950s, but to gain a full understanding of the problems of the home market also requires a consideration of demand-side factors.

According to George Wilson, the managing director of Raleigh Industries, the problems of the domestic market were different from those of foreign markets. By the mid-1950s the sales of pedal cycles in the UK had not reached the levels they had achieved prior to the war,[48] and this view was echoed by Boulstridge. The latter informed the *Financial Times* that there was a different pattern to the post-war domestic market compared to the export market, and whilst 1 423 542 cycles had been delivered to the home market in 1938, this figure had not been equalled since, and from 1951 'substantially lower levels have prevailed'. Boulstridge offered three reasons for this decline in domestic sales. First, he suggested that increased spending power had been directed towards the consumption of television sets and other consumer durables.[49] Second, and somewhat bizarrely, he blamed 'the incidence of national service' which apparently 'diverted younger men from their ordinary occasions'. Third, he placed the bulk of the blame upon the adverse effect of legislation relating to 'the price and conditions of the purchase of bicycles'. In addition, there was clearly a fourth factor, the expansion of motorised transport. As George Wilson pointed out, the industry could not ignore the 'ample evidence of the degree to which motorisation has affected the lives of the great majority of people in this country'. For both Wilson and Boulstridge, a major factor adversely affecting domestic demand and damaging the future potential of the industry was the incidence of purchase tax. For example, Boulstridge was concerned about the consequences of future levels of purchase tax on creating business uncertainty, and leading to problems of over-stocking in the industry.[50] The disquiet expressed by Boulstridge and Wilson was echoed by Sir Bernard Docker, the chairman of BSA, who attacked the autumn budget of 1955 as a set of policies which 'added to the burden of taxation'. Identifying purchase tax for his main assuault, he claimed that it was a 'financial device' which was 'a tangle of absurdities and anomalies'.[51]

A further irritant concerned government regulations on hire purchase terms, whereby the government could raise or lower the size of the initial deposit and the rate of weekly payments.[52] In this respect, the use of hire purchase regulations was related to government macro-economic policy, and the notorious phases of 'stop-go' which characterised economic decision-making in the 1950s. Governments used purchase and hire purchase terms to constrain inflationary pressures in the economy by attempting to regulate the prevailing level of aggregate demand. Nevertheless it is difficult to accept the view of business leaders, such as Boulstridge, Wilson and Docker, that government legislation was the main factor influencing the demand for cycles. As Margaret Hall has pointed out, 'The control of hire purchase has a sharp impact on the timing of purchases, rather than on the long-run trend of consumption as a whole'.[53] The root cause of the industry's problems was that it was facing a structural decline in the demand for its basic product in the home market, and experiencing intensified competition from abroad. The next sections will examine the industry's responses to these challenges by first looking at a case study of a major firm, J. A. Phillips, and examining changes in its production and organisational strategy during the 1950s. This will be followed by taking a broader view of a key initiative of the period, the attempt by the industry to break into the motorised bicycle (the moped) and scooter markets.

Facing the challenge: a study of J. A. Phillips & Co.

In the mid-1950s the management at Phillips were highly optimistic about future business outcomes. The firm offered 40 distinct models of bicycles for the home market in 1954, and catered for a wide variety of tastes, interests and incomes. For example, prices ranged from its cheapest model at £12 16s. 9d. to its most expensive at £24 6s. 1d., and their sales portfolio included for the first time a sports model for boys and girls, the 'Phillips Junior Sports'. The company deployed an aggressive marketing strategy, and the management were quick to exploit events in the media to stimulate the sales of its products. For example, in the summer of 1953 they seized the opportunity offered by the release by Associated British Pictures of the film 'Isn't Life Wonderful', starring Donald Wolfit. Adapted from the book, *Uncle Willie and the Bicycle Shop*, it represented life in 1904, and Phillips supplied 20 promotional cycles which were displayed in a shop on the film lot. By the end of its run, the film had been exhibited in 300 cinemas, and Phillip's dealers were requested to co-operate with local cinema managers in establishing mutual publicity schemes. The company also announced that their publicity department would 'give full backing (to dealers) by supplying publicity materials for window displays', and arrangements were made to display material in the foyers of cinemas. Other opportunities were taken to use the media industries, and stars of popular radio shows of the 1950s, such as Kenneth Horne and Richard Murdoch, were employed to help sell the Phillips name. The company showed considerable enterprise in the area of marketing, and by the mid-1950s Phillips was one of the leading cycle producers in the world. Celebrating its Diamond Jubilee in 1953, the Phillips company was a world-wide name, and there was coverage of the event not only in the British press, but also from much further afield. For example, the *Singapore Cycling Annual* recorded the great success of the company in producing cycles from its 'four great factories', and also informed its readers that the company was 'also one of the largest cycle ... component manufacturers in the world'.[54] The company's status as a component manufacturer is of particular interest. As we referred to earlier, the emergence of continental and Japanese firms as major component suppliers increased the competitive pressures on the company, and it was this side of the business which was of particular concern to the management at Phillips.

In November 1951 Boulstridge complained about competition in component supply from continental producers. For example, the company's pedals had been superseded in 'construction and finish' by continental makers, a fact that Boulstridge confirmed from a recent visit he had made to the USA and Canada. Boulstridge believed that the problem was due to a lack of investment in best practice technology, and insisted that the company needed to improve its production methods and, as an initial step, he recommended the purchase of 'special plant' to improve the efficiency and quality of their pedals. Unanimously supported by his fellow directors, the decision was taken to 'acquire a bolt making machine with necessary tools', at an approximate cost of £25 000. The new equipment was given an urgent priority, and two directors, Winisper and Fellows, were given responsibility for providing specifications and arranging purchase. By December, the management had decided that their plans for pedal production required an additional bolt-making machine, and a second purchase was sanctioned.[55]

Orders for the new machines were placed with an American firm, the National Machine Co. (NMC). But some 11 months after the original decision to sanction the order, in October 1952, Fellows reported to the board that 'the National Machine Co. have been requested to defer preparations for the second bolt making machine until we get a clear picture as to the full capabilities of the machine'. At this same meeting, Boulstridge reported a 'serious decline' in the sales of the company's pedals, and pointed out that at current production levels and prices they were losing ½d. per pair on pedals, and would need, on his estimate, to sell 'a minimum of 60 000 pairs per week at a reduced price before they could reap a profit'.[56] The delays in installing new equipment, however, seriously hampered Boulstridge's hopes in this direction, and he again lamented the poor quality of the company's pedals. Winisper, who had been charged with delivering improvements in the production system, informed him that 'remedial action' was in the course of being introduced, and promised that this would take affect within a matter of days. Boulstridge was not, however, satisfied, and continued to urge upon the directors the need to enhance quality to meet competition, and he highlighted the inability of the production department in its attempt to mass-produce 100 000 pairs of pedals per week, which had been the main cause of the deterioration in product quality.[57]

Despite a reassurance by Winisper that production was 'at the highest standard and would be maintained', the problems of production at Phillips continued, and as the sales of pedals deteriorated further, the management cancelled the order for the second bolt-making machine in 1953. This decision, however, embroiled the company in a major dispute with NMC who would only accept cancellation on payment of 16 per cent of the purchase price of the machine. In addition, Phillips was obliged to 'accept delivery of the electrical equipment, to the value of $3 017, which had already been obtained by them'. In a magnanimous gesture NMC offered to treat 50 per cent of the cancellation charge as an advance on a repurchase of the machine by 1 May 1954. Nevertheless, the management at Phillips were reluctant to become embroiled in a legal dispute with the NMC, and they reversed their decision to cancel the machine order, agreeing to fulfil the original contract. This episode shows that Phillips was a company with a high level of concern for the technical quality of its products, but management vacillated over the appropriate strategy to pursue. Further, while Boulstridge was alert to the problem facing the company he was ill-served by his fellow directors who, at best, were over-optimistic in their assessment of policy implementation, and at worst were simply slipshod, both in their advice to Boulstridge and in their analysis of the capabilities of the machines they sought to purchase. Vacillation was compounded by problems over delivery dates which involved the company in further disputes with NMC. For example, Phillips were informed that the NMC could not deliver the first machine until at least July or August 1954, some 30 months after Boulstridge had first raised the problem, and the American company could provide no firm date for the delivery of the second machine.[58]

Boulstridge's frustrations concerning technical developments at Phillips were compounded by worries over the firm's organisational capabilities. In 1950 he complained that the company's AGM had become a mere formality which allowed for no detailed analysis of the company accounts. His proposed solution was a separate board meeting at which an 'expert accountant would be present' to facilitate a closer study of the 'implications of the detailed accounts'. In this he was supported by Arthur Chamberlain, a member of the main board of directors of the TI holding company since his appointment as chief executive of Hercules in

1946. Chamberlain pointed out that both at home and abroad customers were demanding greater extended credit facilities and it was the position of the parent company 'that subsidiary companies should be prepared to grant credit terms, for example, 30 days, 60 days or 90 days rather than allow prospective business to pass to their competitors'. He also raised the question of intra-company trading and enquired whether Phillips 'was experiencing difficulties in obtaining adequate supplies of materials for associate companies'. On the whole Boulstridge was satisfied with the service which Phillips was receiving, but was clearly less than impressed with the arbitrary nature of decision-making within the TI group. For example, he referred to a last minute decision to reduce supplies of seat and chain stays from a TI subsidiary, a matter which had caused considerable problems to production at Phillips. In reply, Chamberlain outlined the managerial philosophy of the main TI board concerning the relationship of subsidiaries within the group. It was the responsibility of the main TI board to formulate strategic decisions on 'whether associated companies were to receive their full requirements from within the group regardless of the effect on manufacturers outside the group'.[59]

Chamberlain's pronouncement highlights two key factors concerning organisational strategy within the TI group. First, it would appear to confirm that the holding company form of organisation, adopted by TI in the inter-war years, still persisted into the post-war period. Internal competition of an administered kind was allowed to flourish 'with only minimal policy and financial controls from head office'.[60] However, while Phillips might well have experienced a high degree of autonomy, and had a management style probably not unlike the personal capitalist form characteristic of Raleigh, so too did other associated companies within the group. Hence there was a tendency for tensions to arise over intra-group supplies of materials and components. Second, the issue of component supplies had important implications for the bicycle industry as a whole. Components formed a high proportion of the total cost of manufacturing a cycle. Table 6.5 shows the cost of producing a cycle for a small firm which assembled, enamelled and finished bicycles, with an annual output of 20 000 units per annum in 1965.[61] It was crucial for small fabricators that they could secure adequate supplies of components at competitive prices. As TI's chairman, Stedeford had reassured the industry in 1945, at the time of the purchase of the Hercules Cycle Co., that the group's bicycle division would continue to serve the needs of the bicycle trade as a whole. Any shift away from this strategy would have had serious implications for the bicycle industry, but as will be shown in the next chapter, Raleigh, similar to TI, retained a strong commitment to the 'equity' of supply, and was to merge with TI's bicycle division in 1960.

Table 6.5 Cost of production for a small bicycle manufacturer, 1965

	Cost per bicycle (£)
Components	8.00
Direct labour for assembly	0.25
Other manufacturing overheads	0.75
Total	9.00

Source: Pratten, 1971, p. 158.

In July 1951 Boulstridge referred to 'unprecedented' policy problems facing the company, and urged his fellow directors to discuss 'any matters which were of serious importance to the company'. Over a year later he was still complaining of 'the many complexities which the company is faced', and reiterated the 'importance of more frequent discussions on matters of policy'.[62] One certainly detects a sense of frustration on Boulstridge's part as he attempted to raise, amongst his colleagues, a greater sense of urgency over the difficulties confronting the company. Unfortunately the minutes of the board, all too frequently, do not elaborate on the policy problems, but at a meeting in October 1952 we do get a glimpse of one of the issues facing the company when Boulstridge raised concerns over the performance of the company's planning department. The main problem seemed to be an attitude of complacency by middle management, and as Boulstridge admitted, 'since 1940 the Progress Planning Department had generally escaped their responsibility for the correct planning of the products of the business'. This resulted in a contradictory outcome, whereby some components were in excess supply while in other cases there was an inability to produce sufficiently to meet demand. Boulstridge demanded that the department 'should be placed on a business like footing as soon as possible', and that members of the Phillips board should 'give thought to the matter with a view to deciding precisely what information should be procured, how to procure it, and how best to employ it'. It would appear that within a year, in July 1953, improvements had been effected and Bennett, a Phillip's director, informed the board that the planning department was working 'satisfactorily'. But again Boulstridge was ill-served by his colleagues, for in June 1954 he was complaining bitterly that the planning department 'could not be considered as operating satisfactorily either on the analysis side or in connection with issuance of work tallies'. Consequently Bennett was requested to undertake a full investigation of 'conditions in the department with emphasis on the query whether the senior official is fully capable of controlling the job'.[63]

The fundamental problem of component supply continued into the mid and late 1950s. For example, in October 1955 Bennett complained of the difficulties 'which frequently occurred in the bicycle factory in consequence of shortages, at critical moments, of adequate supplies of components from the Credenda works'. The effect of these shortages was that bicycles were leaving the factory with accessories which were 'a significant departure from standard specifications', and more seriously they were disrupting the volume of output which 'would never be retrieved'. As was mentioned earlier, Boulstridge placed part of the blame for the company's failure to make satisfactory deliveries to the home market in 1955 on inadequate component supply, and Bennett recommended that all the company's bicycle factories should carry a stock of at least one month's supply of components and parts. Some of the causes of the problem were related to the position of Phillips within the wider TI enterprise, for as late as the mid-1950s the parent company had still not agreed an overall policy for intra-company trading amongst its constituent parts. As Arthur Chamberlain admitted in early 1956, TI was not clear whether associated companies were supplying components at factory cost or at prices including the normal mark-up. With the supply of certain component parts, such as pressed steel bottom brackets, the problem became so acute that Boulstridge instructed Fellows to pursue the possibility of purchasing supplies from continental producers.[64] The organisational structure at TI, it would appear, had not evolved by the mid-1950s much beyond the inter-war holding company format. The ability to supply an optimum flow of components and accessories, an advantage one would assume from being part of a larger group, seems to have escaped Phillips, and it is a serious indictment of administrative and managerial inadequacies at TI.

The problems at Phillips were not just organisational, but there were also other constraints operating. For example, in early 1956 Winisper maintained that the maximum output of all types of pressed steel brackets was potentially 14 000 per week, but actual output was restricted to no more than half that number because, 'unfortunately, we have not yet a sufficient labour force to man a night shift'. Boulstridge's main concern was that actual output was falling well short of potential output, and he impressed upon his fellow directors the importance of ensuring that the company reached 'the potential maximum production rather than to rest content if current production ran parallel with incoming orders'.[65] This factor was crucial if the company, and indeed the British bicycle industry generally, was to meet the challenge of growing international competition by the mid-1950s. In the key American market continental bicycle producers were able to profit from an ability to offer delivery of a complete machine within seven days from the placement of the order.[66] Faced with the competitive challenge, there was a variety of responses, which included organisational innovation, the development of new products and a focus on marketing.

In 1956 TI began an organisational restructuring of their bicycle division which attempted to move away from the high level of autonomy which characterised the associate companies. In effect, the associate companies had operated as personally managed, independent concerns, and an executive council, under the chairmanship of Lord Reills, and including Boulstridge and Chamberlain, was established to oversee TI's cycle divisions. The various companies making the cycle division were now brought under the umbrella of the BCC, and a chief executive committee was also set up with a series of subcommittees responsible for production policy, commerce and marketing, costing, and overseas affairs. The costing subcommittee, for example, was given the task of establishing uniform costing procedures, particularly for long-run projects. The most important project was a proposed 'uniform bicycle factory' to replace the numerous and geographically scattered plant of the existing bicycle division.[67] The implementation of this project was to be a protracted one, and it involved various negotiations with companies, including ICI, to purchase an appropriately sized site for the new factory. It is difficult to gauge the success of the reconstruction, not least because BCC was merged with Raleigh Industries in 1960. But there is no doubt that there was a major attempt to revamp the existing structure of the bicycle division. The necessity for this was highlighted in the autumn of 1956 when Boulstridge informed the Phillips board of a loss of £17 000 in July, and, more seriously, anticipated a £50 000 loss in August. With the high cost of organisational reconstruction, it is not surprising that the burden fell most heavily on labour. In the autumn of 1956 1 250 workers, representing one-tenth of its bicycle workforce, were made redundant.[68]

The aim of TI's chairman was to concentrate bicycle production 'in compact and efficient plants', and in November 1958 he claimed that his company would spare 'no expense to make this possible in the cycle industry'. The response of the workforce had been less than enthusiastic, and in January 1958 2 000 workers had struck over redundancies in the Phillips plants in Smethwick.[69] There were, however, broad structural forces at work which placed strong downward pressure on the industry. In 1957 BSA, the smaller of the big three, had bowed to competitive pressure and sold its bicycle division to Raleigh Industries. The mid-1950s were difficult years for BSA, and in response the company had undertaken an aggressive marketing strategy[70] and reorganised its cycle companies into a separate division in 1953. Nevertheless, it continued to lose market share steadily, particularly to Phillips. Despite operating a modern factory at its Waverley site, with a capacity of 8 000 machines per week, the cycle division had been operating at a loss even before the market turned sharply against British bicycles in 1955. In November 1955 BSA announced a decline in profits; for the financial year ending the 31 July 1955 they fell to £2 865 676 compared to £3 079 826 in the previous year. The company directors referred to 'the continued effort to maintain the lowest possible selling prices in the face of increasing costs', and reference was made to 'the struggle to combat ever increasing competition both at home and abroad'.[71]

BSA was then rocked to its core by a scandal concerning its long-time chairman and managing director, Sir Bernard Docker, which also embroiled his high-profile wife, Lady Docker. The upshot of this was that not only did Docker lose his chairmanship and executive position, but was also voted off the BSA board. The problems of the company were compounded by Docker's attempts to fight his way back on to the board in October, and not surprisingly the new chairman, J. Y. Sangster, called for 'stability' at the company, and pleaded that in the future BSA might receive 'only such publicity as its size and position would warrant'. Against the background of falling profits, increased competition and boardroom turmoil, BSA sold its manufacturing rights for Sunbeam, New Hudson and Eadie to Raleigh Industries. *The Economist* claimed that the deal was a welcomed 'accreditation for Raleigh, just as much as BSA should be healthier for the divorce'.[72] What is clear is that in the face of growing competitive pressure, BCC, for example, complaining of increased competition from The Netherlands, Germany, Japan, Russia and China, restructuring and organisational change became a basic requirement of survival. But restructuring by itself was not enough. There was a requirement for a corresponding strategy of product innovation, and this takes us to the experiment with motorised bicycles and the introduction and marketing of mopeds and scooters.

Mopeds and scooters: a missed opportunity

In November 1953 Jim Boulstridge acknowledged the 'usefulness, for some purposes, of power assistance to cycling', and insisted that 'the original idea of the application, which is that of a light, simple attachment, shall remain the objective'. He also maintained that on the Continent 'the tendency had been one of over development of these small motors, and to progress beyond the original conception with the application of higher power, speed gears, and more complicated systems of transition, which had led to the production of what were, in effect, fully powered light motor bicycles'. Boulstridge claimed that this was probably 'an over-development of the original intention', and pointed out that this path 'had not been followed by British makers, who have, in my view, more sensibly kept to the original idea of a light, reliable and simple form of power-assistance to the pedal cycle'. As an endorsement of Boulstridge's limited vision, Phillips brought out, at the end of 1953, a bicycle designed to carry an auxiliary engine, priced at £15 19s., which they somewhat apologetically named their 'motorised attachment model'. Phillips were prepared in the early 1950s, albeit with a certain degree of reluctance, to enter the moped market, but there was clearly no intention to develop scooters.[73]

Raleigh Industries' top management were also reluctant to diversify into the motorised bicycle market based on the premise that they had invested heavily in their traditional product range from which they expected to reap continuing returns. Their managing director, George Wilson, informed shareholders in 1955 that:

> Raleigh has achieved its present position in the world's markets by concentrating its entire efforts and resources on the manufacture of pedal cycles and variable geared hubs and hub dynamo lighting sets, and so bright in our view is the future of these products that we have no intention of departing from this policy unless conditions in our industry shall radically change.[74]

While Phillips, unlike Raleigh, had not 'turned its back on the new market for motor assisted bicycles', both companies, nevertheless, missed out on the growing market for scooters. By the end of 1958 the Board of Trade estimated that there were 'getting on for one-quarter of a million' scooters on British roads, compared 'to next to none at all' ten years previously.[75] Table 6.6 shows the growth of scooters during the mid-1950s and, as can be seen, the expansion of the market was accompanied by high levels of import penetration. Although there was a

Table 6.6   Output of scooters in the UK, 1953–57

	Domestic output (000)	Imports (000)	Total (000)	% of domestic to total
1953	5.0	1.0	6.0	83.3
1954	7.5	3.5	11.0	68.2
1955	9.5	18.5	28.0	33.9
1956	8.5	24.7	33.2	25.6
1957[a]	26.7	41.0	67.7	38.4

Note: [a] For nine months only.

Source: *The Economist*, 11 January 1958, p. 147.

strong response by British manufacturers in 1957 to the foreign challenge, imports still accounted for over 60 per cent of the rapidly growing
British market. By the end of the 1950s the market leaders were the
Italian Lambrettas and Vespas, followed by the cycle-makers Piatti, also
designed by an Italian. The main British contender was the 'Dandy',
produced by BSA, which at 70 cc was half the size of most scooters, but
the company was confident that its scooter programme would secure
for them a 'important share' in the domestic and export market.[76]

It would appear that the conservatism of the British producers allowed the Continental makers to gain a key advantage in motorised
bicycle production. However, there are three important caveats to this
conclusion. First, Italian and German manufacturers, who had built
new factories and re-tooled, were at first prohibited from making heavy
motor cycles. Thus, they concentrated on producing low-priced, eco-
nomically powered cycles which suited the pockets of continental
consumers in the early 1950s. For example, scooters with an engine
capacity of under 125 cc grew in Italy from 300 000 licensed machines
in 1950 to nearly 1 million by 1953. Second, both BCC and Raleigh did
not neglect the motorised market, and focused their attention on mopeds rather than scooters. Phillips, for example, who were first in the
field, had introduced their 'Gadabout' and 'Gladiator' machines in
1956, and by 1958 the motor cycle and cycle show at Earls Court could
boast 50 stands including scooters and mopeds. In October 1958 Raleigh
launched on the British market their first mass-produced moped, an
event which signalled a retreat from the decision taken by Wilson in
1955 not to enter the market. This turnaround no doubt reflected a 13
per cent fall in pedal cycle deliveries between 1956 and 1957. Finally,
companies such as Phillips, Raleigh and Norman Cycles, the latter
another subsidiary of TI, complained that despite their initiatives in
developing moped production their efforts were frustrated by government regulations. In comparison to the Continent, where mopeds were
defined as bicycles and required no driving test or road tax and insurance, in the UK all three were required, and mopeds were placed 'in the
same category as the fastest motor cycle'. In the spring of 1958
Boulstridge led a deputation to the Minister of State at the Department
of Transport, and called for 'a relaxation of the restrictive legislation on
the use of mopeds'. This legislation, he claimed, hampered the British
bicycle industry 'in its battle with Continental competitors who have
long since been freed from such obstacles'.[77]

Certainly, by 1958, the moped was a product innovation which was
seen as of considerable importance to the bicycle industry. Preceding the
opening of the 1958 Bicycle and Motor Cycle Exhibition at Earls Court,
London, there was 'emphatic and wide publicity' concentrated on the

new mopeds to be introduced that year, and Boulstridge, in his role as President of the British Cycle and Motor Cycle Industry's Association, touted the exhibition as the 'show of the century'. A blitz of press, television and radio publicity was followed up by the visit of celebrities to the show, including Lord Brabazon, Stirling Moss and Harry Secombe. The Phillips 'Gadabout' was pictured being ridden by the latest young British film star, Janette Scott.[78] By the end of 1958 there were some 300 000 mopeds on British roads, and potential consumers could 'choose between a wonderfully simple machine like the Raleigh or the Phillips Panda or the Mobylette in the de luxe form'. These machines came in a number of different specifications, including 'single speeders', those with a two-speed capacity and 'an increasing tendency to contract out' of the use of pedals on the multi-geared machines.[79]

Between the two main British producers of mopeds, Phillips Cycles and Raleigh, competition was fierce. For example, in the spring of 1959 Boulstridge bitterly complained to the executive council of BCC that while Phillips had 'been first in the field with mopeds', it was now Raleigh which 'had stolen the initiative'. The competitive failure of Phillips was again related to the problems of adequate component supply, and Yapp, a member of the BCC executive council, explained that there was 'a hiatus on supplies at about the 1.9 thousand mark'. There were shortages of pedal rubbers, Perry Coaster hubs, rubber grommets, cranks and frame tubing. In contrast to Phillips, the Raleigh moped appeared to be a successful product innovation, and with its 49 cc Sturmey-Archer engine it was both inexpensive and simple to operate. In early 1959 a leading trade paper referred to 'The astonishing popularity of the Raleigh moped and there is no doubt that its rising sales made an important contribution to boosting Raleigh's profits in 1959'. In the year ending the 31 July 1959 Raleigh's profits before tax more than doubled, and the company raised its dividend on its ordinary shares from 8 to 12 per cent.[80]

George Wilson, the managing director, highlighted two factors to explain the turnaround in profits: first, gradual improvements in manufacturing efficiency, and second 'the excellent reception by the public of our new moped'. Wilson believed that Raleigh had 'set the moped fashion' in the domestic market, and sales of the Raleigh machine grew at a rate one and a half times faster than the total sales of mopeds in the UK between July 1958 and July 1959. Raleigh's success with its moped was acknowledged by Sir Ivan Stedeford, TI's chairman, who commented that 'everyone in the cycle trade' had been amazed at the demand for the Raleigh moped. His own amazement, however, was followed by a clear warning to Raleigh that their success may be short-lived. As he put it: 'other manufacturers had not been slow to follow the lead and competition in the market was now extremely keen, particularly from the Continent'. This fact was not lost on Wilson at Raleigh, and at the end of 1959 he noted that competition in the moped market, being 'extremely keen', would probably mean that sales of their machine during 1959 would be no higher than in the previous year. Indeed, in the first eight months of 1960 moped sales actually fell back in the UK from their 1959 levels, and a disappointed Wilson was forced to concede that 'Continental moped producers were ahead in development and design'.[81]

By 1960 Raleigh Industries, which had just merged its bicycle interests with TI's BCC, announced its decision to produce, under licence, a moped of French design. This agreement was negotiated with the French company Motobecane, and it allowed Raleigh to produce a Mobylette-type moped. In the same year, an agreement was finalised with Bianchi & Co. of Italy to produce under licence their 'Roma' scooter.[82] The story of the cycle industry's entry into moped production is a salutary one. It starts with a missed opportunity, reflected in the delayed entry by BCC and Raleigh into a rapidly expanding market, and was followed by a brief interlude associated with a burst of optimism and product development in 1958 and 1959. By the early 1960s, however, British producers had accepted Italian and French market dominance, and from the Raleigh experience had consented to produce foreign machines under licence. The initial promise of motorised bicycle production may well have offered a brighter future for companies such as BCC and Raleigh, but their short independent venture into the moped market flattered to deceive. What could not be disguised, however, was the market context in which the moped venture took place, namely a decline in the market for pedal cycles. By 1960 the industry was facing acute problems, and this resulted in the reorganisation of the industry with the merger of the two leading players, TI and Raleigh Industries.

The bicycle industry: decline and merger

In 1959 BCC claimed that its new integrated bicycle works were 'already reaping the benefits of the policy of standard production methods', but the company's production planning was still suffering from the problem of inadequate supplies of components and, as a BCC director put it, there were over 450 cycles on the shop-floor 'at the present time waiting for equipment'. Delays in delivering finished cycles created tensions with the company's key retailer, the high street store chain, Currys. For example, Currys urged the Phillips directors to get their house in order, and provide them with firm information on delivery dates for basic models in order that they could transmit 'a suitable directive ... to their branches'. This request, however, could not be met by Phillips, and as Davis, a BCC director, argued, Currys had contracted for a seven to ten-day delivery date, but their orders were still outstanding after four months. The result was that branch managers of Currys 'were ... refusing to order Phillips machines even against directives from head quarters'.[83]

One can sympathise with the frustration of BCC's chief executive, Jim Boulstridge, when he pointed yet again to the inadequacies of the company in supplying customers, a fact which 'raised the whole question of the efficiency of our material control'. But even more serious was the fact that BCC's problems were set within the context of a secular decline in the demand for pedal cycles. The decline was experienced simultaneously in both the foreign and domestic markets, and by April 1959 Boulstridge was thinking the unthinkable when he raised the question of 'the desirability of eliminating the American market'. For Boulstridge the question was one of profitability, and he had been informed that each cycle sold in the USA entailed a loss to the company of 11s. 7d. Boulstridge's view did not go unchallenged at the meetings of BCC, and a fellow director proposed a compromise to the effect that 'it was beneficial to accept American business provided that it was established that it should not interfere with more profitable work'. Boulstridge was not convinced, and contended that it was difficult to limit the extent to which companies belonging to BCC could participate in the US market. As he argued, 'either Hercules and Phillips were in the market or out of it'. The directors finally concluded that it was probably better to remain in the market, not for any real hope of profitable returns, but rather that pulling out of the USA would damage their 'world wide prestige'.[84] The high hopes of the early 1950s had rapidly faded, and the British bicycle industry faced a declining position in the American market, a trend which was already evident from the mid-1950s (see Table 6.7).

Table 6.7   US imports of cycles from the UK and Germany, 1954–56

	Total imports (000)	Imports from UK (000)	% of total for UK	Imports from Germany (000)	% of total from Germany
1954	964	534	55.4	257	26.6
1955	1 224	538	43.4	433	35.4
1956	1 174	266	22.7	628	53.5

Source: Financial Times, 29 April 1957.

A key factor in Britain's falling market share in the USA, referred to earlier in the chapter, was American import duties on cycles, which were raised by 50 per cent in August 1955. But, as can be seen in Table 6.7, it was the German cycle industry which rapidly caught up and supplanted British producers in this market, a feature which suggests there were other factors at work apart from increased import duties. In TI's annual report of November 1957 the chairman, Sir Ivan Stedeford, was forthright in his explanations of the problems confronting the British cycle industry. 'Industrial effort' was 'being squandered because of disunity between management, labour and government'. This was creating a climate of uncertainty in British industry, an environment which was not conducive to raising levels of business investment. Referring directly to the fall in cycle exports to the USA, Stedeford complained that 'As long as industrial costs, including wages, continue to run ahead of production, we stand in peril of costing ourselves out of world markets'. His report also contained the warning that 'Tomorrow's business in bicycles will depend more than ever on low costs and prices'.[85]

Stedeford's critical commentary was not simply directed at the British trade unions, but he also left enough venom for a condemnation of Conservative government economic policy. In particular, 'the Treasury's attitude to investment has been infuriatingly changeable', and he went on to catalogue a list of direct complaints. These included the granting of investment allowances which had then been revoked, constantly changing restrictions on hire purchase, and the fact that 'bank advances had been stiffened and eased at alarmingly short intervals'. According to Stedeford, investment was being turned 'on and off like a tap', and this was undermining plans for longer-term strategies of factory expansion and modernisation. Placing the emphasis on the need for long-term investment, he quoted T. Barna, an industrial economist, whose analysis of investment in manufacturing industry between 1950 and 1956 had suggested that if the policy of 'fits and starts made inevitable by the Treasury's indecisions' could have been avoided then 'we would by now have had £500 million more new plant and buildings and machinery than we have'.[86] The reference to Treasury 'indecision' was an assault on what has become known as stop-go policies, a feature of economic life in Britain which had become firmly entrenched by the mid-1950s. The cost of periodic phases of rapid growth, followed by rapid downturns, was that investment was greatly reduced in the downturn phase, but not necessarily consumption. Thus, for example, the *Midland Bank Review*, in its monetary survey for 1955–56, commented that 'despite deflationary measures, boom conditions persisted in most branches of industry, employment was maintained at high levels and overtime in industry was still common'.[87]

The specific problem of stop-go for the bicycle industry was that it experienced the uncertainty of these policies on the investment side, but gained little from the buoyancy of consumption. Indeed, as shown in Table 6.8, the output of the industry was on a downward track from the mid-1950s. This sharp fall can be set against the decade's overall decline. Between 1951, when output reached 4 million units, and 1958 output fell by 46.1 per cent, but between 1955 and 1958 it fell by an alarming 39.5 per cent. By the latter date 'production and retail sales ... of cycles had worsened again', and this decline was apparent in both domestic and export markets. The situation was such that the production and sales decline had 'put the industry in a position that is not far short of the parlous state of the Lancashire cotton trade'. The year 1958 marked the cycle industry's lowest recorded domestic sales since the end of the Second World War, and export sales also showed a marked decrease.[88] While leaders of the industry such as Boulstridge blamed government policy and rising wage costs, a writer to the *Motor Cycle and Cycle Trader*, in January 1959, argued that purchase tax and hire purchase restrictions were mere scapegoats to cover the industry's business inadequacies. 'To a retailer', he claimed, 'it looks rather if the two big groups of cycle manufacturers have over-developed their means of production without a corresponding and essential development of their sales effort. Neither at the [Earls Court] show, nor at home in our shops do we witness any sense of urgency or enthusiasm.' Such criticisms, questioning the business acumen of the two big producers, were particularly pertinent given a Ministry of Transport Report of 1959 which showed that cycle traffic in the UK had fallen to about 60 per cent of its 1938 level.[89] What also rankled with the 'big two' producers was that small independent companies frequently received a good press. Thus, the *Oxford Mail* in 1958 referred to 'Several ... independent companies, some of which specialise in making a particular type of cycle, such as the high class machines suitable for the fastidious clubman and tourist or the special racing machine for the sporting rider. These companies take great pride in their individual craftsmanship'.[90]

Table 6.8   UK bicycle production, 1955–58

	Annual production	*% decline on previous year*
1955	3 564 000	
1956	2 875 000	−19.3
1957	2 548 000	−11.4
1958	2 156 000	−18.2

Source: *Motor Cycle and Cycle Trader*, 24 April 1959.

Clearly, by the end of the 1950s the future of the pedal cycle industry was in the balance, as consumers, in an increasingly affluent Western Europe, began to substitute motor power for muscle power. At companies such as Phillips an initial response was to streamline its range of cycles and reduce the choice of colour schemes to a set of basic finishes. The aim was to supply dealers with a limited range of models that would meet consumer demand but avoid an unnecessary multiplication of stock. This would reduce the amount of working capital tied up and release factory space. However, in December 1958, Phillips made redundant 100 workers in its Downing Street factory in Smethwick, and the rest of the workforce of 1 000 was put on a four-day week. A month later there was a 15.6 per cent fall reported in the production of cycles between November 1957 and November 1958, and a decline in export values over the same period from £23.8 million to £21.5 million. As a response to the decline in export sales TI and Raleigh Industries announced in May 1959 a merging of their cycle interests in South Africa, and there was a closer integration of their business activities which followed a merger of their interests in Eire. Both companies were quick to announce that their agreement in Eire and South Africa did not 'affect the activities of TI and Raleigh in the UK', but a year later, in June 1960, TI purchased Raleigh Industries and the two companies were formally merged.[91]

The merger of 1960, in effect, brought the bulk of the British cycle industry under the corporate control of a single enterprise. Raleigh assimilated BCC and became a subsidiary of the TI group. In 1960, Raleigh commanded between 50 and 55 per cent of British bicycle output, and the merger saw them command approximately 90 per cent of all exports and 70 per cent of home sales.[92] The merger was clearly a response to the decline in the British industry, and the hope was that it would help to overcome the three main problems facing the industry: first, intensified competition from continental and Asian producers who were successfully challenging TI and Raleigh in their main overseas markets; second, the problem of import substitution reflected in 'local manufacture', leading to the loss of traditional markets in countries such as India; finally, the decline in the home market for pedal cycles with the hope that this would be substituted by product innovation associated with scooter and moped production. Certainly, the hopes of bicycle men such as Boulstridge and Wilson was that the new merged company could meet the challenges faced by the industry. To probe these challenges further, the next chapter will explore in detail the business activities of Raleigh Industries in the post-1945 period.

Notes

1. 'Social Survey of Bicycles in War Time Transport', reported in *Board of Trade Journal*, 12 January 1946, p. 24.
2. Ibid.
3. Raleigh's post-war activities will be examined in detail in Chapter 7.
4. Jeremy, 1998, p. 222; *The Economist*, 7, 21 December 1946.
5. Eatwell, 1979, pp. 69–70. See also Cairncross, 1992; Pollard, 1983.
6. *Board of Trade Journal*, 10 August 1946, p. 1329.
7. Thomas, 1946; Raleigh Records, DDRN 7/3/3, 'September Story – A History of Hercules'.
8. *The Economist*, 20 April 1946, p. 643.
9. *Motor Cycle and Cycle Trader*, 5 January 1945.
10. *Cycling*, 28 November 1945; Thomas, 1946.
11. 'Who's Who in the Cycle and Motor Cycle Industry', No. 11, 'T. J. Boulstridge', *Motor Cycle and Cycle Export Trader*, August 1947.
12. *Motor Cycle and Cycle Trader*, 25 October 1946.
13. *The Economist* 23 March 1946, p. 72, 26 October 1946, p. 688, 7 December 1946, p. 932, 4 January 1947, p. 45.
14. Ibid., 7 December 1946, p. 932.
15. Ibid., 21 December 1946, p. 1021.
16. Ibid., p. 1021; 'September Story'.
17. *The Economist*, 13 December 1947, p. 982; *Motor Cycle and Cycle Trader*, 10 October 1947.
18. The Board of Trade had set an output target of 60 per cent of output to be exported for the bicycle industry in March 1946; the target for motor vehicles was 50 per cent. *Board of Trade Journal*, 21 March 1946, p. 227.
19. *The Economist*, 20 April 1946, p. 646, 22 October 1949, p. 918.
20. Reported in *National Journal*, April 1948.
21. *The Economist*, 22 October 1949, p. 919.
22. *Birmingham Mail*, 6 October 1948.
23. *Financial Times*, 7 October 1948.
24. *Board of Trade Journal*, 1 June 1946, pp. 693–4, 7 December 1946, p. 1765. Germany accounted for 6.8 per cent and were the fourth largest, with the USA taking third spot.
25. Ibid., 1 June 1946, pp. 693–4.
26. *The Economist*, 21 November 1953, p. 609; *Manchester Guardian*, 7 March 1956.
27. *The Economist*, 21 November 1953, p. 609.
28. *Evening Dispatch*, 21 January 1953.
29. Ibid.
30. *Birmingham Post*, 25 January 1953; Boulstridge, 1953; *Motor Cycle and Cycle Trader*, 7 February 1953.
31. *Birmingham Gazette*, 24 January 1953; *Evening Dispatch*, 21 January 1953.
32. Boulstridge, 1953; *Montgomery County Times*, 18 April 1953; *Birmingham Evening News*, 16 March 1953.
33. For example, within one and a half hours of the opening of the International Cycle Show at Earls Court in November 1953 Phillips had taken an order for 3 000 bicycles from Singapore. *Cycling*, 19 November 1953.
34. *The Economist*, 11 January 1955, p. 147; DDRN 7/1/9/1, The Bicycle

and Motor Cycle Industry. Highlight of 1953–54; *Iraq Times*, 30 October 1954.

35. *Motor Cycle and Cycle Export Trader*, November 1953.
36. *The Economist*, 10 May 1958, p. 9; DDRN 7/13/3, Brief History of the BSA Company.
37. *Board of Trade Journal*, 26 January 1957, p. 167, 17 May 1957, p. 1111; *Manchester Guardian*, 7 March 1956.
38. *The Economist*, 1 June 1957, p. 811; The Bicycle and Motor Cycle Industry. Highlight of 1953–54.
39. *Guardian Journal*, 13 November 1954.
40. *The Economist*, 30 April 1955, p. 399, 10 May 1958, p. 527.
41. In addition, new challenges emerged from the Czechoslovakians. Ibid., 10 May 1958, p. 527.
42. Ibid., 30 April 1955, p. 400, 10 May 1958, p. 527.
43. For a discussion of product life cycles see Duijn, 1983, pp. 21–36; Wells, 1972; Vernon, 1966, pp. 190–207.
44. *The Economist*, 22 November 1958, p. 735; Nottingham Central Library, *Raligram*, February 1953, p. 30; *Nottingham Evening News*, 27 August 1953.
45. *The Economist*, 22 November 1958, p. 735.
46. *Motor Cycle and Cycle Trader*, 7 February 1953.
47. DDRN 1/18/2, Board Minutes of Phillips Cycle Co. Ltd, 5 December 1955.
48. *The Economist*, 13 December 1958, p. 1025.
49. *Financial Times*, 14 November 1953. Boulstridge was referring to the consumption of 'white goods' which are classified as consumer durables, and were associated with the economic growth and expansion in the 1950s. See Howlett, 1994. Boulstridge's view was also articulated by Wilson. See *The Economist*, 13 December 1958, p. 1025.
50. *Financial Times*, 14 November 1953; *The Economist*, 13 December 1958, p. 1025.
51. *The Economist*, 10 December 1955, p. 988.
52. See Boulstridge's comments in *Financial Times*, 14 November 1953.
53. Hall, 1962, p. 435.
54. *Evening Dispatch*, 16 November 1953; *Motor Cycle and Cycle Trader*, 16 May 1953; *Singapore Cycling Annual*, 1954.
55. Board Minutes of Phillips, 2 November 1951, 27 December 1951.
56. Ibid., 28 October 1952. Following the company's usual policy of close co-operation with their representatives and travellers, they were contacted over the extent of the price reduction in an attempt to 'influence a resuscitation of our trade'.
57. Ibid.
58. Ibid., 17 July 1953, 11 June 1954.
59. Ibid., 29 November 1950.
60. Hannah, 1983, p. 86. For a discussion of the origins of the holding company form of organisation in Britain see Jeremy, 1998, pp. 174–6.
61. The cost of production in 1965 would have been in the same order of magnitude as it was in the 1950s.
62. Board Minutes of Phillips, 27 July 1951, 28 October 1952.
63. Ibid., 28 October 1952, 27 July 1953, 11 June 1954.
64. Ibid., 31 October 1955; DDRN 1/26/1, TI Cycle Division Minutes,

17 January 1956; Board Minutes of Phillips, 31 October 1955. The company also sought supplies of strip steel from the continent in the mid-1950s. See Board Minutes of Phillips, 23 June 1955.

65. Board Minutes of Phillips, 2 January 1956.

66. Ibid., 31 October 1955.

67. TI Cycle Division Minutes, 17 January 1956.

68. Board Minutes of Phillips, 6 September 1956.

69. *The Economist*, 22 November 1958, p. 735, 18 January 1958, p. 196.

70. The focus of the BSA advertising campaign was on comfort, economy and safety. See DDRN 4/66/2/3, BSA Advertising and Promotional Material.

71. *The Economist*, 12 November 1955, pp. 598, 988, 1 June 1957, p. 818.

72. Ibid., 1 June 1957, p. 818, 19 October 1957, p. 258.

73. *Financial Times*, 14 November 1953; *Yorkshire Evening News*, 16 November 1953. A moped may be defined as a bicycle having pedals and an engine of not more than 50 cc capacity. It was a direct descendant of the pre-war 98 cc auto-cycle. See *East Anglian Daily Times*, 2 October 1958.

74. DDRN 1/2/6; Raleigh Industries Ltd, Report of Directors, 1955.

75. *The Economist*, 17 December 1955, p. 1199; *Board of Trade Journal*, 28 November 1958, p. 1128.

76. *The Economist*, 11 January 1958, p. 148, 22 November 1958, p. 740.

77. Ibid., 30 April 1955, p. 400, 22 November 1958, p. 742; *Motor Cycle and Cycle Trader*, 16 August 1958; Board Minutes of Phillips, 30 April 1956; *Engineering*, 14 November 1958; *Motor Cycle and Cycle Export Trader*, March/April 1958.

78. *Motor Cycle and Cycle Trader*, 8 November 1958; *Motor Cyclist Illustrated*, May 1958. A trade paper wrote in 1958 that 'Judging by our correspondence the Phillips "Gadabout" is the best loved moped in Britain'. *Power and Pedal*, November 1958. In addition to the trade paper's euphoria, the 'Gadabout' was praised in numerous local newspapers, for example, the *Northants Evening Telegraph*, 13 November 1958; *Blackburn Evening Telegraph*, 13 November 1958; *Bogner Regis Observer*, 14 November 1958; *Kentish Gazette*, 14 November 1958.

79. *Cycling*, 19 November 1958.

80. TI Cycle Division Minutes, Executive Council of BCC, 14 April 1959; *Motor Cycle and Cycle Trader*, 13 March 1959; Raleigh Industries Ltd, Report of Directors, 1959.

81. *The Economist*, 12 December 1959, p. 1104; *Motor Cycle and Cycle Trader*, 18 December 1959; DDRN 3/8/1–12, Raleigh Industries Ltd, Balance Sheets and Accounts together with Reports (1949–60), 1960; *Financial Times*, 7 November 1960.

82. *Motor Cycle and Cycle Trader*, 4 November 1960.

83. TI Cycle Division Minutes, Executive Council of BCC, 14 April 1959.

84. Ibid.

85. *Birmingham Mail*, 15 November 1957.

86. Ibid.

87. Cited in Lloyd-Jones and Lewis, 1998a, p. 177. For an analysis of stop-go in Britain, see Pollard, 1984.

88. *Motor Cycle and Cycle Trader*, 16 August 1958; *Birmingham Post*, 30 January 1959.

89. *Motor Cycle and Cycle Trader*, 2 January 1959, 18 December 1959.

90. *Oxford Mail*, 15 May 1958.

91. *Motor Cycle and Cycle Trader*, 8 November 1958; *Birmingham Post*, 8 December 1958, 30 January 1959; *Financial Times*, 23 May 1959; Raleigh, Balance Sheets and Accounts together with Reports, 1960.
92. *Financial World*, 23 May 1960.

CHAPTER SEVEN

Triumphs and adversities: Raleigh Industries Ltd, 1939–60

In January 1946 Raleigh Cycle Holdings Co., formed in 1934, was renamed Raleigh Industries Ltd, a central holding company which was to co-ordinate the activities of its existing operating companies, and was to acquire additional subsidiaries in the decade and a half after the Second World War (see Figure E.1 in the Appendix). The two key managerial figures were George Wilson, the managing director and joint chairman of the main operating company, Raleigh Cycles, and Harold Bowden, the managing director and chairman of the holding company, and joint chairman of Raleigh Cycles. In 1950 Bowden appointed Wilson as deputy managing director and chairman of Raleigh Industries, and in 1955 Bowden, aged 75, retired from this position, although he still remained active in the business as the company's honourary president until his death in August 1960. It was these two leading managers; Bowden, with his long association with Raleigh, and Wilson, a man who had, in Bowden's words demonstrated a 'zeal and energy' in the interests of Raleigh since the late 1920s, who were to formulate the strategies of the company in the post-war era.[1] In the two decades following the outbreak of the Second World War the Raleigh company underwent profound change. An enterprise that had coped well with the business challenges of the inter-war years, and had emerged as a dominant force in the British bicycle industry, was to contribute to the war effort, and initially was to experience considerable business success. Yet by 1960 the company lost its business independence, when it was absorbed into the TI group through a merger with BCC. This chapter traces the story of Raleigh's business development via an examination of its activities during the Second World War, and probes the evolution of the company's post-war business strategy. This, we will argue, was set within the parameters of the historical evolution of Raleigh's organisational culture. Thus, in just over half a century from the time of the bicycle boom the British pedal cycle industry was effectively dominated by one producer operating under the organisational control of a large corporation, whose main business interest was certainly not the manufacture of bicycles. To begin the analysis, let us start by examining the Raleigh business during the war.

7.1 Photograph of export luncheon at Raleigh Industries, *c.* 1949 (second from left, Sir Harold Bowden, third from left, George Wilson). Photograph from the Raleigh Archive, reproduced courtesy of Nottingham County Archive.

Raleigh at war, 1939–45

In June 1939 George Wilson informed the Raleigh board of a considerable improvement in the company's sales position over the previous year, and announced that the future of the industry looked promising. Wilson was planning to operate the factory at an annual output of 400 000 cycles, and although he was aware of the deteriorating international situation Wilson urged his fellow directors to think ahead, and plan an extension of sales both in domestic and foreign markets. His optimism was fully justified, and domestic and foreign sales both increased slightly in 1939, despite the threat of war (see Table E.1 in the Appendix). Raleigh's consolidated profit rose from £376 515 in 1938 to £430 163 in 1939 (Table 5.5). As the war loomed it was business as usual, and the management prepared 'the finest and most comprehensive programme which had ever been offered to Dealers by this Company', and looked forward to the prospect of expanding export sales.[2] By August, however, as the international situation deteriorated, Wilson's optimism had vanished. The company, and the cycle industry in general, was faced with an uncertain future, and this was reflected in a heightening tension between Raleigh and its main competitors, the Hercules Cycle Co. The company's programme of sales expansion was premised upon fixing prices at levels which were no more than £1 above the Hercules price, but given the uncertainty 'prices could not be fixed until they knew what Hercules was doing'. As war approached business co-operation evaporated, and negotiations initiated by Raleigh and BSA with Hercules for price fixing agreements collapsed, as the latter wished to keep their options open pending the possibility of military conflict. In the same month, Raleigh was classified by the Ministry of Supply as an 'A firm', to be taken over entirely in the event of war. With the declaration of war in September, Wilson now had to steer the company through the difficult times ahead.[3]

Paradoxically the announcement of war, rather than disrupting bicycle sales, brought forth a rush of orders which taxed the company's productive capacity to the full. Sales were given a significant boost by agents and dealers building up cycle stocks to meet future shortages. For example, in September 1939 the company had 90 000 cycle orders on the books, and by November sales were 80 per cent up on any previous year in the company's history. The surge of demand was also evident for Sturmey-Archer products, and as war demands increased they faced the difficulty of adequately supplying gears to the cycle trade. As we have seen in Chapter 5, the company had already began producing munitions as early as 1937, and in 1939 Raleigh was subcontracting munitions and tool work from Rolls-Royce and Rover.

Further, the company was already facing the difficulties of retaining labour due to conscription, and the procurement of material supplies due to the priority given to military production. The increasing pressure this placed on capacity forced the management to postpone further orders from their depots, and to ration supplies to the trade. The policy pursued was to utilise present stocks of materials to produce cycles, as 'it was possible to sell any type of cycle that was available', but the programme for 1940 was abandoned and rationing introduced by raising prices by 12.5 per cent.[4] In November 1939 Raleigh also raised prices in export markets by 7.5 per cent, and noted that it would be increasingly difficult to meet orders, especially given the rationing of steel to the trade which would inevitably curtail output.[5]

Raleigh's strategy was thus to maintain its bicycle trade and meet its commitments to customers, despite the growing constraints posed by the war. For example, Raleigh continued to supply cycles and components in the first half of 1940, and sales to the home market actually showed a small increase on 1939 to 292 205, or 72.6 per cent of total sales, while foreign sales only registered a minor fall (Table E.1 in the Appendix). The philosophy at Raleigh was to maintain its traditional markets, but at the same time to comply with increasing government demands for munitions and the expansion of bicycle exports. In early 1940 the home market was falling off, and although Raleigh had substantial export orders on hand, they now had their first large contract from the Ministry of Supply for munitions. In January 1940 the Ministry sanctioned a capital outlay of £77 000, £12 000 payable by Raleigh, for the production of a weekly output of 60 000 119 fuses, 20 000 221 shells, and 10 000 small Bofors shells. For Wilson, increasing government demands were a matter of negotiation, and on his insistence the Ministry guaranteed contracting for orders six months ahead for the entire output of the company to justify the expenditure on new plant. He clearly viewed investment in new plant for munitions as a matter of business bargaining, rather than any patriotic feeling for the war. There were positive advantages to be gained from new plant. Wilson argued that 'The position of the factory at the end of the War ... would be a very strong one, and would enable us to make full use of our Sturmey-Archer and lamp production, and to undertake the policy for the future which we have already decided upon in this connection'.[6]

This statement, of course, reflects the thinking of early 1940 and the phoney war, but the management were clearly determined to retain a niche in the cycle market with a view to post-war conditions. For example, Wilson, commenting on the decline in the company's gradual payment sales, claimed that 'Everything was being done to stimulate this side of the business and to hold the nucleus of our organisation together'. In February 1940 the management were still optimistic that they could meet orders for cycles and gears, although steel was in short supply, and export targets were constrained by a shortage of packing facilities and space on cargo ships. By March, the management were expressing optimistic views of maintaining exports, and they were consulting with the Motor Cycle and Cycle Manufacturers Union regarding the percentage of output devoted to exports. Indeed, by May home sales were holding up, despite the difficulties in obtaining steel supplies, as the government supported a policy of promoting the export trade at the expense of domestic supply. Shortages of labour and materials, however, were now having a significant impact upon production costs, and the company announced a 20 per cent increase above pre-war levels for the 'Raleigh Popular'. Raleigh was now increasingly committed to munitions work, producing 40 000 fuses per week, but also manufacturing a range of military products, including shell cases, exploder containers and smoke bombs. Wilson's dealings with the Ministry of Supply continued to be on a strictly business level, and he insisted on obtaining 'a firm price for all articles manufactured by us for the government'.[7]

As can be seen in Table E.1 in the Appendix, home sales of bicycles fell from a total of 292 205 machines in 1940 to a low of 60 824 in 1942, although they rose again in the last three years of the war to just over 100 000. Foreign sales were particularly affected by the war after 1941, falling to a low point of just 15 127 in 1943, and continuing at this restricted level throughout the remainder of the war. This is not surprising given the disruption caused to British shipping, but during the early part of the war Raleigh managed to maintain exports at high levels, and raise the share of exports in total sales to 39.7 per cent in 1941 in response to the government's call for increased export activity. Falling sales were accompanied by falling bicycle production, output declining from 409 479 cycles in 1939 to 299 165 in 1940, and to 162 616 by 1942 (Table E.2 in the Appendix). Output remained below 200 000 for the rest of the war, but the fact that Raleigh was producing at this sustained output is testimony to the commitment of management to maintain a niche in this market. The ability to continue bicycle production was aided by increased government orders for military bicycles. Raleigh sold nearly 130 000 bicycles to the government between 1942 and 1944, and this justified the continued use of capacity for cycle production. Government orders came as a welcome relief, for by the end of 1940 Raleigh was moving to full war production. Fuse production was planned to rise from 120 000 a week to 200 000, a new type of shell was introduced with a weekly output target of 250 000, and the new plant cost an estimated £200 000. The cycle business was thus severely curtailed, and although workers were subsidised, Raven recognised that 'the business was not big enough' to justify the outlay. The management clearly feared that the government would order the complete shut-down of bicycle production, a policy proposal which was reversed by the Ministry of Supply at the end of 1941. As Wilson claimed, the 'proposals for the bicycle industry had been completely reversed ... and now it was not part of the Government policy to cut the Company down to a small annual number of bicycles', and this was supported by an order for 50 000 machines from the Royal Air Force. This allowed them to acquire steel supplies under government licence, special sanctions for the maintenance of labour on cycle production, and a capacity to produce 4 000 to 5 000 cycles per week.[8]

At Raleigh caution was the watchword in dealing with government officials, and this was due partly to confusion over the intentions of government policy, and partly to the risks of large capital investments for conversion to munitions production. For example, in June 1940 the management remarked that cycle orders were now sufficient to cover the output from the factory, and the policy was to sell 'high class models' fitted with gears, dyno hubs and gear cases. Raleigh was now producing 6 000 cycles per week, and the export trade, in accordance with government policy, was accounting for 43 per cent of cycle supplies. Wilson, however, was highly critical of government policies to regulate prices, which restricted the company's sales policy in the face of rising costs, and of the damaging effects on home sales by the severe rationing of material supplies. Acknowledging that the government's intention was to promote exports to pay for the war, he nevertheless condemned the confused messages they gave to business. Thus by August Wilson was predicting an output of 60 000 cycles for the domestic market, leaving 90 000 for exports, but complained bitterly of shortages of steel supplies, even though 'the Government had been at pains to advise us that the export business was equally important with the output of munitions'. Acting as the company's liaison with the Ministry of Supply, Sir Connop Guthrie advised that materials would be available for specified export markets, notably the USA, and he felt confident that if substantial orders could be ensured in this market then special steel allocations would be forthcoming. But pressure was now building up on the company's existing capacity, especially its Sturmey-Archer business which was being swamped by war orders, and the conscription of men not engaged on war work also disrupted output. Further, as the war intensified, and foreign trade was disrupted by the Atlantic blockade, the ability to export was restricted, and government promises of special licences for materials were withdrawn. As the management pointed out, 'it was now a question of priority'.[9]

The question of the company's financial commitment to the war effort was raised in June 1940 when Wilson reported that the management had sanctioned an expenditure of £128 000 on plant since August 1939, and asked the board to sanction a further £82 000. In reply, Guthrie urged caution and advised that 'we should not over-commit ourselves at the present time, especially in view of the uncertainty of the future, and also of the fact that income tax would undoubtedly shortly be further substantially increased'. In his opinion Raleigh should seek further assistance from the government for a further increase in capital expenditure, 'rather than tax our own resources which might in future cause us financial embarrassment'. Profits were stagnant between 1940 and 1942 (Table 5.5), and the profit outlook of the company may well have been a major factor in prompting these discussions at the board. Certainly, the evidence suggests that the government was forthcoming in absorbing part of the costs of capital expenditure, and Wilson's irritation with government interference in the operation of the company was somewhat tempered by the introduction in 1940 of war bonuses to employees of 7.5 to 15 per cent in recognition of the rising cost of living. Nevertheless, he continued to insist upon dealings with the government based upon strict business principles and, for example, commenting upon the bureaucratic nature of Ministry of Supply methods on munitions pricing, he argued that if prices could be agreed on it should 'avoid all future government costing investigations in these works'.[10]

Under Wilson's leadership the board was determined to maintain a position in the cycle trade which would prepare Raleigh for the post-war environment, and this was evident from the early 1940s when Britain's prospects of winning the war seemed somewhat doubtful. This is not to suggest that the company was reluctant to commit production fully to the war effort, and when, in December 1941, the government instructed Raleigh to close down the production of Sturmey-Archer three-speed gears and dyno hubs, the output of which had already been gradually falling, the management complied immediately. From the middle of 1941 production capacity at Raleigh was 'at full stretch' for the production of munitions, and in July 1941 the government requisitioned the Vedonis factory of George Spencer Ltd, of Butterworth, which was re-equipped at the government's expense for the supply of cartridge cases to Raleigh for the manufacture of the Oerlikon gun. By early 1942 cycle production was only 3 000 per week, and shortages of component parts in the trade generally was reducing production. Further, Harold Bowden noted that the quality of manufacture was declining and put this down to the increased use of unskilled labour. Despite the constraints on cycle production, and the uncertainty of the military situation, Raleigh continued to plan forward. The strategy adopted to meet initial war requirements was to increase the capacity of the factory to produce spare parts, and thus keep as many machines as possible on the road during the war. Raleigh faced extreme difficulties in the bicycle market, and in April 1942 the export position was described as extremely difficult, especially in terms of obtaining boats for the South African and Indian markets. The contract to the RAF was taking 1 300 cycles per week of the small output of 3 000, but despite this small turnover Wilson instructed their sales manager, A. E. Simpson, to prepare a 'cycle programme', in conjunction with the factory managers, to meet the conclusion of hostilities. This involved the accumulation of stocks of Sturmey-Archer gears in anticipation of the ending of hostilities, and arrangements with the retailers Currys to guarantee 'that Raleighs should become their leading line in all their branches after the war'.[11]

Raleigh's commitment to forward planning was aimed at the need to prepare for post-war competition, especially from the largest British producer, the Hercules Co. As early as September 1940 Raleigh announced its withdrawal from the Cycle and Motor Cycle Traders Union on the grounds that their interests could best be served outside. In this, they were responding to the fact that Hercules were 'outside the restrictions of the Union, and it was felt that we should not be handicapped in any way with our dealings with them'. The aim was clearly to be ahead of the field when the war ended, and in 1943 Raleigh acquired Rudge-Whitworth as part of its plans to increase the range of bicycles under its control. In May 1943 Wilson informed the board that the Rudge-Whitworth trade mark was on the market, and negotiations were opened with Sir Robert McClean, the managing director of the Gramophone Co. Ltd which had acquired the company in 1938. The Gramophone Co. was a subsidiary of Electrical Musical Instruments Ltd (EMI), and Wilson obtained a 'short option' to purchase the share capital of Rudge-Whitworth, and to take over the trade marks and business. By June Raleigh had paid 95 per cent of the purchase price of £180 000, and the sale was finally completed in November. The deal involved the purchase of trade marks, goodwill, stock and the Rudge-Whitworth plant at Hayes, Middlesex. The plant was subsequently dismantled and production transferred to Nottingham.[12]

Rudge-Whitworth offered Raleigh another extension to their bicycle range in addition to the established reputation of the Raleigh, Humber and Gazelle trade marks. In a letter to McClean in April 1944 Wilson emphasised the importance he attached to the deal in enabling Raleigh to increase 'sales in the post-war period'. An added urgency may well have been given by the fact that McClean had also been in contact with four other companies, Cornecroft Ltd, BSA, the Norman Cycle Co. and Hercules. Acquiring Rudge-Whitworth made little appeal to Hercules because the former had only a limited production potential. Thus, the Raleigh decision was not premised on acquiring a large extension to its post-war output capacity, nor for that matter was the management taking charge of a particularly successful pre-war business (see Chapter 4). For example, on moving its production operations from Coventry and Birmingham to Hayes in 1938 the company had aimed to increase output from just 45 000 machines per annum to 70 000. By 1940 this had been achieved, 'but the pre-war years were the basis of the Company's quota for the latter war years, both for the home and the export markets, and in the pre-war years the Company had not pressed sales with any success in the export field'. The pre-war restructuring of the company had also seen a move to decrease the company's capabilities of producing component parts, which were increasingly bought from outside. Thus, with the increasing demands of war, and the shortages of component supplies in the trade, Rudge-Whitworth was at a severe disadvantage. Indeed, it seems likely that as far as the Gramophone Co. was concerned, the ditching of the company was more than welcomed. With increased restrictions on manufacture and export sales Rudge-Whitworth was faced with the prospect of such a limited output as to be viewed as an uneconomical concern. As the Gramophone Co. itself was being pressured by the government to take up new contracts and increase production for war supplies, Rudge-Whitworth became an additional burden. It was concluded that 'the cycle business could only be operated by itself, and not as an adjunct to their normal business'.[13]

As Table E.2 in the Appendix shows, the output of cycles under the Rudge-Whitworth trade mark remained small in 1944 and 1945, and although it rose rapidly after the war it was not until 1948 that it reached pre-war levels. Nevertheless, it represented a key decision by management in 1943 to plan for the post-war market, and Raleigh was to plan its programme on four product fronts: Raleigh, Humber, Rudge-Whitworth and Robin Hood. The latter trade mark had been acquired by the company before the First World War, and Gazelle cycle production and sales were now to be undertaken under the Robin Hood trademark.[14] At the same time as the company acquired Rudge-Whitworth, Wilson decided to reorganise the management structure at Raleigh by dividing the control over various branches of the business. R. L. Jones was given control over the general office, including staffing, accounts, the gradual payments system, and purchases. A. E. Simpson was made responsible for all sales, depot managers and travellers, and L. C. Clarkson was allocated control of the factory, works staff and production. All three of these directors were 'to rank as of equal importance', but were to be 'directly responsible' to Wilson. This reorganisation was part of the company's commitment to plan for peacetime conditions, and referring to the fall off of orders from the Ministry of Supply in October 1943 Wilson called for 'A thorough investigation into the general position of present production with reference to our post-war activities'. By December Wilson had established a control office to co-ordinate sales by the compilation of statistics on sales, stocks, popularity of various designs and to base assessment on the 'population in our various depot territories'. The aim was to identify potential 'weak spots', and to place the company in a position 'to stimulate effort as and when required'. In February 1944 a two-day sales conference was held at Nottingham between executive management, depot managers and sales agents to 'formulate a blue print for the post-war position', involving planning for models, sales policy and the depots. The executive management were also considering the range of Sturmey-Archer products to be produced in the future.[15]

These decisions were premised upon the belief that government contracts would be gradually reduced, and unless they were renewed, or a greater allocation of supplies made for the home trade, the company's cycle output would be greatly reduced. As Simpson argued, 'In the case of this contingency, it would be necessary for us to absorb our key cycle labour on other jobs in the factory, until such time as they could be re-employed upon the cycle side'. Certainly, the company was acutely aware of the need to invest in design improvements on their cycles in preparation for post-war conditions. Indeed, the company had been actively involved in research and development in munitions during the war, and this was transmitted to the field of cycles. In August 1944 Wilson reported that 'a good deal of development work had taken place with cycle design', and this was viewed as crucial given the fall of turnover in munitions to the government. During the financial year ending August 1944 munitions turnover fell by £750 000, and Wilson reiterated the need for forward planning as the munitions situation facing the company was confused. Wilson bitterly complained that in discussions with the Regional Controller of Labour and the Regional Controller of the Ministry of Supply concerning the shortages of labour, lease lend, plant, and materials supplies, and the continuation of Government contracts, 'little information is available'. But by October 1944 additional allotments of steel to the cycle industry had greatly increased 'sales prospects', and 'excellent progress had been made with ... improved design and equipment on bicycles for post-war', which included improvement in the efficiency of their dyno hub lighting sets. By this stage munitions contracts had been considerably reduced; the production of Hispano and Oerlikon shell cases were halved and the manufacture of 40 mm shells and 20 mm tracers were cut. This, of course, involved a significant reduction in turnover, and a corresponding reduction in labour. However, as Wilson argued, they needed to look ahead, and 'It was the policy of the company to keep all our old people who might be involved in these [government] contracts, and to get them into other work'.[16]

By the end of 1944 management was looking optimistically to the post-war trading environment, a factor reinforced by the sway of the war to the allied powers. For example, negotiations were opened with Hercules for the supply of gears to that company after the war, and also the issue of post-war pricing was discussed. Further, Wilson instructed Simpson to co-ordinate the sales between the company's various marks, and to plan future production and labour strategy. The latter was of major concern to management, and as Wilson pointed out, the ability of Raleigh to increase supply depended not only upon the procurement of material supplies but also on labour, 'which at the moment was extremely tight'. Plans were implemented to exploit what the management believed were exceptional opportunities in the cycle markets of Britain and the world after the cessation of hostilities. In particular, the management prepared schedules of supplies to reactivate the Sturmey-Archer gear and dyno hub business to ensure supplies not only for Raleigh machines but also for other cycle manufacturers. The company looked ahead to a healthy sale of these components after the war, although they warned against complacency, and the possibility of intense competition from rival products. Special attention was given to the competitive strengths of Hercules, and this was reinforced by the failure to secure trade agreements to supply gears and lighting sets to them. Trade agreements, however, were forged with BSA, a company with which Raleigh had good working relations. The fear of post-war competition was instrumental in the decision to establish an experimental shop for the development of new lighting sets and variable gears, and this was extended to the formation of an experimental and research department which also included cycle design. As Wilson argued in June 1945,

> In view of the competition which we should face in the post-war era, it was felt we should without delay start to form a self-contained department which would be responsible for our design and production keeping ahead of our competitors, as had been our experience over the past fifty years.[17]

The formation of Raleigh Industries Ltd in January 1946 also signalled a response to the competitive environment after the war, and the holding company was designed to tighten up central control over Raleigh's growing number of operating companies. As we shall see in the

relationships between Raleigh Industries and Sturmey-Archer, the holding company remained a loose confederation of autonomous firms,
each with their own board and managing directors. The next section
examines the strategy of Raleigh Industries from 1945 to its merger into
TI in 1960, and explores how the historical evolution of its company
culture impacted upon managerial decision-making.

Business strategy and business culture at Raleigh Industries Ltd, 1945–60

'The Post war programme ... which we shall be putting before you in
the New Year will place the Raleigh Cycle Co. and its Associated
Companies once more in the forefront of the Cycle Industry.' This was
the promising message relayed to Raleigh's agents and dealers by A. E.
Simpson, sales director, at the end of 1945.[18] How was this vision put
into practice, and what were the strategies employed? Raleigh's post-
war business strategy was directed towards the achievement of three
major outcomes: to increase output capacity; to direct an increasing
proportion of that increased capacity to export markets; and to continue to make and sell a high-quality product designed to meet customer
need. Bowden, as chairman of the company, accepted that the first
objective, capacity expansion, required long-term planning. Rejecting
short-termism, he believed that business success was best achieved by a
'master plan', a programme of output expansion premised on the belief
that the market environment facing Raleigh was a positive one. As he
informed the company's shareholders in 1951: 'World demand is still
unsatisfied.' This meant that Raleigh's products still 'remained rationed
in all parts of the world', and he went on to claim that 'never before
have bicycles been so popular at home and abroad'. This conclusion no
doubt satisfied the audience of shareholders, and he boasted that 'cycling is in fact definitely on the increase, a fact that augurs well for the
future prosperity of your company'.[19]

In order to expand capacity Raleigh pursued two main strategies.
First, in the immediate post-war years the company embarked on a
modernisation programme at its central production plants in Nottingham. The aim was to expand and upgrade facilities to enable mass
production and to effect time-saving economies by reorganising the
layout of the shop-floor. The modernisation scheme began in earnest in
1947 when 'a great network of conveyors' was introduced 'spanning
the 28 acre Raleigh plant'. The intention was to increase greatly the
flow of production, and the new integrated system consisted of a main
conveyor which carried the frames and cycles and secondary or 'feeder

conveyors', which carried made-to-order components and products from the tool rooms and the Sturmey-Archer assembly department and serviced the central conveyor. The technological advantages of the new system, it was believed, would allow Raleigh to supply its customers with a 'light weight tubular structure produced to the highest standard of accuracy and capable of withstanding the many strains imposed upon its every day use'. Raleigh's commitment to a high-quality product remained paramount, and the reasons for this will be explored later. By 1953 the company could legitimately boast that its frame production plant was 'one of the best equipped in the world', and Raleigh could take pride in the fact that its factories had been purpose built by their own engineers. It would appear that Raleigh was making a determined effort to expand capacity, and was responding positively to a set of market signals which were clearly pointing to a seller's market after the war. By 1950 a new 1.5-acre factory was operational for the production of Sturmey-Archer gears, and within three years this was producing 2 million units per annum. The capital investment programme continued with the building of a 10-acre extension to enable an increase of frame capacity in 1953, at a cost of £1.25 million, and culminated in 1957 with the opening of a new Sturmey-Archer factory costing £5 million. Capital spending was not confined to domestic UK production, but the programme also allowed for the establishment of overseas factories in South Africa and India. The company's intention was to exploit the potential of these expanding post-war markets, to overcome import restrictions and, in the case of South Africa, to compete directly with the bicycle division of TI, who had also established plant in South Africa.[20]

In addition to direct investment into new plant, both at home and abroad, Raleigh embarked on an acquisition programme which led it to absorb a number of bicycle companies during the 1950s, a clear objective of the company signalled by the renaming of the holding company as Raleigh Industries in January 1946. The structure of the holding company, with its various subsidiaries, is shown in Figure E.1 in the Appendix. Raleigh's policy of acquisition reached its apex in 1957 when it absorbed the bicycle division of BSA into the holding company, at a cost of £500 000. The deal now allowed Raleigh to sell pedal cycles under the trade marks of BSA, Sunbeam, New Hudson and Eadie, all companies which came under the BSA umbrella. As we saw in the last chapter, BSA retained its successful scooter interest, but Raleigh in 1957 acquired some of the most famous trade marks in the industry. Raleigh Industries presents the appearance of a dynamic company pursuing an aggressive policy of expansion, but how successful was it in meeting its strategic commitments?

Tables E.1 and E.2 in the Appendix provide data on output and sales. Cycle production rose rapidly from just 182 682 units in 1945 to 674 565 by 1949, and then accelerated to over 1 million by 1951. By this date Raleigh was supplying approximately one-third of the total UK bicycle output, and also succeeded in its second strategic mission of meeting its increased export targets. By 1949 63.7 per cent of Raleigh's enlarged output was being sold in overseas markets, including Eire, and this compared to 30 per cent in 1939 and 23.5 per cent in 1945. In the early 1950s the export share of output had risen to approximately 70 per cent, and the company was now supplying over 100 foreign markets throughout the world. In 1947 Raleigh had welcomed the Labour government's 'call for more exports', and in particular Bowden and Wilson had focused the company's efforts on the strategically important 'dollar markets'. Raleigh's management confidently reported, in 1949, that the USA and Canada were 'fast becoming a substantial factor in our export sales'. Raleigh's business leaders believed that their success in the export drive, facilitated by the increase in productive capacity, was based on the third component of their overall strategy, selling quality products tailored to customer needs. Bowden, for example, reiterated his core philosophy which, as we saw in Chapter 5 was central to his thinking in the inter-war years, and was adamant that at Raleigh 'quality has never been sacrificed to quantity'. He claimed in 1953 that as output had expanded 'our watchword now as ever is quality'. It was Bowden's firm belief that it was Raleigh's commitment to quality that resulted in 'our favoured position in the cycle industry today'. This focus on exporting a quality product was backed up by an extensive network of foreign dealers, who numbered some 10 000 by 1953, and guaranteed that the company's customers would be supplied with 'the type of machine they require'.[21]

Despite the ambitious investment programme, and the market success outlined above, the company could be accused of missing a window of opportunity. That is, it failed to sufficiently supply domestic and world markets with Raleigh bicycles. Raleigh, not unlike Phillips, as we saw in the previous chapter, may be held to account concerning its seeming inability to meet the rising demand for pedal cycles which characterised the first decade following the end of the Second World War. For example, in the case of overseas demand the company's failure to supply foreign markets adequately may be illustrated by problems encountered in the important Indian market. In 1950 the Indian government granted Raleigh an open import licence for 100 000 bicycles, but the company failed to exploit the opportunity, and its in-house magazine, *Raligram*, complained bitterly that 'our company could have taken up to 80 per cent of these but all we could accommodate, and this with difficulty, was 20 000'. Four years later, despite new capacity coming on stream, the company still admitted that export orders of over 100 000 cycles were still outstanding. Such difficulties were not confined to overseas markets, and as a Raleigh director lamented in October 1953, while the home trade 'was keeping up very well so late in the season... it was nothing short of a tragedy to see the business which has been lost this year to our company because of our inability to supply'.[22] How do we account for this tragic loss of business?

In part this was a result of an exogenous factor, which absolves the Raleigh management from direct blame. In the early 1950s there were severe restrictions on the supply of steel and components to the manufacturing sector, and these restrictions were government imposed. Following the British decision to support the USA over the Korean conflict, the burden of rearmament fell particularly on the domestic metal and engineering trades, and there is little doubt that acute shortages of key production inputs adversely affected the export drive.[23] Bowden was certainly worried over the company's future prospects, and he claimed in January 1952 that 'The realisation of all our plans for the future, and indeed our ability even to hold our present position, depends entirely upon the supply of raw materials'. While Bowden may well have been overstating the problem, a 40 per cent cut in Raleigh's allocation of strip steel in early 1952 forced the company to rely on foreign imports costing three times the price of domestic supplies, and this had the obvious effect of pushing up production costs. Above all, what concerned management was that restrictions on output, due to input shortages, could lead to a 'surrender' of 'markets to our foreign competitors, among whom Germany and Japan are playing an increasing role'.[24]

While not discounting the negative effects of government imposed restrictions on Raleigh's input supplies, this was not the only factor which explains the company's problems in satisfactorily expanding capacity. There are good grounds for arguing that factors internal to the company itself frustrated the form and extent of its investment strategy. In particular, we suggest that Raleigh's business strategy was both shaped and steered by a dominant company culture which had evolved over the previous half century.[25] As outlined in earlier chapters, Raleigh was characterised by a set of core values which sustained an organisational style based on personal capitalism, and this committed the company to producing quality products tailored to meeting customer needs. These cultural patterns, informing the business strategy, led to three basic problems. The first was related to the pace at which the investment programme was implemented; the second concerned the form or type of production technology that was introduced; and the third was to do with the consequences of the allocation and sequencing of capital spending between different constituent elements of Raleigh Industries.

Turning to the question of the implementation of the investment programme, the attachment of the Raleigh organisation to a core belief in personal capitalism meant that Bowden and Wilson were committed to an investment strategy based upon retained profits. Following the easing of government controls the expansion of capacity could have been funded by bank loans if Raleigh had been prepared to accept outside finance. The company could have accelerated its expansion programme by widening its access to capital finance, but the commitment to personal control, which was deeply embedded at Raleigh, excluded this possibility and outside funding was not considered to be a viable option. As Bowden stated in 1950: 'without increased profits in an expanding business it's quite impossible to finance and accumulate the necessary reserves'. The new factory extension that had been opened in 1953 was financed entirely out of retained profits, and indeed the whole expansion programme was dependent on this flow of funding. Thus Bowden announced in December 1954 that 71.5 per cent of total profits would be retained in the business, 'in view of our programme for the extension of our factories'. While such a policy could be described as prudent, it was at the same time, if expansion was to proceed, heavily dependent on a healthy profit earning capability. Unfortunately for Raleigh, as Table 7.1 shows, total profits after tax fell between 1950 and 1952, and even though profits rose in 1953 they were still below the level of 1950. In addition, Raleigh's strategy was vulnerable to shifts in government fiscal policy, and in 1952, for example, Bowden was complaining about the high level of taxation which he maintained 'made it almost impossible for a company to retain sufficient costs (sic), to support the expansion of its business'.[26] As was seen in Chapter 3, from its beginnings financial independence was central to the control of Raleigh by its founders and heirs, and this core belief in financial autonomy, which persisted into the post 1945 period, clearly affected the pace and timing of the expansion programme.

Raleigh, with some justification, took pride in its production technology, and, as we saw earlier, could boast in the early 1950s that it had one of the best equipped frame production plants in the world. Nevertheless the company's production methods constituted a peculiar half-way house between mass production and batch production methods. Why did Raleigh choose this form of technology, especially when the advantages of continuous flow production, to mass-produce standardised products, over batch production systems were well known?[27] The choice of technological and labour inputs cannot be understood without

Table 7.1 Raleigh Industries, group net
trading profit after tax, 1949–61

Year	Net profit (£)
1949	583 147
1950	688 764
1951	675 176
1952	551 631
1953	714 467
1954	1 036 903
1955	1 211 157
1956	1 195 507
1957	770 661
1958	353 424
1959	831 817
1960	905 370
1961	600 366

Source: Compiled from Lloyd-Jones, Lewis
and Eason, 1999, Table 5.

recognising the company's commitment to the historical association of
the Raleigh name with quality products, and meeting customer needs.
Thus, Raleigh from its early days had manufactured a variety of product lines, and this in turn led to non-standardisation in component
production which required the use of specialised machines and tools
built to order by its tool-room staff. The Raleigh bicycles, and its other
trade marks such as Rudge-Whitworth and Humber, were specially
designed and equipped to meet the needs of particular customers, and
indeed particular countries. For example, bicycles for the Canadian
market were made with sloping top tubes to meet specialist customer
requirements, and special colour schemes were introduced for the South
African trade. This meant that Raleigh was required to manufacture a
wide range of components and parts to provide its sales force 'with a
service organisation which gives complete satisfaction'. To meet the
special requirements of its export markets in frames and wheel forks
alone, Raleigh produced 500 separate types, and each 'pair of replacement forks' had to 'be identical to the original'.[28]

The Raleigh strategy, in what management believed to be a 'seller's
market', was to produce a wide range of products for differentiated
markets, a business approach recognised by *The Economist* when it
observed that the majority of exhibits at the 1953 Cycle and Motor

Cycle Show were 'old fashioned upstanding designs produced for colonial markets'.[29] The outcome at Raleigh was that from a technological perspective, craft traditions still continued to permeate the work processes, and this was reflected in the company's education and training programme which gave a high priority, under its craft apprenticeship scheme, to training workers for tool-room operations.[30] This is not to suggest that Raleigh failed to invest in new automatic technologies, it did, and as new factories came on stream in the 1950s they were equipped with new machinery and more automatic processes were introduced. The company did increase the speed of throughput in its production plants, but the emphasis on diversification required the duplication of component parts, increased the number of machine operations, and reduced efficiency levels. For example, *Raligram* boasted that to produce a four-speed gear hub took the time of 21 machine operations using 48 separate machine tools and 46 gauges to produce the axle alone, and a further 37 press tools and 22 gauges to produce the hub shell. It also pointed out that all the tools, machine attachments and gauges were produced in the company's own tool room. Production systems combined automatic technology with a 'vast amount' of operations which were continued by hand, including all the machining and welding.[31] That Raleigh's top management was prepared to innovate new production methods there is little doubt, but the commitment to core values, which were still manifest in the 1950s, meant a curious ambivalence which inhibited the exploitation of the full potential of the new technology. It also created tensions between management and labour in the second half of the 1950s, at a time when Raleigh faced growing competitive pressure and the need to reorganise. In short, the diversity of styles, sizes and colours meant that their manufacture was generally organised on a batch basis.[32]

A third factor which connected the investment strategy at Raleigh with management's identification of core values was the decision of the company to expand its Sturmey-Archer gear capacity ahead of its frame capacity. The commitment to product quality, as a core value, and the personal style of management, led it to expand component production first, and direct investment resources to the subsidiary firm of Sturmey-Archer. Thus, the post-war investment plan allocated resources first to a new Sturmey-Archer plant which came on stream in 1950, while a major extension of frame capacity had to await until 1953. Also in 1950 the decision was taken to provide Sturmey-Archer dyno hubs and three-speed gears to the entire bicycle industry. According to George Wilson these components, which during and after the war had been 'a feature exclusive' to Raleigh cycles, were 'now available to the markets of the world, and comes with a name long famous for quality and service'.[33] Why should the management have made such a decision? It is understandable as a demonstration of the impact of core values on business strategy. Management firmly believed that past success was based on quality which was unmatched by its competitors, and these values acted as a 'compass' to guide their sales strategy. They saw no danger in supplying customer needs with a quality component, and as Wilson boasted in 1956:

> The policy pursued by Sturmey-Archer gears is calculated to be in the best interest of the bicycle trade. It is entirely independent from the policies of our cycle companies. Raleigh has no advantage whatever from its association with Sturmey-Archer. In fact in times of shortage Raleigh takes its cut with all the other customers. You need never fear that Sturmey-Archer will ever adopt any other policy than what is absolutely fair.[34]

The problem with this strategy was that it gave two distinct advantages to Raleigh's competitors. First, the decision to expand Sturmey-Archer gears, and make them freely available to the industry, offered competitors what amounted to a free gift. High-quality components could be purchased and fitted to lower-quality and cheaper frames. This was an important gain for small producers in particular, and as Pratten has shown, components formed a high proportion of total costs. He estimated that for a bicycle manufacturing firm, manufacturing 20 000 units per annum, compared to Raleigh's 1 million in the early 1950s, component costs per bicycle would be approximately £8 compared to a total ex-works cost of only £9.[35] Consequently, if smaller firms could purchase their components at competitive prices, the declared aim of Sturmey-Archer, then the cost advantage of larger producers such as Raleigh over their smaller competitors would be extremely limited. Second, in order to supply its competitors, Raleigh limited its own frame capacity, and consequently as late as 1955 Wilson was forced to acknowledge that Raleigh Industries was still 'unable to meet the demands of some of our principal export markets'. The Sturmey-Archer strategy also suggests that the organisational structure at Raleigh Industries was more or less a loose federation of semi-autonomous companies. The dominant company culture at Raleigh led management to assume that subsidiaries operated in the wider interest of the organisation overall, loyal to the spirit of the 'Raleigh family'. Thus George Wilson, a former Sturmey-Archer man, warmly endorsed the policy of D. S. Robinson, the managing director of Sturmey-Archer, when the latter proclaimed 'That the policy of my company is to give priority to the requirements of the cycle trade all over the world'.[36] But the Raleigh organisation was characterised by ambiguity and there was a potential contradiction between the wider company interest and the role of subsidiaries. A product-related subsidiary was given a high priority in the allocation of scarce investment resources, sold its components to the parent company's main domestic and foreign competitors without any favour to Raleigh Cycles, the main operating company, and delayed the expansion of frame capacity. In an important sense the organisational culture was acting as a 'defective compass'.[37] Management's belief in the notion of the 'Raleigh family' blinkered its need to supply its own customers adequately, both at home and abroad, with Raleigh cycles.

A combination of exogenous and endogenous factors acted to constrain Raleigh's capacity expansion programme, and this was to have serious consequences for Raleigh's continuation as an independent company. Before we look at the story of the merger with BCC, the cycle division of TI, a brief sketch of the business environment facing the company in the 1950s will provide a background context. In general terms the decade of the 1950s was characterised by relatively high rates of economic growth, rising prosperity, full employment and expanding international trade. Indeed, the 1950s have been described as the 'Golden Age' in the economic history of the advanced capitalist economies.[38] In the first half of the decade Raleigh seemingly prospered within this growth inducing environment, producing record levels of output and exporting some 70 per cent of its bicycles and bicycle components. But in the second half of the 1950s Raleigh's performance faltered, and the firm experienced worrying falls in both profits and sales. It can be seen from Table 7.1 that net profits peaked in 1955, and then fell by 71 per cent to a low of £353 424 in 1958. Profits did recover over the next two years but remained below their 1955 level, and in 1961 profits fell back again to only half their level of the mid-1950s. At the beginning of the decade the ratio of net profits after tax to total capital employed was 12.2 per cent; by 1961 this had fallen to 2.5 per cent. Net sales also faltered in the late 1950s, and after peaking in 1956 they fell over the next two years by 10 per cent, before recovering in 1960 to just under their 1956 level. Raleigh's deteriorating performance was principally a result of three factors: the problem of rising domestic costs; the increase in external competition; and a shift in the demand for bicycles associated with a rise in living standards.

The issue of labour and raw material costs exercised the minds of Raleigh's top management throughout the decade. As early as 1951 Bowden was complaining 'that the rate of profit on turnover was lower than previous, owing to the burden of increasing costs of material and labour, which we have largely absorbed'. In July 1952 Bowden further warned of the 'essential' need to halt the rise in costs 'if we are to maintain our position in the export field in the face of increasing world-wide competition'. Indeed, the chairman believed that Raleigh's prices should be falling rather than rising, but he acknowledged that this could 'only be achieved' if there was 'a fall in costs'. However, by 1955 Raleigh 'had reluctantly decided to increase prices' of all its products in order for the company 'to meet continually rising costs of labour and raw materials'. Raleigh had managed to hold prices stable over a two year period between 1953 and 1955, but in the latter year the company was faced with a number of labour awards and the now chairman, George Wilson, estimated that these would 'add at least £225 000 per annum to the wage bill'. Indeed, Wilson claimed that between November 1950 and early 1956 there had been 'no less than six national awards', which represented 'an increase of no less than 57.32 per cent on the consolidated rates'. 'At the risk of repetition', Wilson proclaimed, 'I must sound the warning that to load our industry ... with additional costs can only lead to still further inroads by our foreign competitors into our traditional markets, with an increase in short-time working and redundancy as the inevitable result.' In what amounted to a plea, Wilson concluded that 'I only hope that the leaders of the Confederation of Unions who are pressing this latest application may yet grasp the vital significance of this simple but fundamental truth before it is too late'. It would appear that Wilson's plea went unheeded as two years later he was arguing that a major contributing factor to Raleigh's fall in net profits was 'the rising tide of increased costs over the last few years'. In particular, what concerned Wilson was that while the bicycle industry had attempted to absorb, 'in whole or in part the additional costs arising out of a continuous process of labour awards and increased prices of raw materials', such was the squeeze on profits that rising costs would have to be passed on to the consumer in the form of higher prices. Raleigh had consequently increased its prices in the domestic market but in its important export markets it had found that this was 'not possible to do so' without losing market share.[39] This latter point raises the issue of foreign competition, the second factor which impacted on Raleigh's performance, particularly from the mid-1950s.

As was seen in the previous chapter, foreign competition hit the British bicycle industry hard, particularly from the mid-1950s. Raleigh was no exception to this trend, and indeed was rather exposed as it exported 70 per cent of its output. In 1956 Wilson acknowledged that foreign competition 'has now for the first time since the war began to make serious inroads into markets traditionally associated with British bicycles'. It was in the important US market where Raleigh faced the full blast of foreign competition, Wilson admitting that overseas competitors had made 'spectacular advances'. The British share of American imported bicycles had fallen by 30 per cent between 1954 and 1956, and by 60 per cent between 1950 and 1956. According to Wilson the

American market was 'a price market', and he attributed the sales decline 'almost entirely ... to the fact that foreign manufacturers'' were 'able to sell at a price which their British counterparts have been quite unable to match on account of their relentless build up of their labour and material costs over recent years'. In 1958, while Wilson could announce that Raleigh was still doing relatively well in East Africa, Holland, India and Eire, the latter described as 'one of the few markets in the world where the cycle industry has been able to improve on its past performance', the situation in North America was still deteriorating. The year was a difficult one for Raleigh in the USA, and Wilson bemoaned the fact that 'this is yet another market where the return is quite disproportionate to the scale of the business done'. Reference was made to the increasingly keen competition which was 'emanating from continental sources, often from behind the Iron Curtain'. Wilson acknowledged that Raleigh was making little or 'no return' on its American and Canadian business, but he committed the company to staying in North America, taking the view that to withdraw from this important dollar market 'would be a very short-sighted policy'. Raleigh's top management decided to 'ride out the storm', based on the expectation that 'saner trading conditions' would return. But demand patterns were changing and this requires a brief account of the third factor which affected Raleigh's business performance.[40]

As was demonstrated in Chapters 4 and 5, during the inter-war years companies such as Raleigh largely concentrated their activities on the home market, with exports mainly confined to the Empire. After the war the demand pattern for pedal cycles changed, and the sale of bicycles in the domestic market never attained their pre-war levels. According to Wilson there was a number of reasons for this change, but he did place emphasis on 'the improved standard of living of the population which had given rise to an enormous increase of motorised transport'. In addition, he claimed that bicycles were more recently becoming exposed to the 'introduction of so many forms of heavily advertised domestic appliances'. This reflected the growing market for consumer durables during the 1950s as the British people embraced a new consumerism, perhaps best typified by Harold Macmillan's famous 1959 slogan, 'You have never had it so good'. But Wilson was sceptical about pedal cycles sharing in the new consumerism, and he did not expect 'to see the demand for pedal cycles in this country again equal the pre-war levels'. He was more optimistic when it came to overseas markets but, as was seen above, the increased weight of foreign competition was bearing down on Raleigh, and the worry was that the company was losing its price competitiveness.[41] Did Raleigh's management have a strategy to combat this trend? There appears to have been two survival strategies: first, management appealed to its workforce to moderate their wage claims; and second, Raleigh executives stressed the key importance of increasing productivity.

During most of the 1950s Raleigh enjoyed, as it had done through most of the 1920s and 1930s, good industrial relations with its workforce. In 1950 Bowden had been keen to inform workers that there was a social dimension to profits which could be used to subsidise 'various social amenities', including a profit sharing scheme. A year later he returned to the theme of good management–worker relations when he claimed that at Raleigh it had long been the practice 'to recognise and reward the achievements of our work people, without whose co-operation and goodwill our excellent results would never have been achieved'. Bowden further announced that an additional Christmas bonus would be awarded, 'to celebrate the production of one million bicycles and tricycles during the year'. By the end of the decade, however, there was little to celebrate and Wilson was forced to sing a very different tune to that of Bowden only a few years earlier. In 1957 Wilson bitterly complained that despite the company's profit sharing scheme the 'persistent demand for increased wages had become an annual event'. Wilson could also have added that Raleigh provided its workforce with an excellent education and training programme, welfare facilities and a commitment, during a period of rapid change, to no redundancies. Raleigh's chairman denied the demands of the trade unions that wage claims were necessary in order for workers to maintain both their living standards and their share in industrial income. He pointed out that between 1954 and 1957, while prices had increased by 14 per cent, weekly wage rates had increased by 22 per cent. Further, Raleigh's profits had declined rather than increased. In obvious exasperation Wilson asked: 'How can it be maintained in the face of this evidence that labour is asking for nothing more than its justifiable share in increasing prosperity?'[42]

While there is no direct evidence of a sub- or counter-culture at Raleigh, nevertheless by the late 1950s it would seem that the relationship between management and the workforce was coming under increasing strain. Top management believed that the commitment to the workforce was reciprocal, that is, management trusted their workforce because they assumed that both parties shared a loyalty to the company – they were all Raleigh people. Yet, although management appealed to the workforce for wage restraint this manifestly failed to impress. While Wilson insisted that for the good of the company all at Raleigh should 'forgo the luxury of paying ourselves more for the same amount of work', this did not resonate with the workforce who were responding to a set of national trends rather than firm specific values. Workers used their increased bargaining strength, in a full employment economy, to enhance their earning power. [43] From the perspective of management the waning of trust in their workforce, as appeals for constraint fell on deaf ears, was compounded by the fact that damage was being inflicted on the company by wage increases outstripping improvements in productivity.

The issue of productivity became of growing importance to Raleigh's management in the second half of the 1950s when productivity gains failed to match wage increases. Between 1955 and 1960 profit per worker fell by approximately 50 per cent (Table 7.2), as the company struggled to absorb the costs arising from a series of national wage agreements, and hence the appeals for wage constraint. But why did productivity growth fail to match the increase in labour costs? There is not a straightforward answer to this question, but Raleigh did experience an unfortunate historical conjuncture, that is, just at the moment when its long-term investment strategy was coming to fruition there was a downturn in the demand for pedal cycles. Wilson explained in 1958 that a trade recession had 'coincided with the completion of our very considerable programme of factory expansion, with the result that we find ourselves, temporarily, burdened with surplus productive capacity, which for the time being is doing nothing to earn its keep'.[44] As Freeman has pointed out, 'below capacity working may have a significant adverse effect on the economies of large-scale plant operations and losses can be on a large scale'.[45] Wilson was well aware that the running costs of Raleigh's surplus capacity was a 'continuing charge', and had to 'be borne by a volume of business which has already sharply decreased'. Not surprisingly, Raleigh's management placed a heavy stress

Table 7.2   Crude estimates of profit per worker at Raleigh Industries, 1950–60

Year	Profit per worker (£)
1950	114.79
1952	78.80
1953	102.07
1954	129.61
1955	134.57
1957	81.99
1960	75.45

Source: Compiled from Lloyd-Jones, Lewis and Eason, 1999, Table 9.

on improving productivity and in addition to their education and train-ing programme, they embarked in the late 1950s on a factory reorganisation scheme which among other things 'set up an entirely new division charged with overall responsibility for research and prod-uct design and development'. Wilson regarded the initiative as of 'immense' importance for the long-run future of the company, and he anticipated that its implementation would lead to 'a number of funda-mental changes ... to our manufacturing processes'. But all this was rather late in the day, and despite schemes of labour redeployment, operated with the approval of the trade unions, and the introduction of 'new blood' management from outside the company, falling profits in the second half of the 1950s delayed investment in modernisation.[46] Productivity levels, albeit measured by the crude indicator of profits per worker, fell sharply from £134.57 in 1955 to only £75.45 in 1960, a fall of 43.9 per cent. (Table 7.2). Two main criticisms may be levelled at Raleigh's top management. First, it remained too strongly wedded to a company culture, which had certainly served the company well in the past, but which by the 1950s was acting as a constraining force slowing down the pace of adaptation. Second, the convergence of rising wage and material costs with intensifying foreign competition placed a pre-mium on increasing productivity, but management spent too much time and effort appealing for wage constraint and trading on their workers' loyalty, rather than driving through technological changes at plant level. Increased wage costs, falling productivity and declining profit margins led, in 1960, to the merger with BCC, and the demise of Raleigh as an independent company. The story of this merger, outlined below, will form the concluding section of the chapter.

The end of an era: the merger with BCC, 1960

Rising wage costs, falling productivity, and declining profits at Raleigh created severe difficulties for management, and in 1959 negotiations were opened for a merger with BCC, the cycle division of TI. This was, in many ways the logical outcome for the two big British cycle produc-ers, as BCC in the 1950s had purchased a large volume of its components from Sturmey-Archer, and in turn Raleigh had depended upon TI for steel and aluminium tubing. In early 1959 the companies had collabo-rated in South Africa, Raleigh closing its plant at Vereeniging and acquiring an interest in the BCC cycle factory at Springs. Wilson clearly had close connections with personnel in the TI group, and Sir Francis de Guingand, the chief executive running TI's industrial interests in South Africa was a close personal friend. Thus, 'Such was Tube Investment's faith in the men at Nottingham that they asked the Raleigh people to take responsibility for integrating the British Cycle Corporation into Raleigh Industries'.[47]

On the 1 August 1960, just 23 days prior to the death of Raleigh's president, Sir Harold H. Bowden, Raleigh Industries was converted into a new trading company to acquire all the assets of its subsidiaries, including the Raleigh Cycle Co. Ltd, Sturmey-Archer and BSA. This company now acquired the whole of the share capital of BCC, which as we saw in Chapter 6 included J. A. Phillips & Co., and was absorbed into the TI group. In effect, Raleigh Industries became synonymous with the British bicycle industry, and its absorption into TI placed it as the primary British cycle producer. The merger with BCC did little to change the managerial structure of the company, and Wilson was made managing director and chairman of Raleigh Industries, a trading company of TI. Indeed, key Raleigh personnel, such as Eric E. Baker, export director, Bryan L. C. Dodworth, secretary, and Leslie L. Roberts, production manager, retained their positions on the new board. But change there inevitably was, and leading managers from TI were brought into the executive board: Sir Francis de Guingand, James Boulstridge of Phillips, and Charles Gilbert Smith, the managing director of Norton Motors.[48]

Nevertheless, the old guard still remained, and in his statement from the chair in 1960 Wilson outlined three main reasons for the merger. First, it would strengthen the company's competitive position in the face of intense competition from continental and Asian manufacturers, especially in overseas markets which took the bulk of cycle production. Second, they would be in a stronger position to combat the rise of local manufacturers in export markets which had traditionally been the preserve of the British cycle industry. Third, as we saw in the last chapter both Raleigh and BCC had fared badly in their attempts to capture the British market for mopeds, and Bowden proclaimed that the combined efforts of the two companies would enable them to utilise the full resources at their disposal – and especially the BSA and Phillips divisions – to provide the platform for putting Britain at the forefront of a market which had 'so largely been dominated by foreign makers'. The motivation for the merger was largely defensive, a clear reaction to the growing competitive problems of the British cycle industry, and the pooling of the financial and managerial resources of the 'two leading manufacturers' would allow the company the strength for an effective response. The management, however, had high ambitions concerning the prospects of the moped market, and as Bowden argued in 1961, announcing a 'no change' policy in their range of mopeds, 'We consider that we have the finest range of mopeds in the world, and the performance of our light-weight scooter has already created for itself a wonderful name'.[49]

The new board had the responsibility, with TI, for the control of the combined cycle, component and motorised transport division of the group, and the task facing management was

> to weld into a useful whole the parallel activities of the TI and Raleigh cycle interests, and by integration and rationalisation of sales, manufacture and administration to create the maximum degree of efficiency and economy consistent with the fullest exploitation of the world-wide goodwill attaching to the individual products and trade names of the Companies concerned.

The new group now employed 13 000 workers, and controlled a number of geographically separated factories with a total floor space of 4.64 million square feet.[50] In September 1961 Wilson called a convention of dealers at Nottingham, the first one staged by the company since 1954. This was to be a 'get-together' to discuss the programme for the coming season, but was used by Wilson as a platform for promoting the merger with TI. This, he claimed, placed Raleigh in a key position in the British cycle industry, but he referred to the fact that 'after more than seventy years of independent operation it was a difficult decision ... but we came to the conclusion that, on balance, such a move could only be in the best interests of our shareholders and employees, and of the British cycle industry as a whole'. Referring to the future prospects of the organisation, he made a play on the past experiences of the company, and claimed that there would be 'no change in our policy or outlook. What we need is stability in the industry. The deterioration in the home sales must be halted and confidence restored'. This is a remarkable testimony to the influence of historical experience, built on the evolution of core managerial values, in shaping the perception of management at Raleigh. Wilson concluded his address to the delegates with words that may well have been uttered by Frank and Harold Bowden themselves: 'If the right relationship exists between us, if we produce for you a first class article and if you display the necessary zeal to sell and service it, then I have no fear about the future'.[51] In the longer term the Raleigh name did survive, although its independence was lost in 1960, and it was subsequently acquired by an American consortium in 1970. The history of Raleigh and the British bicycle industry is a story of change and adaptation, but also of the continuity of business leaders in the industry, their unstinting belief in the value of the product, and their personal commitment to building their organisational capabilities.

Notes

1. DDRN 3/8/1–13, Raleigh Industries Ltd, Balance Sheets and Accounts together with Reports for 1949–61, 1950, 1960; DDRN 2/9/6–8, Certificates of Incorporation of Raleigh Industries Ltd, and Change of Name from Raleigh Cycle Holdings Co., 24 January 1946.
2. DDRN 1/2/6, Raleigh Cycle Co. Ltd, Board and General Meetings Minutes with Fortnightly Reports, 3 June 1939. In particular, Wilson was optimistic about Eire and Argentina, and reported a contract for 25 000 cycles with the latter, a doubling of this trade on the previous year.
3. Ibid., 24 June, 12 August 1939.
4. Ibid., 24 June, 12 August, 22 September, 30 November 1939. A similar programme of rationing was followed for gears, and 'orders for Sturmey-Archer gears had accumulated in proportion to the cycle trade, and at the present moment it was just a question of rationing our customers'. Dyno hub lighting sets were also sold off as a bulk order to Currys. Ibid., 22 September 1939.
5. Ibid., 30 November 1939.
6. Ibid., 9 January 1940.
7. Ibid., and 7 February, 18 March, 8 May 1940.
8. Ibid., 19 September 1940, 6 February, 9 October, 11 December 1941. Raleigh designed specialist bicycles for the military, the government approving in March 1941 the Raleigh Mark 5 Government Cycle 'to facilitate competition in the market'. Ibid., 28 March 1941.
9. Ibid., 5 June, 21 August, 19 September 1940.
10. Ibid., 5 June, 8 May 1940.
11. Ibid., 23 July, 11 December 1941, 5 February, 1 April, 23 September, 17 November 1942.
12. Ibid., 19 September 1940, 15 May, 24 June, 12 October 1943, 25 February 1944; DDRN 7/3/8 Special Binder, Rudge-Whitworth and its Acquisition By the Raleigh Cycle Co. Ltd.
13. Special Binder, Rudge-Whitworth.
14. Minutes with Reports, 18 March 1943. This decision was taken to keep Gazelle sales as high as possible in relation to Raleigh and Humber sales, and to overcome the problems of restrictions in export markets because of the rights held by the Dutch Gazelle Co.
15. Ibid., 24 June, 12 October, 9 December 1943, 25 February 1944.
16. Ibid., 21 June, 15 August, 27 October 1944.
17. Ibid., 27 October 1944, 9 January, 18 June 1945.
18. DDRN 11/1/12, A. E. Simpson to Dealers, end of 1945.
19. Balance Sheets with Reports, 1951.
20. Nottingham Central Library, Raligram, the in-house journal of Raleigh Industries, March 1947, p. 5, January 1948, p. 8, January 1950, p. 12, February 1951, p. 8, February 1952, p. 2, July 1953, pp. 10–11, September 1957, p. 2. Minutes with Reports, 11 November 1949.
21. Balance Sheets with Reports, 1950, 1951, 1953; Raligram, February 1952, p. 25, November 1952, p. 20, February 1953, p. 30; Balance Sheets with Reports, 1953; Nottingham Evening News, 27 August 1953; Nottingham Guardian, 11 November 1952.
22. Raligram, February 1950, p. 12, December 1954, p. 14; Minutes with Reports, 1 October 1953.

23. Schenk, 1994, p. 312; Pollard, 1984, p. 37; 'Economic Survey for 1951', *Ministry of Labour Gazette*, **59**, 1951, p. 141; Worswick, 1962.
24. *The Economist*, 5 January 1952, p. 52; Balance Sheets with Reports, 1952; Minutes with Reports, 21 October 1951, 13 February 1952.
25. For an examination of the importance of company culture to understanding business development see Jeremy, 1998, chapter 14; Hofstede, 1994; Alvesson, 1993, pp. 9–26; Casson, 1993; Church, 1996; Griffiths, 1995; Kay, 1993; Lipatito, 1995; Rowlinson, 1995; Schein, 1985; Westall and Godley, 1998. The evaluation of Raleigh's business culture is examined in Lloyd-Jones, Lewis and Eason, 1999.
26. Balance Sheets with Reports, 1950; *Raligram*, February 1953, p. 2; *The Economist*, 25 December 1954, p. 121, 3 January 1953, p. 51.
27. For a discussion of this issue see Freeman, 1982, pp. 35–8.
28. *Raligram*, November 1952, p. 20.
29. *The Economist*, 21 November 1953, pp. 609–10; Balance Sheets with Reports, 1953.
30. For a discussion of Raleigh's education and training programme see Lloyd-Jones, Lewis and Eason, 1999. For a general discussion of technical education and training in British business see Aldcroft, 1994.
31. *Raligram*, September 1949, p. 14, January 1950, p. 12, July 1953, pp. 10–11.
32. For a discussion of batch production systems see Pratten, 1971, p. 158.
33. Minutes with Reports, 16 October 1950; *Raligram*, March 1951, p. 3.
34. *Raligram*, February 1956, p. 18.
35. Pratten, 1971, p. 158.
36. Balance Sheets with Reports, 1955; *Raligram*, February 1956, p. 18.
37. The use of metaphors such as 'defective compass', in evaluating the relationship between company culture and business strategy are explored in Alvesson, 1993, pp. 9–26, and employed in Lloyd-Jones, Lewis and Eason, 1999.
38. See Maddison, 1962, p. 62.
39. DDRN 1267/2, Directors Reports, Chairmen's Statement 1952, 1953, 1956, 1958.
40. Balance Sheets with Reports, 1956, 1958.
41. Ibid., 1958.
42. Ibid., 1950, 1951, 1957.
43. Ibid., 1957.
44. Ibid., 1958.
45. Freeman, 1982, p. 40.
46. Balance Sheets with Reports, 1958, 1960.
47. Bowden, 1975, pp. 77–8.
48. Balance Sheets with Reports, 1960, 1961.
49. Ibid., 1960; DDRN 4/9/11, Notes of Speech by Wilson for Dealers' Conference, 19–21 September 1961.
50. Balance Sheets with Reports, 1960.
51. Dealer's Conference.

Appendix

Table A.1 Early pioneers in the British bicycle industry

Firm	Date of producing	Location	Comment
Mark Edward Norringham	1864	London	The first bicycle maker in the metropolis.[a]
Coventry Machinist Co.	1868	Coventry	Described as parent of other companies.[b]
Humber, Marriott & Cooper	1868	Nottingham/ Coventry	Firm moved to Coventry where Marriott became an alderman. The company claimed that only 'the most skilled men in the world are employed in the manufacture of Marriott, Cooper, Humber cycles'.[c]
Robert Edlison	1868	Stapleford (Leicestershire)	Company moved to Leicester in 1875. Original business combined blacksmiths with cycle-making until 1885.[a]
Henry Clark	1868	Wolverhampton	None
George Pries	1869	Wolverhampton	Lock and safe maker producing 'boneshaker with wheels'.[a]
Tangeys	1869	Smethwick, Birmingham	Hydraulic engineers. Built large number of velocipede bicycles at its Cornwall works and paid royalties to A. Davis, the London agent of the French Velocipede Co.[a]
Snaxell & Spencer	1869	London	Gymnastic apparatus makers.[a]
Newton Wilson	Late 1860s	London/ Birmingham	One of Britain's foremost indigenous sewing-machine manufacturers. Began making cycles in the late 1860s.[a]

Table A.1 concluded

Firm	Date of producing	Location	Comment
Smith & Starley	1871	Unknown	None
Haynes & Jefferies	1873	Coventry	Daniel Rudge, who moved from Wolverhampton to Coventry and was the founder of the Rudge-Whitworth Cycle Co., amalgamated with Haynes & Jefferies.[a]
Thomas Baylis & Co.	1874	Coventry	The firm's founder invented the patent coned bearing and was located at St Mary's Works, Coventry.[d]
Singer & Co.	1875	Coventry	Trained as an engineer in London. The firm made the 'Challenger' cycle with the 'celebrated Trailing break, special steering arrangement, foot rest, etc. – produced in any style required'.[e]
Hillman & Herbert	1876	Coventry	Advertised their 'Premier' cycle as: 'The only machine with front forks, and therefore the only machine that can be ridden with comfort and speed on rough roads.' Brother of Alfred Herbert. Trained as Engineer, London.[e]

Notes: [a] Harrison, 1985, pp. 42–3; [b] *Bicycling News*, 9 August 1878, p. 453; [c] *Bicycling News*, 25 December 1885, p. 243; [d] *Bicycling News*, 18 August 1876, p. 259; [e] *Bicycling News*, 10 November 1876, p. 393, 3 November 1876, p. 391.

Sources: *Bicycle News and Motor Review*, No. 58, 1901, p. 2; Harrison, 1985, pp. 42–3.

Table A.2 Total number of firms making complete cycles, fittings, components and accessories (including tyre manufacturers and enamellers) in the principle manufacturing towns of the Midlands. Figures in brackets are manufacturers of complete cycles where listed in trade directory

	Birmingham	Coventry	Wolverhampton	Nottingham	Leicester
1870	16 (16)				1 (1)
1874/5		2 (2)			
1877				6 (6)	
1879		15 (15)		7 (7)	
1879/80			19 (19)		
1881	51 (43)	17 (16)		7 (7)	
1882	58				13 (13)
1883	52	21 (14)		8 (8)	
1884			24 (24)		14 (14)
1886/7	78 (54)				
1887			17 (17)	11	
1888				14 (10)	14 (14)
1889/90					16 (16)
1890	95 (72)				
1890/91		30 (22)			
1892	140 (114)	69 (42)	40 (34)		
1893		64 (35)		31	
1894/5			39 (34)		
1895	198 (152)			46 (42)	25
1895/6				51 (42)	37 (36)

Source: Harrison, 1985 p. 43.

Table A.3   Value of British overseas trade in cycles and parts, 1895–1913 (£000)

	Imports[a]			Exports	Exports – retained imports
	Gross[b]	Reshipped	Retained		
1895				1 386	
1896				1 856	
1897	527	93	434	1 430	996
1898	613	219	394	961	567
1899	287	92	195	662	467
1900	195	48	147	531	384
1901	144	35	109	718	609
1903	99	23	76	849	773
1904	82	10	72	740	665
1905	131	12	119	936	817
1906	158	16	142	1 140	998
1907	171	10	161	1 288	1 127
1908	156	12	144	1 420	1 276
1909	177	14	163	1 638	1 475
1910	210	20	190	1 957	1 767
1911	223	15	208	2 014	1 806
1912	254	16	238	2 059	1 821
1913	334	17	317	2 087	1 770

Notes: [a] Not specified before 1897; [b] 1897–1901 includes motor cycles and parts.

Source: *The Economist*, 16 May 1925, p. 956.

Table B.1   Profits of the Raleigh Cycle Co., 1889–1914

	Net profit (£)	Dividend on ordinary shares (%)	Dividend on deferred ordinary shares (%)	To reserve (£)
Jan. 1889–Dec. 1889	1 862			
Dec. 1889–Sept. 1890	4 395			
Oct. 1890–Aug. 1891	7 503			
Sept. 1891–Aug. 1892	7 072			
Sept. 1892–Aug. 1893	7 366			
Sept. 1893–Aug. 1894	14 175			
Sept. 1894–Jan. 1896	14 537			
Sept. 1894–Aug. 1895	7 448			
Sept. 1895–Aug. 1896	19 296			
Sept. 1896–Aug. 1897	9 035			
Sept. 1897–Aug. 1898	8 500			
1899[a]	11 661	10	0	8 000
1900[b]	11 632	10	0	2 000
1901	8 312	10	0	12 000
1902	9479	10	0	6 000
1903	10 069	10	0	6 000
1904	1 301	0	0	0
1905	6 988	5	0	3 265
1906	16 206	5	0	8 000
1907	18 811	5	0	8 000
1908	15 246			
1912	36 415			
1913	41 191			
1914	49 512			

Notes: [a] For 5 months to August; [b] From 1900 accounts from September to August.

Sources: DDRN 3/1/1–22, Company Ledgers; DDRN 2/7/1, AGMs of the Raleigh Cycle Co., 1896–98; 1899–1914.

Table B.2   Value of goods sold, Raleigh trading account, 1889–96 and
1910–14 (£)

1889–96

January 1889–December 1889	7 148
December 1889–September 1890	17 471
October 1890–August 1891	36 696
September 1891–August 1892	45 633
September 1892–August 1893	62 133
September 1893–August 1894	85 845
September 1894–January 1896	88 722

Year ending August:	1910	1911	1912	1913	1914
Raleigh Cycle Co.	81 019	87 861	95 171	110 234	102 180
Robin Hood cycles	31 478	37 690	45 187	46 280	50 572
Gradual Payment Department	8 998	11 298	7 922	8 162	10 013
Motor hubs			6 771	53 700	68 442
Sturmey-Archer Gears Ltd	26 448	23 918	29 512	36 556	64 291
Depot consignments	85 784	118 852	129 219	141 741	157 825

Source: DDRN 3/1/2–3 Company Ledgers.

Table B.3 Profile of directors and managers of the Raleigh Cycle Co. Ltd, 1891 and 1896

After restructuring of company, 1891

Sir John Turney	Chairman and Managing Director of Turney Bros. Ltd, Nottingham
George Fellows, JP	Of Lloyds Bank
Joseph Lazonby, JP	Solicitor and Manager of Cumberland Union Banking Co. Ltd, Wigton
Paul Angois	Director of Raleigh Works
R. M. Woodhead	Manager of Raleigh Factory
Frank Bowden	Managing Director and Chairman of Raleigh
Edward C. Farrow	Secretary of Raleigh

After formation of new company, 1896
Directors

Frank Bowden	Chairman and Managing Director of Raleigh Cycle Co. Ltd, Nottingham
John Pearson Cox	Chairman of Moore & Robinsons Nottinghamshire Banking Co. Ltd
Ernest W. Enfield	Late Partner in Hurst, Fellows & Co., bankers of Nottingham, and now amalgamated with Lloyds Bank
William Lambert	Director of Nottingham and Nottinghamshire Banking Co. Ltd
Joseph Lazonby	Solicitor and Manager of Cumberland Union Banking Co. Ltd, Wigton
William Wright	Director in Moore & Robinsons Nottinghamshire Banking Co. Ltd
Arthur John Chamberlain	Solicitor, Nottingham

General Manager
D. W. Bassett

Works Manager
G. P. Mills

Secretary
Edward C. Farrow

Bankers
Moore & Robinsons
Nottinghamshire Banking Co. Ltd, and their agents, Glyn, Mills, Currie & Co., Lombard Street, London

Brokers
G. Lacey Hillier (London)
Arthur E. Blake (Nottingham)
W & F Cuthbert (Birmingham)

Solicitors
Wells & Hind (Nottingham)
Hind & Robinson (London)

Auditors
Mellors, Basden, & Mellors (Nottingham and London)

Sources: DDRN 10/3/9/3 Prospectus of the Raleigh Cycle Co. Ltd, 1891; DDRN 10/3/9/4/1 Prospectus of the Raleigh Cycle Co. Ltd, 1896; DDRN 3/1/2/2 Raleigh Cycle Co., Agreement for Sale and Purchase of Business Upon Reconstruction, 4 March 1896.

Table B.4 Reconstructions of the Raleigh Cycle Co., 1896 and 1899

Scheme for reconstruction of Raleigh Cycle Co. Ltd, 4 March 1896

Every member of the old company shall be entitled to receive, in respect of shares therein held by him (except founder's shares), as consideration of the purchase of the company for £180 000:

1. Ten shillings in cash in respect of shares in the old company, raising £32 900.
2. The allotment of one fully paid £1 6 per cent cumulative preference share of the new company in respect of every two shares held in the old company, raising £32 900 for sale.
3. The allotment of one fully paid £1 ordinary share of the new company in respect of every two shares held in the old company, raising £32 900 for the sale.
4. The allotment of one fully paid £1 ordinary share of the new company in respect of every two shares in the old company, or ten shillings in cash if the new company exercises its option of paying the sum of £32 900, part of the said consideration for the purchase, in cash instead of fully paid ordinary £1 shares.
5. The residue of £48 400 is at the option of the new company, either by allotment of fully paid preference shares, or fully paid ordinary shares in new company, or in cash, or partly in preference and/or ordinary shares, and partly in cash. The said shares shall be allotted to the liquidator or his nominee.

Source: DDRN 10/3/1/2/2, Raleigh Cycle Co. Ltd, Agreement for Sale and Purchase of Business Upon Reconstruction of the Company, 4 March 1896; DDRN 2/7/1, *Nottingham Daily Express*, 4 February 1896; Wells & Hind, solicitors, Circular to Shareholders, 30 October 1896.

Capital and share issue in the new Raleigh Cycle Co., incorporated February 1899

	£
Debentures	
First with power to increase to £40 000	35 000
Second and third	17 000
Total	52 000
Nominal share capital	
480 000 ordinary shares at 2s. 6d. each	60 000
600 deferred ordinary shares (entitled to 5% after payment of 10% on ordinary shares and providing for reserves) at £1 each	60 000
Total	120 000
Distribution of ordinary shares	
100 000 to be subscribed by preference shareholders in the old company	12 500
100 000 to be subscribed by ordinary shareholders in the old company	12 500
48 000 to be issued to creditors in old company	6 000
68 000 to be issued to Gazelle Co., in recognition of trade debts owed by that company	8 000
Present issue 312 000	39 000
Reserved for future issue 168 000	21 000
Total	60 000
Deferred ordinary shares	
40 000 to preference shareholders in the old company subscribing for ordinary shares (2 for every 5 in old company)	40 000
20 000 to ordinary shareholders in old company subscribing for ordinary shares (1 for every 5 in old company)	20 000
Total	60 000

Sources: DDRN 10/3/4/6/1 Memorandum and Articles of Association of the Raleigh Cycle Co. Ltd, Incorporated 15 February 1899; DDRN 1/39/1, 3rd AGM of the Raleigh Cycle Co. Ltd, 3 January 1899; Minutes 29 November 1898.

Table B.5 Range of Raleigh cycle models and prices, 1898 and 1901

1898 Model	Price (£)	1901 Model	Price (£)
No. 1 Nottingham Make Ladies	30. 0. 0	No. 7 Nottingham Make Path Racer	29. 0. 0
No. 2 Lenton Make Ladies	26. 0. 0	No. 8 Nottingham Make Road Racer Plus Extras	29. 0. 0
No. 3 Nottingham Make Light Roadster			+ extras
a) Without Brakes and Mudguard	28. 0. 0	No. 9 Nottingham Make Tandem Racer	39. 0. 0
b) With Brakes and Mudguard	30. 0. 0	No. 10 Nottingham Make Tandem Racer Plus Extras	39. 0. 0
c) With Brakes Only	29. 5. 0		+ extras
d) With Mudguards Only	28. 5. 0	No. 11 Nottingham Make Roadster Tandem	42. 0. 0
No. 4 Lenton Make Light Roadster		No. 12 Nottingham Make Ladies	30. 0. 0
a) Without Brakes and Mudguard	24. 0. 0	No. 12 Lenton Make Ladies	26. 0. 0
b) With Brakes and Mudguard	26. 0. 0	No. 12 Radford Make Ladies	22. 0. 0
c) With Brakes Only	25. 5. 0	No. 13 Radford Make Ladies	22. 0. 0
d) With Mudguards Only	24. 5. 0	No. 14 Radford Make Light Roadster	
No. 5 Nottingham Make Road Racer		a) Without Brakes and Mudguard	20. 0. 0
a) Without Brakes and Mudguard	29. 0. 0	b) With Brakes and Mudguard	22. 0. 0
b) With Brakes and Mudguard	31. 0. 0	c) With Brakes Only	21. 5. 0
c) With Brakes Only	30. 5. 0	d) With Mudguards Only	20. 5. 0
d) With Mudguards Only	29. 5. 0	No. 15 Nottingham Make Roadster Tandem	47. 0. 0

1901 Model	List price (£)	Net cash price (£)
No. 4 1st Grade Raleigh Roadster	18. 18. 0	12. 12. 0
No. 6 1st Grade Raleigh Road Racer	18. 18. 0	12. 12. 0
No. 17 Lady's 1st Grade Raleigh	23. 12. 6	15. 15. 0
No. 5 1st Grade Raleigh Light Roadster	23. 12. 6	15. 15. 0
No. 7 Special Raleigh Pathracer	25. 10. 6	17. 0. 0
No. 8 Special Raleigh Roadracer	25. 10. 6	17. 0. 0
No. 1 Lady's Special Raleigh	30. 0. 0	20. 0. 0
No. 3 Special Raleigh Roadster	30. 0. 0	20. 0. 0
No. G Lady's Gazelle	15. 15. 0	10. 10. 0
No. G Raleigh-Gazelle	15. 15. 0	10. 10. 0
No. G Gazelle Road Racer	15. 15. 0	10. 10. 0
No. 16 Lady's Modele Superbe	37. 10. 0	25. 0. 0
No. 20A Gents Modele Superbe	37. 10. 0	25. 0. 0
No. 20B Cross (X) Frame Raleigh	30. 0. 0	20. 0. 0
No. 20C X Frame Path or Road Racer	30. 0. 0	20. 0. 0
No. 20D X Frame Raleigh Light Roadster	31. 10. 0	21. 0. 0
No. 10 Raleigh Patent Frame Racing Tandem	35. 5. 0	23. 10. 0
No. 11 Raleigh Patent Frame Roadster Tandem	42. 0. 0	27. 10. 0
No. 15 The Famous Raleigh Tandem	42. 0. 0	27. 10. 0

Note: All prices are in £. s. d.

Sources: DDRN 4/10/1/5, The Raleigh Cycle Company Ltd, Nottingham, 1898, pp. 56–70; DDRN 4/10/1/7, The Book of the Raleigh 1901.

Table C.1 UK exports of cycles and motor cycles, 1907–36

	Volume cycles	Value cycles (£)	Value per cycle (£)	Value cycle parts (£)	Volume motor cycles	Value motor cycles (£)	Value per motor cycle (£)	Value motor cycle parts (£)	Value cycles as % of value parts	Value motor cycles as % of value parts
1907	102 399	508 822	4.97	779 222	800	27 970	34.96	25 252	65.30	110.76
1910	129 106	542 511	4.20	1 414 776	3 341	122 582	36.69	37 894	38.35	323.49
1913	147 633	609 482	4.13	1 143 026	16 850	732 369	43.46	217 330	53.32	336.98
1916	58 878	286 171	4.86	861 251	12 847	594 969	46.31	258 692	33.23	229.99
1918	28 015	202 977	7.25	323 786	5 652	363 104	64.24	156 138	62.69	232.55
1919	62 959	610 186	9.69	1 334 913	8 330	575 848	69.13	322 140	45.71	178.76
1920	159 678	1 541 920	9.66	317 912	21 304	1 672 903	78.53	667 654	48.63	250.56
1921	39 117	381 277	9.75	1 418 957	8 104	662 736	81.78	316 948	26.87	209.10
1922	68 119	468 943	6.88	1 600 051	7 280	484 078	66.49	261 646	29.31	185.01
1923	121 670	705 784	5.80	2 019 403	16 156	870 621	53.89	419 530	34.95	207.52
1924	200 603	1 023 975	5.10	2 060 254	37 911	1 626 396	42.90	738 224	49.70	220.31
1925	278 260	1 307 977	4.70	2 140 297	47 114	1 857 025	39.42	1 023 801	61.11	181.39

1926	275 902	1 194 109	4.33	1 803 510	48 121	1 804 750	37.50	807 006	66.21	223.64
1927	283 462	1 190 260	4.20	1 638 277	53 000	2 139 051	40.36	930 675	72.65	229.84
1928	339 046	1 358 160	4.01	1 753 693	59 906	2 522 812	42.11	1 244 688	77.45	202.69
1929	368 030	1 390 160	3.78	1 650 574	62 377	2 663 316	42.70	1 351 438	84.22	197.07
1930	247 147	945 401	3.83	1 214 006	42 689	1 833 196	42.94	1 067 861	77.87	171.67
1931	172 950	608 591	3.52	918 057	23 247	987 455	42.48	672 157	66.29	146.91
1932	164 074	519 567	3.17	1 064 815	19 537	747 966	38.28	503 652	48.79	148.51
1933	204 625	579 599	2.83	1 411 577	17 731	670 712	37.83	456 718	41.06	146.85
1934	281 991	784 645	2.78	1 744 212	16 807	649 110	38.62	482 291	44.99	134.59
1935	377 301	1 052 664	2.79	1 904 901	18 074	701 938	38.84	344 629	55.26	203.68
1936	519 173	1 393 659	2.68	1 827 510	20 460	799 414	39.07	314 367	76.26	254.29

Source: *Bicycling News*, 1 July 1937.

Table C.2   Net profits of firms in the British cycle industry, 1914–40

	BSA	Rudge-Whitworth	New Hudson	J. A. Phillips	Hercules Cycle and Motor Cycle Ltd
1914	190 429				
1915	408 455	33 141			
1916	381 770	No accounts			
1917	427 976	No accounts			
1918	435 207	No accounts		6 315	
1919	393 090	No accounts		5 750	
1920	No accounts	No accounts		No accounts	
1921	–355 000	No accounts		40 075	
1922	–46 000	98 316		9 622	No accounts
1923	250 000	–25 795		18 264	No accounts
1924	300 000	–2 634		26 698	No accounts
1925		20 227		29 442	33 324
1926	300 000	27 681		32 438	12 073
1927		–5 244		23 693	31 529
1928	72 063	8 767		46 606	42 540
1929		9 179	1 200	38 414	–2 851
1930		14 685	–17 600	35 417	39 405
1931		–18 880	–17 800	35 911	27 726
1932	–331 000	–33 667	–25 800	35 282	34 382
1933	245 531	No accounts	7 600	41 287	101 304
1934	127 550	–6 025		65 666	148 877
1935	112 182	–25 513		78 752	24 383
1936		–66 734		52 305	83 059
1937				70 675	32 616
1938				54 852	12 240
1939				29 670	48 257
1940				28 106	1 358

Note: No accounts relates to the fact that company recorded that no balance sheet was compiled for that year.

Sources: BSA in BSA Monograph; New Hudson in *The Economist*; Rudge-Whitworth in DDRN 1/29/21–38 and 1/30/1–3, Rudge-Whitworth Annual Reports and Balance Sheets, 1915–32, 1934–36; J. A. Phillips in DDRN 1/18/1 Directors' Minute Book of J. A. Phillips & Co. Ltd, 1918–40; Hercules, from DDRN 1/15/1 Minute Book of the Hercules Cycle and Motor Co. Ltd, 1922–40.

Table C.3 Sales of Rudge-Whitworth cycles and motor cycles, and expenditure on advertisement, 1910–32

	Value of cycle sales (£)	Expenditure on cycle advertisement (£)	Value of motor cycle sales (£)	Expenditure on motor cycle advertisement (£)
1910	44 531	28 701		
1911	41 949	23 561	661	
1912	34 374	10 846	3 247	8 178
1913	30 013	9 847	3 030	8 310
1914	24 771	12 284	3 643	8 104
1915	13 143	4 180	2 225	2 956
1916	7 494	1 167	1 090	1 247
1917	8 903	2 471	746	945
1918	7 841	2 706	130	1 190
1919	8 110	7 852	1 124	7 656
1920	14 151	15 331	3 600	7 667
1921	17 273	11 967	2 846	13 614
1922	17 550	13 070	1 469	16 048
1923	19 544	9 497	1 460	13 735
1924	32 583	7 881	3 068	8 245
1925	43 764	13 932	7 453	9 839
1926	55 197	8 483	8 275	15 473
1927	50 709	9 668	6 091	20 845
1928	39 969	5 861	6 441	10 303
1929	47 418	3 878	5 726	7 586
1930	40 032	5 568	6 735	7 817
1931	46 115	4 473	3 446	7 110
1932	44 207	3 593	3 016	3 463

Source: DDRN 1/44, Rudge-Whitworth Ltd, Statement of Accounts for Creditors, 2 November 1932.

Table D.1   Profile of key management figures at Raleigh, 1914–39

Barnsdale, Major J. D.	A cousin of Harold Bowden. Appointed a director in 1921, retired in 1934.
Bowden, Frank	Founder of Raleigh. Retires as joint managing director in 1916, but retains chairmanship of board until death in April 1921.
Bowden, Harold H.	Becomes joint managing director with Frank in 1915, and succeeds him in 1916. Managing director and chairman of Raleigh Cycles and Sturmey-Archer, and after 1934 held similar posts in newly formed Raleigh Cycles Holding Co. Retires as Managing Director of Raleigh Cycles Co. in 1938, retains chairmanship of the company as well as the managing directorship and chair of the holding company.
Bush, Frederick C.	Became general manager in 1920, replacing Monks, and appointed a director in 1922. Retired as general manager in 1936.
Guthrie, Sir Connop	A Director of Suffolk Trust, the promoters of the flotation in 1934. Joins board of both Raleigh Cycle Holdings Co. and Raleigh Cycles Ltd.
Holland, H. R.	Appointed to head Raleigh's motor cycle department from BSA in 1920, became works manager in 1922. Resigns this position in 1929.
Lazonby, Joseph	A director at Raleigh since its foundation, and a close associate of Frank Bowden. Retires in 1923.
Lees, J. M.	Formerly works manager of Willys, Overland & Co. Appointed to Raleigh in 1928 to head a newly established planning department. Becomes works manager on resignation of Holland in 1929.
Linter, George	Secretary of Raleigh Cycles and after 1934 also Raleigh Cycles Holding Co.
McCraith, Douglas	A Nottingham solicitor and close associate of the Bowdens, appointed to the board in 1915. Retires in 1919.
Monks, Harry H.	Formerly London manager, becomes general manager in 1915. Retires in 1920.

Table D.1   concluded

Raven, W. H.	Appointed factory manager in 1908 after the resignation of G. P. Mills, having joined Raleigh from the New Hudson Cycle Co. Becomes manager of the cycle department in 1922, a 'working director' in 1934, and remained with the company until his retirement in 1942.
Wilson, George H. B.	Elected to board of Raleigh Cycle Co. in 1931, after joining the staff of Sturmey-Archer in 1927 and becoming a director of that company in 1929. Before the First World War he had worked on the staff of the Campion Cycle Co., and during the war was a captain in the RAF being awarded the MC and Air Force Cross. In 1918 he had joined Dunlop and remained there until his appointment with Sturmey-Archer. Elected to the Board of Raleigh Cycle Holding Co. Ltd in 1934, and appointed general manager of the Raleigh Cycle Co. in 1936. In 1938 succeeded Harold Bowden as managing director of the latter.

Source: DDRN 7/2/27, Raleigh Company Executives, 1887–1962.

Table D.2   Raleigh prices of cycles, 1923 and 1927,
and motor cycles, 1923

Cycles	(£. s. d.)	
	1923	1927
Boys and Girls Junior	8. 0. 0	6. 15. 0
Popular Gents	8. 10. 0	7. 17. 6
Popular Ladies	9. 0. 0	7. 17. 6
Popular Light Roadster	8. 10. 0	6. 17. 6
Standard Road Racer	9. 5. 0	—
Standard Gents	10. 10. 0	8. 17. 6
Standard Ladies	11. 5. 0	8. 17. 6
Standard Light Roadster	10. 10. 0	8. 7. 6
Special Gents	15. 0. 0	12. 0. 0
Special Ladies	15. 0. 0	12. 0. 0
Superbe Gents	18. 10. 0	15. 0. 0
Superbe Ladies	17. 10. 0	15. 0. 0
Carrier Bicycle	12. 10. 0	9. 17. 6
Ladies Lightweight	—	10. 10. 0
North Road Racer	—	9. 2. 6
Popular Road Racer	—	6. 7. 6

Motor cycles	1923 (£)
2.75 hp, 2 speed, chain cum belt	55.0
2.75 hp, 3 speed, chain cum belt	58.5
2.75 hp, 3 speed, all chain	60.0
3 hp, 3 speed, all chain	63.0
2.75 hp, 3 speed, all chain sports	70.0
2.75 hp, 3 speed, all chain sports with sidecar	90.0
5/6 hp flat twin solo	100.0
5/6 hp flat twin solo with standard sidecar	125.0
5/6 hp flat twin solo with deluxe sidecar	130.0

Source: Minutes with Reports, 11 October 1922; 9 August 1926.

Table D.3 Data from Raleigh factory trading account showing gross and net profit by product and the percentage of each on sales, 1926–30

	Cycles		Motor cycles (including engines)		Countershaft gears		Cycle gears		Total	
	£	%	£	%	£	%	£	%	£	%
Net profit by product and % of each on sales										
1926	116 785	15.72	19 420	4.00	52 184	21.26	29 488	26.32	217 877	13.73
1927	49 995	9.19	471	0.13	52 762	23.69	13 389	13.27	116 617	9.45
1928	47 318	8.20	45 729	9.83	76 519	24.17	45 829	29.34	215 394	14.21
1929	48 968	8.45	15 969	4.46	47 964	21.32	42 118	27.66	155 019	11.80
1930	4 969	0.91	-18 368	-7.23	36 478	19.29	37 347	27.86	60 426	5.39
Gross profit by product and % on sales										
1926	304 709	41.00	124 381	25.61	117 812	47.99	63 051	56.29	609 956	38.45
1927	230 400	42.34	104 173	28.40	115 490	51.86	47 537	47.13	497 600	40.31
1928	222 594	38.54	141 723	30.46	144 808	45.75	85 538	54.77	594 663	39.24
1929	236 598	40.80	98 961	27.66	107 010	47.54	82 137	54.52	524 706	39.95
1930	209 689	38.52	58 406	23.00	90 074	47.62	73 862	55.10	432 031	38.52

Note: Before deducting selling expenses etc.

Source: DDRN 3/11/1, Auditors Reports and Accounts 1926–30.

Table D.4 Results of manufacturing operations: percentage of costs on sales, Raleigh, 1914–18 and 1920

	1914	1915	1916	1917	1918	1920
Material consumed & carriage	38.77	37.41	33.47	28.02	35.37	33.33
Productive wages	18.86	22.85	22.80	25.88	24.52	28.20
Prime cost[a]	57.63	60.26	56.27	53.90	59.89	61.53
Factory running charges	13.28	17.27	14.69	18.20	20.42	21.60
Factory running charges on prime cost[b]	27.03	28.66	26.14	33.77	34.11	35.10
Gross factory profit[c]	29.09	22.47	29.04	27.90	19.69	16.87
Sales and consignments	100.00	100.00	100.00	100.00	100.00	100.00

Notes: [a] Prime cost = material and carriage + productive wages; [b] Factory running charges on prime cost = the percentage of running charges to prime cost; [c] Gross factory profits = the residual after charging all costs from sales and consignments.

Source: DDRN 1/40/5–9, Auditor's Reports and Balance Sheets, 1914–18, 1920.

Table D.5 Raleigh factory trading account, value of sales and percentage of total factory sales, 1923 and 1925–1930

	Cycles		Motor cycles (including engines)		Countershaft gears		Cycle gears		Total	
	£	%	£	%	£	%	£	%	£	%
1923	199 116	36.92	115 237	21.37	162 800	30.19	62 109	11.52	539 262	100
1925	280 617	37.57	125 169	16.76	246 399	32.99	94 717	12.68	746 902	100
1926	743 202	46.85	485 657	30.61	245 512	15.48	112 008	7.06	1 586 379	100
1927	544 109	44.08	366 760	29.71	222 734	18.04	100 864	8.17	1 234 467	100
1928	577 629	38.11	465 280	30.70	316 499	20.88	156 186	10.31	1 515 594	100
1929	580 041	44.16	357 744	27.23	225 114	17.13	150 652	11.48	1 313 551	100
1930	544 347	48.54	253 930	22.64	189 143	16.86	134 074	11.96	1 121 494	100

Note: Sales are calculated after deducting finished stocks and work in progress.

Source: DDRN 3/11/1, Auditors Reports and Accounts 1926–30; DDRN 3/17, Private Ledger of Raleigh Cycle Co. Ltd.

Table D.6 Raleigh factory running charges and selling expenses and percentage of productive wage, 1924–30

	Productive wage (£)	Running charges (£)	As % of productive wage	Selling expenses (£)	As % of productive wage	% of Productive wage – Running and selling charges combined
1924	240 210	191 105	79.51	101 668	42.37	121.88
1925	278 933	207 391	74.35	106 310	38.11	112.46
1926	300 250	235 386	78.40	117 665	39.18	117.58
1927	232 014	215 799	93.00	165 184	71.20	164.20
1928	292 919	209 535	71.53	169 734	57.94	129.47
1929	261 327	205 458	78.62	164 229	62.84	141.46
1930	231 251	194 685	84.18	176 920	76.51	160.69

Source: Auditors Accounts and Reports 1926–30.

Table D.7   Raleigh cycles sales and production, 1935–39
(machines sold and produced for year ending August)

	Home sales			Foreign sales			
	Raleigh	Humber	Gazelle	Raleigh	Humber	Gazelle	Total
1935[a]							306 234
1936	283 031	46 068	—	42 902	6 206	—	378 207
1937	280 959	44 279	—	120 433	13 136	—	458 807
1938	218 684	34 398	—	118 362	16 523	—	387 967
1939	208 866	30 806	36 140	102 208	16 486	1 984	396 490

	Production				
	Raleigh	Humber	Gazelle	Tandems	Total
1935	283 186	48 031	—	1 177	332 394
1936	321 742	50 216	—	319	372 277
1937	412 894	60 097	—	873	473 864
1938	343 082	50 684	—	—	393 766
1939	313 066	46 839	49 574	—	409 479

Note: [a] Raleigh sold 263 772 and Humber 42 462, no distinction was made
between home and foreign.

Source: Compiled from Minutes with Reports for August of each year.

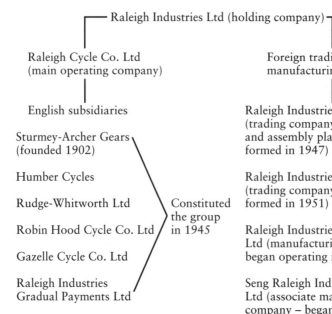

Raleigh Industries Ltd (holding company)

Raleigh Cycle Co. Ltd
(main operating company)

Foreign trading and
manufacturing companies

English subsidiaries

Sturmey-Archer Gears
(founded 1902)

Humber Cycles

Rudge-Whitworth Ltd

Robin Hood Cycle Co. Ltd

Gazelle Cycle Co. Ltd

Raleigh Industries
Gradual Payments Ltd

Constituted
the group
in 1945

Triumph Cycle Co. (acquired 1954)

BSA Cycles Ltd (acquired July 1957)

New Hudson Cycle Co. (subsidiary of
BSA – acquired 1957)

Sunbeam Cycles Ltd (subsidiary of BSA
– acquired 1957)

J. B. Brookes (Saddles) Ltd (acquired
December 1958)

Carlton Cycles Ltd (acquired December
1959)

Raleigh Industries of America Inc.
(trading company – distribution
and assembly plant – subsidiary
formed in 1947)

Raleigh Industries of East Africa
(trading company – subsidiary
formed in 1951)

Raleigh Industries of South Africa
Ltd (manufacturing company –
began operating in January 1952)

Seng Raleigh Industries of India
Ltd (associate manufacturing
company – began operating in
November 1952)

Raleigh Cycle Industries (Canada)
Ltd (trading company –
subsidiary formed in July 1954)

Sturmey-Archer Gears (Holland)
NV (trading company –
subsidiary formed in 1955)

BSA Cycles (Ireland) Ltd. (trading
company – subsidiary acquired in
1957)

Deutsch Sturmey-Archer Gears
GMBH (trading company –
subsidiary formed in 1957)

Irish Bicycle Industries Ltd
(renamed Irish Raleigh Industries –
subsidiary acquired in December
1959)

Consolidated Cycle Industries Ltd
(acquired in 1960)

Figure E.1   Company structure of Raleigh Industries Ltd.
Source: Lloyd-Jones, Lewis and Eason, 1999.

Home sales:

Table E.1 Sales figures for Raleigh, 1938–49 (machines sold for year ending August)

	Raleigh	Humber	Gazelle	Rudge	Robin Hood	Tricycles	Total home	Government sales[a]
1938	218 684	34 398	—	—	—	—	253 082	—
1939	208 666	30 806	36 140	—	—	—	275 612	—
1940	217 431	32 569	42 205	—	—	—	292 205	—
1941	63 716	10 762	22 222	—	—	—	96 700	33 022
1942	49 676	5 082	6 066	—	—	—	60 824	36 093
1943	91 767	12 544	6 266	—	—	—	110 577	63 210
1944	60 302	10 623	—	13 490	16 296	—	100 711	11 066
1945	73 698	12 567	—	19 656	11 694	—	117 615	2 573
1946	126 317	23 639	—	25 599	16 093	—	191 648	—
1947	165 666	28 255	—	35 842	19 250	—	249 013	—
1948	142 295	26 372	—	46 079	17 648	1 516	233 910	—
1949	149 591	21 755	—	41 316	5 292	28 209	246 163	—

Note: [a] All models

Table E.1   concluded

Foreign sales and sales to Dublin:

	Raleigh	Humber	Gazelle	Rudge	Robin Hood	Tricycles	Total foreign	Dublin[a]
1938	118 363	16 523	—	—	—	—	134 886	—
1939	102 008	16 486	1 984	—	—	—	120 478	—
1940	91 323	16 769	2 359	—	—	—	110 451	—
1941	68 755	14 381	2 381	—	—	—	85 517	—
1942	25 801	6 819	713	—	—	—	33 333	18
1943	11 063	4 022	42	—	—	—	15 127	783
1944	12 294	3 463	—	1 335	—	—	17 092	868
1945	28 643	4 151	—	2 598	—	—	35 392	1 556
1946	81 238	20 040	—	13 189	—	—	114 467	13 146
1947	128 546	30 723	—	28 362	73	—	187 704	23 752
1948	174 242	44 349	—	48 327	2 144	37	269 099	37 652
1949	235 810	68 756	—	56 079	4 046	3 163	367 854	52 166

Note: [a] Includes all models

Total sales:

	Home	% of total	Government	% of total	Foreign	% of total	Dublin	% of total	Total
1938	253 082	65.2	—	0.0	134 886	34.8	—	0.0	387 968
1939	275 612	69.6	—	0.0	120 478	30.4	—	0.0	396 090
1940	292 205	72.6	—	0.0	110 451	27.4	—	0.0	402 656
1941	96 700	44.9	33 022	15.3	85 517	39.7	—	0.0	215 239
1942	60 824	46.7	36 093	27.7	33 333	25.6	18	0.0	130 268
1943	110 577	58.3	63 210	33.3	15 127	8.0	783	0.4	189 697
1944	100 711	77.6	11 066	8.5	17 092	13.2	868	0.7	129 737
1945	117 615	74.8	2 573	1.6	35 392	22.5	1 556	1.0	157 136
1946	191 648	60.0	—	0.0	114 467	35.9	13 146	4.1	319 261
1947	249 013	54.1	—	0.0	187 704	40.8	23 752	5.2	460 469
1948	233 910	43.3	—	0.0	269 099	49.8	37 652	7.0	540 661
1949	246 163	37.0	—	0.0	367 854	55.2	52 166	7.8	666 183

Source: Compiled from DDRN 1/2/6, Raleigh Cycle Co. Ltd, Board and General Meetings Minutes with Fortnightly Reports, reports for August of each year.

Table E.2   Cycle production at Raleigh, 1938–56

Figures for 1938–46

	Raleigh	Humber	Gazelle	Rudge	Robin Hood	Total
1938	343 082	50 684	—	—	—	393 766
1939	313 066	46 839	49 574	—	—	409 479
1940	233 844	36 882	28 439	—	—	299 165
1941	136 914	25 933	25 112	—	—	187 959
1942	137 670	16 704	8 242	—	—	162 616
1943	139 550	17 829	8 380	—	—	165 759
1944	151 742	13 529	—	16 674	12 160	194 105
1945	127 064	19 763	—	23 883	11 972	182 682
1946	235 744	54 059	—	47 318	16 652	353 773

Figures for 1947–49

	Raleigh	Humber	Rudge	Robin Hood	Tricycles	Total	% home/ foreign
1947							
Home	183 833	32 379	43 150	19 466	—	278 828	59.9
Foreign	144 539	1 075	37 167	3 633	—	186 414	40.1
Total	328 372	33 454	80 317	23 099	—	465 242	100.0
1948							
Home	151 467	27 664	49 575	18 320	1 600	248 626	43.0
Foreign	203 564	55 797	62 345	7 509	49	329 264	57.0
Total	355 031	83 461	111 920	25 829	1 649	577 890	100.0
1949							
Home	145 937	20 506	41 113	5 554	32 000	245 110	36.3
Foreign	263 078	75 507	76 739	9 702	4 429	429 455	63.7
Total	409 015	96 013	117 852	15 256	36 429	674 565	100.0

Figures for 1950–56 (includes all Raleigh's English subsidiaries)

1950	872 845
1951	1 010 077
1953	1 222 000
1956[a]	1 404 000

Note: [a] Figures for 9 months only.

Sources: Compiled from DDRN 1/2/6, Raleigh Cycle Co. Ltd, Board and General Meetings Minutes with Fortnightly Reports, reports for August of each year. Figures after 1950 taken from Lloyd-Jones, Lewis and Eason, 1999, Table 4.

Bibliography

Abbreviations: NRO: Nottingham Record Office; references to material in the Raleigh collection indexed as DDRN; CRO: Coventry Record Office.

Business records of the British bicycle industry

Birmingham Small Arms Co., BSA, NRO, DDRN 4/3/6, DDRN 4/3/66; DDRN 7/13/3; Solihull Record Office, BSA collection.

British Cycle Corporation, BCC, Cycle Division of Tube Investments Ltd, NRO, DDRN 1/26/1.

Cluley & Clarke Ltd of Coventry, CRO 1233.

Coventry Premier Ltd, NRO, DDRN 1/35.

Humber Cycles. Merged with Raleigh in 1932. NRO, DDRN, Raleigh Records.

Hercules Cycle Co., NRO, DDRN 1/15, DDRN 7/3/3.

Jane Cycle Co. of Birmingham, NRO, DDRN 1/36.

James Cycles, NRO, DDRN/25.

Phillips, J. A. & Co., NRO, DDRN 1/18.

Raleigh Cycle Co. and Raleigh Industries Ltd, NRO Raleigh Records, DDRN 1–7; Nottingham Central Library, *Raligram*, the in-house journal of Raleigh.

Rudge-Whitworth Ltd, Coventry Record Office, CRO 849; Nottingham Record Office, Raleigh Records, DDRN 1/29–30; DDRN 1/44; DDRN 7/3/8.

Sturmey-Archer Gears Ltd, Nottingham Record Office, Raleigh Records, DDRN 1/23.

Newspapers, trade and other journals

Trade journals for the bicycle and motor cycle industries are located in two main collections: Coventry Central Library, Bartlett Collection, and Nottingham Record Office, Raleigh Records, Raleigh Trade and Newspaper Cuttings, DDRN5.

Aberdeen Evening Express.
Accelerator.
Bicycling News.

Bicycling News and Motorcycle Review.
Birmingham Evening News.
Birmingham Gazette.
Birmingham Mail.
Birmingham News.
Birmingham Post.
Blackburn Evening Telegraph.
Board of Trade Journal.
Bognor Regis Observer.
Clarion.
Constabulary Gazette.
CTC Gazette.
Cycling.
Cycling Times.
Cyclist.
Daily Herald.
Daily Mail.
Donegal Democrat.
East Anglia Daily Times.
Engineering.
Evening Dispatch.
Evening Standard.
Financial News.
Financial Times.
Financial World.
Garage and Motor Agent.
Guardian Journal.
Hercules Cycle Magazine.
Hercules News.
Hull Daily Mail.
Indian Cycle and Motor Journal.
Iraq Times.
Irish Cyclist and Motor Cyclist.
Irish Times.
Kentish Gazette.
Labour Gazette.
Leeds Mercury.
Lincoln, Rutland and Stamford Mercury.
Lloyds Sunday News.
Manchester Guardian.
Ministry of Labour Gazette.
Montgomery County Times.
Motor Cycle and Cycle Export Trader.

Motor Cycle and Cycle Trader.
Motor Cycling.
Motor Cyclist Illustrated.
Motor Export Trader.
National Journal.
News Chronicle.
Northants Evening Telegraph.
Nottingham Daily Express.
Nottingham Evening News.
Nottingham Evening Post.
Nottingham Guardian.
Nottingham Journal.
Oxford Mail.
People.
Police Chronicle.
Power and Pedal.
Singapore Cycling Annual.
Star.
Swindon Evening Advertiser.
The Economist.
The Times.
Yorkshire Evening News.

Trade directories and rate books

Birmingham Trade and Commercial Directory (1901), (Birmingham: Kellys).
Birmingham Trade Directories for 1920s and 1930s (Kellys: located in Birmingham Central Library).
Birmingham Rate Books, Aston District, 2, Birmingham Central Library Archives.
Coventry Complete Directory (1894), (Coventry: Robertson & Grey).
Coventry Trade and Commercial Directory (1874–75), (Coventry: Anslow & Roden).
Coventry Trade Directories for the 1920s and 1930s (Kellys, located in Coventry Central Library).
Nottingham Directory (1900), (Nottingham: Wrights).

Books, articles and theses

Aldcroft, D. H. (1986), *The British Economy*, Vol. 1, *The Years of Turmoil 1920–51* (Brighton: Wheatsheaf).

Aldcroft, D. H. (1994), *Education, Training and Economic Performance, 1914–1990* (Manchester: Manchester University Press).

Allen, G. C. (1929), *Industrial Development of Birmingham and the Black Country* (London: Allen & Unwin).

Alvesson, M. (1993), *Cultural Perspectives on Organizations* (Cambridge: Cambridge University Press).

Andrews, P. S. and Brunner, E. (1955), *The Life of Lord Nuffield: A Study in Enterprise and Benevolence* (Oxford: Basil Blackwell).

Barnsdale, J. D. (1922), 'Raleigh's Bids for Overseas Markets', *Motor Export Trader*, January, pp. 56–8.

Beeley, S. (1992), *A History of Bicycles: From Hobby Horse to Mountain Bike* (London: Studio Editions).

Boulstridge, J. (1953), 'Records in the Bicycle Industry', *Financial Times*, 14 November, pp. 16–17.

Bowden, G. H. (1975), *The Story of the Raleigh Cycle* (London: W. H. Allen).

Bowden, H. H. (1922), 'How We Cut our Price to Selling Level', *Motor Cycle and Cycle Trader*, 13 January, pp. 33–4.

Bowden, H. H. (1934), 'The Four Ms of Industry – Men, Management, Machinery and Money', Address to Birmingham Rotary Club reported in *Birmingham Gazette*, 16 October, pp. 21–3.

Bowden, S. (1994), 'The New Consumerism', in P. Johnson (ed.) *Twentieth Century Britain. Economic, Social and Cultural Change* (London: Longman).

Briggs, A. (1952), *History of Birmingham*, Vol. 2 (Oxford: Oxford University Press).

Broadberry, S. N (1986), *The British Economy Between the Wars: A Macro Economic Survey* (Oxford: Oxford University Press).

Broadberry, S. N. and Crafts, N. F. R. (1990), 'Explaining Anglo-American Productivity Differences in the Mid-Twentieth Century', *Oxford Bulletin of Economics and Statistics*, **52** (4), pp. 375–402.

Burgess, K. (1975), *The Origins of British Industrial Relations* (London: Croom Helm).

Cairncross, A. (1992), *The British Economy Since 1945* (Oxford: Blackwell).

Capie, F. (1983), *Depression and Protection: Britain between the Wars* (London: Allen & Unwin).

Casson, M. (1993), 'Entrepreneurship and Business Culture', in J. Brown and M. B. Rose (eds), *Entrepreneurship, Networks and Modern Business* (Manchester, Manchester University Press).

Casson, M. and Rose, M. B. (1997), 'Introduction', *Business History*, **39** (4), Special Issue on Institutions and the Evolution of Modern Business.

Chandler, A. D. jnr (1962), *Strategy and Structure: Chapters in the History of the American Industrial Enterprise* (Cambridge, MA: MIT Press).

Chandler, A. D. (1990), *Scale and Scope: The Dynamics of Industrial Capitalism* (Cambridge, MA: Harvard University Press).

Church, R. A. (1966), *Victorian Nottingham, 1815–1900: Economic and Social Change in a Midland Town* (London: Frank Cass).

Church, R. A. (1993), 'The Family Firm in Industrial Capitalism: International Perspectives on Hypothesis and History', *Business History*, **35** (4), Special Issue on Family Capitalism, pp. 17–43.

Church, R. A. (1995), *The Rise and Decline of the British Motor Industry* (Cambridge: Cambridge University Press).

Church, R. A. (1996), 'Demonstrating Nuffield: The Evolution of Managerial Culture in the British Motor Industry', *Economic History Review*, **49** (3), pp. 561–83.

Coleman, D. C. (1987[a]), 'Failings and Achievements: Some British Businesses, 1910–90', *Business History*, **29** (special issue), pp. 1–17.

Coleman, D. C. (1987[b]), 'The Uses and Abuses of Business History', *Business History*, **29** (2), pp. 141–56.

Cottrell, P. L. (1980), *Industrial Finance, 1830–1914: The Finance and Organisation of British Manufacturing Industry* (London: Methuen).

Davenport-Hines, R. P. T. (1984), *Dudley Docker. The Life and Times of a Trade Warrior* (Cambridge: Cambridge University Press).

Davies, J. McG. (n.d.), 'A Twentieth Century Paternalist. Alfred Herbert and the Skilled Coventry Workmen', in B. Lancaster and T. Mason (eds), *Life and Labour in a Twentieth Century City: The Experience of Coventry* (Coventry: Cryfield Press)

Demaus, A. B. and Tarring, J. C. (1989), *The Humber Story, 1868–1932* (Stroud: Alan Sutton).

Donnelly, T., Batchelor, J. and Morris, D. (1995), 'The Limitations of Trade Union Power in the Coventry Motor Industry', *Midland History*, **20**.

Duijn, J. J. van (1983), *The Long Wave in Economic Life* (London: Allen & Unwin).

Eatwell, R. (1979), *The 1945-51 Labour Governments* (London: Batsford Academic).

Farnie, D. A. (1979), *The English Cotton Industry and the World Market, 1815–1896* (Oxford: Oxford University Press).

Fitzgerald, R. (1988), *British Labour Management and Industrial Welfare 1846–1939* (London: Croom Helm).

Florence Sargent, P. (1933), *The Logic of British and American Industry: A Realistic Analysis of Economic Structure and Government* (London: Routledge & Kegan Paul).

Floud, R. (1976), *The British Machine Tool Industry, 1850–1914* (Cambridge: Cambridge University Press).

Freeman, C. (1982), *The Economics of Industrial Innovation* (London: Francis Pinter).

Garside, W. A. and Gospel, H. F. (1982), 'Employers and Managers: Their Organisational Structure and Changing Industrial Strategies', in C. Wrigley (ed.), *A History of British Industrial Relations, 1875–1914* (Hassocks: Harvester).

Glyn, S. and Booth, A. (1996), *Modern Britain: An Economic and Social History* (London: Routledge).

Gospel, H. (1992), *Markets, Firms and the Management of Labour in Modern Britain* (Cambridge: Cambridge University Press).

Grew, F. W. (1921), *The Cycle Industry* (London: Isaac Pitman).

Griffiths, J. (1995), 'Give My Regards to "Uncle Billy": The Rites and Rituals of Company Life at Lever Brothers, c. 1900–1990', *Business History*, **37** (4), pp. 25–45.

Hall, M. (1962), 'The Consumer Sector', in G. D. N. Worswick and P. H. Ady (eds), *The British Economy in the 1950s* (Oxford: Clarendon Press).

Hannah, L. (1976), 'Strategy and Structure in the Manufacturing Sector', in L. Hannah (ed.), *Management Strategy and Business Development: An Historical and Comparative Study* (London: Methuen).

Hannah, L. (1983), *The Rise of the Corporate Economy* (London: Methuen).

Harrison, A. E. (1969), 'The Competitiveness of the British Cycle Industry, 1890–1914', *Economic History Review*, **22** (3), pp. 287–303.

Harrison, A. E. (1977), 'Growth, Entrepreneurship and Capital Formation in the United Kingdom's Cycle and Related Industries 1870–1914', University of York, unpublished PhD thesis.

Harrison, A. E. (1981), 'Joint Stock Company Flotation in the Cycle, Motor Vehicle and Related Industries 1882–1914', *Business History*, **23** (2), pp. 165–90.

Harrison, A. E. (1982), 'F. Hopper and Co. – The Problems of Capital Supply in the Cycle Manufacturing Industry', *Business History*, **24** (1), 3–23.

Harrison, A. E. (1984), 'Bowden, Sir Harold', in D. J. Jeremy (ed.), *Dictionary of Business Biography* (London: Butterworths).

Harrison, A. E. (1985), 'The Origins and Growth of the UK Cycle Industry to 1900', *Journal of Transport History*, **6** (1), pp. 41–70.

Hofstede, G. (1993), *Cultures and Organizations. Intercultural Cooperation and its Importance for Survival: Software of the Mind* (London: HarperCollins).

Howlett, P. (1994), 'The Golden Age, 1955–1973', in P. Johnson (ed.), *Twentieth Century Britain: Economic, Social and Cultural Change* (London: Longman).

Jeremy, D. J. (1998), *A Business History of Britain, 1900–1990s* (Oxford: Oxford University Press).

Jones, G. and Rose, M. B. (1993), 'Family Capitalism', *Business History*, **35** (Special Issue on Family Capitalism), pp. 1–16.

Jones, H. (1983), 'Welfare Schemes and Industrial Relations in Inter-War Britain', *Business History*, **25** (1), pp. 61–75.

Kay, J. (1993), *Foundations of Corporate Success: How Business Strategies Add Value* (Oxford: Oxford University Press).

Kirby, M. W. (1992), 'Institutional Rigidities and Economic Decline: Reflections on the British Experience', *Economic History Review*, **45** (4), pp. 637–60.

Kynaston, D. (1996), *The City of London*, Vol. 2, *The Golden Years, 1890–1914* (London: Pimlico).

Lancaster, B. (n.d), 'Who's a Real Coventry Kid? Migration Into Twentieth Century Coventry', in B. Lancaster and T. Mason (eds), *Life and Labour in a Twentieth Century City: The Experience of Coventry* (Coventry: Cryfield Press)

Lane, J. (1977), *Report of Business Records of Coventry and Related Areas*, (Coventry: Lanchester Polytechnic).

Lazerson, M. H. (1988), 'Organisational Growth of Small Firms: An Outcome of Markets Or Hierarchies?', *American Sociological Review*, **53** (3), pp. 330–42.

Lewchuck, W. (1987), *American Technology and the British Motor Industry* (Cambridge: Cambridge University Press).

Lipatito, K. (1995), 'Culture and the Practice of Business History', *Business and Economic History*, **32** (2), pp. 1–41.

Lloyd-Jones, R. and Le Roux, A. A. (1984), 'Factory Utilisation and the Firm: The Manchester Cotton Industry, c. 1825–1840', *Textile History*, **17** (1), pp. 119–27.

Lloyd-Jones, R. and Lewis, M. J. (1988), *Manchester and the Age of the Factory* (London: Croom Helm).

Lloyd-Jones, R. and Lewis, M. J. (1994), 'Personal Capitalism and British Industrial Decline: The Personally Managed Firm and Business Strategy in Sheffield, 1880–1920', *Business History Review*, **68** (Autumn), pp. 364–411.

Lloyd-Jones, R. and Lewis, M. J. (1998a), *British Industrial Capitalism Since the Industrial Revolution* (London: University College of London Press).

Lloyd-Jones, R. and Lewis, M. J. (1998b) 'British Industrial Capitalism During the Second Industrial Revolution: A Schumpeterian Approach', *Journal of Industrial History*, 1 (1), pp. 56–87.

Lloyd-Jones, R., Lewis, M. J. and Eason, M. (1999) 'Culture as Metaphor: Company Culture and Business Strategy at Raleigh Industries, c. 1945–1960', *Business History*, 41 (3), pp. 93–133.

Maddison, A. (1962), *Phases of Capitalist Development* (Oxford: Oxford University Press).

Marrison, A. J. (1996), *Businessmen and Protection* (Oxford: Oxford University Press).

Mason, S. A. (1994), *Nottingham Lace 1760s-1950s* (Stroud: Alan Sutton).

Middlemass, K. (1979), *Politics in Industrial Society: The Experience of the British System Since 1911* (London: A. Deutsch).

Millward, A., (1989), 'The Cycle Industry in Birmingham, c. 1890–1920', in B. Tilson (ed.), *Made in Birmingham: Design and Industry 1859–1985* (Studley: Warwick & Brewin Books).

Millward, A. S. (1972), *The Economic Effects of the Two World Wars on Britain* (London: Macmillan).

Morley, D. (1991) *Classic Motorcycles: BSA* (London: Osprey).

Morris, B. and Smyth, J. (1994), 'Paternalism as an Employer Strategy, 1880–1960', in J. Rubery and F. Wilkinson (eds), *Employer Strategy and the Labour Market* (Cambridge: Cambridge University Press).

Nockolds, H. (1976), *Lucas. The First 100 Years*, Vol. 1, *The King of the Road* (Newton Abbot: David and Charles).

Payne, P. L. (1967), 'The Emergence of the Large-Scale Company in Great Britain 1870–1914', *Economic History Review*, 20, pp. 519–42.

Payne, P. L. (1984), 'Family Business in Britain: An Historical and Analytical Survey', in A. Okochi and S. Yasuoka (eds), *Family Business in the Era of Industrial Growth* (Tokyo: University of Tokyo Press).

Peden, G. (1988), *Keynes, The Treasury and British Economic Policy* (Basingstoke: Macmillan).

Piore, M. J. and Sabel, C. F. (1984), *The Second Industrial Divide: Possibilities for Prosperity* (New York: Basic Books).

Pollard, S. (1983), *The Development of the British Economy, 1918–1980* (London: Edward Arnold).

Pollard, S. (1984), *The Wasting of the British Economy* (London: Croom Helm).

Pratten, C. F. (1971), *Economies of Scale in Manufacturing Industry* (Cambridge: Cambridge University Press, Department of Applied Economics Occasional Papers, 28).

Reynolds, B. (1977), *Don't Trudge It: Rudge-Whitworth Coventry* (Yeovil: Rudge-Whitworth & Co.).

Rollitt, A. K. (1900), *Annual Meeting of the Associated Chambers of Commerce of the UK*, 13–15 March (London: Associated Chambers of Commerce).

Rosenberg, N. (1994), *Exploring the Black Box, Technology, Economics and History* (Cambridge: Cambridge University Press).

Rowlinson, M. (1995), 'Strategy, Structure and Culture: Cadbury, Divisionalization and Merger in the 1960s', *Journal of Management Studies*, **32** (2), pp. 165–97.

Ryerson, B. (1980), *The Giants of Small Heath: The History of BSA*, (London: Haynes).

Sabel, C. F. and Zeitlin, J. (1985), 'Historical Alternatives to Mass Production: Politics, Markets and Technologies', *Past and Present*, **108**, pp. 173–6.

Sako, M. (1992), *Prices, Quality and Trust: Inter-Firm Relations in Britain and Japan* (Cambridge: Cambridge University Press).

Saul, S. B. (1968), 'The Engineering Industry', in D. H. Aldcroft (ed.) *The Development of British Industry and Foreign Competition* (London: Allen & Unwin).

Schein, E. H. (1985), *Organizational Culture and Leadership. A Dynamic View* (San Francisco: Jossey-Bass).

Schenk, G. R. (1994), 'Austerity and Boom', in P. Johnson (ed.), *Twentieth Century Britain. Economic, Social and Cultural Change* (London: Longman).

Scranton, P. (1989), *Figured Tapestry. Production, Markets, and Power in Philadelphia Textiles, 1885–1914* (Cambridge: Cambridge University Press).

Scranton, P. (1991), 'Diversity in Diversity: Flexible Production and American Industrialisation, 1880–1930', *Business History Review*, **65** (Spring), pp. 27–90.

Soltow, J. H. (1980), 'Origins of Small Business and the Relationship between Large and Small Firms: Metal Fabricating and Machinery Making in New England, 1890–1957', in S. W. Bruchey (ed.) *Small Business in American Life* (New York: Columbia University Press).

Swedberg, R. (ed.) (1991), *Joseph Schumpeter: The Economics and Sociology of Capitalism* (Princeton, NJ: Princeton University Press).

Thomas, R. H. (1946), 'British Industry Gets Down to It', Series No. 4, on 'J. A. Phillips & Co. Ltd', *Motor Cycle and Cycle Trader*, 25 October, pp. 11–15.

Thoms, D. (1990), 'Technical Education and the Transformation of Coventry's Industrial Economy, 1900–1939', in P. Summerfield and E. J. Evans (eds) *Technical Education and the State Since 1850: Historical and Contemporary Perspectives* (Manchester: Manchester University Press).

Thoms, D. and Donnelly T. (n.d.), 'Coventry's Industrial Economy, 1880–1980', in B. Lancaster and T. Mason (eds), *Life and Labour in a Twentieth Century City: The Experience of Coventry* (Coventry: Cryfield Press).

Thoms, D. and Donnelly, T. (1985), *The Motor Car Industry in Coventry Since the 1890s* (London: Croom Helm).

Tolliday, S. (1986), 'Management and Labour in Britain 1869–1939', in S. Tolliday and J. Zeitlin (eds), *The Automobile Industry and Its Workers* (Oxford: Oxford University Press).

Tolliday, S. and Zeitlin, J. (1986), 'Introduction', in S. Tolliday and J. Zeitlin (eds.), *The Automobile Industry and Its Workers* (Oxford: Oxford University Press).

Tweedale, G. (1995), *Steel City: Entrepreneurship, Strategy and Technology in Sheffield, 1743–1993* (Oxford: Oxford University Press).

Vernon, R. (1966), 'International Investment and International Trade in the Product Life Cycle', *Quarterly Journal of Economics* **180** (2), pp. 190–207.

Watling, H. (1937), 'British Cycles and Motorcycles Abroad: How the Industry is Regaining Lost Markets and Winning New Ones', *Bicycling News*, 1 July, pp. 1–5.

Wells, L. T. (ed.) (1972), *The Product Life Cycle and International Trade* (Boston: Division of Research, Harvard University Graduate School of Business Administration).

Westall, O. and Godley, A. (eds) (1998), *Business History and Business Culture* (Manchester, Manchester University Press)

Wigglesworth, N. (1996), *The Evolution of English Sport* (London: Frank Cass).

Wilson, J. F. (1995), *British Business History, 1720–1994* (Manchester: Manchester University Press).

Worswick, G. N. D. (1962), *The British Economy in the 1950s* (Oxford: Clarendon Press).

Wrigley, C. (ed.) (1993), *A History of British Industrial Relations 1914–1939* (Brighton: Gregg Revivals).

Index of business firms and leading business men

Subject and author index